THE COMPLETE
PARKHURST TALES

THE COMPLETE
PARKHURST TALES

NORMAN PARKER

BLAKE

Published by John Blake Publishing Ltd,
3 Bramber Court, 2 Bramber Road,
London W14 9PB, England

www.blake.co.uk

First published in paperback in 2006

ISBN 1 85782 592 6

British Library Cataloguing-in-Publication Data:

A catalogue record for this book is available from the British Library.

Design by www.envydesign.co.uk

Printed in Great Britain by Bookmarque Ltd, Croydon, Surrey

1 3 5 7 9 10 8 6 4 2

Papers used by John Blake Publishing are natural, recyclable products made
from wood grown in sustainable forests. The manufacturing processes
conform to the environmental regulations of the country of origin.

For the ultimate 'chap', honourable, loyal, courageous,
my mum.

CONTENTS

FOREWORD

TOM MANGOLD, FREELANCE TELEVISION
JOURNALIST AND AUTHOR

I first met Norman Parker after discovering that he held more power inside prison than the Home Secretary. We had arrived at Long Lartin, *permessos* in hand, cleared by the Home Office, the Prison Department, the Prison Officers' Association, the Governor and probably the Secretary-General of the United Nations too. All we wanted to do was film a sequence inside one of Britain's more modern nicks. Norman, however, thought otherwise.

We were met by an Assistant Governor, Peter Quinn (then and now symbol of the new breed of enlightened and caring prison officials), wringing his hands with embarrassment. Yes, he knew we had clearances from everyone, but there was . . . ah . . . a little problem. The inmates were not happy. They couldn't . . . ah . . . quite see what was in it for them. We smiled indulgently. That's your problem, we smirked, we are the media; what's more we have clearances. You sort your nick out. But it was not to be. Quinn held his ground, no one interfered with the chemistry of his prison without good reason. Impasse. Four coffees later I suggested I met the little bastard who was standing in our way. Quinn had me sign a form that exonerated the prison from any nastiness inflicted upon me, then inserted me thankfully into a cage full of lifers. And that's how I met 083395 Parker, N., their leader.

It was the beginning of a fifteen-year relationship conducted for the most part by correspondence, and although it wasn't exactly *84 Charing Cross Road,* both of us did sharpen our wits and our writing styles against each other, and I hope he enjoyed the experience as much as I did.

Not once in the whole exchange did Norman ever whinge, gripe or display an ounce of self-pity. I lived with him through the endless parole knock-backs, the disappointments clinging like nettles to his mail, but he held on to his sense of humour and never gave up believing the day would come when he would eventually walk out. He was almost certainly one of hundreds of victims to endless government law-and-order campaigns engineered to bring the bluerinse shires to their feet at party conference. Political convenience, not penal realities, kept Norman inside for two decades.

I can remember, as a young reporter, the days when the average sentence for murder was fourteen years, of which the average time served was nine. Why nine? Because it was held that the personality begins to disintegrate in nick after ten years. It is a small tribute to Norman that his bottle has not gone after all this time. To the contrary. He kept himself half alive by watching Panorama as often as he could (even forcing groaning fellow cons to watch the most boring of our political problems), by reading various subjects for various degrees, and by honing his literary potential, usually at my personal expense. His letters to me are littered with unkind references to my occasional penchant for Krug '82, or to the general decadence of the Fourth Estate, to which I belong with such pride. There were times, goddamit, when Norman just didn't take me seriously.

Because, sociologically, Norman is not part of the famous criminal class, he has a detachment, awareness and objectivity that allow him the vision and insight to reflect not only with passion but also with sardonic understanding on those twenty years. Wasted? Well, not quite. He knew he had to do his bird; he just didn't know he had to do so much.

Together with the United States (and the old, white South Africa) we imprison more people, for longer, than most other civilized societies. Yet the recidivism rate is so appalling I cannot understand why there is not a taxpayers' revolt of poll-tax proportions at such a pointless waste of public funds.

I haven't been to any more prisons since I met Norman, thank God, but I doubt if much has changed since the late seventies. I'm sure the Barmy Army still trundles its tiny tumbrels around Leeds Prison every dawn, collecting the little faecal parcels thrown out of the cell windows every night by men (three to a cell) not too happy about spending hot nights living with their own shit inside a bucket next to their beds. I'm sure they still do the penitential conga around the courtyard, zombies taken out on a leash for a breath of Leeds air. I'm sure Wormwood Scrubs still keeps its Cat. 'A's in a large cage within the wing, filled with men going palpably crazy with nothing to do, year in, year out. And does the Scrubs still have all those psychopaths making life intolerable for screws, the rest of the cons and staff alike?

There are good men in prison, caring POA officers, AGs, some governors. Equally there are prisoners who regret what they have done and who would dearly like to atone and get out. There are, too, sadly some who must stay inside for a very long time indeed. The system's apparent inability in finding those who need help and in giving men back their dignity, while restraining their liberty, is a national scandal. But, as the great cliché has it, there are no votes in prison. So we shall continue to inflate our sentences, waste their time and our money, and pander to a public half traumatized by fear into believing that prison will answer that deeper malaise that crime inflicts on us all.

Norman's contribution to the debate is important. He has the credentials, and we should listen to him, for his is the authentic voice from inside, and it has something vital to tell us.

PREFACE TO HOLLYWOOD

Dear Hollywood,
Thank you for the murderous images that filled and fuelled my younger
years. Thank you for Bronson, Schwarzenegger, Stallone and all the other
violent killers who rampaged across the screen. At times I became quite
confused. Could murder and mayhem be so wrong when all my favourite
heroes were doing it?

Mickey and Mallory were really cool; Natural Born Heroes, they killed
by the score.

Thank you especially for Hannibal Lector. Urbane, charming, witty,
interesting, what a shame he killed and ate people on the side. How was
I to know that this glamorized, sanitized portrayal was not the true nature
of the serial killer?

For decades I travelled through the bowels of our prison system,
searching for the heroes of my youth. You can imagine my disappointment
when the man never once bore much resemblance to the myth. The serial
killers were all sick, disgusting people; the rapists singularly unattractive;
the gangsters often selfish and mean-spirited. You have misled a whole
generation.

But perhaps my journey hasn't been completely in vain. From my
experience, let me now show you the true nature of the beast. Come into

my world for a while and marvel at the abominations in human form. Bad, most certainly. But also quite mad. Sad even. Glamorous and attractive? Not ever.

Hollywood, how could you have got it so wrong?

NORMAN PARKER

INTRODUCTION

HEART OF A KILLER, SOUL OF A POET

I don't think I was born a criminal; perhaps I just worked at it. Undoubtedly, I have always been a troubled spirit. A deep sentimentality, combined with a profound feeling that the world is oh so unfair, made me too sensitive. I always lived on the borders of pain and unhappiness. Ergo my crimes. Heart of a killer, soul of a poet.

My parents were very ordinary: father a clerk, mother a civil servant, both Jewish. However, it was a marriage in name only. They didn't get along.

I was the eldest child, a small, slim, quiet boy. My sister, three years my junior, was both beautiful and volatile. There were always tempestuous times.

Susan and I were both 15 when we met. If opposites attract, then we were a classic couple. I came from a good background, did well academically and was largely non-violent. Hers was a criminal family, she suffered a learning disability and she was very violent. She regularly attacked other girls, in an age when the gentler sex were just so. Susan and her family were Nazis. Both brothers were personal bodyguards to Sir Oswald Mosley. She slept with a picture of Hitler above her bed and, beneath her pillow, a .45 revolver that her brothers had for armed robberies. (I was persuaded to look after the rest of the guns.) An interesting situation, with me a non-practising Jew!

At times, Susan and I loved each other deeply. But living with a clinical kleptomaniac, whose violent outbursts kept her permanently under a psychiatrist's care, was never easy. It had a predictable end.

Mad with jealousy over her latest infidelity, I confronted her. She fetched the revolver from beneath her pillow; luckily for me, her best friend was a witness to this. Alone now, we argued violently. The shot carne from the pistol I had been carrying in my belt. She died amidst a scene I can still recall graphically these 30 years later.

Murder with a firearm was then a capital offence. At 18, I stood trial for my life at the Old Bailey. In the event, I was convicted of manslaughter and sentenced to six years. I couldn't have cared if they had hanged me.

The memory of what had happened was with me all the days of my sentence. It was worse when I got out. By now though I was clinically depressed and consumed with rage. It was just a matter of time.

John was a violent Scots robber. We went on several bits of work together. A climactic argument saw him pull a gun on me. While I struggled with him, a friend hit him with a hammer. I wrested the gun free and shot John several times. Then we tried to hide the body.

This time I got 'life' for murder; my friend was acquitted. In 1970, at 25 years of age, I faced the rest of my life in jail.

But I was the irresistible force against the immovable object. My rebelliousness took me on a bizarre and incredible journey through the bowels of the system. My spirit drove me forever onwards. I am just emerging now, a quarter of a century later.

Along the way, I witnessed terrible things, some of which I recount here. For *Parkhurst Tales* is the story of that journey. The telling does not purge the memories though, and they are with me constantly.

So if you would be a warrior and walk the path of the mad and the bad, come into my world for a while. This time you can leave; the next you might not be so lucky.

Welcome to my world, come walk with me a while and feel my pain.
You may see things that disturb you,
but you will also see feats of strength and courage.
There will be men like beasts
Free-world values will be inverted.
It will be a festival of the bizarre,
For in the Kingdom of Parkhurst, nature imitates art.

NORMAN PARKER

1 THE PLACE BY THE POND

If Parkhurst was an unlovely prison, then Parkhurst hospital was absolutely in keeping with the rest of the place. An ugly red-brick building, it stood on its own, away from the main wings. Cracked brickwork, peeling paint, broken slates and gutters clogged with leaves all added to a general air of decrepitude.

There were large sliding sash windows, but they were begrimed and massively barred. Heavy steel gates that were permanently locked stood in the place of doors. You could be forgiven for mistaking the building's function because it certainly didn't look like a place where people were nursed and cared for.

And it wasn't. The hospital screws were mean-spirited to a man. Perhaps, long ago, the milk of human kindness had flowed in some of them. But no more. Long years of watching the most abject human suffering had inured them to the daily misery that they were part of. If there was such a thing as a bedside manner here, it was characterised by indifference and downright cruelty.

The few 'medical' patients were confined to a surgical ward where they waited for, or recovered from, operations. The rest were detained in the hospital under mental-health 'sections', awaiting certification and transfer to one of the 'special hospitals' for the criminally insane.

These patients were mostly regarded as dangerous animals to be contained and their violent behaviour curbed. They were locked in cells for all but a few hours each day, the loneliness of solitary confinement exacerbating their already parlous mental state. Small wonder that, on occasion, some would attack the screws.

Then, they would be beaten; flung naked into strip cells; filled with mind-numbing drugs; or left for days in a strait-jacket. For these were not normal men, easily coerced. They were men driven by obsessions so intense that their sanity had crumbled under the pressure. Men whose every waking second was a painful torment. In some cases, they were men for whom death would come as a merciful release.

Yet in the midst of all this ugliness and suffering, there was a place that was an oasis of peace and beauty. Out of a side door from F2 landing was a small enclosed yard. In the middle lay a pond surrounded by neatly mown grass. Running around it was a white flagstone path.

On a fine day, the water of the pond would glisten with reflected light. Fish would swim lazily beneath the lily pads. Small insects would skitter across the surface. It was an idyllic setting, far from the smells of F2 and the haunting cries of lunatics locked behind doors.

For a short while, a man could remember he was human again. That there was another world, apart from the one of concrete floors, brick walls and iron doors. He could lie on the grass and think of days when he played with his children in a similar setting. Of days when he held hands with a wife or girlfriend and basked in the warmth of her love.

The frantic heart would still, the frenzied mind would clear and a man could regain something of his sanity.

But it was all too short. Hardly had they laid down but a screw would call out that exercise time was over for another day. Men would climb reluctantly to their feet and amble back into the building. The sweet, fresh air would be replaced by the acrid, all-pervasive smell of piss. In places, the sickly sweet smell of shit would assail the nostrils. Unfriendly screws would shepherd men back into their cells. The doors would crash shut with an awesome finality, leaving each man incarcerated with only his loneliness and recent memories of the place by the pond.

Vic was one of the lunatics. He was seriously, certifiably insane and waiting for a place in Rampton or Broadmoor. It was said that, on two occasions, he had been taken to the very gates of Broadmoor in a van, only to be refused admission because he was too violent.

And he was extremely violent. To himself and others, too. A powerfully built man in his early 30s, he was doing five for GBH. From gypsy stock, his swarthy skin gave him a Mediterranean appearance. Long, lank, greasy black hair hung down around hunched, muscular shoulders. His inordinately long arms were covered with hundreds of scars caused by self-mutilation. He walked bent over, with his long arms hanging down by his sides, giving him a definitely ape-like appearance.

Vic was on heavy medication. Every morning, noon and night, he was given tots of various psychotropic drugs. He would drink each of these like an alcoholic taking his first drink of the day. With each swallow, he would shake his head. He rarely spoke to anyone, just ambled about in a drug-induced stupor.

He could be tranquil for months at a time. He would stumble, beast-like, through his daily round, sedated from the intrusions of reality. But, when the medication wore off, he could become especially dangerous.

Vic liked to sit by the pond. Each day, he would amble out into the yard and lie in the same place. There was a small mound at one end of the pond. He would stretch out there with his head on the mound and stare at the sky. It was comfortable and comforting just lying there. The vast infinity of space seemed to pour in through his eyes and cool his fevered brain. It was nice by the pond.

For the past few months, Vic had had a friend of sorts. Tom was a young intense Scouser, with a pale emaciated face and a frail drug-raddled body. His corpse-like appearance only served to emphasise his eyes. They burned with a fierce intensity, reflecting the flames of madness that raged in his brain.

In the course of their solitary lives, Vic and Tom rarely met, except on exercise. Then Tom would come and sit by Vic as he lay by the pond. They hardly ever spoke, and then only in monosyllables. It could hardly be described as a friendship. Just two lost souls, warming each other with their company.

It was a fine summer's day. The heat in the hospital was stifling. There was no breath of wind, and the myriad smells just hung in the air. When their doors were unlocked for exercise, the patients hurried towards the brightness flooding in from the yard. As Vic burst free from the building, the sweet, fresh air filled his nostrils and his heart swelled in his chest. He headed for his usual place, then stopped.

There, lying in his place by the pond, was a new fella. He was stretched out, head on the mound, staring at the sky. It was exactly the position Vic usually adopted.

Vic stared at him more closely. The newcomer was plump, balding and middle-aged. His clothes were unbuttoned, his hair unkempt, his face unshaven. He stared upwards, totally oblivious to his surroundings, through dead-fish eyes glazed by drugs.

Vic moved past him to the other side of the pond. Tom shuffled along behind. Not a word had been spoken.

Vic looked around the yard. Three screws were supervising exercise. They were stood in a group by the doorway to the wing, engrossed in conversation.

Vic bent down. Pushing his fingers into the earth either side of a large white flagstone, he pulled it from the path. He walked quickly around the pond. Coming sideways on to the new fella, he raised the flagstone high above his head. With all his considerable strength, he smashed the edge of the flagstone into the unsuspecting face.

There was a dull, meaty thud, as stone struck flesh and bone. With a grunt of effort, Vic fell to his knees and rained more blows into the mess of blood and gore that, seconds earlier, had been a face.

A high-pitched scream rent the air as Tom appeared at Vic's shoulder and began smashing at the face with a smaller piece of flagstone.

The noise alerted the screws. One hurried to ring a nearby alarm bell. The other two ran towards the pond.

The first rushed at Tom and pushed him roughly aside. The second grabbed Vic's upraised arms firmly, but gently. 'Come on, Vic,' he said. 'Away you come.'

Vic rose slowly to his feet. He lowered the blood-spattered flagstone, then let it drop in the grass. He allowed the screw to lead him away, back towards the building.

Tom had also dropped his flagstone and was being gently pushed in the same direction. The new fella lay motionless on the ground. Not a word had been spoken.

Now there were dozens of screws in the yard. They poured in from F2 and through a gate in the wall. Some shepherded the rest of the patients in from exercise. The others stood in a semi-circle about the newcomer.

A stretcher appeared and he was lifted on to it. They carried him into the hospital. The bloodstained flagstones were left where they had fallen. They would eventually be examined by the police, for they would have to be called in. To the experienced eye, the newcomer looked like he would die.

But he didn't. Perhaps it would have been more merciful if he had. Massive brain damage would ensure that he never moved a muscle again. He was totally paralysed, a complete cabbage both mentally and physically.

At the subsequent trial, Vic and Tom were charged with attempted murder. Both were sentenced to life imprisonment. Strangely, their obvious insanity wasn't a mitigating factor. They were shunted off into different parts of the prison system, where they probably amble around under heavy medication to this day.

Back at Parkhurst hospital, everything was as usual. The water of the pond glistened in the bright sunlight. The grass grew lush and green, the blood long since washed into the mound by the rain. There were two holes in the path where flagstones had once been. Other lunatics lay in the sunshine. The place by the pond looked peaceful and idyllic, unmarred by its terrible secret.

2 ARRIVAL

I woke immediately and sat halfway up. It was purely a reflex action. I couldn't actually recall hearing the bolt being drawn, the lock shooting back or the door opening, but something had roused me. Now, through sleep-dazed eyes, I could see the crush of screws wedged in my doorway. There must have been ten of them, all hatless.

A frisson of fear followed by a rush of adrenalin brought me fully awake. Whatever it was, the situation was serious. You just didn't have ten screws coming into your cell at 6.30 on a Saturday morning.

'Pack your kit,' said the white shirt, who was obviously a PO or an SO.

I knew that it was a waste of time to argue. These were just foot soldiers acting under orders. You might as well argue with robots. The decision had already been made, and they hadn't been part of the decision-making process.

'Just tell me if I'm going to the chokey or out of the jail,' I said to the white shirt.

He looked at me, pausing while he made his decision. 'You're going out of the jail,' he said.

So I was being shanghaied. It wasn't the first time. My only concern now was to take all my stuff with me. If I left it behind to follow me on, all sorts of things could go missing.

'I'm not going without my kit, guvnor. So just give me 15 minutes to pack up,' I said.

He weighed this up, then agreed. He probably figured that if he had me dragged out it would take time anyway. Then there would be the legacy of dealing with my pals when they were unlocked later. It was a sensible decision.

I quickly threw everything into four large kit boxes that I had under my bed. I'd been in that cell in Wormwood Scrubs for two years, yet every trace of my occupation was boxed and gone in 20 minutes.

I sat in reception, reflecting on what I was leaving and what lay ahead. I felt a deep sadness for the loss of the friends I was leaving behind. But I had to stifle these feelings to gear myself up for the challenge to come.

By the time the escort was ready to leave, it was nearly 9.00 a.m. I was expecting a visit from my mother and sister that morning. Now I would miss it. It wasn't worth mentioning. As an 'A' man, they wouldn't tell my family I was leaving.

Ironically, as we drove out of the gate in the green van with the tinted windows, we passed my mother and sister waiting to come in. They were close enough to touch, yet I couldn't let them know I was in the van. How I hated those bastards for the unnecessary suffering they caused.

Soon, we were on the road. I had no idea where I was going and wouldn't give the screws the satisfaction of asking. They might not have told me anyway. I sat there and tried to work it out for myself. The further we went, the easier it would be to figure out my destination.

We were heading south, so that made it easy. There were only two category-A jails south of the Scrubs: Albany and Parkhurst, both on the Isle of Wight. I couldn't see it being Albany, as I'd been shanghaied from there two years previously for an escape attempt followed by a tear-up. They certainly wouldn't want me back. The feeling was mutual.

The thought of Parkhurst didn't exactly frighten me, but I didn't take it lightly either. I had heard so many stories about the place. It had the reputation of being Britain's toughest jail. There had been a bad riot there in '69, brutally put down by the screws.

Parkhurst had seen several murders and countless stabbings and coshings. It was a jail to sort the men from the boys. I felt that I could handle it but, as with any serious challenge, couldn't help but have some misgivings.

We duly reached Southampton and drove on to the ferry. Any thoughts of a breezy walk on the deck were quickly dashed. We all sat in the darkness of the hold. Half an hour later, we drove off at Ryde.

The 'Island', as always, looked quite beautiful. It was a sad irony that such a place should be blighted by the presence of Albany and Parkhurst. The lovely surroundings made the jails seem that much grimmer.

Suddenly, we turned off the road to be confronted by a massive pair of wooden gates, set in a weather-beaten gate lodge. The immediate impression was one of age. The chipped brickwork, the rusting iron, all showed the decay of years.

'Grim' is a word often used to describe jails, but Parkhurst personified all that was grim. It was as if all the grief and misery it had witnessed had lined and cracked its façade, just as misery cracks and lines an old face.

There was an air of hopelessness about the place. Nothing new could come to Parkhurst; it had experienced it all before. It had eroded the youth of so many spirited young men, and it would do the same to so many more.

Inside the gate lodge, it was just as depressing. Surly, chunky, middle-aged screws went about their business at their own pace.

The outside world would have to slow down. It was now in the domain of Parkhurst, and Parkhurst wasn't going to be rushed for anyone.

We drove through a big green iron gate, past some low buildings and stopped outside the reception. We all got out of the van and I went in with the screw I was handcuffed to. While the others unloaded my boxes, the cuffs were removed.

A stern-faced screw was waiting behind a counter. There was no negotiation. He stated what was allowed at Parkhurst and what wasn't. I had entered the reception with several boxes. I left with one. The rest would stay in the property room until I moved on to a more liberal jail.

Carrying my box, I walked up a steep hill towards the wings. There were no neat paths or flower beds, just dirt, gravel, weeds and rubble.

We entered 'D' wing through a dingy corridor. It was quiet and deserted. I realised that it must be the dinnertime bang-up.

There was a con sitting on the hot-plate, just inside the gate. As he looked at me, a smile lit up his face. It was Jeff Bunning, a little raver who had been in the Albany trouble with me two years before.

'Hello, Norman,' he said. 'You've come to a right piss-hole here.'

I nodded a quick 'Hello' as we swept past. Within seconds, we were through into 'A' wing. A cell was open on the ones and I went inside with my box. The door banged shut behind me. I sat down in a dirty, dusty cell that obviously hadn't been occupied for weeks. Apart from my encounter with the reception screw, not one word had been said to me. I had arrived at Parkhurst.

Just before 2.00 p.m. the wing was unlocked. I heard a considerable hubbub as men hurried along landings and clattered down stairs. As I left my cell, I nearly bumped into someone coming in. The fat, balding face above the massive chest broke into a broad grin. It was Ken Cohen, an old pal of mine who I hadn't seen for several years. Then, he had been doing a five for long-firms. In the early Sixties, the Twins had several front-men running frauds for them. Sometimes, these front-men would forget who was really running things. It was Ken's job to remind them.

A Jewish boy who knew his way around a pound note, Ken was a big lump. A fattish 16 stone with a bull neck, his most striking feature was his chest. Heavy bench presses had pumped it up to enormous proportions.

Ken was no lumpen thug, though. He had both intelligence and style. His trademark had been to walk into the office of the offender all booted and suited, complete with an expensive briefcase. He would start off reasonably enough but, at some point in the conversation, would suddenly pull a steel hatchet from the briefcase and embed it in the desk in front of the petrified fraudsman. If the latter had had the presence of mind to look carefully, he would have noticed that Ken had gone to the trouble of having the hatchet gold-plated. No doubt this concession to style was lost on most of them.

'Glad to see you, Norman,' he said now, as he threw his arms around me and hugged me. 'Come and meet some of the fellas.'

We walked out on to the ones to find that a small crowd had gathered. I was introduced to about ten fellas. I immediately felt at ease, realising that I was in the company of my own kind. They were all Londoners. Most were robbers, but a couple were in for just violence. Although I had never met any of them before, some I had heard of and most were friends of friends.

About half were 'A' men like myself. I began to feel more at home. In most jails, Londoners stick together. It was almost traditional that they welcome one of their own on arrival.

Saturday afternoon is a time of high activity in the majority of jails. Most cons arrange to do something or other. There were visits, racing and sport on the telly and outside association in the compound. The fellas made their various excuses about prior commitments and said they would see me later.

'Come on, I'll show you about the place,' Ken said. 'It's a bit of a filthy piss-hole, but the screws leave you right alone here. That's why I don't mind it at all.'

We walked through to 'D' wing, then along the corridor through which I had entered a couple of hours earlier. We stepped outside on to the same steep hill, but this time I was going down.

Ken pointed out the chokey on the right, with its tiny wire-covered exercise yard. On the left was a separate building surrounded by high walls. This prison within a prison, the 'Security Wing', housed Ron and Reg Kray (universally known as 'the Twins'), a couple of IRA men and several others doing exceptionally long sentences. The place bristled with security devices. There were cameras pointing in all directions.

At the bottom of the hill, we turned sharp right, then came to an open gate on our left. We went through into the compound. There were several workshops at the far end, both brick-built and prefabricated. Immediately in front of us was a large tarmac football area. It adjoined a tarmac basketball court.

Both were full of people. The football area, however, was ridiculously overcrowded. There must have been 40 players crammed on to the three-quarter-sized pitch. They were dressed in a wildly differing and bizarre assortment of clothes. One big athletic-looking fella was dressed from head to toe in white – white vest, white shorts, white socks and white trainers – making him look like a professional sportsman. Others had on drab prison-issue gym kit and looked like the 'Bash Street Kids' at play. Most were dressed in their normal prison clothes, though, charging about in overalls, shirt and shoes.

Right in the middle of this motley throng was an elderly fella with a badly crippled leg. He was dressed in overalls and a very long khaki-coloured raincoat. A blue beret was pulled down tightly around his ears. It could have been Benny Hill. He certainly wouldn't have looked out of place.

Needless to say, under these conditions the quality of the

football left a lot to be desired. In fact, it wasn't football as I'd ever seen it played. The pitch was so crowded that it was impossible to run with the ball. As soon as it appeared, the players would lash at it wildly with their feet. It reminded me of those amusement arcade games where, at the flick of a lever, miniature wooden footballers swung a leg at a little plastic ball.

'There are a lot of nutters here, Norman,' said Ken, probably feeling that some explanation was due. 'Some of them are quite dangerous, but we're a strong firm here and none of them come near us.'

I had been looking carefully at the cons and had already noticed the high proportion of crazy-looking ones. Nearly everyone looked aggressive or tough. Central casting could have hired them out *en masse* as a prize crew for a pirate film. It was immediately obvious that Parkhurst was half prison, half lunatic asylum. It was quite depressing to think that this was how the authorities classified me.

We turned right, past the tarmac area. The path led between some prefabricated workshops on the left and another football pitch on the right. I use the term 'football pitch' loosely, for I had never seen one like it. There were vast areas of bare earth. Where the halfway line should have been, the Works Department had at some time dug a trench. Insufficient backfill had caused the ground to subside, leaving a concave depression about four inches deep. It went right across the pitch. Any player dribbling across the halfway line would have to flick the ball over the dip and jump after it.

The two touch-lines were a study in extreme contrast. On one side there was, tight to the line, a raised path a good two-and-a-half feet above the level of the pitch. This meant that any player forced into touch on that side would crash into the hip-high bank and roll on to the path.

Tight to the other touch-line was a brick retaining wall, its top level with the pitch. Beyond this was a two-foot drop on to a concrete path. Players forced into touch on this side would find that the ground had suddenly disappeared from beneath their feet, sending them crashing. Not surprisingly, broken legs were a regular occurrence.

In any other setting, this pitch would have seemed bizarre. In Parkhurst, though, it was just right. It could have been designed for the place.

As we walked, Ken told me about the nick in general. All the cons had several previous convictions and were rejects from other jails. Many had seriously assaulted either screws or cons before being moved here. Consequently, Parkhurst had the reputation of being the end of the line. It was full of people the system had given up on.

It came as no surprise that the parole rate was negligible. All that the vast majority of cons had to look forward to was nine months on the 'hostel scheme' at the end. On a long sentence, this was hardly enough to motivate anyone.

According to Ken, Parkhurst wasn't just one jail, it was four. There was the main jail, comprising wings 'A', 'B' and 'D'. This was the normal location for most people.

Second, there was the Security Wing with its dozen or so extra-high-risk cons. People whose escape couldn't even be contemplated.

Third, there was 'C' wing, which was especially for psychiatric cases. This wasn't the only criteria, though, because, if it had been, most of the jail would have qualified. 'C' wing was for highly dangerous psychiatric cases. All of them had severely injured screws or other cons. A couple had committed murders in jail and got a life sentence on top.

The 'C'-wing regime was all kid-glove treatment and unlimited psychotropic drugs. The atmosphere was extremely heavy. Some nutter or other would regularly go berserk and try to kill another nutter, for little or no reason. It was all very unpredictable.

Last, there was the hospital. This housed patients waiting for, or recovering from, operations. It also housed very violent cons awaiting certification, or those certified and waiting for a place at Rampton or Broadmoor. The former were kept in a locked ward, the latter on a landing called F2.

F2 was a legend throughout the prison system. The hospital screws could handle anyone on F2. They would either beat them senseless or drug them until they didn't know whether they were coming or going. Men would be left in strait-jackets for days on end. Any complaints were ignored as the ravings of lunatics.

I had a glimpse of F2 a couple of days later. I was called over to the hospital for an interview with Dr Cooper, the senior psychiatrist. As I sat waiting in a small reception area, I noticed a large partition that ran from floor to ceiling. I wandered over and peered through a window. I was looking at F2 landing.

I was immediately struck by its strange appearance. Everything looked so terribly antiquated. The decor matched the dull creams and browns of the mental hospitals of the Fifties.

The hospital screws seemed all of a type. Middle-aged, squat, corpulent and powerful-looking, there wasn't an ounce of compassion in their manner. They looked like men who had seen so much suffering that they had long since become inured to it. There would be no mercy at their hands.

Suddenly, several of them moved purposefully towards an open area further down the landing. Here, the cells spread out in an arc, with a circular, open space in front of them. There was bright daylight coming from the opposite side. I took this to be an open door to an exercise yard.

The screws took up positions around the circular area. They stood with their backs to the wall, spaced ten feet apart. When they were all in position, a screw went to one of the cells in the arc. Without looking through the spy-hole, he unlocked the door and opened it outwards, keeping himself behind it. Then he walked quickly to join the others, staying close to the wall all the time.

I watched this performance with amazement. It was as if they were letting out a dangerous animal. I stared with mounting anticipation to see who or what would appear.

For several seconds there was nothing. Then a figure shuffled into view He was a black man of indeterminate age. It was difficult to discern his build, because he was bent almost double. He was no giant though. He ambled forward lopsidedly, with an ape-like gait.

The screws kept their faces pointed straight ahead, but their eyes swivelled to follow his every move. As he disappeared into the daylight, they broke from their positions along the walls and followed him outside. The hospital screws at Parkhurst weren't known for overreacting. I wondered what manner of man could demand such a healthy respect from them.

Although the hospital screws ruled F2 with brutality and fear, this wasn't the case in the rest of the jail. Ken explained that, after the riot in '69 and all the bad publicity, they had to pull in their horns a bit. The heavy mob who gave out all the kickings was broken up and dispersed to other jails. It wasn't a liberal regime now by any means, but the regular organised beatings were no longer a feature. This was something I grew to be grateful for in the months to come.

The exercise period came to an end. All the various footballers, basketball players, runners, walkers and watchers made their way out of the compound and back to their wings. Ken and I walked with the crowd. As we entered 'D' wing, we saw that tea was about to be served. It was the usual Saturday prison tea of eggs, cheese and salad. We went through into 'A' wing and joined the queue.

As we waited, Ken explained that 'A' wing was the reception wing. Everyone started off there. Then they either stayed or moved over to 'B' or 'D' wing. 'D' wing was supposed to be the most easygoing. However, Ken had got used to 'A' wing and would stay there for the duration.

I was still taking it all in. My main priority was to escape, so good wings and bad wings didn't come into it. I would go to the one that offered me the best chance. And, from what I had seen of Parkhurst so far, I couldn't wait to have a pop.

Ken finished his seven and never looked back. He became a wealthy and successful businessman in Southampton.

3 THE OLD BAILEY

At six o'clock, we were unlocked for evening association. As I came out of my cell, I met Dave Bailey who was in the cell next door. He had been introduced to me earlier by Ken.

Dave was a quiet, unassuming sort of fella in his late 20s. Of medium height, slim, with short black hair and black horn-rimmed glasses, he looked like a bank clerk. Nothing could have been further from the truth, for he had, in fact, been a bank robber and a very active one at that. He considered himself lucky to be doing only eight years.

Dave told me that anyone who didn't go up to the stage rooms for association would be banged up for the evening. They didn't allow cell association on 'A' wing, which had the reputation of being the worst wing as far as privileges were concerned. I walked with Dave to the stage rooms.

We went up a flight of stairs, through a couple of gates and along a dingy corridor. Suddenly we came to a number of large rooms. Two were in darkness except for the neon glow from the TV sets. A third had a full-sized table-tennis table in it. The last was a large kitchen-cum-dining room. There were two gas cookers against a wall and a pair of tables surrounded by chairs in the middle.

We had been sitting there for about ten minutes when a fella entered the room and approached our table. A big man, in his early 30s, he had two striking features: very broad shoulders that swung as he walked, and a wicked-looking scar that ran all down one side of his face and across his chin. Jet-black hair and a certain swarthiness combined with the scar to give him a thoroughly intimidating appearance. He looked like just the sort of fella you wouldn't want to have a row with.

Dave's face registered surprise, then he jumped up from the table with a 'Hello, John'. They walked over and sat down at the table.

As Dave introduced me, I realised that I had heard of John Harrison. He was a well-known armed robber. Although the English police don't officially have a 'ten most wanted' as they do in the States, unofficially he had been the Met's 'Public Enemy No. 1'. This was undoubtedly reflected in the 15 stretch that he had drawn.

Like me, John had also arrived at Parkhurst that morning. He was still suffering from the effects of a shotgun wound to his upper arm, caused accidentally on a bit of work. He hadn't been able to go to hospital with it at first, which had caused complications to set in. Eventually, he flew to Spain for treatment. The outcome was that, although it had happened several months previously, he was still passing blood. That was why they put him in the hospital wing first. After a quick check-up, he had been put on 'A' wing.

Dave and John were old friends and had been on several bits of work together. There was no immediate hostility between John and me, but there was a certain wariness, a degree of feeling each other out.

It didn't really help matters when it transpired that the Jock I had killed had been a pal of John's down the Moor. It was balanced somewhat by the fact that I was good friends with John's cousin, Clive. However, at that moment, John and I were just comrades, fellow Londoners in a prison a long way from home. There was no sense in falling out. We had enough common enemies among the screws and some of the crazier cons.

If Saturday evening was boring, Sunday was an even longer and more tedious day. We went out to the compound in the morning and again in the afternoon. In the evening, we sat up in the stage rooms talking. After three hours of conversation the previous evening, we were rapidly running out of things to say.

This was barely preferable to a solitary evening banged up in a cell. But I wouldn't give the screws the satisfaction of having me behind my door voluntarily. As it was, they had us locked up far, far too long anyway. On a long sentence, you had to protect yourself from the damage that solitary living does to the personality. I intended to be out and interacting with others as much as possible.

They didn't waste a lot of time allocating work to John and me. First thing Monday morning, we were told to start in the tin shop right away. Neither of us really minded. We knew that, if we weren't at work, they would bang us up. An added incentive was the fact that Dave, Barry Hurley and several of our pals worked in there, too.

The tin shop was a one-storey prefabricated building with a corrugated asbestos roof. It stood in the compound about 30 feet from the fence. There were heavy bars on all the windows, which were set in old wooden frames. It had a decidedly ramshackle appearance.

In reality, the tin shop occupied only half the building. The other half was the press shop. Whereas the latter contained large sophisticated machinery which cut and shaped metal, the tin shop was a low-technology, labour-intensive production line. It mainly turned out metal wastepaper bins.

Each grey bin came in several pre-manufactured parts. The job of the production line was to assemble the bins by fitting the thick round bottom to the curved sides. They were finished off by curling the top rim around a steel hoop.

There was a machine that resembled a giant tin-opener, complete with a handle that turned. Instead of cutting metal, though, it stitched the sides of the bin to the bottom. The finishing touches were provided by beating the rim with a hammer until it neatly curled around the metal hoop.

Not only was the work boring and repetitive, it was also extremely noisy. All day long the shop rang with the crashes and shrieks of worked metal.

The tin shop was potentially a very dangerous place. There were quite a few unstable and dangerous cons working there. Hammers, iron bars and screwdrivers were all readily available. There was always the possibility that some nutter would creep up and bash you with something.

About six of our crowd worked in the shop. We were no strangers to violence ourselves and had inflicted more than our fair share on other people. In the event of trouble, we would all stick together.

Even by Parkhurst standards, we were a strong firm. There was no great fear of anyone coming at us unprovoked – marauding bullies would look for softer targets. There was always the chance, though, that one of our group might upset a nutter who would then creep up and go berserk with a deadly weapon. So we were always on our guard. We regularly laughed and joked between ourselves, but we could never completely relax.

I settled into the shop quite easily. I liked to do a bit of work to pass the time, provided it wasn't too objectionable. The rest of our group felt the same. We would knock out a certain number of bins each day. It didn't take long and it kept the civvies happy. They never bothered us at all. We took our tea-breaks when we liked and for as long as we liked. So, compared to some shops, the tin shop wasn't bad at all. Each morning and afternoon before work, all our London crowd would meet in Dave's cell. We would discuss the latest gossip, reputations would be scrutinised and we would judge whether someone was a decent fella or not. It was a bit like putting them on trial in their absence. We came to refer to Dave Bailey's cell as the 'Old Bailey'.

There was a nucleus of about ten of us who were pals and would stick together if any trouble started. There were a few more on the fringes who dropped in regularly. A couple of these were tolerated rather than liked. They hung around with us for the laughs and for the security that membership of the group brought. But we knew that, if it was really off, we couldn't expect too much help from them; consequently, they didn't have our total loyalty.

One morning, several days after we had started in the tin shop, John and I were sitting in Dave's cell waiting to go to work. It was getting late and still there had been no work call. However, this wasn't unusual. Security checks or trouble often caused delays.

The fellas had drifted in and out until there were just the three of us left. Dave was sitting upright at the top of his bed, his back against the bed-head. John was slouched across the bottom. I was sitting in Dave's chair on the other side of the cell, with one arm resting on the table next to Dave's radio which was playing softly. In the background, we could hear the occasional *crash* as a cell door slammed. At first, we took no notice, but the noises grew louder and closer. Suddenly, our landing screw was standing in the doorway.

Every landing has a screw who is responsible for it. The landing screw for the ones was a right pig. The animal metaphor wasn't too much of an exaggeration either, because he even looked the part.

Only about 30 years old, he was a bloated 18 stone. Massively flabby thighs led up to an enormously fat arse that stretched the normally baggy and shapeless uniform trousers skin tight. Several rolls of fat of decreasing girth ran from his waist to his chest. Piggy eyes, peering out from the swollen face, gave him a decidedly porcine look. But, whereas many pigs are stamped with the name of their country of origin, nature had stamped this one with a bright-red tomato-shaped birthmark on the nape of his corpulent neck. Our crowd always referred to him as 'Tomato Neck'.

He was a small-minded, uncaring, petty man who never took into consideration any suffering that an order might cause. To him, orders were like holy scripture, sacrosanct and unchangeable. They were there to be obeyed.

He came from a long line of screws. His father and grandfather had been screws. There were rumours that even some females of the clan had also earned a living locking people up. I suppose you could say that the secret of Tomato Neck's nature lay in the breeding.

His fat red face seemed to fill the doorway. 'Away to your own cells and bang up then,' he said. 'The tin shop's flooded and there's no work this morning.'

The tin shop was so old and ramshackle that it was not surprising that the roof leaked when it rained heavily. But it was hardly our fault. Why should we have to spend a morning locked up in our cells just because their roof leaked?

'It ain't our fault that the roof leaks, guvnor,' I said. 'Why don't you leave us unlocked?'

'I'm not having a dozen "A" men running about my landing all morning,' he responded immediately, in a tone that brooked no argument.

'Why don't you bang the three of us up together,' interjected John.

Tomato Neck didn't even hesitate. 'No, I want you all away to your own cells.'

His dismissive arrogance suddenly made me very angry. 'Well, you'd better go and get some fucking help then,' I said aggressively.

For a second he was taken aback. 'Right,' he said petulantly, 'I will.' With that, he spun around and stormed away.

Back in the cell, no one spoke. We all knew the situation we were in now. It looked like there was going to be a confrontation. One side or the other would have to back down, otherwise there would be a row

Now that we had made a stand, we could hardly back off at a show of force. Any credibility we ever had would be gone. The screws would know that, if they wanted to, they could take liberties with us. It would be the start of a long and slippery slope to humiliation. Now, it was a matter of pride.

For me, there were also other considerations. Even though I had been at Parkhurst for just a short time, I hated the place. Rather than suffer a couple of years of constant aggravation, maybe it would be better to have a serious tear-up right now and get moved to another jail.

Dave, John and I weren't under any illusions about the coming row. We weren't going to win. There were hundreds of them and only three of us. We might be able to hurt a few of them before we went under, but we were in for a good kicking and a hard time in the chokey before we departed.

I couldn't help feeling sorry for Dave. John was doing 15 and I was doing life. They wouldn't bother to take us to an outside court in the event of a serious tear-up. Any more time on top would be almost irrelevant. Dave, though, was only doing an eight. Therefore, he had far more to lose than we did.

We knew he would stay with us out of loyalty. Normally he was an easygoing fella who didn't get into much trouble in prison. It wasn't lack of bottle. He just didn't look for trouble.

We sat there, not talking. The time for talking had long since passed. There was no strategy to discuss; we would be vastly outnumbered. We sat there in strained silence, staring straight ahead, waiting to see what developed.

We heard more doors banging. They must have been locking up the wing cleaners now. If it was going to be off, they didn't want other cons about who might join in against them.

The distant slamming and banging was an ominous sound. It

was almost like an artillery bombardment before an enemy offensive. In one way, it was just that. It was meant to intimidate us psychologically, to show that they meant business.

Suddenly we heard the clatter of many pairs of metal-tipped boots coming down the stairs to the ones. Then there was the growing thunder of marching feet drawing closer to Dave's cell. We looked at each other resignedly, but no one said anything. I remember thinking to myself, Here we go.

The doorway darkened as the screws came to a halt outside. It was impossible to count how many there were. The front ones crowded into the narrow doorway. There was just a mass of dark-blue uniforms, fronted by taut, threatening faces.

The wing PO stepped across the threshold. He was a humourless, cold man, with a face pallid from too much time spent indoors, short cropped hair and gold-rimmed spectacles that gave him a distinctly Germanic appearance. Our group called him 'Goebbels'. This was more than just a prison joke. We detested the man and felt that he and the original Goebbels were of a type. If there was a difference, it was only a matter of degree.

We had reached an absolutely crucial moment. What happened now would determine the outcome of the confrontation. We all realised that to show any fear or weakness would encourage Goebbels and his men to press forward. I didn't even look up at the PO, just continued to stare fixedly past him.

He faced me and said, 'Parker, I'm giving you a direct order to leave this cell.'

Precisely as he sounded the last syllable, I replied, 'Stick your direct order up your arsehole.'

Fighting hard to keep his face impassive, he turned to John. He started to repeat the order. He only got as far as 'I'm giving you …' when John replied with a throaty 'Bollocks'. The tension was electric. This was it. There would be no compromise now.

Very slowly, I slid my arm across the table and closer to Dave's radio, which was still playing softly. I consciously resolved to smash the black plastic casing into the side of Goebbels's face the instant the tear-up started. If I was going to get a belting, I might as well have the satisfaction of knowing that, somewhere, Goebbels would be sitting with a very sore and swollen face.

'Right,' said Goebbels with all the finality of someone reaching a momentous decision.

I sat tense as a spring. I was only seconds away from serious injury. 'Right,' I thought, 'this is it.'

'Right,' said Goebbels again. Immediately, I felt that something was wrong with his performance. One 'Right' was enough, then came the action. There was no need for the second 'Right'. It seriously detracted from the finality of the first.

'Right,' said Goebbels a third time. Now that certainly wasn't right. One 'Right', obviously. Maybe two 'Rights' at a push. But a third 'Right' smacked of dithering. I suddenly had the feeling that there wasn't going to be a tear-up after all.

Turning to the screws crowding in the doorway, he barked, 'You first two stay here, the rest of you come with me.' With that, he was out the door.

We heard the thunder of many boots again, but this time going away from the cell.

We turned to each other and started laughing. Partly it was relief, but it was also very comical to see Goebbels mount such an elaborate display of force only to back down at the last moment.

'Looks like a bit of arsehole trouble,' said John, roaring with laughter.

'Perhaps he's gone for reinforcements,' I chipped in. 'Look, he's left a couple of sentries.' I pointed to the backs of the two screws standing either side of the doorway.

After a few seconds, these left, too, walking away quietly across the ones. There was no aggressive stamping of feet now.

Although we were laughing, we were considerably relieved. The screws had backed down, but it wasn't because they feared they would lose the fight. They knew that a couple of them would probably get hurt and that might have deterred them a bit. The real deterrent, though, was that it would have been a serious incident. Parkhurst didn't want any more bad publicity about brutality. It could all have easily ended up in a court case; certainly it would have gone before the VC. Then there was the distinct possibility of more trouble from the rest of our crowd when they were unlocked again.

However, it was a significant victory on our part. We had made a stand against the hard-line regime that was peculiar to 'A' wing. John and I both knew that, as new arrivals, we would be blamed, and we would be top of the screws' 'hate list'. It didn't bother us. We hated them with a passion, too.

Now there was a new and deeper relationship between John and me. We had both stood together in the face of a mutual threat. There was trust and loyalty now. We both knew that, in a similar threatening situation, we would stick together again. From that moment, we were good pals.

Suddenly, we heard the sound of screws going along the landings unlocking doors. There was the usual hubbub, as men who had been locked up hurried back to what they had been doing before.

The sound of the doors opening grew closer. Once again, Tomato Neck's face appeared in the doorway. Trying hard to sound as if nothing had happened, he said, 'OK, everybody who isn't working go up to the stage rooms for association.' With that, he was gone.

We had only contempt for him. He had had the added humiliation of having to tell us that we had won. Going up to the stage rooms might not be the same as association on the landing, but it was a lot better than being locked up every time the workshop was closed. Also, the screws wouldn't be able to just sit in the wing office drinking tea now. They would have to man the stage rooms. We had set a significant precedent.

The incident emphasised the difference between the screws and us. They were just mercenaries, conditioned to obey. They would say one thing one moment, then be ordered to say the opposite the next. But, if we believed in something, we stood by it and fuck the consequences. At least we had the courage of our convictions. Therefore, we considered ourselves to be more honourable men than them. For that reason, we considered ourselves to be better men than them.

John served eight years out of his 15, then got a bit of parole. His marriage broke up when he got out. He has served a couple of short sentences since then.

Dave Bailey married and settled down. His only contact with prison now is when he occasionally visits a friend.

Tomato Neck had a fatal heart attack.

4 TOP-CAT

If the 'Old Bailey' had been a meeting place before our confrontation with Goebbels and his men, afterwards it became something of a rallying point. Not that we were actively pursuing a campaign to force better conditions on 'A' wing, but, having made a stand there, it was a bit like liberated territory. The screws might totally control the rest of the jail, but they knew they wouldn't have it all their own way with the fellas who frequented the 'Old Bailey'.

As the days passed, I got to know some of the fellas better. A constant visitor to Dave's cell was Barry Hurley. That first Monday morning, about eight of us had been sitting there laughing and joking when he walked in. He seemed instantly on the defensive. When Dave introduced him to John and me, he said, 'Hello,' but there was no warmth or enthusiasm in his greeting. It was as if he felt a bit threatened by us new fellas. Not afraid in any way, but viewing us as some kind of rivals. He obviously had his own particular status within the group, and it was as if he feared that a newcomer might usurp this role. He wasn't overtly hostile, but I immediately felt that relations with him could well be awkward.

Barry had darkish ginger hair, done in an elaborate curly style that fitted his head like a German helmet. It was perhaps his best physical feature. He must have regularly spent a lot of time on it, but you would never have got him to admit it.

His face, especially his cheeks, was very red, which made him look permanently flushed and angry. He wore gold-rimmed glasses through which he occasionally squinted, an indication that his sight was quite bad. I got the impression that he was embarrassed by having to wear glasses.

He was on his way to work like the rest of us, but was wearing a neatly pressed set of denims that hung well on his tall slim frame. He was carrying a large radio, with enormous headphones looped around his neck. Barry clearly had a lot of style.

He had the nickname 'Top-cat', but it was one of those nicknames that was used virtually exclusively by its owner. Referring to himself, he would say, 'The old Top-cat did this' or 'Top-cat did that.' We always said, 'Where's Barry?' or 'Hello, Barry.' Apart from the fact that 'Top-cat' sounded a bit silly among grown men, with someone as paranoid as Barry you never knew whether he would think you were taking the piss if you used the nickname. 'Barry' was both sensible and safe.

He had been a professional boxer, fighting at lightweight. You wouldn't have known it by looking at him. Apart from a broken nose, he didn't have that punched-about look that most pro fighters have. He had been neither very good nor very bad. Poor eyesight had prematurely ended his career.

He was an occasional bank robber, but was presently doing a five for violence. He had chased a fella in a car, pursued him into a house and fired several shots at him. If the judge had realised how poor Barry's eyesight was, he would doubtlessly have viewed the incident less seriously.

Barry worked on the waste-bin production line with the rest of us. However, he seemed to do very irregular hours. In my first week, he was hardly ever there and, when he was, he didn't work at all. He either stood talking to Dave, or sat at a workbench drinking tea and listening to his radio through the headphones.

When we met, we acknowledged each other but, although we were in the same group, this was still very much the 'feeling each other out' period. I could sense the anger and general hostility in him and was content to stay my distance.

A couple of days after the incident with Goebbels, we were working in the tin shop as usual. John wasn't there. Because he couldn't get on with all the noise and dirt, he had managed to get a job in the laundry. He got his job change very quickly. Presumably the screws had jumped at the chance to split us up.

Our group had been working for about an hour when Barry came in. He had been to the gym for remedials – in his case, to reduce tension. He had done several rounds on the punchbag, followed by half an hour skipping. His normally red face looked especially flushed and angry. He dumped his radio on a workbench and went to talk to Dave. I was working further down the line, hammering the tops of the bins down. I had been talking to Alec Good and Tom Morris, working close by, when Barry came in. With my back half-turned towards him and Dave, I carried on with my hammering.

At first, their conversation was inaudible because of the noise, but then I heard raised voices. Without making it too obvious, I turned slightly so I could see what was going on. I had already booked Barry as being a bit volatile. I didn't fancy having my back to him if he went into one.

As their voices got louder, I could make out their conversation. Barry had obviously been talking about those times when he had gone into one – there had been a couple of violent incidents in the past. Barry was saying that he couldn't help it, that he got carried away in certain situations and that it was all beyond his control.

Dave had known him for years, and was clearly aware that, 99 per cent of the time, Barry was as normal as any of us (a reasonably easy standard of sanity to attain). Dave was saying that

Barry knew exactly what he was doing when he went into one and was doing it deliberately.

The argument grew heated, especially on Barry's side.

'You know what you're doing,' Dave would say.

An increasingly agitated Barry would reply, 'I can't fucking help it,' emphasising each word with dramatic gestures.

Each time the statement was repeated, Barry's voice would go up an octave and increase in volume. Dave should have known what was coming. From where I was standing, I could see Barry inexorably losing control.

Finally, after about four rounds of statement and response, Barry's voice rose to a shriek. 'I can't fucking help it!' he screamed, his eyes wide, his mouth open, his face red as a beetroot, his arms moving in synchronised karate chops.

The shriek rose above the background din. Everybody immediately stopped whatever they were doing and all eyes turned. Dave had gone very quiet, suddenly realising that Barry was on the brink of the very type of episode they had been discussing.

Out of control now, Barry stared around wildly. I knew that, at any second, things were going to be flying about. I hid the hammer I was holding out of sight beneath the top of the workbench. One of our crowd or not, if the demented Barry came near me with one of the heavy pieces of metal that were lying about, I was going to clump him. In the middle of the shop were piles of the shiny metal rings that went around the tops of the bins. Barry ran over to them and began throwing armfuls in the air. Everybody stood stock still. No one wanted to attract Barry's attention by making any gesture that he could misconstrue as hostile. Some did it out of fear, some genuinely reluctant to fight a man who had truly lost control.

The rings bounced off the metal racks and benches. They made plenty of noise, but they could hardly hurt anyone. We were more concerned with what he would throw next.

Suddenly, Barry stopped. He spun around to glare at the screw sitting in the observation box next to the door. A frisson of fear ran through me. If Barry ran over and chinned him, we would all be involved. For when the heavy mob ran in and tried to grab him, we wouldn't just stand there and watch him fight the screws alone. Too many of us had bad memories of being jumped on by a heavy mob ourselves. The outcome would be a full-scale tear-up. The screws would pull their sticks, the fellas would wade in with iron bars. It could well end up in an outside court case with people getting more bird on top – that is, as well as a good belting and months in solitary.

If it had to be, then so be it. It would be nice to be on something like even terms with the heavy mob for a change, instead of being outnumbered ten to one, them with sticks and you with bare hands. But you always left your name and address behind in jail. We would certainly be well nicked for it. If any screws were badly hurt, we could expect from six to ten on top. So, if it could be, it was best avoided.

If someone could have got between Barry and the screw in time, he would have done so. Not at all for the screw's sake, but for Barry's and for everyone else who would be dragged into the ensuing free-for-all. But Barry was nearer to the screw than any of us. He ran to the box and jumped up on the side. With his face thrust right into the screws, he screamed, 'Have you rung that fucking bell?'

Clearly afraid, the screw hurriedly replied, 'I was going to, Barry, but, now that you've calmed down, I won't '

Barry might have been wild at that moment, but he wasn't stupid. His sense of self-preservation suddenly took over. The alarm bell was inside the box, right by the screw's knee. It could be pressed secretly, without anyone seeing. The screw's illogical answer just served to confirm Barry's suspicions.

In amazement I watched as Barry grabbed a nearby broom and ran into the middle of the shop. Holding it in both hands by the top of the handle, he swung it backwards and forwards at arm's length. Now I was convinced that he had really flipped. It looked like he was going to play a bizarre game of croquet, with the broom as the mallet. Barry wasn't as crazy as he seemed, though. Next to the screw's box was a pair of wooden doors. A little way further up the shop was a second pair. Almost simultaneously, both pairs crashed open. A blue-serge tidal wave of screws burst in, all breathless and hatless. When the alarm bell rang at Parkhurst, every available screw ran to answer it. Later, I heard that someone had actually made a count: there were 42 of them.

They surged in, filling up the aisles between the racking. They stopped in a rough semi-circle facing Barry.

I could now see the reason for the broom, which Barry swung backwards and forwards, ready to strike out. 'OK, who's first?' he challenged.

A PO took a tentative step forward out of the ranks. Holding out an arm in a consoling gesture, he asked, 'What's the matter then?'

Barry ignored him. 'Come on then,' he repeated, still swinging the broom.

For long seconds, nobody moved. Everyone had become part of a frozen tableau. But it was a tableau that could explode into violence at any moment – for, when the screws had rushed in, every con in the shop had picked up a lump of metal and held it by his side.

The situation was very heavy now. It had almost taken on a life of its own. All the actors were standing there, irrevocably committed. One wrong move could spark it off. If the screw stepped forward, Barry would do him with the broom. Then it would be off. Unless one of us did something.

Still holding the hammer by my side, I walked from behind my workbench and went to stand between Barry and the screw. My back was to Barry, so the immediate danger was that he might hit me with the broom.

Subconsciously I cringed, waiting for the blow to the back of my head. But at the same time I had to deal with the PO. Facing him, I said, 'You can see he's upset. Why don't you back off and let him calm down?'

The PO was an old hand, a veteran of scores of situations like this. He wouldn't have been at Parkhurst if he wasn't. He realised that things had become very dangerous. He didn't fancy hand-to-hand combat with wooden batons against iron bars. If there was a chance to defuse the situation peacefully, he would take it.

'What's the matter with him then?' he asked me.

Unfortunately, the answer was beyond me. I was as mystified as anyone else as to why Barry had suddenly gone into one. I turned and asked, 'What's the matter, Barry?'

I could see his eyes turn thoughtful. He could see a way out of the mess he had got himself into. 'Those cunts haven't given me my treatment again,' he shouted.

I turned back to the PO. 'They haven't given him his morning medication from the treatment room,' I said, catching on immediately.

'Does he want to walk over to the hospital and get it?' offered the PO.

Barry was instantly aggressive again. 'You're not getting me over the hospital so they can beat me up!' he shouted.

The PO realised he had said the wrong thing. He quickly calmed Barry, saying, 'OK, OK, we'll send over to the hospital and get it.' Turning to me, he asked, 'What's he on?

'I don't know Ask the hospital screws, they'll know. In the meantime, I'll sit him down and make him a cup of tea until it gets here.' With that, I took Barry by the arm and led him away to the bench where we had our tea-breaks.

For the moment, the situation was defused, but we weren't out of the woods yet. Barry was on regular treatment, so I knew that part of the story would stand up. Now it all depended on whether they were going to nick Barry for throwing the rings about and threatening the screw in the box. If they tried to take him away to the chokey, it would be off all over again.

Barry sat at the bench and I plugged in the kettle. I busied myself getting the tea things out, not looking at the screws who still remained in a semi-circle.

The PO wandered slowly down the shop towards the bench. 'What's the matter then, Barry? What happened?' he asked, standing so that I was between him and Barry.

Barry's head spun around. 'How would you like to keep hearing German voices?' he challenged.

There was really no answer to this. Whether it was sheer inspiration or merely a vestige of his previously demented state, I couldn't tell. But its effect was perfect. Obviously thinking himself in the presence of a madman, the PO turned and walked back to join the rest of the screws.

I looked at Barry. He started to laugh. 'Hold up,' I said under my breath. 'If they think you're just fucking about, they'll come back and nick you.' Barry managed to keep a straight face.

Just as the tea was ready, a hospital screw appeared carrying a tot of medicine. He handed it to the PO who handed it to me. I gave it to Barry. He drank it immediately, as if it was an antidote to whatever had beset him. He pulled a face, then drank some tea.

The screws withdrew. Like the tide going out, they flowed back out through the doors and locked them behind them. Suddenly, the shop was as it had been before.

The rest of the fellas came over and joined Barry at the bench. He couldn't restrain himself any longer and started laughing. We all laughed with him. Partly because it had been a funny situation, partly from relief. We lived on the edge all the time. Laughter and fear were often only seconds apart.

'That was a bit strong about the German voices,' I said to Barry.

'Good, wasn't it?'

The screw in the box could see us all laughing, but he was out of earshot. Anyway, it was all over now. Nothing would come of it. Another report would go into Barry's record about how violent and unstable he was. The screws would hate him even more and wait their opportunity to get him on his own and then bash him. But for now it was finished.

Back at the wing, Barry walked with me to my cell. He grabbed my hand. 'Thanks for what you did in the shop, Norm,' he said with genuine emotion in his voice as he shook me by the hand. All reserve and hostility were gone now. I'd found another pal.

As I got to know Barry better, I grew to like him. He could be very funny at times. He wasn't at all as flash or as arrogant as he had seemed at first sight. Among his friends, he regularly put himself down. But only among friends.

He was very paranoid. He would regularly come to me and say that he was going to do someone or other because of some half-imagined slight. There was never any real substance to it. Everybody knew he was quick-tempered and could have a right row. No one would go out of their way to provoke him for no reason.

If I had been mischievous, I could have used him like a weapon, pointing him at anyone I didn't like. But I felt that I should protect him from himself. I always told him he was imagining things and that there was no need to steam into someone.

Although Barry could regularly get you into trouble, in some ways it was reassuring to have him on the firm. He was very loyal. If John or I ever looked like having a row with someone, he would be right there with us.

The more I hung around with him, the plainer it became that he had a definite mental problem. There was a background of mental illness. He had a brother at home who was mentally subnormal.

On a previous sentence, Barry had been doing a two stretch at Camp Hill. He had started to play up, so they put him in the chokey. To wind the screws up, or so he said, he had begun to act like a dog. He would run about his cell on all fours and, whenever they opened it up, he would bark at them.

They had sent him for observation to Parkhurst, only half a mile from Camp Hill. They put him in a cell in the hospital. He continued to run about on all fours and bark.

The next day, the resident psychiatrist came to his cell. The door was opened and Barry ran up to him, barking.

'What's the matter with you?' asked the psycho.

'I think I've got hard-pad,' said Barry.

Now this was all very funny stuff, vintage Top-cat in fact, but the hospital staff at Parkhurst weren't known for their sense of humour. Barry was put in an observation ward with several other nutters. The screws told him he was going to have electro-convulsant therapy. This didn't mean very much to Barry. He just continued to play the role to see where it would take him.

One morning, they had given him an injection to relax his muscles. Then they loaded him on to a trolley and took him to a small room. Here they strapped him to a table and fitted electrodes to various parts of his body.

I don't know what Barry expected. Perhaps some electrically induced transcendental state, like an acid trip with heat and light. He certainly wasn't expecting the paralysing surge of current that lifted his rigid body clear of the table top.

His back arched as his hands and feet strained against the straps. He felt the most tremendous pain he had ever felt in his life. It was so intense that it left him paralysed and helpless as he slumped back to the table when the power was switched off. Then, his every nerve tingling with pain, a second jolt of power surged through his body sending him rigid again.

This was repeated several times. When it was over, they had wheeled him out of the room on a trolley and dumped him unceremoniously on his bed in the ward. He lay there unmoving, literally numb with shock.

As he had drifted in a semi-conscious limbo, Barry couldn't figure out whether it was treatment or punishment. The dog hadn't liked it either. In fact, it was never seen or heard of again. Barry had been moved back to Camp Hill to finish his sentence.

As soon as my reception period on 'A' wing was finished, I was allowed to move on to 'D' wing. Barry and most of our crowd were on there, and it was a much more liberal wing. If you didn't want to go up 'on stage' for the evening, you could hang about on the wing and go in and out of each other's cells. No one was banged up during association time.

I was put in a cell on the ones, close to the hot-plate. We called it the ones – that is, the ground-floor landing – but there was a basement landing beneath it for the nonces. We never saw them. It was down a flight of stairs and through a door that was always kept locked. As none of us ever saw this landing, as far as we were concerned it didn't exist. For us, the landing with the hot-plate was the ones.

I had only been on 'D' wing for a week when the younger brother of a close friend of mine arrived. I felt duty bound to look after him as best as I could, whatever he was like. I had heard that he was only 21 and was doing life with a big rec. I waited by 'D' wing gate for him to come from reception.

As I laid eyes on Stewart Down for the first time, my heart sank. He was quite short, which didn't really concern me, but he also had a soft, round baby face that made him look no more than 18. He didn't seem tough at all. I wondered how he would cope with the rigours of Parkhurst. It looked like I would have a full-time job playing nursemaid.

I needn't have worried though. As he came through the gate, most of our crowd appeared. Some knew him from outside – in spite of his youth, he had been quite an active armed robber. They gathered round and welcomed him.

I shook his hand and introduced myself. He had heard about me from his brother and had been told to look out for me. The baby face was soon wreathed in smiles.

Stewart's mind was very sharp. He wasn't at all intimidated by Parkhurst. Within a couple of days, we all found that he had a lively sense of humour. When he wasn't playing jokes on us, he was taking the piss. Far from needing protection, at times it was us who needed protection from him.

One of his first tricks was to catch a wood pigeon and put it in John's locker. As John came back from work, Stewart and I walked with him to his cell. He went straight to his locker to make a cup of tea, exactly as Stewart knew he would.

John was just starting his 15 and his nerves weren't in the best of shape. They certainly weren't improved when the terrified bird burst out of the darkness of his locker and began flapping around.

'Get it out, get it out!' he screamed, throwing himself across the cell.

Stewart and I rushed in to find John cowering on his bed, while the bird flew around and around, making desperate attempts to get out of the window. There were feathers and bird shit everywhere.

It was very funny and all our groups laughed and laughed, but we couldn't help but think how we would have handled it. Your own cell was just about the only place in the whole jail where you could relax and feel reasonably safe. Now, with the arrival of Stewart, those old familiar surroundings might conceal a nasty surprise.

Stewart and Barry hit it off straight away. They both had a highly developed sense of humour, and life around them was rarely dull. In prison, where boredom is the worst enemy, they were good company.

Barry's second wobbler came right out of the blue, just like the first one. I soon came to realise that, no matter how well you knew him, you could never predict when he would go nuts.

By now, Stewart had done his reception period and had moved on to our wing. We had just been unlocked for the evening. He was standing with Barry on the ones, right outside my door. I was in the recess opposite, washing some cups for tea. We were talking backwards and forwards across the landing, trying to decide what we were going to do for the evening.

As we were talking, Big Mick Wilson, a giant mixed-race pal of ours, came along the landing. He had been an active bank robber and was now doing a 14 for a big bank robbery in Cardiff. At a time when very few black fellas had been into 'the heavy', Mick had worked with some of the best white firms in London. In the main, he was an easygoing fella. But he wouldn't stand for any bollocks, especially from the screws. He'd had countless confrontations with them and hated them with a passion. He was very loyal and was one of the central figures in our group. Unlike Barry, he rarely started trouble for little or no reason. But, if trouble started, he would be right there with us.

Mick stopped to talk to Stewart and Barry. He was carrying a magazine in his hand. He looked at them both and asked, 'Can you do puzzles?' It was an innocuous enough remark.

Barry's reply was innocuous, too. 'Can I do puzzles?' he echoed.

As Mick and Stewart stood looking at him, he said it again, but this time he shook his head from side to side and waved his arms in time with each word. When he repeated it a third time, his voice rose to a shout and the head and arm movements became wildly exaggerated. From the recess, I was trying to figure out if he was just playing about or was really about to go into one.

Stewart and Mick still stood there, smiles frozen on their faces. 'Can I do fucking puzzles?' screamed Barry at the top of his voice. There was a new screw on the wing, one we had never seen before. He was a swarthy, miserable-looking fella of about 30, whose craggy face exuded a confident, arrogant attitude. I guessed he must have just arrived from some hard-line local nick like Winchester where the screws had it all their own way.

He was standing outside the office, close to the hot-plate. I had seen him earlier, looking up and down the wing in an aggressive manner. He had been a good 40 feet from my cell though, so I had taken no notice.

Alerted by Barry's fourth and loudest outburst, the screw stared into the gloom of the poorly lit landing. As Barry turned his head, his eyes met the screw's. Their gazes locked.

Suddenly, Barry's full attention was on the screw. 'Who are you fucking looking at?' he shouted.

I was already starting to move. I had put the cups down and was just leaving the recess on my way to grab hold of Barry.

'Who are you looking at?' replied the screw in a challenging tone.

I had only got halfway to Barry when, with a roar of rage, he suddenly charged down the landing towards the screw. I was five feet behind him, running with my arms outstretched, but I wasn't going to catch him in time.

The screw now realised he had made a serious mistake. His swarthy face turned pale with fear. He backed into the office doorway, never once taking his eyes off the rapidly approaching Barry.

If Barry had decided to punch him, there was nothing anyone could have done to stop the blow. Luckily, though, Barry had set his mind on hitting him with the small wooden cell table that stood against the wall just outside the office.

It took a second or so for Barry to bend down and grab the table by the legs. He swung it upwards, above his head. The screw stood paralysed in the doorway. Realising that he was about to be hit with the table, he fell straight back into the office to avoid it, without moving his feet.

The leading edge of the table sliced downwards in a vicious arc. It passed through the space where the screw's head had been a second earlier, and smashed into the brickwork of the doorway, cutting a long groove into the paintwork.

The table shattered, but, as it continued its downward arc, it struck the outstretched hand of the screw as he overbalanced backwards into the office. There was a dull thud as his body hit the office floor, followed by a noisy clatter as several pieces of table fell to the landing.

But now I was on Barry. Grabbing him from behind, I pinned his arms to his sides, lifted him bodily off his feet, spun around and ran back along the landing with him.

Suddenly, Stewart was next to me. The three of us crashed through my half-open cell door. As Stewart and I threw Barry on to my bed, we both fell on top of him.

Inexplicably, we all burst out laughing. I jumped up and ran to close my door. For the next minute or so, we laughed helplessly. Perhaps it was from relief after the tension. Perhaps it was just our bizarre sense of humour. In Parkhurst, you could be doing mundane things one second and the next you could be in a heavy situation, heart racing and adrenalin pumping.

We wiped tears of laughter from our flushed faces. 'You *are* a cunt, Barry,' I said, still laughing. 'I suppose I had better go and see what's happening.'

Things had been very quiet since we had dragged Barry away from the office. As far as I knew, the whole heavy mob could be standing outside on the landing. I opened the door and looked out. The landing was deserted. Big Mick had disappeared and there wasn't a screw to be seen anywhere. Putting a serious expression on my face, I walked along to the office.

The wing SO was sitting inside on his own. He was a small sharp-featured man of about 40 with a permanently pasty face and sad, tired eyes. There was nothing nasty or vindictive about him. In many ways, he was an anomaly. Battle lines were rigidly drawn at Parkhurst, but he was always civil and tried to be helpful when he could.

However, it was a warrior society where kindness was inevitably taken as weakness. His concern or lack of spite was hardly appreciated. Because of his reluctance to nick people, he was actually put on more. Fellas would take out their ire on him where they wouldn't have with another SO.

Although I recognised his kindly qualities, I never acknowledged them in any way. I hurt with too much pain. I burned with too much anger. I seethed with a surfeit of frustration and desperation. He was still the enemy. He was one of those who kept me here. One of those who locked me away each night with my loneliness. There was no place for gratitude or compassion at Parkhurst or in my soul. And, if I should have reciprocated his kindness in any way, there was always the danger that it would be misconstrued by the rest of the fellas.

The SO looked up as I walked in. His eyes met mine and held them for a second. In that short time, volumes were spoken yet nothing was said. He knew it was about Barry and the recent incident. It was significant that the heavy mob hadn't been called. That undoubtedly had been his decision. So already we had cause for thanks. 'Could you phone the hospital please, guv, and ask them to send over some Largactyl for Barry?' I asked, breaking the spell. 'He didn't get it at teatime.'

The SO nodded silently and picked up the phone. He spoke to someone, mentioned Barry's surname and asked for the medication to be brought over. He replaced the receiver and said, 'It's on its way over. I'll give you a shout when it arrives.'

Nothing else was said. No mention was made of the incident. I noticed that the new screw was nowhere to be seen. No doubt he had been sent on to another wing for the evening. I left the office and walked back to my cell.

About five minutes later, I heard the SO calling my name. I went out and saw him standing outside the office. I walked up to him and he handed me a small medicine tot containing a clear oily-looking liquid. 'Thanks, guv,' I said and turned away.

In a small quiet voice, he called after me. 'Parker, I would be obliged if, the next time that Barry misses his treatment, you'd tell me. I'll get on to them straight away.' His deep, sad eyes met mine, and for a moment I felt guilty. I knew he had done the decent thing and not had Barry nicked. But what could I do? We were both so trapped by our respective roles. I had said it all when I had thanked him, yet that one word was too inadequate.

'OK, guv,' I said quietly and nodded in acknowledgement. Then I walked away.

Back in my cell, I handed the Largactyl to Barry. He realised that he wasn't going to be nicked. They would have come for him already. The Largactyl was an added bonus. He liked a tot of medication.

'Top-cat,' I said shaking my head, 'you've just used up another one of your lives. I don't know how many more times you can get away with this.'

Top-cat drank the medicine in one gulp and laughed.

For weeks at a time, Barry would be all right. There would be regular periods of 'the hump', and paranoid mutterings about doing someone for something or other. But it was all smoothed over.

However, if we had thought that Barry's wobblers had finished, we were greatly mistaken. Perhaps these troughs of relative tranquillity were actually the calm before the storms.

The third time Barry went into one, I wasn't there to influence events. He had gone over to the hospital one morning to see the dentist. He had mentioned that he was going, but I paid no attention. Barry always had some kind of pain or ache. He needed a full-time medical team all of his own. Perhaps this time he actually had toothache.

Now a Top-cat with toothache is a very unstable animal indeed. Especially when he is entering the inner sanctum of the Kingdom of Parkhurst. Even if I had realised, there was little I could have done. I suppose I could have gone over to the hospital with him just to see that he was all right. But that would have been taking things a bit too far. By the time a hospital screw had gone to the various wings to collect all the fellas who wanted to see the dentist, he had a group of seven of them. They all trooped over to the hospital and sat in a side corridor on a long wooden bench, at one end of which was the door to the dentist's room. The top half was opaque glass with the legend 'DENTIST' inscribed on it in large black letters. In the same side corridor was a psychiatrist's office. There were two chairs outside this, both unoccupied.

For most of the week, the dentist's room was empty. The dentist, who worked outside, only came in when there were enough people who wanted to see him, usually once a week.

He didn't choose who came to see him, or the order in which they would enter. On arrival, he was given a list of names by the screws. He worked strictly to that list, calling men in the order given.

Shortly after the seven fellas arrived, the dentist called the first one in. After about an hour, four men had been called, Barry still sat on the bench.

Suddenly, the gate at the far end of the corridor opened and a screw let in Big Mick. He had been called over to the hospital to see the psychiatrist. He headed along the corridor towards the two unoccupied chairs.

In the confined space of the corridor, his massive physique seemed even more enormous. He ambled along, a dusky mountain of flesh and muscle. He worked out every day on the weights and ate like a horse. He carried some fat, but he was such a big man that he still looked muscular.

He wasn't particularly close to Barry, but they both had mutual friends in our group. Now they acknowledged each other, then Mick went to sit in one of the chairs outside the psycho's office.

Another half-hour passed. Another two men had gone in to see the dentist. Barry sat alone on the bench, but now, at least, he was next. Mick still sat outside the psycho's.

The door to the dentist's office opened and the previous patient came out. He was followed by the dentist, who looked at Barry sitting on the bench. 'I'm sorry,' he said, 'but I've run out of time. You'll have to come back next week.' With that, he turned around and went back into the office, closing the door behind him.

The previous patient walked along the corridor towards the gate, passing Big Mick still sitting outside the psycho's. On reaching the gate, he rattled it for the screw to come and let him through.

Back on the bench, Barry still sat there. He stared straight ahead. His face had gone very red, his body very stiff.

Suddenly, without a word, he jumped to his feet. He grabbed the bench in his arms and, with one fluid motion, rammed it through the opaque glass of the dentist's door.

Inside the office, the dentist, finished with his weekly session, was gathering his tools together and washing up. The crash of breaking glass rudely shocked him from his tired reverie. In a panic, he threw himself at the alarm bell and pressed it.

Outside in the corridor, Barry stood with the bench cradled in his arms like a battering ram. He faced the gate at the end aggressively. It was flung open and several white-coated hospital screws poured through. Halfway along the corridor, Big Mick had stood up. He was between Barry and the heavy mob, caught right in the middle.

The screws stopped. A PO pushed his way to the front. He looked at the agitated Barry clutching the bench at the end of the corridor, then at the muscular giant who stood between them. He recognised the two cons as old adversaries. As he looked, Big Mick backed along the corridor to stand next to Barry. Both sides glared at each other. The battle lines were drawn.

Once again, Barry's luck held. No one had been hurt. There was only a broken window and a shaken dentist. A full-scale tear-up would be a worse incident. Negotiations were started.

Mostly it was Mick who did the talking. The PO glared at Barry and Barry glared back. He was convinced that, had he been on his own, they would have steamed into him without hesitation. Big Mick had added another dimension to the equation.

Barry and Mick were allowed to leave the hospital. They were escorted back to the wing. There were no charges. Barry had slipped out of trouble again without so much as a nicking. He laughed as he told me about it later.

Mick wasn't amused at all though. He had nearly got involved in a major tear-up for nothing. It was a measure of his loyalty that he had stood by Barry over what was no more than a fit of temper. In the same circumstances, he would do the same again. However, perhaps Mick would be more careful about being in Barry's company in future.

One morning Barry came up to me looking very red in the face and extremely agitated. I immediately recognised the telltale signs.

He told me that there was a fella on his landing who he was definitely going to do that very morning. There was much twisting of face and grinding of teeth. He punched his fist into his palm a couple of times.

'What did he do, Barry?' I asked.

He was strangely reticent. Usually he would blurt out the fella's supposed offence. This time I had to drag it out of him.

'I didn't like the way he slopped out this morning,' he admitted sheepishly.

Now, as far as I knew, there was only one way to slop out. You took your piss-pot, walked to the recess and threw the contents into the slops sink. The scope for improvisation was minimal.

What had the fella done? A quick pirouette before he chucked the contents into the sink maybe? Perhaps he had approached the sink backwards and thrown it over his shoulder.

No, it was none of these. I finally dragged out of Barry the fact that the fella had thrown the contents of his pot into the sink aggressively, and it had splashed a bit.

I paused to show Barry that I was thinking about it. Then I pointed out two things. Firstly, no doubt the fella was glad to see the back of whatever had been fermenting in his pot overnight. Secondly, the only person he was really going to splash was the person nearest, namely himself. It took some doing, but Barry finally accepted this logic. However, not without a good deal of thought.

There were occasions, though, when there was no time to sit down and rationalise. I was in the gym one morning working out with Eddie from South London and a young giant called Mark. Mark was one of those fellas who had come into prison a skinny teenager and with a combination of regular meals, regular sleep and regular workouts had completely transformed himself.

He weighed about 15 stone, had the build of an American quarterback and didn't have a scrap of fat on him. He seemed to grow bigger and stronger by the day. He developed an interest in boxing and, although he didn't have much style, he could punch with devastating effect. To see him hit the medicine ball was awesome. In the end there were few people strong enough to hold it for him.

On the debit side, he wasn't overendowed with brains and could be a bit flash. He wasn't the best thief you'd ever meet either. He was doing five years for robbing his local butcher, who knew him. Having said that, he had plenty of bottle and could have a fearsome row.

Mark regularly worked out with Eddie and me. This particular morning we were doing some heavy bench press with the Olympic bar. I was 'repping out' with 200 pounds, doing sets of ten.

Mark, however, was repping with 250 pounds for sets of 12 and 15. The massive 20-kilo plates either end of the Olympic bar clanged and jangled as he powered through the sets.

I had just finished my set and was having a breather. Eddie was spotting for Mark. Suddenly, a very agitated Barry grabbed me by the arm and pulled me away from the bench. He had been working out on the punchbag, and his face was red and running with sweat.

'Norm, I'm going to do that fucking Mark,' he panted, face twisted, teeth clenched and hands gripped in fists. 'Next time he's bench pressing I'm going to smash him in the face with a twenty. Will you go and stand in the way of the screw's window when I do it?'

I was amazed. This had come completely out of the blue. I had been working closely with Mark and couldn't recall him even so much as looking at Barry. Barry was absolutely adamant though. He was right on the verge of actually doing it.

Now this was no mere punch-up he was talking about. A 20 was an all-steel plate the diameter of a car wheel, which weighed 20 kilos. It would do Mark serious damage to be hit in the face with that while lying on his back. Then there was the 250 pounds that he would be holding at arm's length, which would come crashing down on his head. It could easily kill him and would certainly rank as attempted murder.

It would be no problem for me to obscure the screw's view. He was locked in a separate room and could only look out through a small observation slit. That wasn't the point though. There would be a degree of treachery involved on my part, and it wasn't as if Mark had done anything to deserve such an attack.

'Look, Barry,' I said, 'I'm working out with the fella. He ain't a pal of mine, but you can't ask me to do a treacherous thing like that to him. What's he done anyway?'

It transpired that Mark was supposed to have looked at Barry in an aggressive way. In a gymnasium, where everyone was psyched up to get through their workouts, aggression was everywhere. It was a measure of Barry's paranoia that he thought Mark's was directed at him.

I managed to talk Barry out of it quite quickly. It was a high-risk strategy, but I just said that I wouldn't be party to it under any circumstances, turned my back on him and walked away to join my workout partners.

Policing Barry was always a hit-and-miss affair though. I couldn't always be there right on cue. There would be times when none of our crowd would be near enough to influence events.

I was standing in the breakfast queue one Sunday morning. I always found it amazing how much the fellas liked their cornflakes in the nick. Admittedly, the normal diet was unbelievably boring and, more often than not, badly cooked. But, if they liked cornflakes that much, I couldn't see why they didn't just buy several packets from the canteen.

Sunday was the one day of the week that porridge wasn't served. You would see people queuing up, who never usually got up for breakfast. Passions could run high. If rations were perceived to be too short, then the screw serving them could expect a volley.

It was a 'touch' – a bonus – if someone who wasn't getting up for breakfast said that you could have his ration of milk and cornflakes. Sometimes there was competition between fellas to have this extra ration.

There was a big queue this morning. Barry was about 20 places from the front, and I was several people behind him. I didn't walk forward to join him, because no one pushed in at Parkhurst. There were too many lunatics who might take violent exception.

Barry turned to me and said something jokingly. It was mildly piss-taking, but there was nothing malicious in it. Perhaps it was just too early in the morning for me. I hated queuing up anyway. Stung, I searched for some rejoinder. Something that would sting Barry in return.

Looking past him along the queue, I saw a tall rangy fella of about 35. He had bright-ginger hair. Next to him was his mate, an enormous 17-stone Brummie, who was more fat than muscle. He had an extremely large head, which prompted our crowd to refer to him as 'Pig's Head'. They were both on Barry's landing, and he detested the pair of them. He especially disliked the big ginger fella (Barry was ginger himself). As usual, I could never find any real reason for it.

However, there was some competition between them to collect

the cornflakes of a fella called Brian. At different times, Brian had given them to whoever asked first.

On one occasion, Barry had asked the screw for Brian's ration of cornflakes only to be told that the ginger fella had collected it a few minutes earlier. Barry was still fuming when he spoke to me about it 20 minutes later.

'The big greedy slag,' he raged. 'If he ever does it again, I'll do him.'

This all came back to me as my eyes fell on Ginger. Without really thinking, I said, 'Oi, Top-cat. You mind that Ginger doesn't nick Brian's cornflakes again,' and pointed up the queue.

It had an instant effect on Barry. He spun around and peered along the queue. Because of his poor eyesight, he hadn't noticed Ginger before. But he saw him now.

'He'd better not,' he snarled. 'Brian has already said that I can have them.'

I immediately regretted mentioning it. If Barry had already asked Brian, then there shouldn't be any confusion. If Ginger had asked first, then Brian would have told Barry when he had asked for them. Unless, of course, both just assumed that they could have them.

The queue moved on. Ginger collected his breakfast and set off back up to the fives. A minute later, Barry reached the screw who was giving out the cornflakes. Suddenly, I saw them arguing. Barry was instantly very red. He turned to me, pointed upstairs, made a gesture with his fist and mouthed some angry-looking words. Then he stormed away from the queue, up towards his cell on the fives and the direction Ginger had gone.

I realised that, very shortly, it would be off. But I was only half-a-dozen places behind Barry in the queue. I was actually in the process of getting my own breakfast. I couldn't just drop everything and run after him.

Within seconds, I was out of the queue and hurrying towards my cell. I couldn't run because I had on thonged shower sandals, not the ideal footwear in which to have a row. I calculated that Barry would have to drop off his cornflakes at his cell first. I quickly pulled on a pair of trainers, then ran a couple of cells along the landing to get Stewart Down. Ginger and Pig's Head were both big fellas. If there was going to be a row, I might as well have some help.

Stewart jumped up from eating his breakfast and ran out of his cell after me. I only had time to explain briefly. Stewart had started to laugh.

As we ran up the first flight of stairs, we realised that we were already too late. In the distance there was an intermittent rumbling sound. It was the muffled thuds and crashes of two large bodies falling about a small wooden-floored cell.

It was an instantly recognisable sound. One that might herald dire consequences. It could be a pal who was being attacked. Within seconds, you might be involved in a tear-up with knives and lumps of metal.

We increased our pace up the second and third flights. Stewart's expression was serious now. We were both breathing heavily when we reached the fives.

We ran along the landing in the direction of the sound. It had grown louder now. Fellas were stopping on the landing and looking towards the cell. But, at Parkhurst, if it wasn't anyone you knew, then you didn't get involved.

I burst into the cell first. It was a strange sight that met my eyes. Barry and Ginger were locked in combat. There were cornflakes and milk everywhere – in their hair, clinging to their clothes and all over Ginger's bedspread.

I guessed what had happened. Barry had dropped off his cornflakes at his own cell, then run along to Ginger's. As he ran in, Ginger had been standing up with a bowl of cornflakes and milk in his hands.

Barry must have hit Ginger with a good right-hander. You could see the angry red mark on his chin, which was already swelling. The shock and pain showed in his face.

As the punch had gone in, Barry's fist must have caught the edge of the bowl. The contents had flown skywards. The welter of cornflakes had risen, only to fall back quickly. Now Barry and Ginger were wearing them like beads in their hair.

You could see that Ginger didn't really want to know. He was grappling with Barry more in an attempt to stop any further blows than to hurt him. The arrival of Stewart and I only served to reinforce his reluctance. If it wasn't the immediate punch-up that worried him, then it was the heavy comeback afterwards that was his concern. He was looking for a way out.

'Hold up for fuck's sake,' I shouted. There were plenty of things to fight about at Parkhurst, I just didn't think that a bowl of cornflakes was one of them.

Both men continued to cling together. I stepped forward and prised them apart, getting my body between them. As I turned, I noticed Pig's Head standing terrified in the corner. He realised that, if it looked like he had been joining in against Barry, then we would steam into him.

I gently forced Barry backwards and, with Stewart's help, got him out of the cell. We led him along the landing towards his own cell. His face was now white with anger. He was definitely in no laughing mood. Stewart, though, was already giggling. To see the usually immaculate Top-cat bedecked with soggy cornflakes was very funny indeed. I started laughing as well.

As we got him into his cell, we saw his own bowl of cornflakes lying on his table. Turning to us he said, 'Well, he never got to eat the extra bowl, did he?' and burst out laughing himself.

Top-cat liked nothing better than an audience to perform to. The worst thing we could do was to ignore him, and he hated to be left out of anything. Most of the time we did spend with him though. We went to the gym with him, watched TV, went on exercise and ate in the same food-boat. On the odd occasion, however, we would do something he didn't do.

Barry hated cards. He was no good at them and got the hump very quickly. John Harrison and I both liked a game of kalooki. We both fancied we could play a bit. A lot of the London chaps liked to think they were good at kalooki. Some would play in various London 'spiels'. A lot of money could be won or lost.

John and I were nowhere near that good. John loved a gamble, and I did it for enjoyment. I limited myself to two ounces a week. Once I'd lost that I'd turn it in. And I invariably lost.

We played in a cell up in a corner of the fives. It belonged to a fattish, middle-aged Birmingham fella. He had some kind of stomach disorder, which gave him permanently bad breath. He wasn't one of our crowd, we just played cards in his cell sometimes. In our usual irreverent fashion we used to refer to him as 'the Breath'. The card school was sometimes known as the Breath's, but more often as the 'Green Dragon' after a well-known spieler in the East End of London.

On a Saturday evening, especially if we had won a few quid on our racing book, John and I would go up to the Green Dragon for a couple of hours. Big Mick was always there, Eddie from South London and Brian, he of the disputed cornflakes. The Breath would make a jug of tea, and we would settle down for a quiet Saturday-night game of cards and a chat.

This Saturday evening, Barry was over in his cell sulking. We wouldn't have him in the cell with us when we were playing cards. He just couldn't sit quietly. Sooner or later he would have done something and had the whole school in an uproar. Top-cat and cards just didn't go together.

Barry's cell was right across the landing from the Breath's, about 20 feet away. He was tidying up noisily, just to let us know he was there. We pushed the door to and carried on playing. After a while it grew very quiet. We were right up in the far corner of the wing and most people were either up in the stage rooms or down on the ones.

Suddenly, there was a muffled crashing and banging from the

direction of Barry's cell. It was that sound again, the tumble of heavy bodies rolling about a wooden floor in combat. There were muffled shouts of rage and pain too.

In the Green Dragon, we all froze the moment we heard the rumbling sound. A second or two passed as we looked at each other, deciding if it really was what it sounded like. Then, without saying a word, we all jumped up from the card table and ran across the landing to Barry's cell.

Our faces were tense, our hearts beating faster as increased adrenalin coursed through our veins. We just didn't know what we were running in to. In the crazy world that Barry inhabited, it could be anything.

We pushed the door open and crowded into his cell.

Everything was tidy and in its place. There were no signs of the disarray we had expected. Barry was down on his hands and knees in the far corner. He had his back to us. Shouts and groans came from his direction. He turned to face us, and the noise stopped. He had a large stone in each hand. He had been banging them on the floorboards and shouting, to imitate the sound of a fight.

It had been very convincing, but we weren't amused. We had jumped up from a serious game of cards and run over to what we thought was a heavy tear-up. The adrenalin was still pumping.

As we stood there looking at him, Top-cat suddenly burst out laughing. 'That will teach you to ignore me' was all he said.

Nothing was ever mundane with Barry. Whatever the situation, he had some little act to stamp his own particular mark on it.

Every weekend we went to the pictures. The show was held in the chapel, up by 'A' wing stage rooms. It was a serious outing. You could get a couple of hundred fellas there from 'A', 'B' and 'D' wings.

If the film was watchable, it was a good way to escape the boredom for a few hours. The initial settling-down period, though, could be a bit hectic. Fellas would be milling about, speaking to mates from other wings.

Our crowd, a nucleus of born-and-bred London criminals, always sat in a group. We liked each other's company anyway, but it was as much to show solidarity as anything else. There were a lot of dangerous little firms in Parkhurst. We weren't looking for any aggro with anyone, but we wouldn't walk away from it either. What, in effect, we were saying was that, if we sat together, we stood together.

Barry would be somewhere in our midst. If he hadn't got a seat with us, there would have been an instant tantrum. He liked to sit next to me. Sometimes, in the scramble for seats, he might end up a couple of chairs away.

We would all get to our places early, talk through the credits, then shut up once the film started. Others, though, would arrive late. Then they would carry on talking through the credits and into the film. They would all shut up eventually, but there could be quite a hubbub for a couple of minutes.

It was very annoying for someone who had come to see the film, but it wouldn't last long. There was little you could do about it anyway. It would have been very dangerous to shout out at particular people to shut up, because, if anyone said anything back, then you would have to jump up and have a row right away. So we let it go.

Barry wouldn't though. The lights would dim. The film would start. But some fellas would still carry on talking. Suddenly, he would scream out at the top of his voice, 'Shut up.'

Now, merely to say 'shut up' hardly does justice to the way that Barry did it. The first part of the 'shut' was a rising scream ending in a shriek. The 'up' was a deep-throated roar, ending in a bellow. The whole thing sounded like a madman who had finally come to the end of his tether and couldn't stand the distraction any more.

It always knifed through the hubbub of chatter and silenced everyone immediately. Every time it shocked, even those who were expecting it. We would all jump, and Barry would laugh. So would other people who knew him and had heard it before. But it was always dangerous. It could just happen that some week someone would shout something back. Then Barry would have been clambering over seats, trying to get at the fella.

On 'D' wing our crowd used to put hooch down now and again. It would have been no use trying it on 'A' wing. The screws always made themselves very busy and were forever tearing the wing apart, looking for anything illegal. But 'D' wing was much more relaxed.

With hooch, it was almost like a game with our screws. Many of them enjoyed a drink themselves and could understand our wanting one too. Even if they caught you with it brewing, they would invariably make you pour it down the drain rather than nick you. Once you had it in a cell, though, and had started drinking, they would leave you alone. They didn't want a confrontation with several drunken men that could easily lead to a full-scale punch-up.

In return, sensible people policed themselves. If someone got falling down drunk, the others would take him to his cell, put him to bed, make sure he had some fresh water and a sick bucket, then bang him up.

If anyone started to get violent and wanted to smash the place up, the others would calm him down. In general, it was an arrangement that worked quite well. There was no love lost between the screws and the cons on 'D' wing, but there was some degree of live and let live.

I was the brew-master on our firm. Over the years I had learned how to make hooch from various old Paddies and the occasional Italian, for whom it was something of an art.

I had a flair for organisation and was clever at hiding things. With the right ingredients, I could make a passable brew that tasted a bit like gin and orange. I know what they say about only being able to get up to a certain proof with homebrew, but I found that if I kept 'bombing' the brew with more yeast and sugar it could get very strong indeed.

I got together a couple of clean one-gallon liquid-soap containers, a block of yeast from the kitchen, about 12 pounds of sugar and an assortment of fruit.

The first few days were always the worst. The reaction between the yeast and the sugar always generated vast amounts of gas. It was a sickly sweet smell, reminiscent of rotting fruit, instantly recognisable to con and screw alike.

There were a variety of tricks used to try to disguise the smell, like sprinkling talcum powder about or smearing wintergreen over the door jamb. None was very effective. You just had to keep moving the stuff about.

By day the two containers were moved around various cells on the wing. At night, when there was little chance of a cell search, I had them in my cell. I would nurse them gently, keeping them warm by the pipes and occasionally 'bombing' them with extra sugar and yeast. Usually it took about three weeks. This was a reasonable length of time for a good brew.

The nearer we got to the time of drinking, the more nervous we would become about losing the hooch. On this particular occasion I wanted to drink it on Saturday evening. There were rarely searches on a Saturday, and there was no work so we had all day to strain it off and get everything into position. Also, you had all day Sunday to get over the effects.

Big Mick, though, wanted to drink it on the Friday. He didn't want to take the chance of waiting the extra day and losing it. As I was looking after it, however, this time I had my way. Saturday it would be.

Barry agreed to have the party in his cell. It was an ideal place, right up in the corner of the fives. We would be out of the way, and the screws wouldn't hear too much noise. At least, that was the theory.

It was a brave decision on Barry's part for several reasons.

Firstly, you could always count on plenty of mess at a hooch party. Fellas would knock things over and occasionally spew up. Once the hooch hit you, these things could become unavoidable. Barry had a nice tidy cell that he took a pride in. We all swore we wouldn't mess it up.

The second danger was that, should there be any trouble, you could hardly leave the party if it was in your own cell. Bearing in mind the volatile people who would be attending, trouble was always a distinct possibility.

We were all pals and rarely rowed among ourselves. However, we still promised Barry that we'd be on our best behaviour. It was quite a novel situation, with us promising to behave while Barry acted the responsible one.

Saturday arrived. I strained the hooch and took it up to Barry's cell. I poured it into a clean two-gallon plastic bucket and left it in a cool corner. As soon as we were unlocked that evening, our crowd was to make its way up to Barry's cell, and the party would start.

The doors were unlocked at six o'clock, and I climbed the stairs to Barry's cell. It was all laid out ready. The bucket of hooch was in the middle with the lid off. On a nearby table stood several half-pint china mugs. Next to them were a couple of plates bearing neatly made sandwiches. His record player was playing softly in the corner. Barry had clearly gone to considerable trouble for us.

I arrived first, closely followed by Big Mick and Stewart. Then Eddie came in with Mick, a prolific and well-respected robber out of North London. There was a lot of laughing as we greeted each other. Stewart was especially tickled by the sight of Barry playing the serious, if genial host. We took our seats and settled down to wait for John.

About five minutes later he hurried in. He was lucky to be there, because he lived on 'A' wing. He had been trying to move on to 'D' wing for weeks, but the screws wouldn't let him. They didn't like to let too many of us get together on the same wing. On this occasion, though, Eddie had asked our SO if John could come on the wing for the evening. Much to our surprise, he agreed.

The atmosphere was just like a party outside, minus the women of course. Everybody was in good spirits and looking forward to a break in the usual monotony. You had to have these breaks, these high points, otherwise life was all boredom and gloom. We each took a china mug. Barry filled a jug from the bucket and topped each one to the brim. The golden-orange liquid had just a trace of effervescence on top. The slightly nauseous smell of the brewed fruit made our noses wrinkle.

We had no time for those who would gingerly sniff the brew, though, then sip it. We observed the tradition of the 'first cup'. Holding our breath, we said, 'Cheers,' then drank the whole cupful straight down. No doubt the rush of alcohol to the brain was responsible for much of the drunkenness caused by hooch. It also helped you get used to the rather sickly smell.

I experienced an extraordinarily sweet taste all down the back of my throat. I shuddered involuntarily as the alcohol hit my stomach. Then, an ever-growing warm sensation suffused my whole body.

In no time at all the party was in full swing. The music was blaring, and everyone was laughing and shouting at the top of their voices. We had almost forgotten that we were in prison.

Top-cat was in his element. He had a captive audience and could show off to his heart's content. He told all his old jokes and ran through several of the incidents we had been involved in. It all seemed very funny now. We laughed and laughed.

In a spirit of peaceful coexistence, someone suggested we invite in a couple of the Jocks for a drink. There were a lot of Scots fellas at Parkhurst, and, on the whole, they were staunch people. The Londoners and the Jocks got on quite well. There was some rivalry, and we moved in different firms, but there was a degree of mutual respect. (At this time it was the epitome of success for a Scottish criminal to come down to London and make it.)

John went out and came back with Hughie and Jamie, two Jocks in their late 20s. At first, they were ill at ease, but after a couple of drinks they were laughing and joking with the rest of us. We were all very drunk by now.

From time to time people would wander off. They went to have a piss, to clear their head or just to stretch their legs. Those less drunk would regularly go out and tour the landings to make sure that one of our crowd wasn't lying drunk somewhere.

Suddenly, I realised that Stewart was missing. I still felt responsible for him. If anything had happened to him, I wouldn't have been able to face his brother, Ian, who was doing 25 years in another jail and who was also a close friend of mine.

Before tea, I had taken pains to ensure that Stewart was prepared for the evening to come. I explained how, after drinking hooch, it was very easy to spew up. It often came after you lay down and the room started to spin around.

I took him into my cell and showed him how I had laid it out. There was a new plastic washing bowl on the floor beside the bed. A clean towel lay next to it. I explained that if you were sick you would need to drink lots of water. I had a jugful on my table. These were all the things that an experienced hooch drinker needed to know, I had told him.

I left Barry's cell looking for Stewart. I wasn't too steady on my feet myself. I staggered along the landing to the recess, thinking that he might have gone for a piss. As I drew close, I could see some movement in the gloom.

South London Eddie and Mick had a mop each. They were dancing with them in the recess. I had never seen anything so ridiculous in my life. Here were two of London's better-known villains acting really foolishly. But that was what the hooch could do to you. It was all harmless fun really. Part of it was laughing the next day at the way you had made fools of yourselves the night before.

I carried on looking for Stewart. The stairs down from the fives had never seemed so steep. I clung on to the hand-rails with both hands. As I staggered down each flight, I stopped only to look in each recess. There was no sign of Stewart.

There were no screws about either. Once they had heard the noise of the party and realised who was involved, they had come down from the landings and retired to the relative safety of the office.

Finally, I reached the ones. I staggered across to Stewart's door, only to find it locked. I looked through his spy-hole and could see him lying in his bed fast asleep. Clearly, he had had enough for the evening.

I suddenly realised that so had I. My cell was just across the landing. Before I knew it I was inside and banging the door behind me.

Back at the party things were getting a bit out of hand. John and drink were like fire and gunpowder, a volatile combination. He was falling down drunk by now and had started throwing playful punches. He was a powerful fella, though, and a playful punch from John could hurt. Especially when he was off balance and his timing was out.

Within no time at all he had not only punched Big Mick on the chin but both of the Jocks as well, laughing helplessly all the while. Tempers were becoming frayed. Already pride had been hurt. Luckily, it was nine o'clock, and time for John to get back to his own wing.

As Eddie had been responsible for bringing him over, it was his job to get him back. He steered him out of Barry's cell on the long journey down to the ones. With Eddie leading him, John partly walked, partly fell down the three flights of stairs. By now it was just after nine. The door through to 'A' wing was open, and a reception committee of 'A'-wing screws was waiting.

'Hold up. Look at these slags,' said John, laughing hysterically. He went into a fit of continuous laughter. He stood in the middle of the ones and wouldn't move. With Eddie pulling on one arm and the 'A'-wing screws shepherding him along, but not touching him, they gradually got him into 'A' wing.

Finally, they pushed him into his cell and banged him up. John was still laughing uproariously. The screws, though, definitely weren't amused. Any chance he had ever had of moving on to 'D' wing was now gone.

When I awoke the following morning, the first thing I became aware of was a terrible stench. It smelled like a combination of all the most loathsome things imaginable. The second thing I noticed was that the side of my face, where it touched the pillow, felt wet and sticky.

I gingerly lifted my head from the pillow. The room spun before my eyes. Looking around, I could see that I must have been sick as I lay asleep. On one side there was vomit all over the pillow and up the nearby wall. On the other I had missed the bed completely and been sick on the floor.

I levered myself up on to my elbows so that I could see more of the cell. Bleary-eyed, I saw the new plastic bowl, still where I had put it the evening before. But there was something in it. It was a brown bowl, and whatever was in it was of a similar colour. Suddenly, the smell hit me, the very distinctive smell of shit. Next to the bowl, lying on the floor, was the clean towel I had so carefully laid out. It had a long brown smear on it.

I cringed as I realised what must have happened. As I had banged my door the night before, I must have suddenly realised that I wanted a pony very urgently indeed. My pot was on the other side of the bed, which I had across the cell. I needed to climb over the bed to reach it. No easy task for someone who was failing down drunk and on the verge of an imminent bowel movement.

I must have realised that I wasn't going to make it in time. I didn't remember dropping my trousers, shitting in the bowl and wiping my arse on the towel before I climbed into bed, but I must have done it, because the evidence was all there before me.

I couldn't believe it. I considered myself to be a very clean-living fella. I was extremely scrupulous about personal hygiene. My cell was always clean and tidy, and I never, ever shit in my pot.

I felt very embarrassed. I felt even more so when I realised that the night screw must have looked through my spy-hole to check that I was in. Heaven knows what he made of the bowl of turds and the towel with the skidmark. He must have thought I was an animal.

My immediate problem was to get rid of the bowl and its contents without anyone seeing it. I would obviously have to empty it down the slops sink. The trouble was that, first thing in the morning, everybody else was throwing something down there too.

Right next door to me lived a little raver called Jeff. If he saw me slopping out with shit in my washing bowl, you could bet your life that it would be all over the nick by dinnertime. But I couldn't hang about too long, because it stank. Anyone coming in would smell it.

As my door was unlocked, I went straight to the recess with my water jug on a dummy run. Sure enough, there were dozens of people about. I emptied the old water from the jug and filled it with fresh.

When I got back to my cell, I poured some of the water into my empty piss-pot. I went over to the khazi and emptied that.

By now, the early rush was thinning. I went back to my cell and hovered in the doorway. Suddenly there were only people going away from the recess, no one was on their way to it. I dived into my cell, grabbed the bowl and walked quickly to the slops sink. I was committed now; I couldn't turn back.

It went sweet as a nut. Straight into the recess, down the sink, a quick rinse of the bowl, which was then thrown underneath, and I turned around and walked out again.

Later that morning, we all met at Barry's. He was cursing the state of his cell. There were dog-ends everywhere, spilled hooch and a smashed cup. For once, he had been on his best behaviour. It was the rest of us who had acted like fools.

We laughed at Mick and Eddie for dancing with the mops. We jokingly chastised John for setting about people. He wouldn't be allowed on the wing now, and we had to contend with all the Jocks walking about with long faces.

We mocked Stewart for slipping away early and going to bed. In fact, we laughed at all the foolish things that people had done under the influence of the hooch. Except, of course, the foolish thing I had done. But that was because no one had seen mine.

The dentist incident was the third time that Barry had seriously confronted the screws and got away with it. They didn't go out of their way to nick people at Parkhurst. The vast majority of trivial offences were ignored. Fellas were doing far too much bird to be messed about. However, it was very unusual for incidents like the three Barry had been involved in to go unpunished.

It wasn't that they were worried about him physically: there were many dangerous people at Parkhurst who could have a right row. It wasn't even fear of repercussions from our crowd: if the screws ever thought that they were losing control, they would soon confront us and move people out. It had to be something more.

Several months previously, Barry had been at Wandsworth. He had just got his five. It was a long hot summer and there had been some discontent, including a couple of minor 'sit-downs' on the yard.

This was unprecedented. The screws ran Wandsworth; there was no such thing as prisoner power. The POs were proud of Wandsworth's reputation as a hard-line jail. Other prisons might run liberal regimes, but at Wandsworth you got the absolute minimum you were entitled to and nothing more.

Barry hadn't been one of the ring-leaders of the 'sit-downs', but had been involved on the fringes. Now, the jail was closed down tight. All workshops were shut and exercise periods were heavily supervised. There were hundreds of screws all over the place.

One afternoon, Barry had been unlocked for a visit. He was still on appeal so, although he was expecting his wife, he was using an appeal visit when, strictly speaking, only legal matters should be dealt with. It was a common ploy. Most times no attention was paid to what the visit was used for.

The screw had taken Barry across the centre and into the closed-visits area at the end of one of the wings. His wife was sitting in a visiting box, on the other side of a reinforced glass window. Barry sat down opposite her.

There was a vent set in the woodwork at the base of the window. You had to tilt your head forwards to speak into it. Barry leaned forward and began speaking to his wife.

First, he had asked how she was. Then he enquired after relatives, friends and the general social trivia that makes up most people's lives on the outside.

Suddenly, the screw – who had been standing behind him supervising the visit – had stepped forward. 'This is an appeal visit and you haven't been discussing legal matters. The visit is terminated,' he said peremptorily.

Barry turned around quickly. He didn't want any trouble in front of his wife. 'OK, guv,' he said. 'I'll just talk about legal matters.' He turned back to his wife and started to give her instructions to pass on to his solicitors.

No more than 30 seconds had passed when the door to the visits room bust open. Dozens of screws poured in. They grabbed Barry and dragged him from the visiting box. On the other side of the glass, he could see his wife being manhandled away by more screws. He was lifted bodily and carried from the room. Kicks and punches rained on him from all directions. As he was carried along, he could see screws everywhere. There were hundreds of them. They stood all along the landings and around the centre. It looked like the crowd at a screws' football match.

They had run straight across the centre with him and down the stairs to the ones on 'E' wing. There wasn't another con in sight; everyone was banged up. Still punching and kicking him, they tore all his clothes off and carried him naked into a cell.

By now, the screws were in a frenzy, especially a couple of the younger ones. Perhaps the tension of the past few days, coupled with the euphoria of the massive show of strength, had got to them. They had been given *carte blanche* to crush all resistance and they hadn't known when to stop.

One of the screws unbuckled the belt from around his waist and slipped it around Barry's neck. As the others lifted Barry up, the end of the belt was tied to the window bars. Then they let him go. He hung there, choking, as the belt tightened around his neck.

Frantically, his bruised and battered hands had torn at the belt to try to loosen it from the bars. But he couldn't reach them. He was helpless. His legs kicked desperately as he felt himself slowly losing consciousness.

Rocky was a short, stocky screw who had worked on the chokey landing for years. In his youth, he had been a boxer, hence the nickname. Now, in middle age, all he had to show for it was a broken nose and extensive scar tissue. He wasn't a kindly man by any means, but he was a man's man. He had a certain sense of fair play.

He rushed into the cell, pushing several screws out of the way.

'You're not doing this on my fucking landing!' he shouted. 'Give me a hand to get him down.'

The screws seemed to come to their senses. Sheepishly, they helped Rocky lift Barry down and laid him, semi-conscious, on the floor.

'Go and get the doctor,' said Rocky to a young screw, who hurried off. Rocky massaged Barry's neck and splashed water on his face from a nearby water jug.

About 15 minutes later, the doctor arrived. By now, Barry was conscious again, but he still lay on the floor, dazed and shocked.

The doctor examined him. He ran his fingers over the angry red weal that extended all around Barry's throat, but didn't remark on it.

'He's all right,' he said to the four screws who had remained in the cell. He hadn't spoken one word to Barry, who still lay there naked. One of the screws fetched his clothes and threw them to him, then they banged him up.

The following morning, Barry appeared on adjudication before the governor, charged with assaulting a screw. This hadn't surprised him. If they could try to hang him, they could certainly fit him up for an assault. Anyway, he had been expecting it. However, they would have to do something to justify the bruises and scratches he had all over his body. Because it was a serious charge, he had been remanded to appear before the VC.

The VC at Wandsworth wasn't known for its independence. Mainly it functioned as a rubber stamp for the screws. If it ever came down to the word of a con against that of a screw, they always believed the screw, irrespective of any other evidence. Most fellas either pleaded guilty in the hope of getting a lighter sentence or just simply refused to take part in the proceedings.

Two days after the incident, Barry appeared before the VC. He still had an angry weal, dark purple now, around his neck. On closer inspection, you could see small pinpricks of lighter colour where the belt holes had been. The mark of the buckle stood out clearly where it had bitten into his neck.

This physical evidence just couldn't be explained away. Cons weren't allowed belts in Wandsworth and, even if they had, they certainly wouldn't have been allowed them in the chokey.

Then there was Barry's wife. She had written in complaining that she had been assaulted and had seen Barry being assaulted, too. It made for an unusually strong case. Barry was found not guilty of assaulting the screw.

That left the authorities in an awkward position. If the screws hadn't been restraining a man who was assaulting them, then why was his body covered with so many bruises and scratches? And where had the belt that he was hanged with come from?

At this stage, some of the fellas thought that Barry should have followed it through and had the screws nicked. If not for his own benefit, then for others who might follow. But then, they hadn't been nearly hanged in Wandsworth chokey.

Also, Barry would have had to get up in court and give evidence against the screws, which went against the grain for him. He just wanted to get away as soon as possible. A deal was struck. He had been moved to Parkhurst the following day.

The legacy of the incident was that it gave Barry some degree of protection. In any future incident, he could claim that his experience at Wandsworth had unhinged him and left him with a violent antipathy towards screws. If charges were pressed, it would only serve to publicise an incident that the Prison Department would prefer to keep secret. Top-cat now had several lives.

Cynics might say that the 'Wandsworth Factor' was used by Barry to get himself out of tight corners. However, it took a thoroughly disturbed person to get into these situations in the first place. The Wandsworth incident had deeply affected Barry. He carried it with him every day of his life.

5 SHUFFLING BOB AND THE SLOW-WALKERS

Comparatively speaking, the average age of the cons at Parkhurst was older than at other prisons, and there was also a sizeable group who were in their 60s and 70s, some of whom were infirm. When it came to getting about the place, they were much slower than their younger brethren. Consequently, they would have been condemned to be forever last in meal queues, treatment queues and so on. There was also the very real danger of being knocked over in the rush by their more boisterous fellows.

Therefore, as a special dispensation, anyone falling into this category could be classified as a 'slow-walker', which meant that they were allowed to leave their workplace or cell a good five minutes before the rest. It wasn't a privilege that caused any jealousy and went largely unnoticed and unremarked.

'Scots Bob' Cassidy was one of the 'slow-walkers'. In the early Sixties he had gained considerable notoriety for being involved in a gangland shooting outside a well-known London nightclub. He was also a robber of some repute. Now, though, he was in his early 60s and suffering from the first stages of Parkinson's disease.

He wasn't part of our group, but then we were particularly

cliquey. Unless you were a Londoner, a robber and known to one of us, you weren't on. There were sound, practical reasons for this, not the least of them being that we knew there were no grasses or slags in the company. However, there was also a considerable degree of elitism involved.

Bob failed for membership on the grounds that he was a Jock and he was old. Having said that, he probably wouldn't have chosen to sit with us anyway. He had his own pals among the other Jocks and older cons.

We all got on quite well with him, though, and held him in some respect. He had a fiery temper and wouldn't stand any nonsense from the screws. He was staunch and game. If the chaps were involved in any sort of revolt, Bob would be there. This was all the more remarkable because his advancing disease made his hands shake and he could only walk with a slow, shuffling gait. This prompted Barry to nickname him 'Shuffling Bob'. It was typical of Barry's jaundiced view of the world. Our group didn't particularly approve of this less than respectful nickname, but Barry only used it in our company anyway.

At times, 'Shuffling Bob' could be very cantankerous. Although his mind was clear on most other matters, he was totally fixated on being everywhere first. Whether it was the dinner queue, treatments, going to the cinema or stage rooms, Bob just had to be the first one there. What he gained from this, no one really knew. We took it to be an irrational fixation of a sick old man who had done too much bird.

It was quite comical to see him setting off with the 'slow-walkers', shuffling along furiously with his arms working like pistons. The other old boys would stroll along sedately while Bob rushed ahead.

We laughed about this privately, but it didn't bother us. So what if he wanted to be everywhere first? None of us was going anywhere. We had all the time in the world. So who cared?

It bothered Barry though. In fact, at times, it got right up his nose. He was a classic elitist who liked to think that he was good at most things. Perhaps the thought of Bob coming first all the time irked him.

'Look at that old bastard,' he said on several occasions. 'I'd like to trip him up.'

We knew he didn't really mean it. To trip up old Bob would have been severely out of order. Everyone would have been outraged. It would have been a liberty, and none of us liked liberty-takers. Also, Bob was a game old bastard. Barry would have had a fight on his hands.

The wings were always unlocked at six o'clock for evening association. 'D' wing stage rooms were a couple of minutes' walk away. We would have to walk the length of the ones of 'A' wing, up a long flight of stairs, across the twos and left into a 20-foot-long corridor, then sharp right into a 90-foot-long corridor. This would bring us to several large rooms. In all, it was a walk of about 150 yards, up steps and stairs and around corridors.

Depending on what was on TV, there was sometimes a rush for seats. There were two large TV rooms, each with a set high on one wall, but the seats at the front were always sought after. This didn't bother 'Shuffling Bob', though. He always had a good five minutes' start over the rest of us.

One particular evening as I came out of my cell at six o'clock, both Barry and Stewart were waiting for me. This was unusual because, although Stewart lived on the ones, only a couple of cells from me, Barry lived right up on the fives. He always got to the stage rooms after we did.

We hurried into 'A' wing, intent on getting seats at the front of the TV room for a particular programme we wanted to watch. As we entered, we were just in time to see the back of Bob's head on the twos as he turned into the first corridor.

'Let's catch the old bastard up and beat him to the TV rooms,' said Barry mischievously.

Stewart, Barry's perfect foil, was equally mischievous and

readily agreed. I'm not usually easily led but, before I knew it, I was running along the ones of 'A' wing in hot pursuit of 'Shuffling Bob'.

We pounded up the stairs and turned left into the first corridor. As the three of us charged into the long corridor, we saw 'Shuffling Bob' already halfway along it. He was beetling along in his usual brisk fashion.

Hearing the noise of us behind him, he quickly turned his head. Then he hurried on at an even more frenetic pace.

By now, I was thoroughly caught up in this childish game. For a long time, we had ignored Bob's fixation with being first, but now it was out in the open. We were actually trying to get somewhere before he did. What's more, we were closing on him quickly and he knew it. He spurred himself on to an even faster pace, his feet trying frantically to keep up with his speeding body.

Parkhurst is an old jail and there are many strange architectural quirks in its construction. Halfway down, the long corridor is broken by two steps which take the floor 18 inches higher, and for some unknown reason, at the same place the ceiling dips about a foot. This still left seven feet of headroom, more than enough for normal purposes.

As the three of us thundered along, we suddenly came to the steps. In full flight, we leaped up them without even breaking stride. This presented no problem to Stewart or me, who were both only five foot six tall. Barry, though, stood all of five foot eleven.

We heard a deep, meaty thud and a gasping cry of pain as the top of the leaping Barry's head came into sharp contact with the dip in the ceiling. We spun round to see him rolling on the floor in agony, both hands clasped to his forehead.

We ran back, thinking he was badly injured.

'The old bastard, the old bastard,' he moaned over and over again through gritted teeth.

We helped him to his feet, too concerned about the extent of his injuries to acknowledge the humour of the situation. As he leaned against the wall, I pulled his hands from his face. I was relieved to see that there was no blood. There was, however, an angry-looking, egg-shaped lump that seemed to be growing larger by the second. Evening TV was now clearly out, so we helped him back to 'D' wing.

We sat Barry down in my cell and I fetched some cold water to bathe the lump. Seeing that he wasn't badly hurt, Stewart suddenly burst out laughing. That started me off. The pair of us were rolling about on my bed, shrieking uncontrollably.

Barry's normally flushed face was now an angry shade of purple. He fought his mounting rage, while at the same time trying hard not to look ridiculous. He could see that it was a funny situation and, had it happened to either Stewart or me, he would have been laughing, too. All he could manage, though, was to keep repeating, 'That old bastard, that old bastard.'

The following day, all our group knew about it. We chuckled about it as we sat in our usual meeting place, the 'Old Bailey'. When Barry put in an appearance, complete with bump, it prompted fresh peals of laughter.

'I'll have that old bastard,' he said between the roars.

'That's what comes of being wicked to an old man,' said Dave, who was a kind-hearted, even-tempered fella.

Every dinnertime, 'Shuffling Bob' would leave his workshop in the compound five minutes early and head back to the wing with the rest of the 'slow-walkers'. He always arrived first, but this served no immediate advantage as dinner wasn't dished up for another ten minutes.

I was now working as a wing cleaner and saw Bob each day as he hurried in. I would watch him go into his cell and wait until he heard the sound of dinner about to be served. The end table was level with his door, but on the other side of the landing. By the time he reached it, a queue would have already formed, but this didn't faze him at all. He would shuffle right to the front and push in. He was served first every day.

I had observed this little scenario scores of times. Part of my duties as a wing cleaner was to fetch the meals and serve them. I could see the annoyance on people's faces as Bob pushed in front of them, but he was an old man, and sick, so they just let it go. If he had been younger and fitter, there would definitely have been serious trouble. Nobody pushed in at Parkhurst.

The fetching and serving of meals was quite a performance. The kitchen was just past our stage rooms, a 200-yard trek up stairs and around corners. No food trolley could make this trip, so about eight of us would set off each mealtime on a bizarre safari. We returned carrying trays and canisters of meat, mash, cabbage, peas, duff, custard and gravy.

By the time we reached the wing, our arms were quite tired. Consequently, we would heave the metal containers on to the hot-plate and tables, causing a cacophony of sharp crashes and bangs. It was this noise that always alerted 'Shuffling Bob' to the fact that dinner was about to be served.

I suddenly thought of a plan. If I covered the hot-plate and tables with the thick quilted hot-plate covers and got all the cleaners to put the meal-containers down gently, then perhaps we could start serving without alerting 'Shuffling Bob'. We could probably serve a couple of people before he tumbled what was going on. By then, it would be too late. He would still rush out and push in but, for the very first time, he wouldn't be served first.

I told Barry about the plan and he loved it. Later, I told all our group in Dave's cell. They laughed, but were genuinely concerned that 'Shuffling Bob' would go into one. He was a cantankerous, fiery old fucker and no one knew how he would react.

Several vowed to stay out of the way and watch from a distance. They weren't physically worried about him if it came to a punch-up; they just didn't want to be in the immediate vicinity if he started to throw things about.

The following dinnertime, word had gone around about what

was going to happen. 'Shuffling Bob' came in as usual and went into his cell. Up on the landings, about 50 fellas were leaning on the railings waiting to see the fun.

I covered the hot-plate and tables with the thick cloths. I had already spoken to the other cleaners about what I wanted to do. They were all for it. They, too, had the hump with Bob pushing in all the time.

When we returned with the dinner containers, we very gently placed them on the cloths. There was hardly a sound to be heard above the usual hubbub of conversation from the fellas waiting to be served. We gingerly removed the lids from the containers and carefully picked up the metal serving implements. We started to serve.

The queue moved forward as we put meat, gravy, cabbage, potato and duff on to the metal trays. As the first man held out his tray for a serving of custard, the edge struck the side of the metal canister sharply. This familiar sound must have alerted 'Shuffling Bob' because he suddenly burst out of his cell with a plate in one hand and a bowl in the other.

For a second, he hesitated, bewildered. Then he plunged forward into the queue. It was no use his going to the front. The first fella was getting his custard and Bob would have missed all the rest of the dinner. Thrusting his plate between people, he loaded up with food as he rushed up the queue.

There was no chance of Bob being first today, though. He managed to finish fourth as he collected his custard, a very creditable performance in the circumstances. Bob clearly didn't think so, though. He could only glare at the backs of the three fellas who had been served before him as they walked off with their dinners.

He rushed back into his cell and put his dinner on the table. Then he rushed out again to stand in the middle of the ones. There was a wild, deranged look on his face. His routine had been utterly disrupted and it had thrown him right out of gear. He was bewildered. He knew that something strange had happened, but he couldn't quite figure out what.

Everyone who was privy to the joke now looked anywhere but at Bob. Servers suddenly became intent on the act of serving. If anyone had laughed, Bob might have tumbled the plot and steamed into them. Now the situation wasn't quite so funny. There was a confused and angry old nutter on the loose, who just might go berserk at any minute. I stood on the other side of the hot-plate, serving the cabbage. I may have seemed to be taking an inordinate interest in the quality of the greens, staring fixedly into the tray, but I was watching 'Shuffling Bob' very closely. When he had stormed back out of his cell, I had instantly gone on 'battle alert'. I didn't want to but, if he came anywhere near me, I had resolved to clump him with the metal serving spoon. He might be old, but he could still be dangerous.

Bob stood there for a couple of minutes, staring around wildly. Finally, he slowly turned and went into his cell and banged his door up.

Out on the landing, there was an audible sigh of relief. No one wanted to show that they were worried; however, there was an appreciable lowering of tension.

Later, we talked about the incident in Dave's cell. We remarked on how confused old Bob looked when he ran out of his cell. We laughed and laughed, although Dave still thought it a liberty to take the piss out of the old fella.

Barry was especially pleased. 'Did you see the look on the old bastard's face?' he shouted, laughing all the while.

Most of us agreed that it had been very funny and that no real harm had been done. However, we decided not to stage any kind of repeat performance. We had got away with it once. We didn't want to push our luck.

6 LENNIE AND THE PHANTOM

If there was one thing that set Parkhurst apart from other jails, it was that the bizarre was accepted almost as normal. Freakish events set the tone of the place. A classic example was the shit flood.

I had been at Parkhurst about a fortnight, still in a cell on the ones in 'A' wing. It was convenient for the recess, just across the landing. This was a mixed blessing, though, because of the never-ending background noise of chains being pulled, toilets flushing and water running.

One morning, just as I sat down in my cell to eat breakfast, Dave came running in. 'Quick, Norm, throw some old sheets across your doorway!' he shouted urgently.

It was a bit early in the day and the request quite unusual. 'What for, Dave?' I asked, looking up.

'The recess has overflowed and it'll run in here any second, so hurry up!'

Dave was a serious fella, not at all a practical joker. He didn't get excited easily either, so I realised that this must be something serious. I grabbed a couple of dirty towels, ran to the door and laid them across the threshold.

As I raised my eyes, I saw a dark-yellow stain spreading across the landing. The effect was almost surreal. It was as if a yellow shadow was moving across the ones. Looking more closely, I could see countless objects, bobbing along on the surface and also moving – an obscene flotsam of shit, toilet paper, dog-ends and other soggy items of indiscernible origin. Then the smell hit me: the acrid whiff of piss immediately followed by the gut-churning stench of shit.

The foul-smelling yellow sea spread ever outwards. The leading edge lapped up against my towel barrier, then swept past. Luckily, the landing was wide and the volume of water finite. As it spread out ever thinner, it left the flotsam marooned all over the ones.

I suddenly realised that Dave and I were trapped. If we left, we would get the filth all over our shoes and bring it back into our cells. I pushed my door to; after the stench of the flood, I didn't feel much like finishing my breakfast, so we sat back and talked. Dave explained that Parkhurst's sewers were old and couldn't always take the vast amount of waste flushed into them each morning. Sometimes they would get blocked, and then the waste would back up and flow back out of the slops sinks.

As Dave talked, I became very annoyed. This was the latest of a whole series of things that were wrong with the prison. Parkhurst was a physical fight for survival at the best of times. Now there was another potent threat to everyday existence: the danger of disease from living in an extension of a sewer.

After a while, Dave and I heard movement out on the landing. We looked out to see several cleaners scooping up the worst of the mess with dust pans and tipping it into buckets. Then they mopped up the rest. Within 20 minutes, it was all gone. The smell, however, lingered on.

As the cleaning up was completed, two screws appeared, and I recognised one of them as someone I had been told was on the local POA committee.

The union line at Parkhurst was a very hard one. Everything

had to be done by the book, otherwise the POA committee would bring it up at their next meeting with the governor. But it was all one way. Their way. It was all about manning levels, meal breaks and pay. Never about the conditions under which we were forced to live.

I walked right up to the screw. 'You're POA, aren't you, guv?' I asked without any preliminaries. Both screws turned to look at me. 'Well, you have to work in these conditions that we have to live in. Why the fuck don't you get your union to do something about the sewers?'

The POA screw, a taciturn man with a permanently sour expression, just stood there looking at me and said nothing.

'Perhaps the Home Office don't give a fuck about you either,' I said, incensed at his silence.

It suddenly occurred to me that, maybe, he had as little control over building improvements as I had. The Home Office would have to allocate significant funds for the sewers to be rebuilt. It was a sorry indictment of how little they valued the screws, that they weren't willing to spend the money.

There was considerable humour at the next meeting in the 'Old Bailey'. Not that shit was funny in itself, its smell was far too all-pervasive in Parkhurst for that. But the idea of my being put off my breakfast and having to block the doorway with towels tickled the fellas.

Excremental tales were commonplace in prison. There was a constant fund of stories where it had been used in a variety of situations: as a weapon against the screws; as a defensive weapon, when fellas covered themselves in it down the chokey to deter the screws from giving them a beating; and even as a means of sabotage and wind-up. It was a story from this last category that I suddenly remembered. I told it to the fellas as much to distract attention from my recent inconvenience as to entertain.

Lennie Mason was a big fella. Massive shoulders bulging with muscle provided the firm foundation for a thick powerful neck which, in turn, supported an enormous head. Large muscular arms, a thickish waist and hips completed a build that was both symmetrical and strong. At just under six foot tall, the huge frame carried his 16 stone well. The overall impression was of a powerhouse. Lennie had been a seaman for years, and he still had the rolling gait. In fact, with his muscular build he resembled a pumped-up Popeye.

He had a gruff, bluff, easygoing personality. He did tend to take advantage of his size, but not in a nasty or vindictive way. He feared no one and always stood up for himself. Although tough, he wasn't vicious. He was an old-fashioned punch-up merchant rather than a tool man.

He had done several bits of bird, his present four stretch at Albany being the longest. He could hardly be classed as a professional criminal, though, as most of his crimes had been spur-of-the-moment jobs, invariably carried out when drunk.

Len had lived his rough life to the full. He drank in and around West London in the company of three other fellas, all of whom were bigger than he was. They consumed prodigious amounts of booze. The evening would often end in a drunken rampage down the High Street. There were regular punch-ups. One of their favourite tricks was to run into a shop, pick up the till and run off with it. Needless to say, they regularly got nicked. In fact, Lennie's present sentence was for stealing a till while drunk. Perhaps the court would have been more understanding of a younger man, would have seen this behaviour as just part of growing up. Lennie, however, was 32 years old.

Apart from his size, Lennie was hardly remarkable. Albany held many who were far more unusual and bizarre than he was. He did, however, have one feature that made him stand out from the crowd and gave him a unique personality all of his own. Lennie had the most amazing voice. It wasn't that it had a distinctive tone or pitch or was tuneful. It was just very, very loud. Whenever he spoke, a booming sound would emanate from his massive head and fill the room, a deep, husky, throaty roar produced with little or no effort. Lennie only had two volume controls: one minute he would be silent, the next in full cry.

It was awesome to listen to. He wasn't deliberately noisy; in fact, it was doubtful if he realised the din he was making. But a din it was. Words would just pour out at top volume, colliding with earlier words ricocheting back off walls and ceilings. The result was a cacophony that was as powerful and uncontrolled as the booming of the surf. This was the origin of his nickname: 'Boomer'. You could hear him all over the jail.

Len lived on 'D' wing. There were hardly any faces on the wing, so he liked to take a leading role. His was the word of moral authority on how things should be. His was the rallying point to which lesser individuals would gather. His influence wasn't just restricted to 'D' wing. Other than his voice, his main claim to fame was that he was the leading light of the 'yard party'.

Now as far as jobs went at Albany, the yard party was a very good one. Most fellas were confined to the wings or workshops for security reasons. Those with a short time left could get on the outdoor parties. The yard party was a group of four cons under the supervision of a screw, who went around the jail picking up litter.

It might not sound much to free-world people, but for those caught in the claustrophobic confines of small prison wings, to be able to wander around in the fresh air was a considerable privilege.

Albany, a comparatively new jail, was laid out more like campus accommodation than a prison. In between the wings, there were squares of close-cropped grass, bordered by narrow concrete paths. Each area lay in a quadrangle, open at one end. This was where most of the detritus would accumulate.

Lennie's gang would appear, pulling a four-wheeled barrow. Each carried a broom, a rake or a shovel. They would pick up the rubbish and put it in the barrow. On any average day, there would be bottles, jars, newspapers, tissues, scraps of food and various articles of prison clothing.

The littering wasn't done deliberately as some specific act of vandalism. Rather, it was merely laziness on the part of people who were forced to do all their living in one small room.

When they were locked up, unwanted items tended to be just thrown out of the windows as if into some cosmic rubbish chute. Occasionally – unusually – there would be the odd shit-parcel. Someone who had been caught short while locked up would shit in newspaper and throw it out of the window rather than use their pot. It was a filthy habit and no decent con with any self-respect would do it. No one liked to shit in their pot but, in the circumstances, what else could you do?

In the old Victorian jails in towns, shit-parcels often reached epidemic proportions. Squalid conditions bred squalid behaviour. There were scores of dossers and other lowlifes whose general standards were abysmal. A job on the yard party in such a jail was no sinecure at all. Many wouldn't do it.

One morning, Lennie was out with the yard party. The bright spring sunshine bathed the wings in a golden hue. The air was fresh, vibrant and invigorating, as only a spring breeze can be. The grassy areas between the wings were lush and green. Here and there, daisies and buttercups peppered the sward.

Lennie strode out ahead of the party like some medieval lord. Immediately behind him came his 'retainers' – the other three cons – pulling the barrow and carrying the tools. Bringing up the rear was the screw. You could have been forgiven for thinking that Lennie was in charge of the party.

Every now and then he would call out loudly to someone he knew. And he knew a lot of people. Increasingly, it was becoming less like a work detail and more like a lap of honour. Lennie loved every minute of it. He was the most visible con in the nick. People no longer spoke of the 'yard party'. It was always 'Lennie's yard party'.

They passed 'E' wing and turned into the grassy area between 'C' and 'D' wings. Lennie always took special care of this patch. The bit outside 'D' wing was home turf. He took pride in the fact that it was the cleanest, most intensively policed area in the nick.

He opened his mouth, ready to shout instructions to his minions, when suddenly he stopped. There, on the edge of the concrete path, right where it met the grass, was a large shit-parcel. The impact of being thrown from a height had sundered the sodden newspaper it was wrapped in. It had split wide open, revealing its chocolate-coloured contents. They lay there, like the entrails of a freshly killed beast, steaming gently in the early-morning sun.

The parcel was like a slap in the face to Lennie. He stood there speechless, mouth agape. Shit-parcels were unusual in Albany, unheard of in the area outside 'D' wing. It was sacrilege. Worse than that, it was a direct challenge to Lennie.

Suddenly, he found his voice. A roar of sheer outrage burst from his lips. 'What dirty, stinking bastard has done that?' he boomed. The words rebounded from the surrounding wings as he continued with a tirade that betrayed his maritime background.

Faces began to appear at windows. Passing screws and the cons they were escorting stopped to look over. Roosting birds flew from rooftops. Lennie was at the epicentre of a verbal shockwave that spread rapidly ever outwards.

Then, abruptly, in mid-sentence, Lennie stopped. It had dawned on him that the more attention he attracted, the greater would be his humiliation. Someone on his very own wing had deliberately thrown a shit-parcel out, well knowing that Lennie and his party would have to pick it up. This was something to keep quiet about until he had dealt with it.

'Well, pick it up then, pick it up,' ordered Lennie in a husky shout that was a determined attempt at a whisper. His minions, frozen into inactivity by the explosion of rage, hurried forward with brooms and shovel. The parcel was scraped up and thrown into the barrow.

'Well, cover it up, cover it up,' he said, exasperation raising his voice by several decibels.

The others quickly heaped rubbish over the parcel, hiding it from sight. Lennie didn't want to parade around the nick with it in full view. Cutting their usual round short, they went straight to the rubbish tip to dispose of it.

That dinnertime as he lay in his cell, Lennie ran over the events in his mind. Perhaps it was just a one-off. Some fella who had been caught desperately short, whose pot was already part full, had thrown it out. Maybe it was a new reception who hadn't heard that you didn't do things like that at Albany. The more fuss that Lennie made, the more likely it was to encourage either a repetition or copycat behaviour. No, he would keep quiet and hope that it didn't happen again.

That afternoon, he swore the rest of the yard party to secrecy. His normally cheerful face was uncharacteristically grim as he made his rounds. Partly, it was continuing pique at the phantom shit-bomber. Partly it was to deter any humorous remarks by cons who had heard about the parcel. He couldn't help a shiver of apprehension as he turned into the grassy area next to 'D' wing.

There was some wind-blown paper in the corner and several slices of bread on the grass, but there was no soggy parcel wrapped in newspaper. Inwardly heaving a sigh of relief, he strode on.

The following morning, the sense of unease was back as he neared the 'D' wing area. The previous afternoon had proved nothing really. The fellas could get out to use the toilet during the day. It was at night that they could be trapped, locked in with an imminent bowel movement.

But he was worrying unnecessarily. The area was clear. There was even less rubbish than usual. Despite Lennie's efforts at secrecy, it had quickly gone around the wing that he had come across a shit-parcel. No one wanted to be caught throwing anything out of the window now

A couple of days passed. Lennie had returned to being his old self again, and he set out on the morning round with a spring in his step. Like Ward Bond with a severely depleted wagon train, Lennie blazed a trail around the jail. He swept past 'E' wing, into the 'D' wing area. And froze.

He stopped so abruptly that he was nearly run over by the barrow. But he was oblivious to the near-miss. He stood transfixed, eyes glued to the newspaper-wrapped bundle that lay on the grass.

This time, the grass had cushioned the landing and the paper hadn't split. This was absolutely no consolation to Lennie, though. It was obvious what it was. The dampness seeping through and the accompanying whiff that carried on the early-morning breeze attested to its contents.

'Pick it up,' barked Lennie to no one in particular. The others scurried to do his bidding. He glared up at the windows of 'D' wing as if challenging them to reveal the perpetrator. They winked blankly, the sunlight reflecting from their panes.

The yard party continued on its way with Len strangely silent. Clearly, he was thinking deeply about what had happened. Not even the screw spoke, lest he become the object of Lennie's wrath. For he was obviously very angry indeed. The silence was ominous.

But the expected explosion never came. Lennie continued on the round with a calm that the others found unnerving. No one laughed or joked in case Lennie thought they were laughing at the presence of the shit-parcel. They were relieved when the morning's work was over. Every mealtime, the fellas would file out from the wing into a dining hall. Each wing had its own, a large room about 60 feet long by 25 feet wide. The entrance doors were at one short end, the hot-plate at the other. Along the two longest sides were a line of tables and chairs. There was seating for 90 men, a wing's full complement. Mealtimes were always noisy and hectic with so many people confined in such a comparatively small place. It was a time of day when everyone was together, almost like a large family at dinner. Unlike most large families, however, it could be a flashpoint. Jokes and insults were shouted across the room. It was very much a public stage on which many of the fellas acted out whatever roles they were into.

That dinnertime, Lennie waited until everyone was sitting at a table eating. He stood up from his chair and walked to the centre of the dining hall. 'Just a minute, boys,' he shouted above the din. 'I've got something to say.'

For a split second, the throats of 89 men vied for supremacy over the lone voice. But it was no contest. The booming tones cannoned off the walls, smothering all other conversation. The room fell deathly quiet. All eyes turned to Len.

Rotating slowly to look at everyone in turn, he started to speak. 'Fellas, we've got a phantom on the wing. Some dirty, stinking bastard keeps throwing shit-parcels out of the window. Not only is it an embarrassment for our wing, but me and my party have to pick them up. It's up to us all to catch him. And, when I get my hands on him, I'm going to punch his fucking head in.'

As he warmed to his subject, his voice rose. The final few words were delivered *fortissimo*. It was an impassioned rallying call, and provoked an immediate and involuntary response from the fellas. They bayed their approval and thunderous shouting and clapping shook the room.

Over the next week, 'D' wing's phantom shit-bomber was the talk of the nick. Lennie stalked about the jail like a man on a mission. Occasionally, friends would call out, 'Have you caught him yet, Len?' He took it all good-humouredly. Now it was out in the open, he couldn't let people see how much it had got to him. 'I'll have the fucker,' he would reply.

Several days went by, then another parcel was sighted outside 'D' wing. That dinnertime, Lennie exhorted the fellas to increase their vigilance. They were hardly going to stand at their windows all night long, though, just on the off-chance that they might see the perpetrator. Days passed, and still no culprit had been identified.

The parcels began to appear with increasing regularity now. At least twice, sometimes three times a week, there would be one lying on the grass waiting for Len as he came around with the yard party. Every one was split open now, revealing its foul contents. The bomber was firing them into the ground with deliberate force.

Secretly, up in his cell, Lennie fumed. It was so frustrating. He couldn't fight an enemy he couldn't see. Yet somebody was deliberately and very publicly taking the piss out of him.

He had been looking very closely at suitable suspects on the wing. There were about six soapy bastards who he felt to be quite capable of such a dirty trick. For a while he contemplated bashing all six of them, but there would still be no guarantee that he had got the right fella. He would just have to suffer the situation, but it was really getting to him now

On the party with Len was a young Geordie called Ben. He was the unfortunate who always carried the shovel, and it always fell to him to scrape up each parcel and throw it in the barrow. He wasn't particularly quick-witted, but you didn't have to be a graduate to out-think Len.

It was Ben who noticed what everyone else had missed. One morning, as he threw the latest offering from above into the barrow, he called out to Len, 'Hey! Have you noticed the paper the fella is wiping his arse on?'

The question hung in the air. Lennie glowered at him. Was this cretin taking the piss? He briefly contemplated punching him into the barrow along with the parcel, but Ben looked serious. 'What about the paper?' Lennie growled.

'Well, they're all pages from the same cowboy book. It looks like the fella is keeping it just to wipe his arse with.'

Lennie walked over to the barrow. Picking up a piece of stick, he poked at the parcel. He bent closer to scrutinise the pages at the centre of the newspaper wrapping, wrinkling his nose in disgust as the smell hit him. Sure enough, the shit-smeared pages were from a Hank Janson book, *Bad Day at Black Rock*. And what's more, they were consecutively numbered. It was an important clue, Lennie realised that much. But what did it mean? What could he do about it?

So now they knew the phantom was a cowboy book fan. That wasn't uncommon. In fact, Lennie liked a western himself. He looked at Ben for further inspiration. 'Well?' he said impatiently.

'Well, if we slip around all the cells that overlook this area while everyone is at work, we just might find the rest of this book,' said Ben as if he was explaining something to a querulous child.

Like a light coming on in a darkened room, this solution burst into Lennie's consciousness. He smiled but without a hint of humour. 'Are you sure it was the same pages in the other parcels?' he asked.

'I'm sure,' said Ben. 'I was just waiting for this next one before I told you.'

'Don't say nothing to anyone else,' Len said earnestly. 'We'll slip around the cells this afternoon.'

That teatime, Lennie was one of the first to collect his meal. He hurried to his table and ate quickly, then sat back in his chair, hands clasped behind his head, watching the rest of the fellas as they filed in for tea.

He waited until the last one had sat down to eat, then he stood up and walked to the centre of the room. This time he didn't speak immediately. He just stood there, savouring the moment as, one by one, the men noticed him and fell silent.

'Fellas,' he began, 'as you know, some dirty, stinking bastard has been throwing shit-parcels out of the window Well, I've been making my own investigations.' Now Len was clearly enjoying himself, walking up and down in a passable imitation of the counsel who had prosecuted him.

'I noticed,' he continued, 'that the phantom always wiped his arse on pages torn from the same book.' Ben lived on another wing and wasn't present to deny Lennie's claim. 'Well, this afternoon I went around a few cells looking for the book …' He paused for effect, looking around at the sea of faces. 'And I found it!' he shouted exultantly. 'And here it is!' he roared, pulling a torn book from under his jumper and holding it out at arm's length like some trophy.

An answering roar came from the fellas sitting at the tables, all of them caught up in the excitement of the moment. They had stayed with him as he built to this crescendo. They had followed each step in his impassioned argument. Now they were waiting for the final thrust.

Holding the book aloft, with the sound of the mob ringing in his ears, Len turned to look intently at one particular table. As he started to walk towards it, his eyes locked on to those of a small slim, dark-haired fella who sat facing him. He was a young weaselly-looking Irishman with a partial harelip. He was totally anonymous on the wing, with few friends. A small-time thief, more inadequate than criminal. He sat there, terrified, like a rabbit at the approach of a snake.

'And it belongs to you!' screamed Len in an apocalyptic climax as he thrust the book at the Irishman.

The whole dining hall erupted. Fellas jumped to their feet howling and pointing at the culprit. Others pounded their tables in a frenzy of excitement. The Irishman cowered back in his chair, totally paralysed in the face of such hostility.

Suddenly, he made a break for it. He launched himself from his chair, cannoning into a neighbouring table. Stumbling, he threw himself headlong towards the door. With the screams of the mob following him, he burst from the dining hall and headed for the chokey.

He beat and kicked at the gate, looking over his shoulder fully expecting the mob to pursue him. He rang the bell and the gate finally opened. He pushed past the screw standing there, shouting, 'I want to go on Rule 43, put me on Rule 43!'

Back in the dining hall, the uproar continued undiminished. Tears of laughter ran down Lennie's face as the fellas crowded around, asking about how he had found the book. After all the weeks of tension, he felt as if a heavy weight had been lifted from his shoulders. The anger had built up in him, but there had been no direction for him to release it. He was glad that he hadn't bashed the fella, though. It was best that it should end like this.

The Irishman never came out of the chokey. After about a month, he was shipped out.

Once more, Lennie could be seen striding out at the head of the yard party. His booming voice rang out all over the nick again.

There was only one nasty moment. About a week after the phantom had been caught, Lennie and the yard party swept into the 'D' wing area on the morning round. There, right in the corner, lay a familiar newspaper-wrapped bundle. The night-time rain had soaked it so that it lay there a sodden mass.

Lennie froze. A terrifying sense of *déjà vu* overcame him. All the old bad memories came flooding back. But his mind just refused to accept the possibility that he'd have to go through all the pain and frustration again. He marched towards the sodden bundle, positively daring it to be a shit-parcel.

He poked at it with his toe and turned it over. The empty newspaper flopped soggily on to the concrete path. It contained nothing more substantial than yesterday's news. And Lennie had little to fear from history.

'Pick it up,' he barked as he turned on his heel. He strode away, head up, shoulders back, ready to confront whatever new challenge life might bring. It would all be as nothing now, compared to the recent trauma of the phantom.

7 SCOUSE ROY AND THE TWINS

Parkhurst Security Wing, officially known as the Special Security Block or SSB, was very much a self-contained unit. The dozen or so prisoners had their own hot-plate, bathing facilities, exercise yard, association rooms and garden plots. The only time they ever stepped outside was to go over to the visiting room or hospital or to attend church.

They had their own specially trained screws. The regime was very relaxed and liberal. No one had to work and there was little work for them anyway. Most of them spent their days playing games, cooking, gardening or just pottering about.

The wing was claustrophobic in the extreme. The same 12 cons saw each other every day. They also saw the same screws. All the cons were doing very long sentences indeed. For some, the prospects of ever being released were slim. It wasn't surprising then that, from time to time, tensions built up.

Despite all the other notorious cases on the wing, the Twins were undoubtedly the stars of the show. Although they didn't go out of their way to promote it, by and large the wing revolved around Ron and Reg. They were far and away the most notorious. They were also the most dangerous.

They were always surrounded by a small coterie of inmates. This was by invitation only, though. Some were quite content to keep their distance. Others would have jumped at the chance to join 'the Firm'.

A considerable mystique had grown up around the Twins over the years. They had been an institution and a legend in the East End. Many others had been described as gangsters, but Ron and Reg were really in a class of their own. They had had influence and power that stretched way beyond the East End.

This mystique extended into prison. London criminals regarded them as something of a rallying point. However, for many of the chaps their feelings about the Krays were somewhat ambiguous. On the one hand, the fact that the Twins were Londoners appealed to their elitist nature. On the other, they couldn't approve of some of the things they had done. Foremost among these were some of the liberties they had taken. Then there was Ronnie's poofery.

In private, among their own, some criticism was aired, but, in public, nothing was ever said against them. Apart from any feelings of London solidarity, they were still very much feared. Although they were confined to the Security Wing at the moment, at some time in the future they would do their bird in normal jails. The Twins had countless friends and hangers-on. An indiscreet remark could always filter back to them. No one wanted to bump into them several years hence and have to account for something they had said. Especially to Ron.

Ron was by far the more dominant twin. He was also the more mentally unstable. Sometimes, deep depressions would come over him and he would sit or lie in his cell, with the light out, for several days at a time. During these periods, only his brother and another lifer called Joe Mason could go near him; even the screws stayed away until the mood had passed.

At other times, Ron was polite to a fault. Many of the chaps were well mannered – there was nothing tough about being uncouth. Ronnie, however, was solicitous and considerate in the extreme.

If you hadn't known who he was, you would have thought that he was just some well-bred man with impeccable manners. On meeting you, he would ask how you were, how your family was and whether you needed anything. It was all done with an intense sincerity. Knowing who he was and his capacity for viciousness, this was all very unnerving.

Strangers and mugs couldn't make him out at all. Some had taken his overpoliteness as a sign of fear or weakness. This was a very dangerous mistake. You rarely got an immediate response from Ron to any impoliteness. Overfamiliarity or rudeness would be met with a stony look, followed by a muttered 'Goodbye' and his immediate departure. He would go straight to Reg. 'You know that cunt? You know what he said? He can't be allowed to get away with that, Reg.' Plans would be made.

The offender would go blithely about his business, not knowing that deep offence had been taken. In his experience, most people who had felt insulted had said or done something immediately to show what they felt. He would assume that nothing would come of this slight to Ron.

The attack, when it came, would be sudden, unexpected and totally violent. Ronnie would completely lose control, slashing or bludgeoning with no thought of the consequences. Reg would do his part, but with some control. You had a chance with Reg; there wasn't the deep paranoia or the psychotic rage. In fact, when you got him on his own, he was much the same as many of the other London chaps.

However, he was rarely on his own. He and Ron were inseparable.

To be in their company was always an unnerving experience. You had to watch everything you said. You could never relax, in case you lapsed into some perceived overfamiliarity. And never mind what some would say, *everyone* treated the Twins with respect.

Their closest associates on the wing were two other lifers, Joe and Neil. A 'first division' armed robber, who was doing life for shooting someone on a bit of work, Joe Mason was notorious in his own right, but his notoriety was confined to prison where he had spent a large part of his existence. There, he had earned a reputation for toughness and determination. A resourceful escaper and a natural leader, the authorities feared him. He could be very dangerous when roused: he had been middleweight boxing champion in the Army, and could press out reps above his head with over 200 pounds on the Olympic bar. Short in stature, unnaturally strong and highly intelligent, he was a good-natured and fair-minded man who never took a liberty. He was widely liked and respected, a genuine hard man, who behaved like a gentleman.

Neil Adams was entirely different. A small-time thief from Leeds, he had blasted a night-watchman and a police inspector with a shotgun during a warehouse burglary. What he was doing taking a shotgun on a warehouse burglary in those days, no one could figure out. After all, it wasn't a robbery. Surely he didn't expect to meet that much resistance? The difference, though, was between 18 months for burglary and perhaps seven years for going armed. Then there was the danger of shooting someone.

This lack of professionalism was typical of Neil. Basically, he was just a crank. His one brief moment of notoriety came when he was convicted of the two murders and lifed off with a 30-year rec.

In prison, his poisonous nature soon became apparent. He was no real physical threat with his bare hands. In his late 30s and just five-and-a-half feet tall, he also had a gammy leg. He couldn't have a punch-up to save his life. However, he had become a very dangerous man indeed.

With no chance of every getting out, he soon lost the will to live. He had actually asked the Home Office for the right to be put down. Consequently, it didn't matter to him if he killed again, and this gave him a decided edge. He would attack an enemy in the shower, in the bath, on the toilet or in bed. He would use as big a blade as he could get his hands on, and he would be stabbing to kill.

He was a bully who tried to intimidate weaker prisoners. For the average con doing a fixed sentence, he was a daunting prospect. It was a choice between jumping him first and putting him out of the game, with the possibility of getting more bird on top, or taking the chance that he would jump you, with fatal results. Most people just didn't want the aggravation.

The chaps detested rather than feared him. If it had come to a confrontation, they would have jumped him before he could get to his blade, and broken his arms and legs. He never picked on the strong, though. It was hard to figure out how he had got on the firm with the Twins. He was a Northerner, with virtually no saving graces. However, the Twins sometimes stood for a sycophantic nutter who showed slavish loyalty. Anyway, he wasn't in their company most of the time; he was more an errand boy than anything else.

This then was the Twins' social circle when 'Scouse Roy' Grant arrived in the Security Wing.

Scouse Roy, as his nickname suggests, came from Liverpool, and in the early Seventies there were very few sophisticated robbery firms in that city. Those that did exist would never have dreamed of having Roy as a member. He was a thug, plain and simple. He didn't lack bottle, but, like life, all his robberies were nasty, brutish and short. He would never take something by wit or stealth if he could cosh someone and grab it. By virtue of this fact, he was regarded by the Liverpool Old Bill as a major criminal. His 11-and-a-half-year sentence was short by Security Wing standards, but then he was a control problem rather than a security risk.

Roy was a right handful. He had been the 'daddy' of every borstal he had ever been in, and he had been in most of the tough ones. He was just naturally big, strong and vicious. He had showed some early talent for boxing and, if he had stuck with it, there was a chance he could have been very good. Now, in his early 30s, it was too late. Its legacy, though, was a broad-shouldered, bull-like man with a partially hunched back, who could fight like fuck.

He was not unintelligent. It was just that he saw most things in terms of brute force. Why bother to try to convince someone, when you can make them do it by force? There were rumours that he had been in Rampton on a previous sentence. He was certainly regarded as a nutter by people who had lived with nutters all their lives.

At the start of this sentence, he had smashed a screw over the head with a full bucket of porridge, then showered him with the scalding contents. It was a miracle that the screw hadn't been seriously injured, because a full porridge bucket weighed all of 40 pounds. Roy was taken to an outside court and was very lucky to get only six months on top of the 11 years he was already doing.

Transferred to Hull, he had then hit a hardnut Jock over the head with a hammer. The fella was seriously injured and a screw had seen it happen. At the subsequent VC, Roy lost a couple of hundred days' remission and got 28 days' bang-up. They wanted him out of Hull, so Roy duly arrived at Parkhurst Security Wing, with most of his bang-up still to do.

No doubt the authorities thought that the liberal regime and close supervision would slow this wild man down a bit. They were right after a fashion, but it didn't happen quite in the way they thought it would.

The Security Wing was very small as prison wings go. Within five minutes of Roy's arrival, everyone knew of it. A couple of people saw the screws bring him on to the wing with his kit. They saw him taken to an empty cell and locked in.

This was unusual because every other new arrival had been allowed to circulate once he had moved in. The screws told a couple of people that he was on punishment. He would be allowed out to mix when he had finished it.

This news soon reached Ronnie. Now in many ways, Ron was

a very honourable man. He had strong beliefs as to how a man ought to behave. This wasn't just a philosophical exercise on his part; it translated into positive action. He believed that certain things were an obligation.

The thought of a fellow con being locked behind his door on punishment troubled him. He felt that he had a clear duty to do something. It wasn't just a question of hospitality. It was much more than that.

Ronnie collected together coffee, tea, sugar, milk and several packets of biscuits. He got a screw to open Roy's door and handed the lot to him. He introduced himself briefly, before the screw locked the door again. Then he sat in the doorway, talking to Roy through the locked door.

Over the next couple of weeks, Ronnie was to be regularly seen talking to Roy through the door. It was an act of kindness to a fellow con in solitary confinement. Roy wouldn't have seen it like that, though. All his relationships were based solely on dominance and submission. He couldn't conceive of one based on kindness and a sense of duty.

He was aware that, in purely criminal terms, his career was rapidly becoming quite spectacular. The obscure Scouse robber had done a screw, hammered a hardnut Jock and been transferred to England's top Security Wing. Now he had Ronnie Kray sitting on his doorstep, keeping him company against the loneliness of solitary. He must have felt that he had really arrived, to receive such an act of homage.

Time eventually passed and Roy's punishment came to an end. He was let out to mix freely with the rest of the wing's inhabitants. As far as Ronnie was concerned, duty had been done, and duty didn't extend to making Roy a permanent member of his small social circle. He would have to make his own way on the wing now. Ronnie went back to his usual daily round of sitting in his cell in the company of Reg and Joe, with occasional visits from Neil.

Roy, however, took to dropping into Ron's cell whenever he felt like it. This was especially irksome to Ron first thing in the morning. He was on heavy psychotropic medication, which played havoc with his moods. The only people he would allow to come near him then were Reg and Joe.

At first, he just asked Roy not to come in early in the mornings. Roy persisted. Then Ron wrote Roy a short letter and put it in his cell. In it, he explained that he liked to be with only Reg and Joe first thing and would Roy mind not coming in.

Ron was sitting quietly in his cell with Reg when Roy suddenly burst in. He had Ron's note in his hand.

'Who do you cunts think you are?' he shouted. 'I don't want to fucking sit with you anyway.' With that, he crumpled the note, threw it at Ron and stormed out. He had just made a very serious mistake.

There are very few potential weapons lying about in the Security Wing, for obvious reasons. Those that are available are of the homemade variety. That night, Ron and Reg emptied out two large glass sauce bottles. Then they carefully smashed them. The result was two necks ending in two wickedly jagged ends.

The following morning, the screws unlocked the wing as usual. Roy never got up for breakfast and still lay in his bed sleeping. Suddenly, his door burst open and in rushed Ron and Reg, the broken bottles in their hands.

Ron pulled the covers off Roy, then jumped across him to sit on his chest. He immediately began slashing and gouging at his face. At the same time, Reg jumped across his legs and slashed at his exposed stomach. Roy thrashed about, but the combined weight of the Twins pinned him to the bed. One moment he had been dozing peacefully, now he was fighting for his life.

A third shadow fell across his doorway as Neil ran in. He had a homemade spear fashioned out of a broomstick, with a jagged piece of glass taped to the end, which he repeatedly plunged into Roy's side.

Screams and angry shouts filled the air. Blood sprayed over the covers, over the walls and over all four men. Ronnie and Neil were in a complete frenzy.

Alerted by the rumpus, Joe ran into the cell. He quickly took stock of the gory scene. Roy, thrashing about on the bed in a welter of blood, looked like a lump of butcher's meat. They were certainly going to kill him, if they hadn't done so already.

Joe grabbed Neil and threw him bodily out of the cell. Then he grabbed Reggie's arms shouting, 'For fuck's sake, Reg! You're going to kill him! Help me stop Ron.'

Reg dropped the bloodstained bottle. He realised that Joe wasn't doing this for Roy, but for him and his brother.

Together, they got hold of Ron. He was completely gone, hacking and slashing at the gory mess that had been Roy's face. Slowly, he became aware of their voices. He struggled in their grip almost involuntarily. Finally, he allowed himself to be pulled from the bed.

By now, there were several screws outside the door. Dozens more were pouring into the wing. But it was all over. This was just as well, as far as the screws outside Roy's cell were concerned. When they had seen who was involved, they had stopped where they were. Now, with the chiefs and the POs running into the wing, they would have to do something.

Joe and Reg led out a blood-splattered Ron. The screws let them take him to his cell. The wing PO and SO had both arrived by now. After some hesitation, they went into Roy's cell.

The SO immediately reappeared. He shouted at a nearby screw, who was carrying a radio, to call the hospital. They would need medical staff and a stretcher.

A white-jacketed hospital screw was already on the landing. He pushed his way through the group of screws and went into Roy's cell after the SO. There was very little they could do. Roy lay naked on a blood-soaked sheet, writhing in agony and shock. The few white parts of the sheet made the thick bloodstains stand out in stark contrast. He was bleeding from so many cuts and slashes that blood covered him from head to toe. They tried to get him to lie still.

Within five minutes, four hospital screws arrived. Seconds later, they reappeared with Roy on a stretcher, wrapped in the blood-soaked sheet. They took him straight to the prison hospital. This is equipped to handle major operations, so there were ample facilities to deal with Roy's injuries.

Back at the Security Wing, the PO and SO had gone to Ron's cell. They pushed the door open and stood in the doorway. Ron, Reg and Joe sat there, all of them covered in blood.

'You'll have to go to the block, boys, until all this is sorted out,' said the PO.

Reg stood up. 'Joe had nothing to do with this,' he said. 'It was me and Ron.'

With that, Ron stood up, too, and they both walked out of the cell. They were led out of the Security Wing and across to the punishment block a short distance away.

Amazingly, it turned out that Roy wasn't seriously hurt. On the outside, though, his injuries would have warranted an attempted murder charge. But security prisons like to consume their own smoke. They don't want the bad publicity or all the security headaches of taking defendants and witnesses to an outside court.

Ron and Reg appeared before the visiting magistrates. As lifers, they had no remission to lose, but a full account of the incident would be written up in their records. They also got 28 days each in the block.

After they finished their solitary, they were moved on to 'C' wing, the special psychiatric wing. There they would be under the direct supervision of Dr Cooper and would join the ranks of 'Cooper's Troopers'.

After serving more than 20 years, Ron and Reg both died in prison. They had elaborate 'gangland' funerals.

Joe was finally released after 34 years. He was only out for a couple of years when he was caught with a gun. In 2005 he was sentenced to 7 years imprisonment and his life licence was revoked..

Neil is still in prison with no hope of release. It is said that he has seriously deteriorated in recent years.

Rumour has it that Scouse Roy committed suicide shortly after being released from prison.

8 COOPER'S TROOPERS

'C' wing was the special psychiatric wing. It housed about 20 men, all of whom were judged to be severely mentally disturbed. They were also very violent. Every one of them had committed a serious act of violence in prison. A couple had even killed other prisoners.

All were doing very long sentences, and some would never get out. There were undoubtedly individuals in the system who were just as dangerous as anyone on 'C' wing, but nowhere was there such a concentration of dangerous men.

Needless to say, to place men of this type in one small wing made for a very volatile mix. The staff were all specially trained hospital screws; several were said to be martial-arts experts. However, the ethos of the wing was therapeutic rather than coercive. These weren't the sort of men to provoke.

The regime was very liberal: cells remained unlocked all day, there were extra recreation facilities, but everything was supervised with extreme care. There was a high ratio of screws to cons.

Ruling over this domain like some medieval prince was Dr Cooper. Not only was he the top psychiatrist at Parkhurst, he was also head of psychiatric services for the South-west Region of the

Prison Service. This made him a very powerful man. He didn't exactly have power over life and death, but he had the next best thing: the power of certification. If Dr Cooper decided you were certifiably insane, you were bound for Rampton, Broadmoor or one of the other special hospitals.

'C' wing was his pet project. For some reason, he didn't like to admit that there were some patients he could do nothing for. Consequently, there were cases on 'C' wing who should really have been in an asylum. It was generally agreed by the rest of Parkhurst's cons that Dr Cooper had the finest collection of nutters outside the mental hospitals.

'C' wing was virtually self-sufficient. It had its own showers and baths. It had its own hot-plate and TV rooms. It even had its own exercise yard, where its inhabitants could sometimes be seen ambling about aimlessly.

Lastly, it had its own workshop, a 200-yard walk from the wing. Every weekday morning and afternoon, there was a recurring ritual. The 20 or so cons would form a ragged column in the exercise yard, usually two abreast. With screws at the front, middle and rear, they would set off for the workshop.

All the cons were on heavy medication, which tended to make some of them unsteady on their feet. One particular nutter looked to all intents and purposes like he was pissed. Nicknamed 'The Major', he had something of a military bearing and supposedly had a military background, but there the martial comparison ended. He would stagger about drunkenly as the column meandered along. Bringing up the rear were the Twins, together with whichever hangers-on they had on the firm at that time.

Because of the vaguely military nature of this marching column, the other cons had nicknamed the 'C'-wing crowd 'Cooper's Troopers'. It was very comical to watch this bizarre group wend their way backwards and forwards to work each day. No one would openly take the piss, though. Any one of these cons posed a serious danger; to provoke the lot smacked of suicide.

Unlike in many small prison wings, there was no camaraderie. There were too many disturbed individuals, too many men driven by their own particular demons for that. They were united in their hatred of the screws and the system that caused them so much pain, but the intensity of that pain forced them to lash out in all directions, even at each other.

Various small groups would form, coalesce, then disintegrate in an ever-changing kaleidoscope of human interaction. For many of them, their inability to form meaningful and lasting relationships with others lay at the heart of their problems. Anger and hatred were easier emotions to deal with than caring and loving. Groups would mostly come together out of mutual convenience, and, occasionally, one would coalesce around a particular purpose.

Alan Pound had been 15 when he got his life sentence. He and his father had tied up an old woman during a robbery. When she was found, she had been tortured and strangled. The father, swearing that she had been all right when he had left her, said that Alan must have slipped back upstairs and killed her. Subsequent events tended to support this. Whereas the father quickly settled down and seemed reasonably stable, Alan had grown more disturbed as each year passed. Intent on establishing a reputation, he had found that the quickest way to do so was through violence and rebellion.

He wasn't a Londoner, but he had soon realised that Londoners were the elite in most jails. He had quickly latched on to the most notorious of the London crowd. In any confrontation with the screws, he immediately became provocative and violent, and he soon established a reputation for gameness. For this reason, some of the Londoners took him to their hearts: they knew that, whatever the trouble, Alan would be with them while the more faint-hearted would back out. The chaps tend to forgive many shortcomings in those who are spirited and loyal. However, it was soon plain to everyone that Alan's basic problem was that he was quite mad.

For a start, he looked like a lunatic. His bulbous fat head sat atop an equally bulbous body, and his black hair was slicked down in a ludicrous parody of the Fifties' style. He always wore carefully tailored and pressed prison clothes. His shirts had extra large collars to emphasise that they were specially made and not the normal issue; the collars were starched so stiffly that he had difficulty turning his head. A thin tie with a very small knot would be done up tightly to the neck.

This was Alan's idea of the conservative and immaculate style that the chaps affected on the out. He tried to look like a gangster, even to the point of swaggering about with his chest sticking out and his arms akimbo.

He liked to be called 'Al'. If friends called him 'Big Al', he would pretend not to like it, while looking carefully to see if they were taking the piss, for, as a roly-poly five-and-a-half footer, the only thing that was big about him was his gut. But his enduring fantasy was to be a sawn-off version of Al Capone.

All these peculiarities could be tolerated. One of the first things you learn in jail is not to judge people by their looks. The gangster fantasy could be tolerated, too, because so many cons adopt a fantasy persona in jail. What the discerning could not tolerate, though, was Alan's underlying personality.

Although he was loyal and sycophantic towards the strong, towards the weak he was cruel and mercenary. That was when he would show his true colours. He was a terrible bully, threatening and intimidating. Bitterly jealous of the talented and the attractive, he was supremely devious and utterly manipulative.

His 'in' with the chaps allowed him to indulge his vindictive nature towards the rest. Many believed that, if they fell out with Alan, they would have the chaps to contend with. They weren't too worried about Alan himself, because he couldn't hold his hands up in a fight. Having said that, he was very dangerous with a blade. He had already cut several people.

He was a deeply unhappy person. Perhaps, knowing the true

nature of his own personality, he couldn't believe that anyone could like him for himself. He viewed all his relationships with a deep paranoia, and was very heavy to be with. When his friendships broke up, as they inevitably did, no doubt he took that as irrefutable evidence of the uncaring nature of people in general. In consequence, his youthful wickedness quickly matured into a personality that was quite evil.

It wasn't only other cons he had trouble with. He had just as much trouble with the screws. If any of them challenged the various liberties he thought he was entitled to as one of the chaps, he would immediately throw a terrible tantrum. Instantly losing control, his face contorted and flushed, he would threaten dire consequences. If the screws didn't back off, he would steam into them. They would drag him off to the chokey, then he would be transferred elsewhere. Often, when yet another friendship had broken down, he would pick a row with the screws just to get moved to another jail. Then he would start all over again.

Before he was 21, he was in Broadmoor. As far as most people were concerned, that was obviously where he belonged. If it hadn't been for a tussle that he had with the screw in the visiting room, no doubt he would still be there today. However, he sued the screw and, after the case, was sent back into the prison system. Shortly after his 23rd birthday, he found himself in 'C' wing at Parkhurst.

Just as soon as he could unpack his kit, he made straight for the Twins. He didn't know them but they were all he could ever aspire to be. They were both notorious and feared.

It is said that when Ron heard that there was a new young fella on the wing, he seemed quite interested. As soon as he set eyes on Alan, though, he quickly lost any romantic notions.

Alan brought messages from people the Twins knew. His adoration and sycophancy were nothing new to them, however. His personality wasn't such that he made good company. Mostly, they spent their time alone together. They certainly didn't want a typical 'C'-wing lunatic with them all the time.

Maybe to get rid of him, perhaps as hospitality, Ron asked Alan if he wanted to fuck. He told him to go over to Taffy in Cell 17 and say that Ron had sent him. Alan agreed: he was that way inclined anyway and he didn't want to seem ungrateful. However, Ron's parting remark couldn't have encouraged him: 'He's an ugly bastard, but it's an arsehole.'

Taffy Morris, originally from a small Welsh mining village, was doing life for killing his wife. It had been the most traumatic of experiences for him. Basically, he was just an ordinary working fella; then, suddenly, he found himself in the most hostile of environments, surrounded by vicious and violent people. Under intense pressure, his life was a waking nightmare. There was no escape from the torment. He knew he wouldn't be able to stand the pressure indefinitely. It was only a matter of time before he cracked.

He was in that most exquisitely painful of situations: knowing he was doomed, yet having to watch his own slow inevitable decline. And, at only 32 years old, it wasn't a time to be contemplating one's own death. Yet every hour, every minute seemed intolerable. His quality of life was so poor that the pain far outweighed any pleasure he might achieve. He constantly felt like screaming with frustration, rage and despair. But he knew that, if he screamed just once, he might never be able to stop. Already his behaviour was bizarre and unpredictable.

It isn't known whether he was homosexual before he came into jail, but, when it was realised how weak he was, he didn't have much choice. This added further intolerable stress to his situation.

Meeting Alan couldn't have done much for his mental balance. Alan liked to exploit people who were weak, and within no time at all he totally dominated Taffy, whose world became filled with Alan's paranoid machinations.

Taffy used to spend some time with a Geordie called George Arms. He was a big rangy man of about 30. Even on the low-protein prison diet, he was still a strapping 15 stone. He was doing a ten, but had lost most of his remission. He mortally hated the screws and, at the slightest provocation, he would steam into them. Even in the chokey, he would fight them whenever they opened his door. He had received some fearsome beatings, but he had the heart of a lion. He was later to be described as Britain's most violent prisoner. With cons, though, he was generally quite easygoing.

George was a bit slow on the uptake, perhaps as the result of all the beatings he had taken. He was certainly no match for the quicksilver deviousness of a mind like Alan's. The pledges of friendship and loyalty would have taken him right in. He probably thought he had found a good and loyal friend.

Alan quickly grew disenchanted with 'C' wing. The constant tension, the incessant surveillance, all served to fuel his paranoia. True, he could sit with the Twins occasionally, but there was no intrigue and very few people weaker than himself to manipulate.

He developed a plan. Calling Taffy and George into his cell one day, he proposed that they all escape. First, he convinced George. He knew that Taffy would go along with the majority.

Bob was a young screw, at 24 the youngest on 'C' wing. He was married with two young children. Alan knew all this, which was why he had picked him. One day, Bob came up the stairs to the twos. He turned and began to walk along the landing, and, as he passed the recess, he said 'Hello' to George who was standing at the urinal. George quickly spun around and came out of the recess. He walked along the landing about eight feet behind Bob.

Taffy was standing in his cell doorway. As Bob reached the cell before his, Taffy suddenly stepped out on to the landing and turned to face him. There wasn't room to pass, so Bob stopped. He thought that Taffy just wanted to talk to him, as he had taken to doing quite a lot recently.

As Taffy stepped out on to the landing, George pulled an old pair of tailoring scissors from his pocket. They were six inches long and had rounded ends. However, one of the blades had been sharpened on stone until it was razor sharp. Alan had got them from a friend on another wing. Holding the scissors in the open position with his fingers around the blunt blade, George closed on Bob and grabbed him around the top of the head with his left arm. Pulling his head backwards, he pressed the sharpened blade to his throat. 'Do as we say or I'll cut your fucking throat,' he growled.

Taffy seized Bob by the shirt front and, with George pushing from behind, they propelled him through Taffy's open cell door.

Bob instantly shit himself. Quite involuntarily, his bowels opened and their contents ran down his legs. He had been taught about hostage situations in training, but this was real life. He was being held by two certifiable lunatics and had sharpened scissors at his throat. They were certainly crazy enough to kill him.

'Don't hurt me,' he gasped, bursting into tears. 'I've got a wife and children.'

'Fucking shut up,' said George, as he pushed him into the corner of the cell and forced him to lie face down on the floor. Kneeling over him, he tied his hands behind his back with strips of torn sheet, then his legs. Finally, he gagged him with a wide strip of sheet. Bob lay there, sobbing quietly.

Meanwhile, Taffy was barricading the cell door. After pulling the iron bed up to the door, he jammed his table and chair between it and the back wall. The barricade wouldn't last long once the screws started to jack the door off, but it would be enough to slow them down for a couple of minutes. They certainly wouldn't be able to get in quickly enough to stop George from cutting Bob's throat.

The scuffle on the landing hadn't gone unnoticed. There were always several screws standing about. A couple had seen George come out of the recess and walk up behind Bob. At first, they had thought nothing of it, but, when Taffy suddenly stepped in front of Bob, sandwiching the screw between George and him, the first mental alarm bells rang. The rest of it had happened so quickly that there was nothing they could do to stop it.

One of the screws ran to the nearest alarm bell and pressed it. Another ran along the landing to Taffy's cell. He saw that the door was banged shut. He didn't want to panic anyone, so he didn't try to open it. He looked through the spy-hole, but there was only darkness. Something was taped over it on the inside.

Putting his mouth to the crack where the door met the jamb, he shouted, 'Don't do anything silly, boys. What do you want? Who do you want to speak to?'

There was no reply.

Screws began pouring into the wing. They had come from all over the jail. Many were breathing heavily from the exertion of running. They had known the alarm was on 'C' wing, an especially high-risk location. Seconds could save a life, more than likely one of their own.

'C' wing's PO approached Taffy's door with the SO behind him. Some of the other cons had started to gather to see what all the fuss was about. The PO gave the order to lock everybody up. The screws moved to clear the landings, saying, 'Away you go, boys. The sooner you go away, the sooner you'll be out again.'

Doors banged all over the wing as the rest of the cons reluctantly went away. None of them had seen the incident, but they knew that something serious had happened.

As soon as they were all away, a roll-check was done. Only George and Taffy were missing. At least the PO now knew how many cons were in the cell with Bob. Putting his mouth to the crack in the side of the door, he shouted, 'Taffy, George, this is the PO. Don't hurt that man. What do you want? Speak to me.'

'We want to speak to the governor, so fetch him over here quickly or we'll cut this fucker's throat!' George shouted back.

'OK, OK,' said the PO. 'It may take twenty minutes or so, but I'll get him over here. I promise. In the meantime, you just take it easy. We won't try to come in, but you must promise me that you won't hurt that officer. Will you promise?'

'Just get the fucking governor over here and hurry up,' growled George.

As he stood away from Taffy's door, the PO saw that the chief and the security PO had arrived. He told them what had happened. The chief took the radio off the security PO. 'We have an officer taken hostage by two inmates here on "C" wing,' he said into it. 'Inform the duty governor immediately and ask him to come over here. They are asking to speak to him. As soon as you've done that, clear all the wings, clear all the workshops. I want everyone locked up. And I mean *everyone*.'

It was early afternoon. The cons had just begun to move towards work. Crowds streamed down the hill towards the compound, others towards the various workshops.

Suddenly, screws who had been standing against walls, passively watching, came alive. They began herding men back to their wings. There was some grumbling and cursing, but the screws were insistent. They were going out of their way to be polite. They didn't want a riot on their hands as well.

As soon as the control room had given the order to lock everyone up, they phoned the local police. This was the established procedure for hostage incidents.

In the local station, arms were quickly issued. Sirens sounded as dozens of police sped to the jail. They were held up at the gate until the last of the cons had been locked away. Then they were let through to begin deploying in and around 'C' wing.

Snipers with rifles climbed on to roofs, to cover the various exits from the wing. One zeroed in on Taffy's cell window. Other police armed with pistols went inside the wing to join the screws.

The inspector in charge of the police team conferred with the governor, who had just arrived himself. They whispered together for several minutes. Then the governor went up to Taffy's cell. Putting his mouth to the door, he shouted, 'This is the governor. Can you hear me?'

There was a muffled acknowledgement.

'You asked to speak to me,' he continued. 'What do you want? Let me say this, though. Once you hurt that officer, there will be no deals done. So just let's keep this all very low-key.'

A voice spoke right next to his head. George had come to the door. 'We want a van with windows brought into the yard and parked right outside our window. We want to be able to see it. Also we want a go-between we can trust. We want you to unlock Alan and send him up here.'

'OK,' said the governor. 'I'll go downstairs now and arrange it all, but it might take a little time. Can you show me the officer? Just so I can see that he's all right. As an act of good faith.'

'We ain't opening the door for anyone!' shouted George. 'Now hurry up, 'cause I'm running out of fucking patience.'

The governor hurried back downstairs. He went into a huddle with the inspector, the chief and the security PO. He explained the demands.

There was animated conversation for several minutes, then the governor hurried off to Alan's cell. Meanwhile, the inspector gave instructions about the van over his radio.

The governor unlocked Alan and brought him to where the inspector was standing. They both explained the situation to him. They emphasised that, if he helped them, it would go well for him. There were several more minutes of intense conversation, then Alan went up to Taffy's cell to tell them that the van was on its way.

He swaggered along the landing. For once, his desire to be important had been fulfilled. He was a key actor in the unfolding drama. He put his mouth to the door. 'Taffy, George, this is Alan,' he whispered. 'Everything is going OK. The van is on its way.'

'Don't forget to check that it's empty,' whispered George back. 'And drive it around the yard a couple of times to make sure they haven't sabotaged it.'

'OK, George,' replied Alan. 'Take it easy. Everything's sweet.' Then he swaggered back downstairs to confer with the governor and the inspector.

About 20 minutes later, a van appeared and drove on to 'C'-wing yard. It was a blue Transit, with several large windows on either side.

The driver stopped opposite Taffy's cell, then got out and walked away. Alan approached the van and got into it. Carefully following the inspector's instructions, he started it up. This bit was quite exciting for him, for he had never driven before. The engine screamed as the clutch slipped. The van leap-frogged forward a couple of times, then, with the engine shrieking in first, drove in a tight circle around the yard.

Taffy and George were watching from the cell window. The nerves of both were stretched tight from all the tension, but they felt that things were going well for them now. They felt safe for the moment, barricaded behind the door, but they wanted to get it over with.

The stench in the cell was terrible. Bob was lying face down in the corner, whimpering like a beaten animal. He was keeping as quiet as he possibly could in the forlorn hope that, maybe, they would forget he was there. But they were constantly aware of his presence all right; when he had shit his pants, he ensured that. George had an irresistible urge to just grab hold of Bob and throw him out the door. But the screw was still vital to their plans.

They knew they would be vulnerable the moment they stepped out of the cell, but, with Alan watching out for any trap, they should be able to reach the van. Bob would be their insurance. Then, at the last moment, Alan would jump in the van with them and they would all drive out the gate with their hostage. Their built-in advantage would be that no one knew that Alan was part of the plot, too. That was the clever part of Alan's plan.

Alan stopped the van roughly where it had been before and got out. Casually now, he swaggered back to the wing. The inspector called him over and they talked for a couple of minutes. Then he went up to Taffy's door again.

'George, Taffy, it's Alan again,' he said. 'The van's OK. It's empty. You can have everything you want. There's an inspector here, though, who says that he can't allow you to take Bob in the van with you. He says that, as he's in charge, you should take him instead. He'll come up to the top of the stairs and cuff himself to the rail. I'll check that the cuffs are done up and I'll take the key. Then you come out of the cell, let the screw go, then run along the landing and grab the inspector.'

There was a moment's silence. George put his face right up close to the door. He spoke to Alan quietly, keeping his voice down. 'This wasn't part of the plan, Alan. Are you sure it's OK?'

'It's better,' whispered Alan back. 'A police inspector is worth more than an ordinary screw. I'll make sure it's OK before I let you come out'

'All right,' said George reluctantly. Alan went back downstairs. He returned with the inspector. They climbed the stairs together, stamping their feet so George and Taffy would hear them coming. The inspector had a pair of handcuffs dangling from his left wrist.

They reached the top of the stairs and Alan snapped the hanging cuff around the landing rail. 'George!' he shouted loudly. 'George! A screw is going to unlock your door. I'll tell you when he's gone.'

A screw appeared at the bottom of the stairs. He walked up, past Alan and the inspector, then along the landing to Taffy's door. Carefully, he unlocked it, but didn't push it open. He returned the way he had come, deliberately making plenty of noise as he descended the stairs.

'George!' shouted Alan again. 'The screw's gone!'

Taffy's door swung inwards slowly. George appeared in the doorway and looked along the landing. He saw the inspector handcuffed to the landing rail by the top of the stairs. He saw Alan standing next to him, waving a small cuff key between his thumb and forefinger.

George sized up the distance he would have to run to get to

the inspector. There were eight cells between them, about 50 feet. For a second, he contemplated trying to take the inspector and keep Bob as well. But that might just complicate the plan. Also, there were some screws at the bottom of the stairs. George could reach the inspector before they could, but not if he was dragging Bob with him. He decided to stick to the plan.

George went back into the cell. After a short pause, he reappeared with Taffy and Bob. They had taken Bob's blindfold off and untied his legs, but his hands were still tied behind his back. He seemed to be having difficulty standing. It looked like George and Taffy were supporting him.

Suddenly, they let go and pushed him roughly away. They started to run in the opposite direction, their eyes fixed on the inspector and the safety he offered them.

If they hadn't been so intent on watching the inspector, they might have noticed that the fourth cell along from Taffy's had its door wide open. And, even if they had noticed, they wouldn't have been able to see the 14 screws in full riot gear who were standing inside in the dark.

As Taffy and George drew level, the screws burst out on to the landing, cutting them off from the inspector. A riot stick caught George a full-blooded blow to the side of the head. His impetus carried him right into it. The force of the blow knocked him off his feet and slammed him against the landing rail. He crumpled and slid to the floor. More blows rained down on him.

Taffy had managed to check his headlong rush and turned to flee. But the sight of more screws coming along the landing from beyond his cell caused him to pause. A riot stick hit him on the back of the head, knocking him flat on the floor.

Frantically, he tried to crawl away and regain his feet, but he was quickly surrounded by screws wielding riot sticks. Soon, he lay motionless and unconscious. The screws continued to beat him with their sticks, caught in a frenzy.

Back down the landing, George had long since lapsed into

unconsciousness. The screws continued to beat his limp body. Blood ran from his ears, his nose and his mouth on to the landing. The only sounds to be heard were the grunts of exertion from the screws.

'OK, OK, that's enough,' shouted the chief as he hurried towards the two unconscious men. 'Take them over to the hospital.'

Grabbing an arm or a leg each, several screws half-carried George and Taffy along the landing. As they were dragged down the stairs to the ones their heads hit every step on the way. The screws then lifted them up and carried then unceremoniously over to the hospital and on to F2. After ripping all their clothes off, they threw them, naked and still unconscious, into two strip cells. They banged the doors and left them.

Twenty minutes later, the prison doctor arrived to examine them. They both had several broken bones and multiple bruising all over their bodies. They were treated where they lay, then locked up again.

Meanwhile, Alan was reaping the fruits of his treachery. The screws were unaware that he had planned the whole episode. They could hardly have been impressed by his dubious antecedents, but, on the face of it, it looked like he had brought a very serious situation to a satisfactory conclusion.

His position on 'C' wing was now untenable. It wouldn't take long for word to circulate about how he had led George and Taffy into a trap. The screws themselves tended to gossip like women.

For his own protection, he was lodged in the chokey overnight, and the following morning he was transferred to the Scrubs. With him went a report of the role he had played, written into his record. This was just the outcome he had wanted all along. 'Big Al' had his reward.

Madness will out, it would seem. Within a few years, Alan was certified again and returned to Broadmoor. He was finally released, but within a very short period of time he stabbed a gardener with a pitchfork and was sentenced to a further 7 years. Rumour has it that he subsequently died of a heart attack.

A few years after the escape attempt, George died in the chokey at Liverpool. The subsequent inquest cleared the screws of beating him to death.

Taffy was certified and sent to Rampton. After a few years, he was returned to the prison system.

Dr Cooper: after a period of illness, the doctor returned to his position as head of psychiatric services for the South-west Region.

9 DAVE THE RAVE

Around every prison, there are always flocks of scruffy, moth-eaten pigeons, and Parkhurst was no exception. You would see a scrum of them out in the yard, fighting over a crust or some other scrap of discarded food.

Suddenly, a seagull would land among the throng. Its pristine white feathers and clean lines made it stand out as a thing of beauty against its fellows. By comparison, it seemed a queen among birds.

Dave Martin's arrival had all the imagery of a seagull landing among pigeons.

Parkhurst was an old down-at-heel prison. The cons, too, were old compared to those in other prisons, the average age being over 30. The weather hardly encouraged stylish dress either. On the other side of the hill to Albany, Parkhurst took the brunt of the cold winds. The all-pervasive stench from a nearby sewage farm added to a general atmosphere of decay.

Consequently, the cons dressed for comfort rather than appearance. Long grey overcoats and shapeless khaki raincoats were the order of the day. Old blue berets were pulled down tightly around the ears to keep out the chill. On the wings, people lounged around in untidy grey jumpers or granddad vests. Had there been an award for Britain's best-dressed con, it would never have been won by an inmate of Parkhurst. You could imagine the entire population being transferred to some Russian gulag and no one looking out of place.

One day, into this sartorial wasteland came Dave Martin. I was lounging in the doorway of Dave Bailey's cell when I saw two screws coming along the ones escorting a con I had never seen before. He was quite tall, but walked with his head bowed, giving him a stoop.

The most striking feature was his hair. It was a cascade of auburn that fell around his shoulders, glistening with a bouncy sheen that any Silvikrin girl would have been proud of. It framed a long angular face with a large hawk-like nose. The nose was a decidedly ugly feature, but such was the softening effect of the hair that the overall impression was one of some beauty.

His neck was long and thin, with a prominent Adam's apple. Fastened around the mid-point was a silver necklace of interlinked shields, each about an inch high. The whole thing looked like a silver band around his neck.

Narrow shoulders gave way to an emaciated chest, flanked on either side by two long and painfully thin arms. Draped around his upper body was what could only be described as a blouse. It was of a black silky material, with an exaggerated collar and long sleeves that ended in butterfly cuffs. From one wrist dangled a gold bracelet.

The next striking feature was his trousers. The length and skinniness of his legs were highlighted by a pair of jeans with a bright yellow stripe down each outside seam. This meant he was an 'E' man and had to wear patches.

Patches usually consisted of a shapeless pair of prison overalls with a piece of yellow material sewn down each side. Dave's patches, though, were a faded pair of denims, tight at the hips and knees but flared at the bottoms. The wide bright-yellow stripe on either side was an integral part of the design. They had clearly been tailored with some skill.

On his feet were a pair of brownish moccasins. The lack of any rigid sole made him drag his feet to cushion the impact.

This was a startling apparition by any standards. On the ones of Parkhurst at 8.30 in the morning, it was incongruous in the extreme. "'Ere, Dave, 'ave a look at this geezer,' I managed to blurt out as he passed.

Dave Bailey came to his door. By this time the figure was just disappearing through the door into 'D' wing.

'Oh, he's all right,' said Dave. 'That's Dave Martin. He's a raving poof, but he's a staunch fella. He's a bit warm at escaping and he's got plenty of arsehole. He was in the pop at Brixton and put a few of the so-called chaps to shame. He must have just been slung out of Albany.'

I took this information in and realised that, as he had gone on to my wing, Dave Martin and I would probably come into contact with each other quite a bit.

Now there was a rather ambivalent attitude to poofs in most prisons, and Parkhurst was no exception. Generally speaking, they were beyond the pale. Although quite a few of the chaps would have a secret dabble at different times and in different prisons, blatant, effeminate poofs were not tolerated in the company.

It was nothing to do with their being weak or not staunch, because some poofs were very violent indeed and would never grass you, no matter what. Quite simply, it was blind, hypocritical prejudice, and I was as guilty of it as anyone else.

When I returned to my wing a little later, I saw the newcomer talking to my next-door neighbour, Jeff Bunning. He was a raver, too. Just over five feet tall, with dark Italian looks and long, flowing black hair, Jeff had been a sometime companion of several of the chaps in other jails. I knew him from the trouble at Albany a couple of years previously, and he had been the first con to welcome me on my arrival at Parkhurst. We weren't close friends, but we talked regularly and respected each other. His sexuality went unmentioned, although he often made a joke at his own expense. We got on quite well.

I suppose I could have guessed that he would pal up with Dave Martin and, as it turned out, they knew each other from Albany. As I approached, Jeff said, 'Norm, I want you to meet Dave, a friend of mine.'

I was immediately struck by Dave's soft-spoken, intelligent manner. His large bony hand shook mine with no trace of effeminacy. I was relieved that, like Jeff, Dave wasn't an exaggeratedly camp poof.

'He's a bit warm at the escape game, too,' Jeff added.

I immediately realised that Jeff must have told Dave who the livewire escapers were and was trying to get him an 'in' with me. But I was having none of that. I was already in with just about the best firm I could be. This fact, coupled with my prejudice, meant that there was no way I was going to get involved in an escape with Dave. I exchanged a few pleasantries and walked into my cell.

My own escape plan was going quite well. My two pals Stewart and John both wanted to break out. Another pal, Mick Trout, had already been at Parkhurst for several months and made some useful contacts. In particular, he had straightened a works screw who would do anything he wanted. The only trouble was that Mick liked to sit back and plan almost as an intellectual exercise. Sometimes, nothing got done. I believed in striking while the iron was hot. After all, in prison anything could happen.

I kept on at Mick until he got his man to bring in two pairs of bolt-croppers, which we would need to cut the perimeter fence with. I had been thinking of the small single-handed variety and had even provided Mick with a British Standard number taken from a catalogue in the tin shop. Although Mick insisted that he knew what he was doing, in the event the screw brought in two pairs of double-handed bolt-croppers, each about two feet long. They were much too big. They would do the job all right, but the problem was hiding them in the meantime.

They were actually handed over on the compound at exercise time. We could hardly stick them down the front of our strides. Luckily, a fella was bringing in a pillowcase full of laundry. We jammed them in, but the ends still stuck out the top. We draped a towel over them and walked in. Several people were coming in with laundry. The screws took no notice of our bag.

Now we had the problem of hiding them until they were needed. With constant searches, it wasn't easy to hide a two-foot pair of bolt-croppers. One pair, we hid inside a partition up on the fives. The other was smuggled back out on to the compound by a gym orderly, who buried it next to the football pitch as he marked it for the weekend game.

Next, I got Mick to ask his man for an impression of a gate key, which would open all the barred gates in the jail. The screw brought in a piece of cuttlefish in a matchbox and pressed a perfect impression in it.

The plan was to put the matchbox inside a soft toy and hand it out on a visit. If it was put right in the middle, the toy would pass the cursory search before being handed back. The only problem would be to get it away from the child to whom it had been given, without the kid throwing a very public tantrum in the prison car park.

The impression was to go to 'The Hun', a well-known key-man in London. It was no mean feat to make a Chubb key, but he was one of the best in the country. However, the visit was still over three weeks away, so, for the meantime, we had to keep the impression hidden.

Over the next few days, I caught glimpses of Dave Martin about the wing. He rarely seemed to be wearing the same thing. There was a stylishly tailored denim jacket made out of an overall jacket. There was a little thing in purple that could have been a tie-dyed gym vest. Two more coloured blouses and a cut-down grey overcoat gave depth to his wardrobe.

The effect on the screws was quite amusing. They obviously knew he was a skilled escaper, but they just didn't know what to make of him. His camp appearance embarrassed them. They were just as much locked into their chauvinistic male codes as we were.

Any screws detailed to give Dave a spin came in for ribbing from the others. Dave took full advantage of this. If, for example, one of the screws insisted on him stripping right off, Dave would say something like, 'Oh, if it's just my arse you want to see …', at which stage the screw would back off.

This was just as well, because one of Dave's favourite hiding places was in his underpants, around his balls. After all, what screw is going to run his hands around a poof's private parts, in full view of another screw?

Most evenings, I would hang around the wing with Barry and Stewart. Often, they would smoke what they called 'laughing baccy' and the screws called cannabis. I thought 'laughing baccy' more appropriate because, when they were on it, they spent an awful lot of time laughing and fooling about.

Sometimes, when they were out of their nuts, one of them would say, 'Let's go to "poof's parlour".' By this they meant Jeff's cell, where he would sit with Dave Martin.

So in we would go. Jeff and Dave knew us all and got on well with us. They would laugh at having the piss taken out of them by Stewart and Barry, who were obviously intrigued that two effeminate, 'bitch' poofs were cased up together. A favourite joke was: 'Whose turn is it to wear the trousers this week?' It was just fun, with no vindictiveness. Everyone would laugh and enjoy themselves.

Although we weren't close pals with them, it is worth mentioning that, if any of the wing bullies had started to trouble them, we would have come to their aid. And this was no small commitment.

A couple of weeks after Dave Martin's arrival, Jeff came up to me one morning outside my cell. 'Look, Norman,' he said, 'we know that you've got the impression of a key and can't get it out for a while. In the meantime, can Dave have a quick look at it and have a go at making a key himself?'

At first, I was annoyed that they even knew about the impression. It wasn't that they weren't to be trusted, because they were. I guessed who had told them. It was just another example of Mick's bad sense of security. He told too many people about his business.

Then I was worried in case Dave damaged the impression while taking measurements. Dave Bailey, who had been at Brixton with him, assured me that he knew what he was doing. This was no light matter, though. In some ways, my very life depended on it. Escape was all I had. I could hardly just sit still and let my youth drain away.

However, there was a chance that Dave Martin could make a key. It wouldn't cost us anything and, if it didn't work, we could still get the impression to The Hun. I handed the piece of cuttlefish over to him, saying that I wanted it back the next day.

The following day, Dave came into my cell and gave me the impression back. At the same time, he showed me a key he had made. I was immediately impressed. It actually looked like a proper key. All shiny metal, silver-soldered together, but with the flag blank and blackened with candle soot.

If I had thought that my involvement with him was at an end, I was soon proved wrong. As he was in patches and in the top-security mailbag shop, Dave would never get an opportunity to try the key out in a gate. He knew that I worked in the tin shop, which had several sets of gates in obscure corners. He asked me to take the key into the shop and try it out.

I felt committed to giving him as much help as I could now. Although I secretly doubted that he would have made a key that worked, I agreed to take it into the shop and try it.

There was a side bay, called the spray shop, that was separated from the main tin shop by two unlocked swing doors. Two cons worked in there on their own. A civvy would go in occasionally, but for most of the day they worked unsupervised.

I didn't know either of the fellas, but I had been told that one of them, a fella called Dennis, was definitely all right. I went into the spray shop and walked up to them both.

'Do either of you two fellas mind if I try a key out in that gate over there?' I asked.

Dennis immediately jumped up, saying, 'You go right ahead, mate. I'll watch the door.' Luckily, there were a lot of staunch fellas at Parkhurst.

I turned the key in the lock and, being a blank, of course, it did not unlock the gate. But where it had struck the levers, it left silver scratches and scuff marks on the blackened flag. I took it back to Dave.

He worked on it over dinner, then gave it back to me. I took it in in the afternoon and tried again. Once more it didn't turn in the lock. There were another set of scratch marks in the blackened flag.

Each day, deeper notches were cut in the flag. Still it wouldn't turn in the lock. After several days, I was beginning to get the hump with it. It was all very well walking backwards and forwards with a key, but, if I got caught with it on a sudden spin, I would be immediately shanghaied.

Nine times I tried the key in the gate, and, on the ninth, I had partially resolved to tell Dave that I had had enough. I had known all along that he wouldn't be able to make a key that worked.

To my great surprise, on the ninth try, it turned smoothly in the lock and the gate swung open. Just to make sure, I locked and unlocked the gate a couple of times. After work, I hurried back to the wing to tell my pals in the escape that we didn't have to send the impression out after all. We had our key.

This immediately put us on an action footing. We could have a 'pop' within a couple of weeks. But it was no good going from the tin shop in the compound because I was the only one of our group who worked there. We would have to go from the wing so that everybody had a chance.

There was still a lot of planning to do. We had a gate key, and bolt-croppers to do the perimeter fences. But we might have to get out of our cells first and, if it was at night, contend with the gates being double locked.

Then there was the problem of getting away. We had some outside help, but you could hardly ask them to come over to the Island. The scream would go up the moment we hit the fence, if not before. The Island would be sealed and our help would be sealed in with us. We would have to make our own way off the Island and link up with the help on the mainland.

Dave Martin, with his enhanced credibility, now sat in with Stewart and John and me when we discussed our pop. Strangely, Mick had become distinctly lukewarm to all ideas of escape. I quickly came to the conclusion that he didn't really want to go. He had been involved in the Brixton pop and all the trauma that a failed escape entailed. He had settled into his bird at Parkhurst and had even got himself a budgie. In addition, his appeal was due to be heard shortly and he was counting on getting some time off. We decided to press on without him.

Dave said that he could easily make a cell-door key. None of us doubted this now. However, he then said that he could take his cell door off from the inside, by sawing through the hinges with a hacksaw blade he had. Once out, he could unlock me and a couple of others. We could then wrap up the night-patrol screws and let out scores of people. The gate key would get us through the single-locked gates. We would only have to find our way past a final double-locked door and head for the fences.

This was a very attractive plan. A mass break-out in the middle of the night would mean that quite a few of us would stand a chance of getting away.

The final double-locked door wasn't an impassable barrier. With the night screws wrapped up, we could afford to break it down, then storm the fences with out bolt-croppers.

The hardest part, in my opinion, would be for Dave to take his door off from the inside. I had never heard of it being done before. With the greatest skill and patience, he would have to silently cut through the two big hinges which were partly concealed by the locked door. He would then have to lift 200 pounds of steel and wooden door out of its lining while the lock and bolt were still shot into the jamb. And, as this would be in the quiet of the night, he would have to do all this without making a sound.

It was a feat that would need incredible patience and a lot of strength. I didn't think it could be done without making a noise and alerting the night screws. And, if it could be done, then it would take more than Dave Martin – he of the 32-inch chest and pipe-stem arms – to do it. I vetoed the idea, much to Dave's annoyance.

At about this time, something happened that made us all want to keep our heads down for a while. We heard on good authority that, after lock-up one night, a dozen screws had stayed behind with the night patrols in their office. This meant that something had been said. Even Parkhurst wasn't free from grasses.

None of our immediate crowd was suspect. But Mick was still being informed of our progress and who knows who he might have told?

Mick immediately declared that he wasn't going to do anything for a couple of months until all the fuss had died down. This didn't surprise me because I had already sussed that he didn't want to go anyway. Reluctantly, though, we also had to concede that we would have to leave things for a couple of weeks.

Dave Martin wanted to keep on working on ideas, though. He lived on such a high state of alert that all the new heat was just meat and gravy to him. We were of the opinion that there was very little we could do for a while, but, if he wanted to carry on, that was up to him. As the days passed, Dave would occasionally pop into my cell and talk about the ideas he had had and what he was up to. To me, it was all largely academic now, because we couldn't make a move anyway, and I only gave him part of my attention. However, while I continued to underestimate him, he continued to surprise me.

One day, Dave said that he thought that he could make a 'doubles key'. Now no one had ever made a double, in any jail or at any time. Some of the old key-men had made singles that worked, but none of them had even tried to make a double. For a start, no one had ever had so much as a glimpse of one. Only the security PO of the day had one. He went around on his own, double-locking strategic doors and gates late in the evening, and unlocking them again early the next morning. Once doubled, they couldn't be unlocked by a singles key.

It was known that the doubles keyhole was set up and out to one side of the singles keyhole on gates and doors. It was believed that the flag of the doubles key didn't fix to the shank at an angle of 90 degrees, like on singles keys. But, as no one had ever seen one and as it was impossible to get an impression unless you straightened a security PO, this was all supposition.

Dave came up with an idea, a quantum leap in key-making logic. He suggested that, if he put the singles key in the single keyhole and turned it, at the same time as he put a straight shank with a prong sticking out at a certain angle into the doubles keyhole and turned that, then the doubled gate would open.

To me, everything that went on in the obscurity of a lock was a total mystery. I couldn't appreciate the problems, so I couldn't offer an opinion. It was all way beyond me, and beyond everyone else for that matter.

Just above the fives was a raised catwalk that led to a gate into the roof space. This was a crucial line of defence. Anyone who got into the roof space could remove some tiles, heave themselves on to the roof itself and climb down a rope to the ground. Therefore, this gate was always kept double-locked.

It would be difficult to get to without being seen. It was right out in the open, so that any screw walking along the lower landings could see anyone trying to tamper with the lock. At dinnertimes, though, there were only two screws on duty and they stayed in the ones office. All the cons were locked up, except for two cleaners. Jeff was one of these. Waiting until the two screws went into the office, Jeff crept along the landing and unlocked Dave with a homemade cell-key. Dave went straight up to the fives and crawled across the catwalk. He inserted his single into one keyhole and the shank with the prong into the other. The lock turned and the gate swung open.

With the gate open, he could now take the whole lock assembly out with a screwdriver. He removed the lock and swung the gate to, to make it look as if it was still locked. Then he hurried back to his cell. Once inside he quickly took the assembly to pieces. He measured all the levers with a small metric ruler. He made careful note of all the measurements.

After reassembling the lock, he hurried back upstairs, replaced it, then double-locked the gate again. He returned to his cell and Jeff gently banged him up. The whole thing had taken less than 20 minutes. You couldn't fault Dave for nerve, and his genius was breathtaking.

The following day, he came into my cell and told me what he had done: he now had a double key. This added an entirely new dimension to any escape plan. It meant that there wasn't a gate or door we could not go through, at any hour of the day or night. In fact, we could go places that the vast majority of the screws couldn't go, because only the security PO of the day had a doubles key.

It raised some extremely interesting possibilities. At various points in the inner perimeter fence were set massive double gates. They stood 18 feet high, the same as the fence, and were made of the same thick wire mesh. Once through these gates, there was only the second perimeter fence which adjoined a 16-foot-high wall. The former could be cut, the latter roped and climbed. We could choose between them.

Normally, the double gates weren't considered a weak point by would-be escapers because they were always locked on the double. To all intents and purposes, they were just a part of the inner fence. With the doubles key, though, it would now be possible to have a mass escape from the exercise yard.

Unfortunately, things were still very hot. It was only a few days since there had been the security alert with all the extra screws staying behind in the wing office. Normal security checks were being carried out with added enthusiasm. It was only sensible to wait for a while until the screws relaxed again.

This time, the secret would be kept between Dave Martin, Jeff, Stewart, John and me. If we did decide on a mass escape, we would only tell the others at the last moment.

At this stage, I was still calling most of the shots. With Mick no longer interested, the singles key was, strictly speaking, mine. Even though Dave had made it, it had been done with my impression. And we could have got it made outside anyway.

However, the situation had become a bit ambiguous because Dave had gone on to make a doubles key on his own. I suppose I should have seen what was coming.

Dave now decided to press on with a plan of his own. An escape at night meant that someone had to get out of his cell first. Dave now knew that, during mealtime bang-ups, there were only two screws on duty, who always stayed in the office, and there were also the two cleaners. After all, it was by using this information that he had managed to slip upstairs and fit up the gate into the roof space.

Screws were especially thin on the ground during breakfast bang-up. Jeff could unlock Dave. They could let themselves out through the wing gate, then through a door to put them outside the wings.

The compound would be totally deserted at that hour. The

civvies didn't start in the shops until nine. The screws didn't patrol the compound because there were no cons in it at that time and it was so far from the wings. Once in the compound, Dave and Jeff could let themselves through the double gates at the far end with the doubles key. They would now be between the fences and could either cut the second fence or scale the adjoining wall.

There was a major problem, however. To get to the compound from 'D' wing, they would have to walk down the hill past the Security Wing. One of the cameras on the Security Wing pointed up the hill; it couldn't fail to pick them up. Once past that camera, they would have to go through the gate into the compound. And just inside this gate was another camera, trained directly on it. The screws in the control room would have to be blind or asleep to miss all the action on their banks of TV screens.

Jeff was one of the only two cleaners left unlocked over mealtime bang-ups on 'D' wing. The second was a South London armed robber called Terry Hillman. Terry was a bit of a funny fella. He had got too friendly with the screws on the wing and, for this reason, a lot of the chaps wouldn't have anything to do with him. But he could be a right rebel at times.

Terry's job was to make tea for the screws. He also made them the occasional sandwich from mealtime extras. He had free access to their tearoom, which was next to the wing office. It was furnished with an assortment of chairs, a table and several lockers. In these, some of the screws kept spare uniforms. There was quite a collection of tunics, trousers, caps, boots, ties, shirts and mats. Some had been there for months and belonged to screws who were now working in other parts of the prison. The lockers were never locked.

Jeff got Terry to slip two complete uniforms out to him. He passed them to Dave. In his cell, he stripped them down and altered them so that one fitted Jeff and the other fitted him. Then Jeff got Terry to put them back again.

At this stage, Dave and Jeff came to see me. Dave explained

the plan to me and said that I could go with them both. Dressed as screws, they could escort me past the cameras and into the compound.

I was instantly very angry. True, it was an excellent plan, but there was no provision for Stewart and John to go, too. I was nothing if not loyal. I knew that, if I went to them and explained, they would undoubtedly give me their blessing and tell me to go with Dave and Jeff. However, it would still look like a slippery move and I couldn't do that to them.

Then there was the second problem. Although I got on well with Dave and Jeff, I was quite hung up about poofs generally. As their homosexuality was a major facet of their characters, it would certainly be mentioned in their records. In the event of my escaping with them, the press could well pick up this fact. I could imagine banner headlines about 'gay escapers'. As silly as it may sound, this was a major deterrent to me. I'm afraid I was still very much into image at this stage.

Last but not least, the plan would work better with just them as screws. The authorities had me down as one of their more dangerous cons. If the control-room screws did pick me up, the screws might well wonder where someone like me was going at that hour. Especially as I was an 'A' man.

I told Dave that I couldn't go with them. I started to ruck him for going it alone without all the rest of us. However, he had put so much of the plan together by himself that the rights and wrongs of the situation had become confused. I could have got heavy and stopped them, but that would have been out of order.

As far as John, Stewart and me were concerned, it meant the end of our escape plan. We would have to start all over again. After Dave and Jeff went, all the locks would be changed. I went and spoke to John and Stewart about it. They were of the same opinion as I was: things had progressed too far for us to do anything about it.

I went back to Dave and Jeff. As I entered, they were sitting, a bit shamefacedly, in the corner together. I couldn't help feeling sorry for them. They were both nice fellas and it wasn't easy for them in the nick.

'And I suppose you want a pair of our fucking bolt-croppers to do the second fence with, don't you?' I said in a tone that still sounded angry.

Dave nodded sheepishly. I told them about the pair hidden in the partition up on the fives, then turned and left.

In the late afternoon, with most of the fellas still at work and the wing nearly deserted, Jeff collected the bolt-croppers from the fives partition. He took them to his cell.

Shortly afterwards, he got Terry to pass the altered uniforms out from the screws' tearoom. He took these to his cell, too. As it was late afternoon, it was unlikely that he would have a spin now. Once evening association had started at six o'clock, there would be no more spins for the day; it was only in very unusual circumstances that the screws would spin someone during association time.

That evening, Jeff took the uniforms and the bolt-croppers along to Dave's cell. Now they were ready for the following morning.

I saw Jeff at breakfast the next morning, but we didn't speak. There was no sign of Dave, but that wasn't unusual as he never got up for breakfast.

The meal served, the screws came round and locked everyone up, except for Jeff and Terry. Then they went off to have their own breakfasts, leaving only the two screws who stayed in the wing office.

Terry made them a cup of tea and a couple of sandwiches. He stood in the office door talking to them. He had left his radio, outside on the table next to the hot-plate, playing loudly.

Jeff immediately hurried along the landing to Dave's cell. He let himself in quietly with the cell-door key.

They quickly put on the altered uniforms. The tunics and trousers fitted closely to their bodies. They tucked their long hair up inside their screws' caps. Their black prison boots were virtually indistinguishable from those the screws wore. The blue shirts and ties added the finishing touch.

They were now wearing what every screw in Parkhurst was wearing. But there the similarity ended, for two more unlikely-looking screws you had never seen in your life.

The tall gangly one was undoubtedly the skinniest screw in the whole Prison Service. The short one was equally skinny, but the striking feature was his height. At five foot three, he failed the minimum-height qualification by at least three inches. Individually, they looked distinctly odd. Walking along together, they looked extraordinarily comical.

They left Dave's cell, carrying the bolt-croppers in a pillowcase, and crept along the landing to the wing gate. This was a tricky bit, because Dave would have to unlock the gate to let them through. Then he would have to lock it again. All without making enough noise to alert the screws in the wing office, which was only 20 feet away.

The heavy gate made its usual high-pitched squeal as it swung open and closed again, but this was drowned by the noise from Terry's radio. Locking the gate behind them, they hurried along the 15 feet of corridor to the door that led outside the wings. It took just seconds for Dave to unlock it and then they were outside. They had overcome the first hurdle, but the second one beckoned.

Walking as upright as possible, with their caps tilted slightly over their faces, they went down the hill towards the camera by the Security Wing. They would find out soon enough if those presumably watching the screens noticed anything untoward.

The camera stayed pointing up the hill and didn't swivel to follow their progress. They were past the second hurdle.

They approached the gate to the compound and the third and most difficult hurdle. Dave let them both through with his key, in full view of the camera only 15 feet away. After locking the gate, they walked below and past the camera. It stayed pointed at the gate. The difficult part was behind then.

They walked quickly but unhurriedly to the far end of the compound and came to the massive double gates set in the inside perimeter fence. There were no cameras to mark their progress now.

Using his doubles key, Dave smoothly unlocked the gates. He pulled down on the long lever that disengaged the lock's bolts and swung one of the gates open. He and Jeff passed through, swung it to and double-locked it again. There was only the second fence that stood between them and freedom now.

Taking the bolt-croppers from their pillowcase wrapping, Dave went to the section of fence that abutted the prison wall. The first snips were awkward, but, once the blades of the cutters were through, he made a yard-long horizontal cut at knee-height.

Turning the cutters upwards now, Dave made a vertical cut, again a yard long. Jeff had put on a pair of heavy canvas gloves taken from the tin shop. As Dave levered the section inwards, Jeff gripped the edge and pulled.

Until now, everything had gone according to plan. But in all plans there is always an element of luck. Their luck now ran out.

It was true that the compound fence was never patrolled at that time of day. However, Parkhurst wasn't the only prison on the Island. Camp Hill, a lower-security, category-B prison, was just a few hundred yards further up the road. One of their dog-handlers had gone home to his quarters for breakfast, taking his dog with him. Returning the way he had come, he walked along the outside wall of Parkhurst. As he reached the point where the wall ended and the fence began, he suddenly came upon Dave and Jeff. Both parties were taken completely by surprise.

By now, Jeff had managed to pull the cut section of the fence inwards, exposing a triangular hole. Dave made a dive for it, thrusting his head and shoulders through. The dog barked furiously and went to bite him. At the same time, the screw pulled his stick and started to beat Dave about the head and shoulders.

Realising that he stood no chance against this determined assault, Dave pulled himself back inside. It would have been awkward enough to crawl through the hole to the outside unhindered. The efforts of the screw and his dog made it impossible. Dave and Jeff had to watch helplessly as the screw pulled his radio from his belt and put in an emergency call.

Dave quickly stepped behind the wall, out of sight of the screw. He didn't want them to find his keys. Within a couple of minutes, screws would be everywhere.

Barely two minutes passed and a crowd of screws came running into the compound. Dozens more appeared outside the fence, alongside the dog-handler. Temporarily, though, Dave and Jeff were still safe. No one had a doubles key to get them through the big gates.

Another few minutes passed and the security PO appeared. He unlocked the double gates and the screws poured through, roughly grabbing Dave and Jeff. They marched them back the way they had come.

The chokey was just outside the compound gate. Its gates were already open as the posse of screws propelled Dave and Jeff inside. They were pushed into separate cells and made to take everything off. Completely naked, they were twisted around so that the screws could see between the cheeks of their arses.

Satisfied that nothing remained hidden, they threw them a boiler suit each and retreated with all their clothes. As the doors banged shut, a thoroughly dejected Dave and Jeff contemplated a grim future. The VC would take away at least six months' remission from them and there would be a couple of months' solitary, too. But, far worse, they would be separated and moved to different jails.

By dinnertime, the escape was the talk of the nick. There were several different versions circulating, but all told of them being nearly through the second fence.

There were a variety of reactions. Some thought it hilarious that a pair of poofs had nearly done what the combined resources of the so-called chaps couldn't do. Some tried to belittle what they had done, purely because they were poofs. But those who gave credit where it was due had to concede that they had done a feat.

Our crowd, who by now knew the full details, had nothing but respect and admiration for what they had achieved. Merely to make a double was unparalleled. In fact, the screws hadn't accepted that Dave had made a double. With the massive gates still double-locked, they thought that Dave and Jeff had climbed over the first fence. The fact that they hadn't found any ropes didn't faze them. They hadn't found the cell or gate key either, so they assumed that Dave had somehow hidden the lot somewhere.

It would have been very embarrassing for them to admit that a con had got hold of a double. It smacked of corruption in high places, and the Home Office would want chapter and verse. And what security PO would want to admit that his was the first jail where a con had got his hands on a doubles key?

Dave and Jeff, languishing in the chokey, were largely oblivious to all the gossip and rumour. Dave was quite used to people knocking him. His answer was simply to shut them up by pulling off something quite amazing. That, in fact, was what he was working on at that very moment.

The screws had carefully searched Dave's and Jeff's clothing for the keys. They had also meticulously searched the area between the fences, nearest the hole in the fence. They had found absolutely nothing, except the bolt-croppers and a set of gloves. Having stripped Dave and Jeff naked, they were convinced that they weren't hiding anything. They could only assume that Dave had thrown the keys over the fence.

In this, they were quite wrong, for Dave still had them all. When he had stepped behind the wall out of sight of the dog-handler, he had taken a metal tube out of his pocket. It was about four inches long and about an inch in diameter and had a screw top. It looked like a shortened cigar tube.

There was already a length of hacksaw blade inside. Dave

quickly dropped the three keys in with it, then screwed the top back on tightly.

Dropping his trousers and pants, he squatted down. He pushed the rounded end of the tube up his arse. As his sphincter muscle closed behind the screw top, the whole tube disappeared from view.

It was now up inside his rectum and safe from everything but an intimate body search. It could be retrieved at any time. Dave often carried things about like this.

Now, locked in his chokey cell in the late evening, Dave reversed the process. After wiping the outside of the tube with a tissue, he unscrewed the top and took out the blade. Very gently, he started to saw at the exposed part of the top hinge of his cell door. After about two hours he had sawed far enough. He started on the bottom hinge. Another two hours saw him satisfied with his progress on this one, too. He put the blade back in the tube, screwed it shut and pushed it back up into his rectum. Then he lay down for a few hours' sleep.

The following morning, Dave slopped out and collected his breakfast and was banged up again. The chokey screws went off for breakfast, leaving just one in the office. Dave immediately went to work on his door again.

He had left just enough hinge to support the weight of the door when it was opened. Now, in 20 minutes, he cut through the remainder. With the hinges severed, he gently eased the hinged side of the door inwards. Once it cleared the jamb, he slid it sideways so that the lock and bolt both disengaged from the other jamb. He was out of his cell. Having moved silently to Jeff's cell, he quietly slid the bolt back and unlocked him with one of his keys. They both padded noiselessly to the gate leading out of the chokey. Dave inserted the gate key and turned. It was a particularly stiff lock and, as the levers sprang back, there was a dull, metallic *clunk*.

Perhaps this was one of the small sounds of the chokey that the remaining screw was familiar with. After being in the quiet of the chokey for a while, you get to know every sound, even the small ones that only register subliminally.

This was an important sound, though. It could be the first warning to a screw doing a crossword or otherwise loafing that a senior officer was coming in.

Alerted, the screw came out of the office. He was astonished to see Dave and Jeff halfway through the gate. Recovering quickly, he pressed the nearest alarm bell.

Dave and Jeff stopped. It was no use their running; the heavy mob would be there in seconds. A chase around the jail would be futile. They both filed back into the chokey.

In due course, news of this latest attempt reached our crowd. I was astounded that Dave had managed to take his door off from the inside. And without making enough noise to alert a screw sitting in an office only yards away. I could have kicked myself for not letting him try it on the wing. A mass break-out in the early hours of the morning had definitely been on.

Either one of Dave's escape attempts rated among the best I had ever heard of. Taken together, they demonstrated a skill, genius and resourcefulness that was breathtaking. How I wished I hadn't taken so much notice of the fact that he was a poof.

Dave was shipped out of Parkhurst several days after his last attempt. The security PO checked his cuffs as he climbed into the van, then watched him go. I imagine he heaved a deep sigh of relief. He wouldn't want to see Dave Martin again in a hurry.

Towards the end of his 14-year sentence, Jeff had a sex-change operation. She is now free and lives in the North of England.

Dave finished his ten, losing most of his remission on the way. Free for only a short while, he was nicked for two bank robberies, but escaped from a magistrates' court. While on the run, he shot a detective in the groin. He was recaptured and sentenced to 25 years. Returned to Parkhurst, he hanged himself in the Security Wing about a year later.

10 THE SUBMARINE

Dave's inspired escape attempts certainly set the jail alight. Suddenly, all the talk was of having a pop. Men for whom the thought of escape had never entered their heads before were now deeply involved in intricate plots. Many of them were incredibly bizarre. Virtually all of them had no chance of success.

The serious escapers now had to keep their heads down. Cell searches and other security checks were being carried out with vigour. John, Stewart and I could only wait in frustration for all the excitement to die down.

In the 'Old Bailey' the talk was all of escapes, too. Of inspired and gutsy attempts that had been made at other jails. Everyone had his own favourite story. I thought the one I told was every bit as good as Dave's pop. An added dimension was that I had been involved myself, albeit only in a supporting role.

In the late Sixties, the Prison Service suddenly found that they had a problem on their hands. There had been a number of well-publicised escapes, by notorious villains, from various top-security prisons. Now a new breed of criminal was emerging. More organised, more resourceful, even while in prison they had access to large sums of money and the help of dedicated friends and associates.

Luckily for the Prison Service, there weren't many of these sorts of cons. Also, they were easily distinguishable by the audacious crimes they had committed and the exceedingly long sentences they had received for them. Clearly, extraordinary measures were called for.

In their own inimitable way, the Home Office went right over the top. Characterising these 'super-criminals' as some kind of lowlife James Bonds, they set out to create super-jails to contain them. And so the Security Wing came into existence.

They took existing wings inside top-security jails and converted them. They were totally refurbished from top to bottom. Specially reinforced bars were put in windows, and all walls, floors, ceilings and doors were strengthened. Every conceivable security device that could be fitted was fitted. No expense was spared. There were pairs of failsafe external doors that could only be unlocked one at a time. TV cameras scoured the inside and outside of the wing, with teams of screws monitoring the results in a central control room. All Security Wing staff underwent special training.

Each wing would be totally self-contained. The men would eat, sleep, shower, work and have their visits inside the wing. If they had to go outside into the main prison for any reason, a small-scale military operation would be put into effect involving several dog-handlers and escorts.

At first, the regimes were harsh and restrictive. Security considerations embraced every aspect of the men's waking lives. They couldn't have the same privileges and possessions that were allowed in any average long-term jail.

It was a recipe for disaster. A small group of tough, resourceful, desperate men, who had little to lose, were subjected to treatment that could only unite them in their resistance.

And unite them it did. There were several riots and disturbances until an uneasy truce was hammered out. The regimes became very relaxed and liberal. Privileges and possessions were allowed that were unique to the Security Wings. Like exotic birds in gilded cages, these top-security cons idled their time away in conditions that were the envy of less exalted prisoners.

Four Security Wings were built, strung out the length of the country, at Parkhurst, Chelmsford, Leicester and Durham. They were quickly filled with notorious gangsters, train robbers, dangerous killers, particularly prolific armed robbers and such few terrorists as were about in those days. In some wings, if you had deliberately tried to assemble a particularly talented group of hardcases, you could hardly have done better.

Each wing held about a dozen men. Living on top of each other under the most intense pressure, feuds and disagreements were commonplace. Security Wings were not easy places to live in.

However, by the very nature of their sentences, the inmates had much in common. They were cleverer than the average con and often had money and help on the outside. They were desperate and determined. Quite often, their thoughts turned to escape.

Leicester was typical of all the Security Wings. A squat two-storey building, it stood away from the main wing, behind the bathhouse. Like all the others, it positively bristled with bars and security devices. Unlike the others, it was restrictively small.

There were only two landings inside, housing 14 men. Attached to the back of the wing was a small exercise yard, totally enclosed by a 20-foot wire fence. Atop the fence sat a roll of barbed wire. This yard stood inside a larger one which was used by the main prison for exercise. Bounding this larger yard was the prison wall, the highest in the country.

The yard was only occasionally open, and, because of the small size of the wing, wherever you went you could never be alone. Add to all this the overshadowing prison wall, and you had a general feeling of claustrophobia. Among Security Wing cons, Leicester was referred to as 'The Submarine'.

Like the *Bounty*, it was rarely a happy ship. This was due in large part to the commanding officer, PO Fred Buck. He was in charge of the daily running of the wing, and invariably made things as difficult as he could for the cons.

A short fat man in his early 50s, his florid face made him look permanently angry. This was in keeping with his general mood, for he was an unhappy man. He had progressed as far in his career as he was likely to go, and he knew it. His generally antagonistic manner had ensured that he had been refused promotion to chief several times. His children were grown up and had left home. Even his wife had rebelled at living with such a morose, ill-tempered man: she had divorced him a couple of years previously. Now, his life revolved around work, drinking in the officers' club and serving on the POA committee.

He had a thoroughly jaundiced view of the world. He was intolerant of all things liberal, favouring the retributive and punitive. He hated cons with a passion. If he had had his way, they would have been locked up behind their doors 24 hours a day. The laidback, liberal regime of the Security Wing was like a red rag to a bull for him. Consequently, he went out of his way to make life difficult.

As wing PO he had considerable discretion in interpreting the rules, and he made a virtue out of saying 'No'. Whatever it was the fellas asked for, PO Buck would find an excuse to refuse it. The only chance they had was to go over his head to the AG, but he was rarely on the wing, having other duties in the main prison. On those occasions when he was there, he often overruled the PO, much to the latter's chagrin.

Not surprisingly, the cons hated PO Buck. Most of them wouldn't even speak to him, except to make an official request. All this made for a bad atmosphere. The rest of the screws were mostly all right. However, as the commanding officer, PO Buck set the tone; from his position of power, it flowed out to permeate the whole wing.

On the cons' side, Joe Mason was the leading light in the wing. Doing life for his second killing, his chances of release were slim. In his late 30s, he was short and powerful, with immensely broad shoulders. Jet-black hair framed a youthful, handsome face. Perhaps the most striking feature was his eyes. At times, they twinkled with an intelligent mischievousness, but, if you looked deeply, there was a glimpse of infinity there.

Prior to his criminal career, he had served in Korea. He excelled at boxing and had won the Army middleweight title. While away from his platoon on a mission one day, their position had been overrun. The enemy didn't bother to try and dislodge them from their fortified bunker; they just poured gasoline into it and set it alight. Joe returned in time to help pull out the charred bodies of his mates. It is said that the experience unhinged him. He was brought back from Korea in a body-belt, restrained by four military police.

He had come to crime comparatively late in life. After a brief flirtation with safe-breaking he went straight into robbing banks. A disastrous raid on a dairy strongroom left the manager dead. Joe's was the hand that had blasted him with a shotgun.

He had a pleasant, open personality, though. He couldn't abide bullies and would regularly take the underdog's part. Possessed of incredible willpower, he had a highly developed sense of right and wrong. In the unfair world of prison, this made him a committed rebel. A fitness fanatic, he was phenomenally strong, and had already been involved in numerous revolts and disturbances. He was a natural leader and a resourceful escaper. If the Security Wings had been built for anyone, they had been built for him.

Bob Wells was one of the Great Train Robbers. His 30-year sentence was seen as excessive by con and screw alike. Formerly a South London club owner, he bore his cross well. Neither bitter nor defeated, he had a likeable, easygoing personality. Intense workouts with weights had packed some muscle on to his tall thin frame, but he was essentially non-violent.

Buster Edwards was another of the Train Robbers. Shorter and more reserved than Bob, his shyness could easily have been mistaken for snobbery. He, too, had a pleasant, easygoing personality and was often disturbed by the antagonisms and intrigues of Security Wing life.

He had been on the run for a couple of years before giving himself up – the pressure had been too much for him. He had been expecting a seven, so the 15-year sentence came as something of a shock. Even so, it was short compared to what some of the others had got. Buster had settled down to do his bird. The Security Wing wasn't necessary for him; he wouldn't have run away from an open jail.

Eddie Richardson was different altogether. Also from South London, he had been nicked with his brother and sentenced after a much-publicised gangland torture trial. He took his 15 very hard. He was a powerfully built fella in his late 30s, his strength developed from a lifetime working in scrapyards. He was dour and humourless. Sitting in his company, it was easy to descend into melancholy thoughts. He never relaxed and let himself go. Eddie liked the image of the gangster.

Frank Fraser had been nicked with Eddie and was also doing a 15. His nickname of 'Mad Frankie' was no exaggeration. He was perhaps the most spirited and rebellious prisoner in the system. He mortally hated the screws and their authority. He had chinned scores of them and done years in solitary for it.

Frank and PO Buck were like cat and dog. Frank had only to set eyes on him to unleash a torrent of abuse. The PO was a rank coward. He would scuttle away into his office, and any retribution was in the form of red writing on Frank's record or a sly phone call of complaint to the governor.

Jack Buck was in his mid-30s and doing life. Originally a country boy, he was a bit out of his depth in such rarefied company, having neither money nor influence. It was purely the violent attacks he had made on other cons that had got him into the Security Wing. However, he was only a problem when provoked; left alone, he was easy enough to get on with.

His size apart, George Bale was a typical London robber. At five foot three and with baby-faced good looks that belied his 35 years, he looked like a boy among men. However, his 15-year sentence reflected the seriousness of his offences.

He was just as violent and determined in his pursuit of freedom. Two serious escape attempts had ensured him a place in the Security Wing. His sentence seemed to stretch out in front of him for ever. He found it especially hard to hold still and watch what remained of his youth slowly ebb away. He was just marking time at the moment. As soon as he got back to a normal prison, he would be making a break for the wall again.

There were also three nonces on the wing. Two were child-killers, the third a particularly bad rapist. They kept to themselves. No one went out of their way to annoy them, but no one spoke to them either. In addition, there were two cranky killers, solitary men who liked their own company. They acknowledged the others and were acknowledged in return, but they didn't mix.

Bill and Ben were equally strange. Two Northerners, they were both in for bizarre crimes involving kidnap. Nicked for separate offences, they had both drawn heavy bird. Neither had much personality or intelligence, but they had become inseparable and could always be seen pottering about the wing together. Nobody troubled to find out what their real names were; in the circumstances, 'Bill and Ben, the flower-pot men' seemed rather appropriate.

These, then, were the inhabitants of Leicester Security Wing. There were others in the system who probably had equal claim to be there, but the Home Office, in its infinite wisdom, had chosen these 14.

The main group consisted of Joe, Jack and the other Londoners. They weren't a gang in any sense and often split up into smaller groupings. But they had much in common and shared a similar outlook. Apart from Frank, who never expressed an opinion one way or the other, and Buster, who couldn't face being on the run again, all dreamed of escaping to start a new life.

The prison chaplain often made visits to the prestigious Security Wing. Generally, the fellas treated him with contempt. They would often ask him how he could have signed the Official Secrets Act if he served only God. What if he saw something that conflicted with his Christian beliefs? Would he speak out about it? He had no answer to this. He would contain his discomfort, ever mindful that he was among this most dangerous of flocks.

He would often make suggestions as to how they could pass the time. One day he happened to mention that it was a shame they could not come over to the chapel, because he had plenty of work there that needed doing.

Now, among his other talents, Joe was a highly skilled carpenter. He asked the chaplain what exactly he wanted done. He was told that there was a need for a section of staging to go before the altar. Always looking for an opening, Joe said that, if the tools and the wood could be brought over to the Security Wing, he would make the stage for him. The chaplain became thoughtful. He could get his much-needed stage made for nothing, while at the same time giving Joe and a couple of the other fellas something to do, thereby winning their approval. The main problem was to get the project approved by the Security Department. Nothing happened in the Security Wing without their say-so. They would immediately be very suspicious if such a suggestion came from Joe. Coming from the chaplain, though, it was another matter. He wasn't without influence in the prison.

Needless to say, PO Buck was totally against the idea and flew into a rage at the very mention of it. The chaplain went over his head to the AG, who referred it to Security with his recommendation.

Probably because they couldn't think of a sufficiently good enough reason to refuse him, the chaplain got permission for Joe to make the staging, and, within a few days, he was working away on the ones surrounded by various pieces of timber and sundry carpentry tools.

He didn't explain to the others why he had suggested the project. If they wondered why the normally rebellious Joe was doing a job for the chaplain, they didn't ask. Nobody could ever accuse Joe of being a governor's man.

However, Frank did pass one remark. As he stood watching Joe mark and cut the various lengths of timber, he suddenly said, 'Well, Joe, at least you'll get your reward in the next world.'

Joe wasn't at all amused. In fact, the whole project, together with Frank, nearly went up in the air right then. There was a lot at stake, though. He already had the next step worked out. He ignored Frank and carried on sawing.

The chaplain was delighted with the finished stage. He marvelled at the professional finish and the clever way it came apart in sections. He said he was just sorry that Joe couldn't see it in position in front of the altar. For the PO hovering in the background, it raised other emotions.

For some time, the fellas had been complaining that they had nowhere to put their training gear which they used on the yard. At the moment, the vests, shorts, trainers, towels, tennis rackets, footballs and gym mats were just stacked on the floor of the short corridor that led into the yard. The next time the chaplain came around, Joe asked him to try to get permission for him to build a locker for them to put their gym kit in. He would make it all out of wood, just as he had the staging. It would go in the corridor.

Not wishing to appear ungrateful (Joe had refused any reward for making the stage), the chaplain said that he would ask.

The Security Department weren't too pleased with the idea. To have any timber construction in the corridor so close to the yard could be a security problem. And the finished locker could possibly be dragged out and used to climb on top of the yard fence. This wouldn't serve any immediate purpose, though, because you would still be within the outer yard bounded by the prison wall. However, it could be a significant breach in their first line of defence.

On the other hand, there were a number of things in its favour which made it difficult for them to refuse. First, it was the chaplain asking. Second, the other project had gone off OK. Third, it would keep Joe, one of their most dangerous prisoners, occupied. And, last, the fitted locker could be classed as an improvement to the wing.

This time, the PO didn't object. Still smarting from his previous defeat, he wasn't going to give them the opportunity to inflict another. He had lost a lot of face with the AG. He said that he could see no reason to refuse permission for the project.

With as much good grace as they could muster, Security approved the project in principle, although they were beginning to wonder where it would all end. However, they stipulated that Joe submit a detailed plan to them.

Joe was well pleased. The most difficult part was over. He was confident that he could put something together that, while looking thoroughly innocuous to Security, would get him out of Leicester Prison.

That afternoon, Joe sat in the exercise yard and ran the several problems that confronted him through his mind. Bob and Buster were playing tennis across a net strung between two short posts. Jack and George were kicking a football about in the corner. Eddie was doing sit-ups on one of the gym mats. Frank was stretched out on another, dozing in the afternoon warmth.

Ignoring all invitations from the others to join in their games, Joe sat with his back against the wire, his face tilted upwards to catch the sun. Out of the corner of his eye, he could see the PO standing at his office window which overlooked the yard. He often stood there when they were out on exercise. It was as if he had to torture himself, watching them enjoying the fresh air and the comparative freedom.

With the locker in the yard, Joe would be able to climb to the top of the surrounding fence. This would be fine if there was nobody about and he had plenty of time, but the opposite would always be the case. There was always a screw in the yard with them. He was standing over in the corner right now, watching the tennis. There was a small gate in the fence, through which reinforcements would run. Also, more screws could come from the Security Wing, along the short corridor that led into the yard.

Security Wing exercise always coincided with general exercise for the main prison. Whenever Joe and the fellas were in their yard, cons from the main would be exercising in the big yard, just the other side of the fence. There would always be a dozen or so screws supervising them, complete with radios and dogs. And, if any of the human eyes should miss some small piece of action, there was a TV camera on a tall pole in the corner of the Security Wing yard, which swivelled to watch anything out of the ordinary. Joe indeed had several problems to overcome.

The first thing he wanted to find out was the distance between the yard fence and the closest part of the prison wall. It didn't look very far, but a guess wasn't good enough. Joe had to know the exact measurement.

For the past week or so, Joe had noticed an old dosser on the outer exercise yard. He stumbled around, eyes scanning the ground for dog-ends. When he saw one, he would hurry over and pick it up. It went into his snout tin with all the rest.

One afternoon, Joe came out into the yard. He went to sit against the fence, on the side closest to the wall. The cons from the main prison were filing out of their wing, spreading out around their exercise yard.

Joe waited until he saw the old dosser appear. Then he took a long dog-end out of his pocket and tied it on to the end of a reel of thick white cotton. He poked the dog-end through the wire and played out some of the cotton.

There was a screw standing a short distance away, against the outer wall. "Ere, guvnor, watch this,' Joe called over to him.

The screw, who had been watching Joe's antics anyway, stared at the dog-end stuck in the fence.

The old dosser was slowly making his circuit of the outer yard. When he was about 20 feet away, Joe suddenly flicked the end of the dog-end sharply. It flew about six feet and landed on the ground.

The dosser drew closer. Suddenly he saw it. A large dog-end like that was quite a prize to him. Shuffling forward hurriedly, he swooped.

His outstretched hand had nearly grasped it when Joe pulled on the end of the cotton. To the dosser's amazement, it flew out of his grasp, up to the fence and the gap through which it had come.

Everyone who saw it roared with laughter. The screw was especially amused. He liked to take the piss out of the cons himself. He liked it even better when another con did it for him.

Three more times that afternoon, Joe flicked the dog-end through different parts of the fence. Twice more, the dosser swooped, only to see it fly out of his grasp. By now, though, he was thoroughly suspicious of any large dog-end lying near the fence. The third time, he ignored it, turning his head sideways to grin at Joe before walking past.

The next afternoon when Joe came out on exercise, the same screw was standing in the same place. Joe went over to sit by the fence again. Once more, he took the dog-end out of his pocket and tied it to the cotton. He poked it through the wire.

"Ere, guvnor,' Joe called to the screw, 'the dosser ain't standing for any dog-ends close to this fence. Do us a favour and put it right up against the wall. He'll never believe I could have flicked it that far.'

The main wing cons hadn't come out on exercise yet, so the screw had a few seconds. It was a harmless request and he didn't mind being involved in the plot. He strolled over and picked the dog-end from the fence. 'Right up close against the wall,' called out Joe as the screw walked over to place it. The screw did as requested.

Suddenly, the main-wing cons started to file out on to their exercise yard. The screw hurried back to his post and scanned the approaching crowd. While he was watching them, Joe quickly pulled the dog-end in again. Now he had only to measure the cotton and he would have the exact distance between the fence and the wall.

There was a 16-foot gap between fence and wall. When Joe drew up the plan for the locker that evening, he allowed for a length of 18 feet. The short corridor was 20 feet long. The locker would just go in.

It wasn't to be just a straightforward locker, however. Joe wanted to make it as complex as possible. If he was going to build detachable ladders into it, there would have to be plenty of woodwork to disguise them.

The finished drawing showed an 18-foot built-in unit that had several separate lockers. There were compartments for vests, shorts, towels, trainers, footballs and tennis rackets.

It was an impressive drawing. Everything was there down to the finest detail. Every measurement and every bolt was neatly pencilled in. What was not immediately apparent though was that two 18-foot sections of framework could be slid out. These were what Joe was going to use to climb the fence and bridge the gap between the fence and the wall.

Security showed the plan to the Works Department. Perhaps civilian carpenters might have been more concerned with the wastage of timber: there was no real structural need for the extra thickness of the sections of framework. But prison Works Departments were profligate in the extreme with material, and especially where Security Wing work was concerned. Everything was massive and over-reinforced. To them, the extra timber didn't look a bit out of place. If they had made the locker, they would probably have used twice the thickness.

Security approved the plan. Within days, the wood arrived and once again Joe was sawing away on the ones. The rest of the group helped from time to time, with the exception of Frank who expressed no interest in the project. By now, Joe had told them what he had in mind, cautioning them against giving anything away by their behaviour.

For a while now, the ill-feeling between Frank and the PO had been increasing. The PO stayed out of Frank's way as much as he could, but, on the occasions when they did meet, you could feel the tension. Given half an excuse, Frank would have steamed into him. It was only the urgings of the others that stopped him.

One Saturday afternoon, Frank had a visit. As an 'A' man, all his visitors had to be vetted by the police. One of his visitors that day was his teenage niece. But she hadn't been vetted, and the PO refused to let her in.

Frank fumed, then raged. The PO, safely ensconced in his office, refused to budge. The visits screws were apologetic. It wasn't their fault. It was the PO's decision. Frank realised that it was futile to take it out on them. He also didn't want to ruin the visit for his other visitors, who came in while the niece remained outside in the car park. As Frank came off his visit, tea was being served. He walked straight past the hot-plate and up to his cell. A couple of minutes passed and he reappeared carrying his piss-pot. His face expressionless, he walked along the landing towards the recess.

Most of the screws were involved with serving tea, and the fellas were scurrying about between collecting their meals and watching sport on the TV. No one noticed as Frank carried on past the recess towards the PO's office.

The PO was sitting behind his desk, listening to the hustle and bustle out on the wing. He was feeling quite cheerful. He would be going off for his own tea in a few minutes; meanwhile, he was still savouring his victory over Frank that afternoon. He looked up quickly as someone came in the door.

Frank whipped the lid off the piss-pot with one hand. 'You dirty bastard,' he roared as the PO rose from his chair, a look of sheer terror on his face. As he opened his mouth to call out, Frank flung the contents of the pot full in his face.

The PO reeled backwards in a frantic effort to avoid the flying piss. Not an agile man at the best of times, his overweight, bulky form blundered into the arm of his chair and, overbalancing, he fell heavily to land in an untidy heap on the floor.

A passing screw heard the disturbance and rushed in. Luckily for the PO, both his desk and his chair were between him and Frank. The screw ran across the office just in time to put himself in the way. Frank was satisfied, though. He backed out of the office, roundly cursing the PO all the way.

A couple of screws appeared and led Frank away to his cell. By now, the fellas had realised what had happened. Gathering on the ones, directly below the PO's office, they cheered and whistled as the PO came out, a large stain darkening the front of his tunic. Red with embarrassment, he hurried along the landing, down the stairs and out of the wing.

The following morning, Frank was shanghaied. Rumour had it that he had gone to another Security Wing. They hadn't even bothered to nick him. There was nothing unusual about this. Frank was so disruptive that he was moved about at regular intervals anyway. Often, he would be in a jail for only a matter of weeks.

It was no great blow to the plan. Frank hadn't been interested in going, and the fella who arrived in his place was a multiple rapist who immediately got a blank from the remaining five in the group.

Joe took his time making the locker unit. Each section was made exactly to plan. The wing screws would often stand and watch. Joe told them he was making it to last.

It took three weeks, but finally it was finished. Each part had been undercoated and glossed. Joe fitted it together and erected it at the end of the ones. It stood there, gleaming as the light reflected from the fresh white paint. Over each separate compartment, Bob had neatly written 'VESTS', 'SHORTS' or whatever in red paint.

There was no ceremony, but the governor came over to see it, accompanied by the chief, the security PO, the Works PO and the chaplain. They congratulated Joe on a fine job. PO Buck stood in the foreground smiling broadly to show the assembled dignitaries that he approved of this one.

Later, Joe and the others carried it into the short corridor that led into the yard. It fitted perfectly, with a foot to spare at either end. They neatly stacked all spare kit in the appropriate compartments, then went out on exercise, leaving the locker in the sealed chamber, protected from the elements.

They played games enthusiastically for a couple of hours. When exercise finished, they carried their kit inside and stacked it in the locker unit. The screw who had been out in the yard came in with them; the yard camera swivelled on its pole to watch them go. As he went in, Joe looked back to check that the main exercise was finishing as well. Sure enough, they were filing back into the main wing. Each day, both exercises finished at the same time.

Now there were only the outside details to organise. Joe got me up on a visit and arranged for a ringer to be left the other side of the wall. Eddie made similar arrangements.

As there would be five of them, it was best that there be two cars. If they set off in different directions, there was a better chance of at least one group getting away.

They wouldn't be going far. The date for the escape had been set for a Saturday when Leicester City would be playing at home. Within half an hour of their going, the streets would be clogged with thousands of cars and people. They should be able to slip away in the crush.

Late on the Friday before the coup, two ringers were driven up from London. Neither driver knew of the other's existence. The cars were parked at either end of the narrow street behind the jail. In the little red Mini I had arranged were three changes of clothing, some money and a double-barrelled sawn-off.

On the Saturday morning, Joe and the rest of the group went through their usual routine, taking pains not to do anything out of the ordinary. All of them were keyed up. Instead of facing years and years of unrelieved boredom and personal decline, they were suddenly on the verge of freedom. For some, this coming afternoon meant the difference between life and death.

Later that morning, the group gathered in Joe's cell to run over the plan for one last time. Everyone had a job to do. Speed was of the essence. If they took too long, the jail would be surrounded by police and no one would get away.

Two o'clock finally came around. The five of them were already waiting by the door when the screw arrived to start exercise. There was nothing unusual in that. They often stood in a group talking, waiting to go out on exercise. If nothing else, it reminded the screws that it was exercise time and not to start late.

The screw pressed the button on the communication box next to the door. There was a few seconds' pause, then a little orange light winked on. 'Yes, what is it?' said a tinny voice from the control room.

'Officer Jones here,' said the screw. 'Open the door for exercise.'

There was a dull *click*. The screw turned the handle and pushed the door open. He stood aside as the five cons filed past him into the corridor. He followed them in, closing the door behind him. There was another *click* as it locked again. Joe and the others busied themselves at the locker as the screw walked the length of the corridor to the door at the other end. He pressed the button on another communication box. Once again an orange light came on and a tinny voice said, 'OK.'

The screw opened the door and the light from the yard flooded in. Joe and Bob picked up rackets and balls and headed outside.

Two others dragged two gym mats from the corridor. They were about five feet square and made of thick rubber, ideal for doing sit-ups on out in the yard.

The screw pressed another button on the wall outside, next to the door. Within seconds, the door had clicked shut again. Then he went to stand in the corner of the yard to supervise exercise.

In the outside yard, the screws were still taking up their posts. They were more in control on the main wing and always took their own sweet time to start exercise. They were never slow to finish it, though. A few minutes before four o'clock, they would start to shepherd the cons back into the wing. On the stroke of four, the outside yard would always be deserted. Joe and the others played the various games. Everything was done at a leisurely pace. No one wanted to injure himself. Everyone wanted to conserve energy. Very shortly, they would be climbing fences and running through streets.

At five to four, they began gathering all the gym kit together. Three minutes later, they were standing by the door waiting to go in. The outside yard was almost deserted. The last of the stragglers were just disappearing inside, pursued by a couple of screws.

The screw who had been supervising the Security Wing exercise spoke into the communication box for the door to be unlocked. The TV camera swivelled on its pole to cover the entrance. As the door swung open, Joe and Bob carried the kit past the screw into the corridor. They were followed by Eddie and Jack dragging two gym mats.

There were a few seconds' delay before George entered carrying a football. Joe and Bob were already hard at work, removing the bolts that held the ladder sections in position.

The screw stepped into the corridor, pulling the door to behind him, but, before he could close it completely, he felt a powerful arm grip him around the neck and a large sweaty hand clamp over his mouth. Jack dragged him backwards into a corner, with George twisting both his arms.

'You make one fucking sound and I'll break your fucking neck,' Jack growled in his ear.

The screw's legs went weak beneath him as he crumpled to the ground, paralysed with fear. He was alone in the small chamber with five of the most dangerous men in the country. It wasn't a time for heroics, even if he had been capable.

Jack and George tied up the screw and gagged him with a piece of rag. Bob hurried over and picked up his hat, which had fallen on the floor behind the door. He brushed the dust off it, then placed it firmly on his head back to front. With a last look at Joe and a parting wave, he opened the door and stepped out into the yard again.

The camera was still fixed firmly on the door. Raising both his arms above his head, Bob waved at it. Then, with his arms still waving in the air, he hopped and skipped and twirled as he headed for the gate at the far end of the yard.

On the control-room monitors, it must have looked an incongruous sight. Normally, Bob was one of the most sensible fellas on the wing. Now he was skipping across the yard, doing some funny kind of dance. And with a screw's hat on back to front.

The control-room screws couldn't make it out. He wasn't being furtive. Everything was being done right out in the open. It didn't look like an immediate security threat. Perhaps his mind had finally snapped under the strain of the 30-year sentence.

The camera swivelled to watch his progress. They saw him stop at the gate in the fence, but they couldn't see what he was doing because he had his back to them.

Bob quickly pulled a long, thick length of wire from the front of his denims. Taking care to shield it with his body, he bent it and pushed it through the keyhole of the locked gate. He worked it around so that the end came back the other side of the metal jamb. Then he twisted both ends tightly together. Now the gate couldn't be opened, even with a key.

While Bob was busy with this diversionary move, the others had been just as busy. As soon as the camera had swivelled to follow Bob, Joe and Jack hurried out with the two ladders. They moved directly to the section of fence closest to the wall. George and Eddie followed them, dragging a gym mat between them.

Within seconds, Jack had thrown his ladder up against the fence. Quickly, he scrambled up it and stood at the top. Joe climbed halfway up, then stopped. As George and Eddie arrived with the gym mat, Eddie hoisted it above his head and passed it up to Joe who, balancing precariously, lifted it up to Jack's outstretched hands. Grunting with effort, Jack swung it on top of the barbed wire, where it nestled in the vee of the fence. Then he climbed on to the mat and stamped it down on the wire. It was still a precarious base, though. The whole fence swayed as he braced his legs against the motion.

Bob was still standing over by the gate with his back to it, secretly watching the others' progress. By now, the screws in the control room were becoming alarmed. Whatever Bob was up to, though, he didn't seem to be going anywhere at the moment. It finally occurred to them that they should check where the others were.

The camera swivelled around on its pole. It panned over the door leading into the wing, then carried on. Suddenly, it was right there on the screen in front of them. A ladder was against the fence. A man was on the wire. The others were gathered around below. A full-scale escape attempt was in progress.

They pressed the general alarm. It sounded in the local police stations; within minutes, carloads of armed police would be on the way. It also sounded all over Leicester jail; every available screw ran towards the Security Wing.

A line of screws burst out of the main wing. They sprinted across the outer yard, towards the gate in the fence. Bob watched as they drew near, a smile on his face.

Just as they had been taught in training school, the leading screw had his key out ready to unlock the gate. He would push it open and step aside, allowing the others to run through.

Reaching the gate, he thrust his key at the lock, only noticing at the last moment that it was obstructed by a piece of wire. The screws following behind didn't even check their pace, expecting the gate to be thrown open immediately. As the lead screw pulled up sharply, the screws following behind cannoned into him. Hats and sticks tumbled to the ground as several fell over. The Keystone Cops couldn't have done it better.

There were a couple of dozen screws in the outer yard by now. Realising they couldn't get in, they hurried around the side. They gathered beneath where the ladder was touching the fence, looking up impotently at the man on the wire.

The PO had been sitting alone in his office when the alarm sounded. The bright, warm sunlight from the window on the back of his neck had had a soporific effect. He wasn't dozing, just lost in a dreamy reverie in which the Security Wing played no part.

Suddenly, his phone rang. The alarm had brought him fully awake, now the shrill ringing of the phone galvanised him into action. He snatched it from its cradle.

As the control room informed him of the escape in progress in the yard, his expression underwent an amazing transformation. His pupils dilated, his nostrils flared and his fat pink face was suddenly suffused by a brilliant-red glow. He launched himself from his chair and ran to the window

He gripped the bars with both hands as he peered through the glass out into the yard. Instantly, he took everything in. He saw Jack on top of the wire, with Joe halfway up the ladder below him. Eddie and George stood at the bottom, passing a second ladder up to Joe.

His mind tried to come to terms with the ghastly tableau. His whole body went rigid with shock, his knuckles white with exertion as he gripped the bars. It was his worst nightmare come true.

Bob strolled across the yard to join the rest. They were safe for the moment because there was no way into the yard. The gate was blocked and one door of the corridor was open. Under the failsafe system, the inner door couldn't be unlocked to let reinforcements through. On top of the fence, Jack was reaching out for the second ladder. Joe passed it to him carefully, mindful of the precarious nature of Jack's footing. Jack wobbled dangerously as he took its weight. Turning awkwardly, he steadied his feet against the mat as best he could.

Bending now, he grasped the ladder closer to the bottom and lifted it to his chest. Bracing his legs, he lowered the top of the ladder towards the wall, his face contorted with the effort.

This was the crucial bit. Once it rested on top of the wall, they would have a bridge across. The screws could only stand below and watch helplessly as Leicester's most dangerous prisoners scrambled across to freedom.

As the end of the ladder neared the wall, Jack started to lose control. Holding it at the bottom, the full weight was concentrated in his arms. Suddenly, it fell the last few feet.

It fell short. Jack hadn't held it out far enough. The end of the ladder grazed the top of the wall, then started to slide down the inside. Almost screaming with the effort, Jack managed to stop it. The end hung there, five feet below the top. The screws below suddenly started jumping in an attempt to grab it, but it was just out of reach. Slowly and with great effort, Jack hoisted it up again. With the others shouting encouragement, he lowered it once more. His arms were tired now, almost numb. He had less control than the first time. Up in the office, the PO stood transfixed. His face looked altogether different now. The colour was completely gone, replaced by a waxy yellow pallor. Suddenly, his face contorted as a spasm shook his body. His hands grasped ineffectually at the bars as saliva dribbled from his lips. Slowly, like a tree toppling in the forest, he fell headlong to the floor.

Back on top of the fence, the ladder suddenly dipped down. The end smashed on to the top of the wall with a force that jarred right up Jack's arms. It bounced upwards and then slipped sideways. The fellas could only watch in horror as it slid down the inside of the wall.

The screws were on it in a flash. Several pairs of hands wrenched it free from Jack's grasp and threw it on the ground. It was all over. Jack and Joe climbed down to join the others. They stood silently in a group, their faces creased with disappointment. For a second, Joe nearly said something to Jack. It should have been Joe's job to lower the ladder across, but in the heat of the moment Jack had got carried away. Now it was too late for recriminations.

They stood in a circle, shaking hands and saying their goodbyes to each other. There would be solitary confinement and heavy loss of remission. Then they would be split up and moved to other jails. After what they had been through together, it was a sad moment.

'Oh, well,' said Joe, breaking the spell, 'I suppose I'd better untie the screw. He's probably waiting for his tea.' The fellas laughed and followed him as he left the yard and entered the short corridor again. The screw was still lying where they had left him. They removed the gag from his mouth and untied his hands and feet. They helped him to stand. He leaned against the wall unsteadily, looking apprehensively at the cons gathered around him.

'It's OK,' said Joe. 'It's all over. Get on the button and take us back into the wing.'

The screw was still unsure of what to do. He hadn't recovered from the shock of being overpowered and tied up. Now the people who had done it were back again. Was this some new devious plot?

He looked at the door that led into the yard to check that it was closed. He walked slowly towards the communication box next to the door leading into the wing, never taking his eyes off the cons surrounding him. He pressed the button on the box.

'Officer Jones here,' he said as it winked into life. 'Open this door and let me and five inmates in, please.'

There was a long delay. Then a voice crackled from the box: 'Will you repeat that again, please, Officer Jones, and state your situation.'

The screw shifted uneasily on his feet. He was becoming impatient now. He couldn't wait to get away from these dangerous and frightening men. He repeated his earlier message, strain showing clearly in his voice now.

Again there was a delay of several minutes. 'I'm afraid there is an emergency in the wing, Officer Jones,' said the voice from the box. 'You will have to remain where you are for just a while longer.'

The screw suddenly pushed his face up close to the box. 'Now you look here,' he shouted, his voice breaking into a sob. 'There's a fucking emergency in here! Now open the door and fucking get me out!' He remained with his face pressed tight to the box as if his close proximity could somehow emphasise the message.

There was a short pause, then the door clicked. The screw pulled it open and rushed into the wing. He nearly cannoned into the 20 or so screws standing just inside with the chief. Each one had his hand on his stick.

'OK, boys,' said the chief to Joe and the others. 'In you come. It's all over.'

Joe walked nonchalantly into the wing, the rest close behind him. The group stopped just in front of the chief. As he opened his mouth to speak, there was a disturbance up on the twos. Every eye turned to see what it was.

Two hospital screws with a stretcher between them were negotiating the descent of the stairs. A bulky figure was strapped to it, a green blanket pulled up to his chin.

As the stretcher neared the bottom, Joe and the others instantly recognised the face of PO Buck. Quite involuntarily, they let loose a bellow of laughter. Men who, seconds earlier, had stood morose and dispirited now roared heartily, their faces animated with pleasure.

The chief and the rest of the screws looked embarrassed. To be truthful, they didn't care much for the PO either. His constant bad humour hardly endeared him to anyone. But he was 'staff' like themselves.

'The PO has had a heart attack,' the chief said to no one in particular.

'Well, thank fuck I never got away just now,' said Joe, smiling broadly. 'I wouldn't have missed this for anything.'

Joe went on to take part in many other escapes. He always came close, but never made it..

Bob was released on parole after 11 years. He lives in retirement in South London.

Buster was released after nine years. A film of his life was made against his wishes, starring Phil Collins. For several years Buster's cheerful face could be seen most weekday mornings, selling flowers from his stall outside Waterloo Station. Tragically, he hung himself in the garage where he kept the stall. His funeral was attended by thousands of mourners.

Eddie served his full ten years with no parole. He then was sentenced to 25 years for cocaine smuggling. He was released a couple of years ago. In jail he became an accomplished painter. He has recently had several showings where his paintings fetched many thousands of pounds each.

Frank served nearly every day of his sentence, a rebel to the end. He was shot in the face several years ago. The police came to his hospital bedside and asked him his name and what had happened. 'Tutankhamen,' replied Frank, 'I'm keeping Mum.' He refused to say another word. In his seventies now, he has since written several books and has become something of an after-dinner speaker.

George is free, whereabouts unknown.

Jack hasn't been heard of for years. An anonymous man at the best of times.

11 BILLY G AND THE DRAINHOLE CELL

By and large, the Londoners stuck together at Parkhurst. Not that we were a large well-organised gang. More that it was considered only the proper thing to stick by your own. Whenever a London face arrived, we invariably gathered around to help him through the settling-in period.

However, in some ways Parkhurst was several prisons in one, and it just wasn't possible to get about all over the place. Especially to parts of the hospital, the Security Wing and 'C' wing, the psychiatric wing.

For some time we had been aware that a good and trusted pal of ours, Billy Gale, had been involved in some kind of personal protest in the hospital. Unfortunately, F2 landing was very much 'home turf' for the screws. It was completely out of bounds except for those patients confined there. The screws' writ ran there largely unchallenged.

Because of who he was, Billy G certainly qualified for some help from us. If anyone epitomised the archetypal chap, then it was Bill. In the Sixties, his well-known London nightclub, The Embassy, was the 'in' place for the chaps, but it also had a famous and international clientele.

Bill was getting over £500 a week from the club, a lot of money in those days, but he still spent faster than he could earn. His lifestyle was colourful and hectic.

He went out clubbing every night of the week. He wore expensive clothes, drove expensive cars and loved a bet. Loyal, kind and generous, he also supported an extensive network of pals who were in the nick. He was often to be seen in the vicinity of some jail or other, handing over a joey of snout and booze for someone to take in to a pal. He was forever doing favours for people in trouble, and no one ever had a bad word to say about him. At a time when there was growing rivalry between the Krays and the Richardsons, Bill was one of the very few who was liked by both firms.

He was also an active bank robber. In an age when blaggers were very few and far between, he worked with some of the best firms in London. He was game and got plenty of money from his efforts. If he had a failing, it was that, at times, he could be clumsy and forgetful. Once, this happened on a bit of work.

Bill was sitting in a ringer with three others, getting ready to go on one. All were experienced armed robbers; one was John McVicar. They pulled on their masks and were checking their guns. Bill was carrying an unfamiliar automatic. Pointing it at the car roof, he pulled the trigger. There was a thunderous explosion which deafened all four of them. A small round hole appeared in the roof.

Unfortunately for them, they were parked outside a block of flats. A woman standing on her balcony heard the shot and phoned the police.

It was equally unfortunate that this was the period just after Harry Roberts had shot the three coppers at Shepherd's Bush. The Old Bill were swarming all over London and any reports of shots brought a lively response. Within minutes, dozens of police cars were rushing to the scene, and soon there was a high-speed chase across London. Bill was leaning out the back window of the fleeing car, firing at the cars following. Bullets ricocheted off lamp-posts and pillar-boxes. It was a real Wild West tear-up.

The police were now convinced that, if it wasn't Harry Roberts himself they were chasing, then it was a very desperate firm indeed. They flooded the area with cars and motorbikes.

Eventually, inevitably, the ringer crashed. All four were badly beaten, then nicked. Bill drew 18-and-a-half years for his part in it.

In the nick, Bill was just as game and determined as when free. Apart from his own potential for escaping, he had scores of friends and admirers both inside and out of prison. The Home Office were taking no chances. They put him in Chelmsford Security Wing.

It was a small wing, housing about 16 cons, all doing very long sentences. The regime was liberal and easygoing. Those who didn't want to work didn't have to. Most just lounged about all day, playing games, lifting weights or cooking.

It was an effective way of buying people off. Many of the fellas adopted the attitude that they could hardly have it any easier; there were a lot worse places they could be. As escape was very difficult, they settled down to pass this period as quietly as possible.

Bill, though, was a man of strong emotions, firm principles and great determination. If he believed in a cause, he would commit himself to it and damn the consequences.

Although separated from his wife, he was devoted to his two young daughters, and his greatest joy was to see them on visits. Bill was on the 'A' list, however, and, as an 'A' man, all his visitors had to be vetted and approved by the police. This didn't directly concern his young daughters. However, they were brought to the visits by Bill's close friend John. Unfortunately, John had a criminal record, so the police refused him permission to visit. This meant that the two girls couldn't visit either.

The prison authorities suggested a compromise. They would find a probation officer to bring the girls up for the visits. Bill immediately refused. He wasn't going to allow a stranger to accompany them. He wanted them to be at their ease, with someone they knew and trusted. It was a stand-off. The irresistible force versus the immovable object.

Unfortunately for the Home Office, however, this irresistible force didn't recognise immovable objects. Bill gave them an ultimatum. Either they give John permission to bring his daughters to Chelmsford nick, or he would start potting up the wing.

One's first reaction to someone throwing piss and shit all over the place could well be one of revulsion coupled with mystification. But piss and shit are very potent weapons in the nick. With the balance of force massively on the side of the authorities, sometimes this was all that was left.

No one likes piss and shit thrown over them, especially when it's someone else's. It has quite a deterrent effect on the screws. It is also a major health hazard. With raw sewage hanging about, a wing could well be closed on medical grounds. (This was long before the days of the AIDS and hepatitis epidemics.)

Before banging up for the night, Bill told the rest of the fellas not to get involved. It was his own private protest.

The following morning as he was unlocked, he came out of his cell and threw a pot full of piss and shit all over the front of the wing office.

It couldn't be allowed to continue. Yet, if the screws tried to grab hold of Bill, there would be a fight; then the rest of the cons would join in. It was a situation that Chelmsford Security Wing couldn't handle.

They moved Bill to F2 landing at Parkhurst hospital the same day. Now F2 landing had seen it all. It had handled the most dangerous and volatile cons that the system had thrown up. One way or another, they were contained – through drugs, beatings or months of solitary.

But the hospital screws had heard of Billy G, and could see that he wasn't intimidated at all. His popularity among the cons was legend. Everyone liked him for his strength, kindness and principles. If the screws tried to beat him up, not only would they have a right fight on their hands – a fight that would be repeated every time they unlocked him – but there was also a danger that news of what was happening would reach the main jail and spark off a riot.

As it was, Parkhurst was still recovering from the effects of the very serious riot in 1969. This had been preceded by months of regular organised brutality. A heavy mob of screw bullies had tuned up quite a few of the chaps in the chokey; eight or nine to one were the sorts of odds they favoured, and several of the fellas had been badly beaten. The riot had been the logical outcome.

It was put down with great force. Many cons were severely injured, as were a couple of screws. The 'so-called' ringleaders were put on trial and got long sentences on top. The whole affair had received widespread publicity.

Evidence was heard of the bad conditions and institutionalised brutality. At the end of the trial, the judge was remorseless in his condemnation: 'The Home Secretary should take a long, hard look at Parkhurst.'

The effect was that the heavy mob of screw bullies were broken up and dispersed to other jails, and conditions improved a little. It was still the same old Parkhurst, but no longer would the screws steam in mob-handed at the least excuse and beat up people wholesale. The powers-that-be at Parkhurst felt they needed a breathing space, with no bad publicity. It was into this new-age Parkhurst that Billy G came with his own personal dirty protest.

On the morning following his arrival on F2, Bill came straight out of his cell and threw a pot full of piss and shit up the nearest wall. Then he walked back into his cell and banged the door. The screws didn't do a thing. They just fetched a couple of lunatics to clean up the mess.

Over the next few days, Bill repeated the process several times. Each time it met with the same response. At first, he suspected that the screws thought he would get tired of it before they did. Well, they would soon discover otherwise. However, through the thick walls of his cell, Bill could hear constant banging and the occasional thud.

A couple of days after the banging ceased, the hospital PO and several screws came to Bill's door.

'You're moving to a new cell,' said the PO.

Bill didn't care what cell he was in. All he was interested in was potting up whatever lay outside. He picked up his few items of personal kit and went with them.

A strip cell was located in the corner of a side corridor off F2. As Bill approached, he could see that they had built a curved wall in front of it. This was covered with white tiles from top to bottom, the floor between the wall and the cell sloped to meet a drain in the middle, and a steel gate sealed off the whole area. The idea was that Bill would throw the contents of his pot up the tiled wall and the excrement would run down into the drain. Clearly, they thought they had Bill now. They locked him in the 'drainhole cell'.

The following morning, he came straight out and threw a pot full of piss and shit up the wall. He repeated the process every time they unlocked him and he had something in his pot to throw. Days passed, weeks passed, months passed. Bill still potted up the wall.

There wasn't the slightest comfort in his cell. He had no books, no papers and no magazines. He didn't write letters or receive visits. His hair and beard grew until they hung down his back and chest. He kept himself scrupulously clean, though, washing several times a day in his plastic bowl.

Seven months passed and suddenly Bill had a visitor. Lord Longford, touring the prison, heard about Bill's dirty protest on F2 and went to see him.

What he made of the strange-looking long-haired man lying in the corner of the cell, we may never know. What Bill made of the strange-looking Lord who so loudly professed Christian beliefs wasn't long in coming.

Longford started off on the wrong foot. He tried to talk Bill out of his protest.

Bill immediately gave him a volley. 'Call yourself a Christian man?' he shouted. 'If you were a Christian man, you'd make these bastards let me see my little girls. Now piss off out of it.'

Longford beat a hasty retreat.

Ritualistically, Bill continued his protest. Another five months passed. He had been potting up F2 every single day for a whole year. Every day he sat alone in a bare cell with absolutely nothing to do. Days ran into nights until there was no distinction between them. Time stretched out in front of him, not in discrete units of hours or days, but in an infinite, unending stream.

On the anniversary of the day he had arrived on F2, his door opened and there stood the governor.

'Bill, it has been decided that you are to go to the Scrubs for your visits. Your friend will be allowed to bring your daughters there.'

Bill weighed up the governor's words. 'If you're fucking me about,' he said, 'I'll only start all over again.'

The same afternoon, an escort arrived to take him to the Scrubs. When he arrived, he was put on 'D' wing, the long-term wing. For the period of his stay, he would be treated as a category-B prisoner, which meant that none of his visitors had to be vetted by the police. Bill had won.

It had never been known before. No one had ever taken on the Home Office and wrung a single concession out of them. It was a matter of policy. Clearly, if one con was seen to demand something and got it, others would try. That the Home Office had given in to Bill was seen as a concession to his unique strength and determination.

Bill started to have his visits. As he'd had none for the past year, he was given as many as he asked for. He saw the girls every morning with John, and most afternoons he was visited by some of his many friends. After all the trauma of that year in the 'drainhole cell', this was a golden period.

Bill had been at the Scrubs for about three months when he was suddenly called in to see the governor. The man was clearly ill at ease. His face was grim as he looked at Bill standing before him.

'I've had a communication from head office that, as from tomorrow, the special arrangement concerning your visits will cease. As a category-A prisoner, your friend will not be able to visit you.' As the governor spoke, he looked down at the table. He couldn't look Bill in the eye.

Bill was instantly very angry. 'OK, if that's the way you want it,' he shouted, 'I'll start all over again.' With that, he stormed out of the office.

That evening, after the nine o'clock bang-up, several screws came to Bill's cell. They told him he had to go to the chokey over on 'A' wing. Bill packed his kit and went with them.

As chokeys go, the one at the Scrubs wasn't very heavy at all. It was spotlessly clean and gleamed with polish. It was strictly run, with no con ever coming into contact with another. The clientele were mostly quite lightweight; all the really wild men were in the tougher jails. There was some intimidation and a few scuffles, but there were none of the heavy duty beatings that went on in some chokeys.

There was one screw, though, a tall Jock, who rather fancied himself. He was always arrogant and petty, and tried to intimidate most of the cons as a matter of course. If anyone played up in any way, he would be the one to threaten them with dire consequences. He had also given a couple of fellas sly digs. He was known all over the nick and was quite proud of his hard-line reputation.

When they unlocked Bill in the morning, the Jock screw was lounging about on the landing. He had heard of Bill. Bill had also heard of him. With a brimming piss-pot, he headed straight for him.

With Bill in hot pursuit, the Jock screw ran along the landing as if his life depended on it. He reached the top of the turret circular stairs and threw himself bodily down them. As Bill arrived at the top, the screw was just disappearing around the first bend. A cascade of piss and shit narrowly missed him as he tumbled down the rest of the flight.

The chokey immediately filled with screws, running to the alarm bell. They shepherded Bill back into his cell and banged him up. They didn't want a tear-up. If they had treated Bill with respect on F2 at Parkhurst, then the screws in a Mickey Mouse chokey like the Scrubs certainly didn't want to start him off. There were over 1500 men in the jail. Bill was known and liked by many of them. He was just the sort of spark that could set the tinder off.

Half an hour passed and Bill's door opened again. The chief was standing there. He knew Bill of old. 'Bill, we've got an escort coming for you. We're going to put you on the yard until it arrives,' he said.

It was a beautiful summer's day. Bill knew that, wherever he was going, he wouldn't have much opportunity to get out in the fresh air, so he picked up his kit and followed the chief.

'A' wing exercise yard was about 50 yards square. On three sides it was bounded by buildings, on the fourth by the prison wall. Bill walked right into the middle and lay down. Several screws took up positions around the perimeter. They settled back in the shade to wait. An hour passed. Bill dozed. The screws nodded as they lounged against walls in the unrelenting heat. Suddenly, the radio each was carrying crackled into life. A Dalek voice informed them that the escort had arrived.

They all moved away from the shade to form a rough circle around Bill. The nearest screw was only 20 feet away, but Bill remained totally oblivious to their presence. He wasn't asleep, but the hot sun had made him very drowsy.

Around the corner of 'A' wing came the chief, walking briskly. Directly behind him came a white police Rover with two uniformed coppers in it. Close behind followed a green Transit van with darkened windows. This was the 'A' van used for top-security escorts. Bringing up the rear was a police mini-van with two dog-handlers in the front and two Alsatians in the back.

The slowly moving motorcade passed through the ring of screws and stopped close to Bill. He had been alerted by the sound of the engines and now was sitting up, watching. He stood, picked up his kit that was strewn around him and walked towards the green Transit.

The chief produced a pair of handcuffs and cuffed Bill to a tall screw who had got out of the 'A' van. They both climbed in the back. The doors were locked and the motorcade slowly set off, back the way it had come.

If Bill ever had any doubts about where he was going, they were quickly dispelled as soon as the escort started to head south. There were only two category-A jails to the south of the Scrubs: Albany and Parkhurst, both on the Isle of Wight.

With sirens blaring, they raced through the city streets. They stopped for nothing: traffic lights, rights of way at junctions and roundabouts or whatever. Coppers immediately stopped traffic and waved them through. Soon they were on the open road, speeding south. Now they only used their sirens when they encountered traffic that could slow them down.

As they reached the county boundary of the Metropolitan District, the two police vehicles dropped off. They were replaced by two identical ones from the Surrey police, which had been waiting at a roundabout. With all the enthusiasm of a new escort, they took off at breakneck speed, sirens blaring.

Before long, they reached the Surrey county boundary. Once again, the two police vehicles dropped off to be replaced by two from the Hampshire constabulary. With hardly any slackening of speed, the escort raced ever southwards.

As they entered Southampton, the sirens were switched on again. Pedestrians turned to stare as the green Transit with its darkened windows and police escort sped by. Soon it pulled up at the ferry terminal. Driving to the front of the waiting queue of cars, the Transit stopped to await the ferry.

They were the first to drive on, unescorted now. No doubt they thought they were safe from an organised escape attempt on the boat. Unlike the passengers in the other vehicles, no one left the van. Bill and the screws all sat there in the darkness of the deserted hold. The thought suddenly struck Bill that, should the ferry sink, he and the screw he was cuffed to would certainly drown together. They drove off the ferry at Ryde to be met by a single police car containing two coppers.

Now there were no sirens and the pace was sedate, almost leisurely. An organised escape attempt on the island was hardly likely and the wealthy and influential 'Islanders' didn't take kindly to noisy, speeding motorcades. Eventually, they turned from an avenue of trees into the driveway of Parkhurst.

The van drove Bill straight to the hospital. As he was led on to F2, he immediately noticed a change. The place seemed cleaner and brighter. While he had been away, F2 had been redecorated. The PO's office looked particularly pristine, with its windowed front picked out in gleaming white paint. On the half-open door hung a toy sheriff's badge.

As the escort uncuffed Bill, the PO came out of the office. His mouth dropped open in surprise as he saw Bill standing there. He thought he had seen the last of him when he had left for the Scrubs. 'What's up, Bill?' he said, concern showing in his face.

'What's up?' echoed Bill. 'Piss and shit. That's what's up.'

He was ushered along F2 and put in an ordinary strip cell. For the moment at least, it wasn't back to the 'drainhole cell'. Clearly, this indicated a degree of wishful thinking on the part of the authorities. For the rest of the day, Bill only came out of his cell to collect washing water. He received his meals without incident.

The following morning, Bill was unlocked for early slop-out. He strolled out and emptied his washing bowl into the slops sink in the nearby recess. He walked slowly back to his cell. He reappeared carrying a brimming pot.

Halfway to the recess, he suddenly spun to his right and ran along F2 towards the PO's office. The full contents of the pot splattered the newly painted front. Some went through the half-open door, splashing over the desk top covered with papers. The sheriff's badge swung crazily, then stabilised, dripping with filth.

Bill turned to go back to his cell, but several screws surrounded him. They gently pushed him along the landing towards his old 'drainhole cell'. As the door banged shut behind him, he contemplated the featureless walls that had been his home for a whole year.

Who knows what went through Bill's mind as he sat there? Solitary confinement under the best of circumstances is the most exquisite mental torture. You can try to lose yourself in the world of a book but, after six or seven hours of reading, a headache comes on. A letter received gives the spirit a lift. A letter sent reaffirms your existence; you can contact and act upon the outside world. The exercise periods twice a day free you from the claustrophobic confines of your brickwork tomb. The occasional visit recharges the emotional batteries and gives you precious contact with another human being. It redefines your personality, for, in the absence of others, there is no such thing as self.

Still, time stretches out in front of you. You count the days left until your solitary is over. You try to wish them away. Yet time passes so slowly. Can it be that you have done only six days, and another 50 stretch out in front of you like infinity?

And, at the back of your mind, the terrible question lurks all the time: What if there comes a time when you just can't stand it any more? Solitary is a form of death, social death. When there is only pain, wouldn't death be a merciful release, a cessation of pain?

And what if you were to scream and hammer on the door? It would be oh so easy. But would you ever be able to stop? Would that snap the thin thread of self-control that is all that stands between you and madness or death?

However, Bill's situation was much worse than normal solitary. He had no books. He got no letters or visits. There were no exercise periods. He didn't know when the solitary would end, because it would last as long as he kept potting up F2. And, finally, he had the knowledge that he could bring his torment to an end at any time, merely by giving up his protest.

The protest continued uninterrupted. Every day, Bill emerged from his cell to throw the contents of his pot up the tiled wall. Every day, after Bill was banged up, a couple of F2's resident lunatics would clean up the mess. Like some bizarre and recurring ritual, the actors played out their roles, day in and day out.

Again, weeks passed, months passed. Finally, after another six months, the governor came to Bill's cell once more. This time the message was one of total capitulation. Bill could go back to the Scrubs and have his daughters brought to him by his friend John. This time, it would be a permanent arrangement.

Bill and the governor looked at each other. Both knew, although it remained unspoken, that any going back would result in Bill starting all over again.

Bill returned to the Scrubs. John brought his girls up to see him every day. This time the Home Office kept their word. There was no going back. The immovable object had had quite enough of the irresistible force.

After the 18-and-a-half, Billy G got another nine years for robbing mail trains with one of the 'Great Train Robbers'. He went back to Parkhurst, from where he was released in April 1994. In 2003, at over 70 years of age, Bill robbed a Post Office van single handed. He was sentenced to 4 ? years. He presently lives in retirement in East London.

12 ALBERT THE TERRORIST

Albert was a terrorist, all the media were agreed on that. And, by their criteria, Albert more than qualified. We chaps, though, were constantly surprised by these so-called 'terrorists'. When they first started to come into long-term jails, we expected men who were tougher, more vicious and more criminal than any we had met before.

After all, according to the police, we were the worst of criminals. We were 'first division' armed robbers, killers and gangsters. Yet none of us had started out by robbing banks or killing people. We had come up through the ranks, as it were.

As teenagers, we were burglars, car thieves and Post Office robbers. Some of us stabbed people, cut people, glassed them or hit them with iron bars. All part of the growing-up process for many working-class criminals. Then, as our confidence grew, we extended our criminal contacts. We went into what the police called 'professional crime'.

Yet none of us ever contemplated blowing up buildings or deliberately assassinating the Old Bill. It was hard enough strapping up to go out and rob a bank. Heaven knows the kind of bottle or craziness it would take to do the terrorist crimes.

Therefore, when we first met the terrorists in the nick, we were curious about their backgrounds. Knowing what we had got up to as teenagers on the streets of London, we wondered what they had done as teenagers on the streets of Belfast. We expected to hear that their fledgling viciousness and criminality had been of a completely different order to ours.

You can imagine our surprise when we found out that the vast majority of them were straight goers, men who went to work for a living. They had never burgled or robbed or stolen for purely criminal ends. They had, quite literally, started at the top. One minute they were building workers, drivers or whatever; the next they were planting bombs and killing people wholesale. Irish criminals we could have related to and understood. These people, though, were totally beyond our comprehension.

Albert grew up in East Belfast. He was a straight goer. To get away from the dead-end jobs and high unemployment, he joined the British Army. They trained him to kill.

He saw action in Oman. They had an insurgency problem there which they tried to solve by taking captured rebels across the border and shooting them. Albert had his first taste of illicit killing.

Returning to East Belfast on leave, he was shocked to find it in a state bordering on civil war. The IRA, as self-proclaimed protectors of the Catholic community, were becoming stronger by the day. The Protestant community felt threatened and set up their own paramilitary groups. As a Protestant, Albert felt involved. He didn't return to the Army.

The military skills he had learned made him very valuable to the Ulster Volunteer Force – the UVF. He became sergeant-at-arms to the East Belfast Brigade.

The UVF's first problem was how to collect intelligence on the IRA. If they were going to attack them, they first had to find out who they were. The trouble was that the Protestant community in East Belfast was extremely insular. Although they had lived alongside Catholics for hundreds of years, sometimes in the same street, they knew little about them. The social life of the two communities didn't intersect at any point. The UVF had to start from scratch.

Albert and his group began to kidnap Catholics at random from off the street, and took them back to various Protestant drinking clubs in the area. The interrogations were held in back rooms called 'Romper Rooms'. The process was called 'Rompering', a euphemism for the crudest and most barbaric torture. Fingers were cut off, red-hot pokers were stuck up arses, men died screaming in agony. Their bodies were dumped in Catholic areas to inspire terror.

By now, Albert was thoroughly out of control. The blood-lust was upon him and he was killing wholesale. He took to knocking on doors and asking whether the occupants were Protestant or Catholic. Those who answered, 'Catholic', he shot. A wave of fear swept the Catholic community. Finally, Albert machine-gunned a bus and threw a grenade into it.

Perhaps this was the catharsis that pushed Albert over the top. He came to England and found himself wandering in a wood just outside Guildford, with a suitcase in his hand. He walked into the local nick and gave himself up.

At first, the local CID just didn't believe the amazing catalogue of shootings, bombings and torture this dishevelled young Irishman confessed to. It was only when two Special Branch men came down from London that they realised just what a prize had fallen into their laps. They flew Albert back to Belfast for further questioning. His crimes were quite sensational on their own. However, his allegations about UVF arms dumps in police stations were political dynamite. He went on trial for his own crimes first, and was convicted of the doorstep killings and the bus outrage. He was sentenced to life, with a minimum recommendation of 25 years. Then he gave evidence in the trials of senior Protestant paramilitaries. However, all these trials collapsed through lack of evidence.

Now he was in a thoroughly invidious position. The IRA wanted to kill him for murdering Catholics. The Protestant paramilitaries wanted to kill him for informing on their arms dumps. He was no favourite with the British Army either: there was embarrassment over the arms dumps, as well as suspicions that, as a sniper, he had shot at British soldiers. Albert was transferred to England to serve his sentence.

Even in English jails, Albert wasn't safe. First, there were scores of IRA, whereas he was often the only Protestant terrorist. Then there was the fact that he had grassed on the UVF. This didn't exactly endear him to the chaps, for whom grassing was anathema. Albert had plenty of enemies.

He could look after himself, though. Ruggedly handsome, with thick, curly black hair, he stood nearly six feet tall and weighed over 13 stone. His broad shoulders weren't just for show either. The British Army had trained him in unarmed combat.

He quickly realised that one way to make friends among the cons was to give the screws a hard time, so he became a committed prison rebel. Soon, Albert was fighting the system all the way.

There was some doubt whether there had been collusion between the security forces and Albert's group. Albert was trying to force an official enquiry. For a while, he went 'on the blanket' – refusing to wear prison clothing – to try to get political prisoner status. All it got him was long periods of solitary. Four years into his sentence, he found himself in the chokey at Parkhurst on Rule 43, 'Good Order and Discipline'.

Albert had been dozing. It was early afternoon and hot in the cell, and the stodgy lunch had made him sleepy. With no structure to his day, other than mealtimes and exercise, it made little difference whether he slept during the day or night. In fact, after a while, day and night seemed to run into each other. At a bodily level, they had become an artificial distinction anyway.

Albert welcomed sleep; it was a merciful release. Every second of consciousness was pain. His nerves were stretched tight from just trying to maintain control. His situation was hopeless; there was no pleasure in his life. He had more than 20 years of this torture still to endure. It was a length of time he couldn't begin to comprehend. Even when he slept, he slept fitfully. His subconscious was filled with the shadows of his waking world. He drifted back to consciousness slowly, reluctantly. He deliberately kept his eyes closed, as if to deny that consciousness a foothold. Eventually, sticky hot eyelids parted to let in the half-light suffusing the cell.

He was lying on his side, looking across at the opposite wall. There was a patch of darkness. A darkness within darkness. Yet there was form there.

At first, his fledgling consciousness rejected what he was seeing. Slowly, the terrifying reality hit him. He gasped as if from some physical shock. His eyes stared in horror as his mind tried to come to terms with it. He was looking at the face of the Devil.

Who knows what Albert saw as he stared with sleep-filled eyes at a blank cell wall? Who knows what demons lived within his subconscious? He had been under so much pressure for the past six years. So many terrifying and bizarre things had happened. At times, it must have seemed as if the line between reality and unreality was becoming blurred. The important thing was that Albert believed he saw the Devil.

He screamed in terror as he threw himself off the bed. He cowered in the corner of the cell like a child, with his head hidden beneath his arms. He was paralysed with fear. He felt sure that, if anything so much as touched him, his heart would stop with the shock of it.

Long minutes he crouched there, rigid. Very slowly, he turned his head and peered through his arms. His heart raced at breakneck speed as the periphery of his vision took in the edge of the dark patch, then encompassed it whole. He stared into the darkness, dreading what he might find. Yet there was nothing. Just a patch of shadow, albeit darker than the rest.

Instead of allaying his fears, this, strangely, served to reinforce them. His memory could recall in full detail exactly what he had seen. It had been as real to him then as the patch of shadow was to him now. He didn't know the meaning of the vision, but he knew that he had to get out of Parkhurst chokey before he cracked up.

But what could he do? It was no use his asking to be taken off Rule 43. Virtually everyone asked sooner or later. The governor would decide in his own time. Albert couldn't wait for that. He had to do something immediately.

Parkhurst chokey was not housed in a separate building. It was merely a partitioned-off section of 'B' wing, composing half of the ones and the twos. The chokey was divided into two sections: the ones was for punishments and Rule 43 subversives; the twos was for Rule 43 protection. The two groups never met.

Albert was located on the ones. It was an old stone-floored landing with ten cells on either side. Entry was from the outside of the building, through gates set in the end of what had originally been 'B' wing. Cons arriving or leaving in a van could be loaded and offloaded right on the doorstep. This was convenient if anyone decided to put up a fight. They would not have to be carried, kicking and struggling in full view of other cons in surrounding wings.

There was another entrance, through the partition separating the chokey from 'B' wing, but this was rarely used to admit cons. The screws occasionally used it themselves for convenience, but they tried to maintain the fiction that the chokey was a completely separate entity from 'B' wing.

The ones landing in the chokey had very rudimentary facilities. It was about 90 feet long by 25 feet wide. At the far end, on the left, was a recess comprising urinal, toilet, slops sink and shower. Opposite was the screws' office, two cells knocked into one. Outside the office was a metal-topped hot-plate from which they served meals.

Just inside the gate, on the right, was a narrow corridor leading to the strip cells and exercise yards. Other than these features, there was nothing. With the vaulted arches over the cell doors, the low ceiling and the painted brick walls, the ones area could have been the basement of an old castle.

Albert never left this area, except at exercise times. Then he was let out into one of the two adjoining yards. To say 'yards' is, in fact, an exaggeration. They were two wire-topped pens about 24 feet long by 12 feet wide. No sooner had you taken a few paces in one direction than you had to turn through 90 degrees to continue.

It was impossible for Albert to get out of the yard. Yet, if he could only climb on to the roof, he could do so much damage and injure so many screws that they would have to move him to another jail. But it couldn't be done. There were always half-a-dozen screws about during exercise time. He would have had to overpower them all, take a set of keys and let himself out of the chokey gate.

During the serving of meals, or any of the other times he was let out of his cell, there were always four or five screws about. And one press of the alarm bell would bring scores more running. The only time he ever got out of his cell with just one screw present was occasionally over dinnertime bang-up.

After a while, the average con could usually control his bowel movements so that they coincided with slopping-out times, but sometimes people would get caught short. Many cons strongly objected to shitting in their pots. Not only would they have to sit in the cell with it and the accompanying odour, but, at slopping-out time, they would have to walk past the screws with a pot full of shit and throw it down the slops sink. This made them feel humiliated.

Albert was one of these people. If he wanted a shit, he would bang on his door to be let out.

During dinnertime, though, there was only one screw on duty in the chokey. There was a standing order that no screw should unlock any inmate while on his own. However, one did. He was an old fat screw who, by Parkhurst standards, was a reasonably decent fella. He wouldn't do it for anyone, but he had done it for Albert a couple of times.

Albert wasn't on punishment, so he was allowed to work. There wasn't much work that was suitable for a chokey cell and a man who wasn't allowed tools. There were mailbags, though. If you sewed a certain number each week, you got wages. Not much, probably about a pound, but you would be able to buy sugar for your porridge and jam to go with your bread and marge. Great treats for a man in solitary. Working also helped to pass the time.

Albert wasn't very competent at sewing. He seemed to be all fingers and thumbs, and, pretty soon, one of the fingers or thumbs would be pierced by a needle. So, instead of sewing, Albert was given the job of waxing the thread.

Mailbag thread had to be waterproofed with black wax before being used. Albert had a large ball of brown twine and a pair of old blunt-ended scissors. He would cut the twine into 30-inch lengths, then pull each length through a notch in a block of black wax. It was a messy job and, before long, his fingers and hands would be black with wax.

As Albert collected his dinner one day, he noticed that the old screw wasn't dressed to leave like the other screws. He was lounging around in the vicinity of the office. Albert surmised that he would be on over the dinnertime bang-up.

As soon as he was behind his door, Albert picked up the old scissors. He climbed on his chair to stand at the window. He began to sharpen one blade of the scissors on the stone sill. Within ten minutes, it was gleaming brightly.

By now, the rest of the screws had left the chokey for their dinner. Only the old fat one remained. Albert waited a further ten minutes. Then he rang his bell and banged on his door. After a few seconds, the old screw was outside.

'What do you want?' he said, pushing Albert's cell flag up.

'I'm busting for a shit,' said Albert. 'It must have been something I just ate.'

The screw drew the bolt back, turned the lock and pushed the door open. 'Don't be too long,' he said, as he turned his back and returned to the office. Seating himself at the desk again, he continued to read a paper.

Albert stepped outside his cell. He looked across to the office and saw that the old screw wasn't even watching. No doubt he would wait for Albert to bang his door up before coming out to check.

Albert re-entered his cell and grabbed the wax block. Quickly, he rubbed it all over his face and neck. Then he rubbed it into his hair, making it very greasy. He took small tufts in his fingers and twisted them so that they stood out from his head like spikes.

He looked like some large malevolent gollywog, but there was nothing cuddly or toy-like about him. The sight that looked back at him from the mirror was frightening, which was exactly the reaction that Albert was seeking to provoke.

Satisfied with his handiwork, Albert took the scissors in his right hand, left the cell and walked quickly to the office. Hurrying inside, he turned and shut the door behind him. Then, with his back still turned, he manoeuvred a large filing cabinet in front of the door.

Hearing the noise, the screw looked up from his paper sharply. Albert turned and, uttering a bloodcurdling scream, ran at the man. Quite involuntarily, the screw screamed also.

The blackened face was suddenly close to his ear as a powerful arm closed around his head. He felt a sharp object prick his exposed neck. He started crying, then blubbering.

'What's the number of Security?' growled Albert in the screw's ear.

The screw was literally too terrified to speak. Losing patience, Albert noticed a list of phone numbers on the desk, next to the phone. He looked down it until he came to 'Security Office'. He dialled the number.

After several rings, he heard a voice at the other end. 'Now listen very carefully,' hissed Albert. 'This is Albert ... in the chokey block. I've got your screw hostage with some sharpened scissors at his throat. If you don't do exactly as I say, I'll kill the bastard.'

Albert paused, then continued. 'Send someone over here immediately. I want to talk. I've got the door barricaded and, if you try to break in, I'll cut his fucking throat.' With that, he put the phone down.

He knew he had a few minutes before anyone arrived. He took a roll of sellotape from a desk drawer and bound the screw hand and foot. Then he piled more furniture, including the desk, against the office door.

Just as he finished, he heard the chokey gate open. Pulling the screw to his feet, Albert pushed him up against the office windows. He held him around the neck with one hand, while the other pressed the scissors against the side of his face. The old screw was still blubbering with fear.

As Albert looked through the windows on to the landing, the security PO stepped into view. He seemed to be on his own, but Albert guessed that dozens more screws would be further down the chokey, out of sight.

The PO looked shocked as he saw the frightening, black-faced man in the office. He carefully scrutinised the old screw, making sure that he hadn't been harmed. Then he put his head close to the barricaded door. 'What is it you want?' he asked.

'I want a closed van, backed right up to the gates of the chokey,' said Albert. 'I also want a helicopter waiting in the car park. Any bollocks at all and I'll kill your man here. Now do it.'

'You'll have to give me a little bit of time,' said the PO. 'You'll get what you want, so don't do anything silly in the meantime.' With that, he turned and walked back down the corridor.

Since he had left, the chief had joined the group of screws waiting out of sight. The PO now told him what he had seen in the office. Leaving strict instructions that no one was to go near the office, they both left the chokey.

When they got outside, the chief took a radio from his belt. He spoke into it, telling the control room that the hostage-taking had been confirmed. 'After you've informed the police, get someone over here with his record,' he ordered. Then he settled back to wait with the PO. Albert's record arrived at the same time as the governor. The chief took it from the screw, then sent him away. There was a four-wheeled barrow parked against the chokey wall. The chief laid the file in the barrow and the governor and the PO gathered round to read its contents.

It soon become clear that they weren't dealing with any ordinary prisoner. Apart from the catalogue of terrorist offences and his normal army training, Albert had also undergone 'Special Forces' training at Fort Bragg in the United States. He wasn't exactly SAS, but he was no ordinary soldier either. They were dealing with a man who had been trained for just the sort of situation they now had on their hands.

Twenty minutes passed and the chief's radio crackled into life, advising him that the police were at the gate. He gave permission to let them in. Two blue Transit vans drove slowly through the grounds. The jail was deserted. All the rest of the cons had been locked up for the duration of the incident.

The vans pulled up just short of the three men by the barrow. An inspector got out and walked over to join them. After a few brief introductions, the chief explained the situation.

The inspector went back to the vans and ordered his men to deploy. Police wearing bulky flak jackets and carrying rifles or pistols scrambled from the vans. Some took up positions both sides of the chokey gate. Two were taken through into the small exercise yard that was overlooked by the office's external window. Others went inside the chokey to join the group of screws already there.

Back in the office, Albert was well aware that now was a very dangerous time for him. He realised that, if he gave them the chance, they would shoot him. Dragging the screw into the corner of the office furthest from the door, he huddled behind him, his back against the outside wall of the chokey.

If they tried to shoot him through the inside windows, he was protected by the screw's body. If they tried to shoot him through the small external office window, they would have to shoot blind, because he was pressed up tight against the back wall.

For the moment, he was safe. But the crucial point would be when he left the office with his hostage and climbed into the back of the van. He needed some kind of extra insurance.

He scrambled forward and snatched the phone off the floor where it had fallen. He dialled the 'Security Office' number again.

Albert spoke as it was answered. 'As soon as the van arrives and is backed up tight against the gates, I want four prisoners to act as go-betweens. Tell them to come to the office windows. When everything is ready, ring me here. I don't want anyone else coming to the window. Understand?'

Security relayed Albert's latest message to the chief. At first, he was alarmed but, when he thought about it more carefully, he could see the possibility of a manoeuvre.

Luckily for them, Albert had come straight to the chokey on arrival. He had no friends in the jail; in fact, he knew no one. If he had, he could possibly have named four staunch fellas who would automatically have sided with him against the screws and the police.

As Albert didn't know anyone, this meant that the chief could pick the four go-betweens himself. At first, he toyed with the idea of using screws or police, dressed up as cons. But they all looked well nourished and had short haircuts and colour in their faces. There was no way that they could imitate the prison pallor and the drained, strained look so prevalent among Parkhurst cons. No, it would have to be other prisoners.

The answer was right on top of him. Quite literally. The landing above Albert's was the Rule 43 protection landing. The cons on it were either bad nonces or grasses, who would have been beaten up on the wings. They would languish on the 43 landing, totally segregated from the other cons, until the authorities decided to move them to another jail.

Understandably, their regime was very restricted. They had a small workshop and limited association facilities, but very little else. Consequently, they were banged up most of the time.

The chief was a sly, devious man, who had been in the Prison Service for many years. For him, treachery had become something of an art form. He could pinpoint a man's weaknesses and exploit them to the full. He would find four men from the 43s to do his bidding.

There were 12 men on the 43 landing. The chief had the records of all of them brought to him. He didn't want men who had so long still to do that he couldn't offer them anything. He also didn't want men who obviously looked like nonces or grasses.

When he had selected four, he went to see each of them personally. All were offered an immediate release in return for their assistance. All readily agreed.

The phone rang in the chokey office. Albert scrambled to pick it up. The voice at the other end said that a van had been backed up to the chokey gates, with its back doors wide open. There was a helicopter waiting in the car park outside. Lastly, the four cons that Albert had asked for were on their way to the office now

Albert stood up, pulling the screw up with him. He cut the tape from around the screw's feet. 'Don't do anything brave,' threatened Albert, 'or I swear to God I'll cut your throat.'

Through the office window, he could see four cons standing outside. They all looked a bit cowed and shifty, but he put that down to their unease at being involved in such a dangerous situation.

Pushing the screw in front of him, Albert approached the office door. He could see that, other than the four cons, there was no one in the immediate vicinity of the office. He unbarricaded the door.

Opening it slightly, he asked each of the cons their name and how long they were doing. 'What I want you to do, boys, is walk with me to the back of the van and check that nobody is inside it before I get in.'

What Albert also wanted, but didn't see fit to mention, was a shield of four extra bodies around him on the walk from the office to the van – just in case someone tried to shoot him. He was well aware that, by now, police snipers would be in position.

The four cons nodded in agreement. Albert pulled the office door open. Holding the screw close to him with one arm, he held the scissors to his throat with the other. Slowly, he emerged from the office.

He looked down the landing and was relieved to see that it was deserted. The back of a large van yawned darkly at him through the opened chokey gates.

Positioning a con in front and back and on either side, Albert moved slowly and cautiously towards the van. Every dozen feet or so, he stopped and carefully looked around for any surreptitious movement. He was relieved to see that all the cell doors on either side were banged shut. This meant that he only had to watch out for an attack from the front or rear.

About ten feet from the back of the van he stopped again. He peered carefully into the darkness to make sure that it was really empty. The back doors nearly protruded into the chokey, so he didn't have to worry about someone standing flush against the outside wall having a clear shot at him as he entered the van.

When he was sure that the van was empty, he motioned to the two cons on either side to join the one at the front. He shuffled the last ten feet to the chokey gate.

He could now see that, although the floor of the van was almost level with the floor of the chokey, the stone steps leading down to the roadway had prevented the van from being backed up flush with the chokey floor. There was a gap of about three feet.

Whether Albert decided to walk down the three steps and

climb into the van or just jump straight across, he would have to let go of the screw for a few seconds.

The three leading cons all jumped into the back of the van. This seemed to make up Albert's mind for him. He pushed the screw bodily across the gap and into the van. He jumped after him.

With his hands tied behind him, the screw plunged headlong towards the interior of the van. Several things now happened simultaneously.

As Albert launched himself across the gap, the three cons turned and threw themselves on him. The fourth con jumped on his back as the front doors flew open to admit several large athletic-looking coppers. Albert disappeared under a welter of bodies.

With his hostage gone and a pair of blunt-ended scissors his only weapon, Albert was clearly finished. He struggled briefly, then gave up, allowing himself to be pummelled by the men on top of him.

A pair of handcuffs pinned his hands behind his back and he was pulled unceremoniously back into the chokey.

Dozens of screws now appeared and several threw punches at him, but the presence of the other cons seemed to inhibit them a bit. He was pushed roughly along the corridor to the strip cells. They tore off all his clothes, ripping them to pieces. They took the cuffs off and threw him naked into the bare strip cell.

As Albert contemplated the end of a brief dream and the beginning of a long, cold night naked on a bare stone floor, up on the 43 landing four cons contemplated the prospect of their release the following morning. Albert had one consolation, though. Now he was certain to be moved from Parkhurst.

Perhaps there was something in Albert's allegations of collusion between his UVF group and the security forces. While every other lifer with a minimum recommendation has served his full term, rumour has it that Albert was released, despite the fact that there were several years of his 25-year minimum recommendation still to go.

13 FREEDOM BEYOND

News of the hostage-taking incident soon filtered up from the chokey to the wings. Whatever the nature of Albert's offence, we all had considerable sympathy for his predicament. We, too, had spent long periods in the chokey. We well knew the damage it could do to a man. I, personally, had spent long months in the chokey, a couple of years previously at Albany.

From the day I was arrested, all my energies had been concentrated on trying to escape. After all, I could hardly just sit still and watch my youth drain away. But it was far from easy to escape from the top-security jails, and Albany was state-of-the-art as far as security was concerned.

I managed to move on to 'E' wing, which was the closest to the perimeter fence. Once I got out of the wing, there would only be a short distance to travel to get to the fence, thus cutting down the risk of bumping into patrolling screws.

There were still several major problems to be overcome, though. First, I had to find a way to get out of the wing. The walls were made of specially hardened German bricks, and to dig through them would take ages and would be very noisy. The window bars were of manganese steel, uncuttable by any blade.

Then, as any escape would have to be made at night, I would have to find a way to climb down to the ground from my cell on the fours, a drop of at least 35 feet.

The next obstacle would be the inner perimeter fence. This stood all of 24 feet high and was topped with a roll of barbed wire. Halfway up the fence was strung another roll of special razor wire. Every 20 feet or so, there was an electronic 'trembler' bell, which would ring in the control room the moment anyone touched the fence. Beneath the gravel path running alongside the fence were buried geophonic detectors which would go off the second anyone stepped on the gravel. Along its complete length, the fence was bathed in the glare of bright lights and scanned by closed-circuit TV cameras. It would be impossible to sneak out of the jail unnoticed.

The outer perimeter fence stood 20 feet beyond the inner one. It had no barbed wire on top, but did have the roll of razor wire halfway up.

Beyond that lay freedom. But 'freedom' was a field that lay in a triangle between three prisons. Parkhurst lay 400 yards to the east and Camp Hill 500 yards to the north. Clearly, I could only run south.

The final problem would be to get off the Island itself. It was a four-mile swim to the nearest point on the mainland, in waters that were beset with dangerous currents, and through one of the busiest shipping lanes in the world. Only a desperate man would even contemplate it.

I was desperate enough, though. I would rather die than just watch my life ebb away. I set about overcoming the various problems. There was plenty of escape expertise among my fellow cons at Albany, but I couldn't just wander around asking everyone. Luckily, there was one old boy called Fred who lived on my landing. He was a store of information and very trustworthy. His help was to prove invaluable.

I also needed a partner. A ladder long enough to reach the top of the first fence would be heavy, and would take two of us to throw it up. Gary was a young fella who lived on the same floor as me, but along the adjoining spur. He immediately expressed a strong interest in escaping, too.

Fred suggested that we use a carborundum stone to cut the bars. This oblong-shaped block, usually used for sharpening chisels, would certainly be hard enough to cut manganese steel; it would also be very quiet. However, it promised to be a long, slow process.

A 24-foot-long ladder would be needed for the fences. We would climb on to the top of the first fence, pulling the ladder up after us. Then we would use it to climb down the first fence and up the second. As there weren't any 24-foot ladders lying about in Albany, we would have to make one. Then there would be the problem of hiding it in a wing that was searched twice a day.

Several fellas on the wing were into keeping and breeding birds. Some had built large aviary-type cages in their cells, containing budgies, cockatiels and finches. I hated the thought of all the noise and mess myself, but, in the interest of the escape, I would suffer it.

Plywood and short lengths of wood were regularly smuggled out of the carpentry section of the woodmill opposite 'E' wing. The screws knew the wood was used as hobbies material and largely ignored the smuggling because it gave people something to do and kept them quiet.

I got several large sections of ply and some two-by-two. The birdcage I constructed was 6' 3" long, 2' 6" high and 2' 6" deep, with a long wire-mesh front. I built a false bottom into it, which gave me a secret compartment 6' 3" long, 2' 6" deep and 3" high. This was where I intended to hide the ladder.

It would have to be in sections. It would be impossible to smuggle a 24-foot length of timber out of the woodmill, even if there was one that long in there.

We waited until there was a particularly thick screw in charge of wing cleaning, then told him that we needed to go over to the woodmill to have a couple of broken brooms repaired. With

Gary and I carrying the broken brooms, the screw escorted us to the woodmill.

We waited while the job was done, then, just as we were leaving, a friend of mine came up to us with an armful of timber. 'Do us a favour, fellas,' said Jonah. 'Take this wood over to the dining hall, will you? It's needed to make some shelving.'

'I ain't fucking carrying it,' said Gary, according to our prearranged plan.

'Give it here,' I said, in a tone that indicated I was disgusted with Gary's negative attitude. 'Here you are, guvnor. You carry some and I'll carry some.'

I handed a couple of lengths to the screw and picked up the rest myself. The lumpen screw said not a word. Perhaps it was my assertive manner: he was used to obeying orders.

'OK, guv,' I said as we arrived back on the wing, 'I'll take it across to the dining hall.'

To my surprise, the screw readily agreed, then wandered off. That had been the crucial point of the operation. We had doubted that any screw would be thick enough to leave us in possession of four six-foot lengths of four by two.

We hurried upstairs to my cell. I quickly took off the fascia panel on the front of the cage, revealing the secret compartment. I slid the lengths inside.

We now had enough wood to make one continuous 24-foot length, but we had to find a way to join the lengths together. I made three 'sleeves', each two feet long, out of thick plywood. I lightly nailed thin ply over the open ends into which the lengths of four by two would slide. Then I put the 'sleeves' in the cage and stood several food pots on them.

This would now give me one continuous 24-foot length to climb the first fence with, but there were no hand- or footholds. I made eight triangles out of six-ply at a hobbies class, saying that I was constructing a geometrical solid as a mobile to hang in my cell. The instructor obviously had a limited knowledge of solid geometry. I walked unchallenged from the class with the triangles that I would screw to the lengths of four by two for handholds. We had our ladder. All that was missing from the cage were the birds that would justify its existence.

I had noticed that most cockatiels I had seen were both bad-tempered and vicious. A bite from one could be quite serious. I bought a large young bird with a thoroughly homicidal bent. 'Nice' would sit in the cage, almost immobile, until someone was fool enough to put his hand in. Then the bird would fall on it in a frenzy of biting, leaving the intruder with a sore and bleeding hand.

I surrounded Nice with six zebra finches who would make a break for the door the second the cage was opened. The screws on searching duty soon learned just to look into the cage without poking about. There wasn't much to see anyway. The false bottom was largely an optical illusion, concealed by the long fascia panel.

It was Fred who solved the problem of how to climb down from my cell to the ground. He stole some webbing from the shop where they made knapsacks. Other than the fact that it was elasticated, it was ideal and strong enough to hold a horse.

That only left the problem of getting off the Island. We did have some outside help, but we could hardly ask them to come on to the Island, because they would be trapped with us the moment it was sealed off. I had noticed on a map in a book by the sailor Chay Blyth that there was a lifeboat station not far from the jail. We resolved to drag the lifeboatman out of his bed in the middle of the night and force him to take us across. Failing that, we would just steal one of the thousands of boats anchored along the Island's coast.

We started to cut my bars with the carborundum block. As expected, it was long, slow work, but, with Gary and I taking turns, and with Fred watching out for the screws, we gradually wore our way through the metal. Each night, I would dummy the bar up with Polyfilla and paint it the same colour as the bars.

Suddenly, there was a security alert. Some fool on another wing had been caught tampering with his bars. We heard that there was to be an intensive bar check using sophisticated electronic equipment. Time was now of the essence.

My bars were now cut, so we dispensed with the plan to cut Gary's as well. Instead, we would cut the ordinary steel frames of our respective doors, just where the locks slid into them. We did this in a surprisingly short time, concealing the cuts with painted cardboard. By late afternoon we were finished.

The wait until nine o'clock bang-up was nerve-wracking in the extreme. If either of us had been subjected to one of the regular special searches, the game would have been up. Gary and I sat in the darkness of the TV room, hoping that out of sight was out of mind.

Just before nine, Gary and I both banged our own doors shut, then waited for the screw to check us through the spy-hole and put the bolt on. This passed without incident. We were safe for the moment.

For weeks now, we had been checking the times of the passing patrols. By 2.00 a.m., the jail was silent and the patrols intermittent. At 2.30 a.m. we made our move.

Gary pulled his door inwards, the lock and bolt both passing easily through the dummy cardboard. He padded around the landing to my cell, withdrew the bolt and pushed the unresisting door inwards.

I had already removed the lengths of four by two from the secret compartment, screwed the triangular 'steps' to them and fixed a 'sleeve' to each of three ends. 'Nice' the cockatiel, not at all amused at being disturbed at this unearthly hour, created a din that threatened to wake the wing.

The knapsack webbing was tied to the bars, trailing out the window to the ground. I sellotaped the small screwdriver to the inside of my left arm. A homemade knife was taped to the inside of my right.

I climbed, feet first, out of my window. It was only a narrow gap and the sawn bar bit into my chest. With Gary pushing on my shoulders, I suddenly slid free. I clutched frantically at the webbing rope as I plunged earthwards.

I seemed to be falling for ages, but this was due to the elasticity of the webbing. Eventually, I bobbed up and down on the exposed wall of the wing, 30 feet from the ground and bathed in the glare of the lights.

Bobbing and turning on the webbing, I climbed to the ground. As I passed the security cage that protected the window of one of the nonces on the twos, I banged into it, waking the fella inside. I saw him come to his window and watch me.

Now on the ground, I called up to Gary. One by one, he threw down the lengths of ladder to me. They smashed into my outstretched arms with surprising force. By the time he had climbed down to join me, the ladder was assembled and ready to go. We set off across the short distance to the first fence.

As we emerged from the cover of the building, it was as if we were stepping out on to a stage. The lights blinded us and made us feel terribly exposed. Every camera seemed to be trained on us.

Any system is only as efficient as the people who operate it, though, and this system was operated by Albany screws. Luckily for us, it was 'situation normal' in the control room: feet up and heads down. A brass band could have marched along the fence and they would have missed it.

Unfortunately, however, the nonce I had woken was also a grass. He had rung his bell the moment he had seen us. It was only because the screw had taken so long to answer it that we had got so far undisturbed.

We threw the ladder up against the first fence with an impact that must have sent every trembler bell ringing. I raced up the rungs. Suddenly, there was a shout from over to our right. Two screws accompanied by dogs emerged from a nearby workshop. They were hatless and with their shirts undone. They must have been having a sly sleep in the shop.

I carried on upwards, hoping I could reach the top before they pulled the ladder away, pitching me into the hanging razor wire underneath. I was conscious of Gary climbing below me. I jumped into the roll of barbed wire atop the fence.

All at once, there was a sharp crack as the ladder snapped. I looked down in time to see the screws throw their weight against it, sending Gary tumbling to land at their feet. Both dogs ran in and pinned him to the ground.

I was safe for the moment, but marooned on top of the fence. I had no ladder now, but there was still a contingency plan. Using the knife and screwdriver still taped to my arms, I might be able to climb the second fence.

Bending down, I gripped the top of the fence. I rolled forward, kicking my legs free of the barbed wire. My lower body crashed into the fence as I hung there by my fingertips. I looked down to see where the ground was, but the grass was long between the fences and the night dark. Everything was blackness. I let go of the fence, hoping for the best.

I had bound my ankles with tape in readiness for just such a drop, but it still jarred me to the bone. I felt one of my ankles go but, as I rose to my feet, I could feel that it was badly sprained rather than broken. I looked up to see both screws standing barely a yard away from me, but separated by the fence.

Hobbling now, I stumbled across to the second fence. I tore the knife from my arm and felt in my pocket for the screwdriver. It was gone. It had obviously fallen out. I looked around frantically. It would be impossible to find in the long grass in the darkness. My escape was over.

The rest was all anticlimax. Eventually, a posse of screws came between the fences and got me. I was led away to the chokey. I was subsequently sentenced to 15 days' bread and water and 56 days in the block. Gary avoided the bread and water, but lost 180 days' remission. Within a day of our unsuccessful attempt, a rope was found on one of the wings. This was the last straw. The screws decided to do a general search of the jail. They went about it in such a bloody-minded fashion that they triggered off a riot. Soon, the chokey was overflowing. Scores of men languished in solitary confinement.

14 HORACE

After a few weeks in solitary, things that would seem mundane and commonplace to free men have the power to capture the attention out of all proportion to their importance.

About a fortnight before Horace entered our lives, we, on the outward-facing side of the chokey, were treated to an amazing sight. A rat was walking along inside the coiled-up roll of barbed wire that sat on top of the first perimeter fence.

Not only did it look thoroughly incongruous to see a rat 20 feet above the ground negotiating the sharp barbs of this deadly tunnel, but also how it had got up there in the first place puzzled us.

The perimeter fence was free-standing, with no building within 30 feet of it. So the rat must have climbed straight up the 20-foot wire fence, through the hanging roll of razor wire and into the barbed-wire tunnel. No mean feat.

I forget who first noticed it as it passed, but we all came to our windows to watch this unusual event. Within a few minutes, the rat had disappeared from view. Some fellas returned to lying on their beds; others stood at their windows making desultory conversation.

Several hours passed. Suddenly a shout was heard. 'There's that fucking rat again!' Wind-ups were common in the chokey, but the urgency of the tone brought us all to our windows. To our utter amazement, the rat came past again, still travelling in an anti-clockwise direction.

It had to be the same rat. Surely there weren't two such intrepid creatures in our jail. Unless it was some new and previously unreported form of rat migration, this rat had made a complete circuit of the jail inside the barbed-wire tunnel.

Now Albany is quite a large jail and, apart from the residential buildings and workshops, there is an extensive sports field. The perimeter, and therefore the perimeter fence, must have been all of 1600 yards long. Yet the rat had travelled this distance walking on barbed-wire.

If you hadn't seen it, you would never have believed it. In fact, it caused arguments with some of the fellas on the inward-facing side, who accused us of trying to wind them up. 'You must think I'm daft,' shouted one fella. It provided a talking point for days.

Due to the totally unstructured nature of our average day, we were accustomed to sleeping at unusual times. Other than mealtimes and exercise, which came with the inevitability of day following night, nothing interrupted the boredom of solitary. Time stretched out in front of us in an unbroken continuum.

Often we stood at our windows, talking into the early hours of the morning. One good thing about Albany was that the cell windows were massive. With the sill at waist height, they measured a good three foot six square. Twelve small glass panes surrounded a larger, sliding window that allowed fresh air into the cell. It was possible to stick your head through this gap and look as far as the eye could see to the right or left.

At night, standing at the window, talking in undertones, you were struck by the peace and tranquillity of a place that was as noisy as a train station during the day. Looking up at the vast inky blackness of the heavens, you couldn't help but feel very small. All this pain and torment that we were going through seemed so important, so momentous to our lives. Yet, in the face of the great infinity, the grand scheme of things, one could only conclude that it was all monumentally insignificant.

The night-time was a time of peace for us. Daytime was the time of shouting and madness. At night, we would commune with the refreshing cool of the moonlight and gather our strength against another day in the chokey.

Like any other group of buildings in the countryside, Albany had quite a selection of wildlife. Not its fair share by any means, because of the security fences. However, there were many mice and rats and the occasional snake. These creatures would hide away during the day. As darkness fell and the grounds became deserted, they would venture out to forage.

Albany was a far from normal habitat for them. The 60-foot light masts cast a brilliant glare over most of the jail. It was only in the lee of the buildings that there were patches of shadow and darkness, and it was here that the small creatures would nervously scamper. All moved furtively and overly cautiously – all except Horace, that is. Horace was a small dun-coloured fieldmouse, who was either very brave, very hungry or very stupid. As things turned out, there was a strong possibility that he was all three.

I saw Horace first. I was standing at my window in the early hours one morning, talking quietly to Aussie in the next cell. Suddenly, I heard a slight rustling in the grass. I stopped talking and looked carefully. I saw a small brownish fieldmouse step out on to the flagstone path that ran between the outward-facing side of the chokey and a corrugated tin fence, fixed to concrete posts. The fence was about eight feet high, with the tin reaching down to a couple of feet from the ground. Its purpose was to prevent us from looking straight out at, and through, the perimeter fence.

Thus, the path lay in an alley some six feet wide. Along its length, it was littered with detritus thrown out of cell windows.

There were the remains of the past week's meals, scattered haphazardly: small pieces of potato, duff, peas and bread. To a fieldmouse, it must have looked like a banquet.

Very quietly, I called to Aussie. 'Nitto the mouse on the edge of the path.'

There was a pause. Then I heard him say, 'I see it.'

Suddenly, the boredom of the night was broken as we became engrossed in secretly watching the fieldmouse going about its nightly business. Hardly drawing breath, we watched, terrified that some sudden sound would send it scampering back into the darkness, leaving us alone with our boredom again.

Totally oblivious of us, Horace ambled down the pathway. He paused at a dry crust just past Aussie Goodwin's window. He had a quick nibble, but most of the discarded food lay further down the path. Horace advanced another ten feet, then stopped to eat at a mess of scraps. After a few minutes, he proceeded further until he was three-quarters of the way down the path. He continued to feed.

Finally, having finished eating, he returned the way he had come. Quite unhurriedly, and still totally unaware of our watching eyes, he trotted back up the path. Pausing for a last look back, he forced his way through the tufts of grass fringing the top of the path, and disappeared.

The following morning, we told the others about the mouse and its night-time feeding habits. Jokingly, I referred to it as 'Horace' and the name stuck. That night, everyone wanted to see Horace and his antics.

There were eight cells on the outward-facing side of the chokey. As darkness fell that night, there were eight men standing at their windows waiting to see Horace.

As I stood at my window talking softly to Aussie, I could hear Scouse Roy and Andy Townsend further down. From time to time, snatches of other conversations could be heard, carried on the occasional breeze.

'Norman, Norman,' came the insistent call from further down beyond Aussie. It sounded like Scouse.

'What?' I asked.

'What time did you see Horace last night?'

'Well, I ain't got a watch, Scouse, but it was very late. Certainly after midnight.'

'Fuck standing here waiting,' Scouse moaned. 'Someone give me a call when Horace arrives.'

A couple of the fellas laughed.

'By the way,' I added while I still had an audience, 'no throwing anything at him. Otherwise he won't come back.'

Sometime in the early hours, I heard the rustling again. I looked carefully and saw Horace emerging from the long grass. Quickly, I alerted Aussie, who passed the warning on down the line.

Exactly as before, Horace came down the path. This time, though, almost as if he knew he was putting on a show, he skipped and scampered from scrap to scrap. He rolled peas with his paws and sat back on his haunches to eat a tit-bit, all in a thoroughly laidback, unhurried manner. Horace obviously thought he hadn't an enemy in the world.

This extended feast lasted about 20 minutes, and took Horace nearly to the bottom of the path, where it ended in the blank wall of the jutting boiler house. With no more territory to explore, he returned the way he had come, giving every one of us a good view of him as he passed our windows. As he disappeared into the grass at the top of the path, there was an audible expelling of breath which we all had been holding in lest we scare him.

Admittedly, it wasn't David Attenborough, and it didn't have the detailed close-ups of a nature programme, but for us cons in the chokey suffering from terminal boredom, it was great theatre. We talked animatedly of Horace and laughed at his antics.

Perhaps realising that it wouldn't last, that Horace would find new pastures or that someone would scare him, I suddenly had an idea. 'Hey, fellas, how about we have a competition to catch

Horace? Any way you like, so long as you get him into your cell.'
There was enthusiastic agreement. Not only would it give us
something to do, planning the traps, but it would also be funny
to watch.

I lay down to think about how I was going to go about it. I was
always going to be at least six feet from Horace, well beyond the
reach of an arm. Anything held on the end of a stick would have
to be moved swiftly and accurately to catch a nimble fieldmouse.
Horace was a very laidback mouse, but I couldn't see him calmly
strolling down the path beneath a hovering butterfly net. No, it
would have to be a ground-level trap.

Casting my mind back to Saturday-morning picture shows and
the way the natives had performed in the Tarzan films, I had an
idea. They had laid a net on the ground with ropes attached to the
four corners. When the prey stepped on to the net, they quickly
pulled up the ropes. I had my plan. No doubt the others had
theirs, but my cell was nearest the top of the path. I would have
first crack at Horace.

During the day, work parties occasionally passed our side of the
chokey. I could see them from my window, before they became
obscured by the corrugated fence. They would always have a
screw with them. If he was half-decent, the cons would sometimes
be allowed to stop and talk for a few seconds. They would give us
news and relay messages.

If the screw was unusually decent, some of the party would
come to my window and pass me a box of goodies that the fellas
up the wings had clubbed together to get for us. Afterwards, I
would share out sweets, biscuits, jam and so on between all the
fellas in the chokey. It was a risky, hit-or-miss business. All our side
of the chokey was scanned by the TV cameras covering the
perimeter fence. A screw spotted letting his party talk with the
cons in the punishment block could get a rollicking over his radio
from the control room. At present, though, they were trying not
to provoke us. We had been comparatively quiet for a while. A box

of goodies into the chokey now and again was a small price to pay for an easy life.

The following morning, I stood at my window to catch a passing work party. After quite a while, one came by and I called out to a fella I knew. He looked sideways at the screw accompanying them, then hurried over to my window.

'Do me a favour,' I said. 'When you go round the back of the kitchen, get me a piece of an onion bag. You know, the netting bags they put the onions in. A bit about a yard square will do.'

The fella looked quite bemused by this strange request. I could see him trying to figure out what I wanted it for. He didn't like to ask and seem nosy. I didn't fancy explaining. If I'd told him I wanted it to catch a mouse, he'd probably have thought that I was cracking up. I could imagine the rumour going around the jail. 'Poor Norman. He's only been down the block a month and his head is going already. He's started collecting fieldmice.'

About an hour later, the party came back again. The fella called to me and, when I came to my window, he hurried over and thrust a yard-square piece of onion bag netting into my hands. Other than that it was bright red in colour, it was ideal. I thanked him, then sat down on my bed to make the trap.

I spread the netting out on the bed. Thankfully, it was roughly square in shape as I didn't have anything to cut it with. The rest would be quite simple. I had a reel of thick black thread. All I would have to do would be to break off four ten-foot lengths and tie an end to each corner of the netting.

I had been sitting there contemplating the problem for no more than a minute, when the door burst open. Reflexively, I leaped up and faced the doorway. I thought for a moment that it was the heavy mob coming in to do me.

Standing at the front of a group of three screws was Punchy, the SO in charge of the block. I immediately relaxed a bit. I was of the opinion that there are only two kinds of screws: dogs and men. Punchy was a man, and a man's man at that. A short, stocky fella of about 40, he had been a professional boxer, and had a badly broken nose and heavy scar tissue around his eyes to prove it. With his craggy chin and broad shoulders, he looked a right handful. Confident of his own manliness, he didn't try to degrade us like some of the more inadequate screws did. He was always fair and treated us with respect. Consequently, we respected him.

Bearing in mind the situation, this was quite remarkable. By now, every one of us cons hated every one of the screws with an intensity born of pain and desperation. The torture of solitary had brought us to a pitch where we could have killed our tormentors and their entire families without the slightest remorse. Sometimes such intense, insane hatred gave us pause. We wondered what we were becoming that we could contemplate such acts in cold blood. But the imperative of trying to find the willpower to survive another day in the chokey made us put these thoughts out of our minds as just another aberration of the bizarre existence we led.

Punchy had won our respect in the early days of the riot. The heavy mob would regularly drag someone down to the chokey, beating them all the way. Once inside, they would really go to town. The fella would be carried along, face down, with a screw holding each arm and leg. A fifth screw twisted on a damp towel wound around his neck. A sixth would run behind, kicking the fella in the bollocks. A couple more would be at each side, beating him about the kidneys with their sticks. Eight to one were the odds they usually liked.

At one end of the chokey were the strip cells. The fella would be carried down a narrow corridor and deposited unceremoniously on the floor. The screws would literally tear all his clothes off, then throw him naked into the bare cell until the following morning. Often, they would follow him in and continue to beat him.

On this particular occasion, Punchy was on duty. The alarm bell sounded and the chokey screws ran around banging up anyone who was out for any reason. One ran down and opened the door to the strip cell. Punchy and two more screws walked down to stand with him.

My cell was strategically placed so that I could see both the entrance to the chokey and the long corridor that led to the strip cells. I could only squint through the pin-hole in the spy-hole cover, so my view was restricted. However, it was enough to allow me to see the majority of the action.

The double doors of the chokey burst open. A bunch of dark-blue uniforms surged in. In their midst was a figure held horizontally. They were flailing away at it with their sticks, fists and boots.

It was impossible to hear anything, because the minute the screws burst through the doors, the fellas had started. We were very solid down the block. Our loyalty to each other was a fine and beautiful thing.

With a bunch of screws beating up a fellow con outside your door, the natural thing to do was to keep quiet in case they started on you. We always did the opposite. We would smash on our doors with our fists, feet or chairs to attract their attention. It would also attract attention to what they were doing. At the same time, we would shout and scream abuse at them. 'You dirty cowardly fuckers!' 'Come in here, you stinking bastards!' Anything to try to distract them from what they were doing.

Mostly it was futile. The screws would just carry on. But it was better than sitting there in silence, listening to the screams of the fella being beaten. And it was good for our morale.

This time, as the crowd drew closer, I recognised several faces. This was the heavy mob of screw bullies who regularly beat up people on the wings. They never worked in the chokey. The governor realised that there would be outright revolt if they did, hand-to-hand fighting every time they opened us up. The regular chokey screws were older, more decent men.

I tried to see the con's face as he was carried past, but it was obscured by all the bodies. They funnelled into the corridor leading to the strip cells, still beating and kicking him in the confined space.

Punchy had been standing quietly at the end of the corridor. As the crowd came into view, his face suddenly contorted in rage. He ran along the corridor to meet them.

There were some big screws in the heavy mob, but they were fat and unfit. The impact of Punchy's short, powerful physique was devastating. Large uniformed figures flew everywhere. He didn't punch anyone; he didn't have to. A couple he just pushed over. Another he grabbed by the throat. 'You aren't doing that in my fucking chokey!' he roared, hoarse with rage.

The heavy mob immediately backed off. The regular chokey screws, coming from behind Punchy, picked up the con from where he lay on the ground. They helped him towards the strip cells and half-carried him inside. Gently, they took his clothes off. A couple stayed with him while Punchy went to the office to phone for the doctor, who later examined him and pronounced him OK. He had some bruises and grazes, but no major injuries. They gave the con some blankets, then banged him up for the night.

For several days afterwards, Punchy's 'rescue' was the talk of the chokey. We had booked him as being a decent fella, a man of principle. Now we knew he would back his principles with action. From then on, whenever Punchy was on duty, the heavy mob never tried to beat anyone inside the chokey.

All this came back to me as I saw Punchy standing there backed by three screws. But just because he was fair didn't mean he was weak. Whatever he had on his mind, it looked serious.

'Parker, I've had a phone call from Security that something was just passed to you through your window,' he said. 'I've been ordered to confiscate it'

I immediately realised that either the screw with the work party had reported it or one of the perimeter cameras had picked it up.

They were obviously still very worried about me following my recent elaborate escape attempt. In my hands, quite innocent-looking objects could have a thoroughly nefarious purpose.

What had started out as a prank to pass the time now looked like leading me into a serious confrontation. Punchy was clearly in an awkward position. He looked at the netting lying on the bed and was puzzled as to what harm I could do with it. However, he had been ordered to take it.

'You'd better have it then, guvnor,' I said, stepping forward and handing him the offending netting.

He took it quickly, muttered, 'Thank you,' and backed out of the cell, banging the door after him.

That was me out of the competition to catch Horace.

Later that afternoon, Aussie called me to the window. 'Here, Norman, have a look at that silly bastard, Scouse.'

I stuck my head through the bars and looked towards the far end of the path. Scouse's cell was about three-quarters of the way down. I could see a large white piece of material lying on the path. Scouse was poking at it with a broomstick.

I guessed it was a plate cloth, a two-foot-square piece of hemmed cotton that was issued as an all-purpose tea cloth. Attached to each of the four corners were lengths of white string, which ran upwards and disappeared into Scouse's window

The contraption looked a bit like an inverted parachute. It was roughly the same idea that I'd had, with emphasis on the 'roughly'. It was intended that Horace would step on to the plate cloth, at which stage Scouse would pull on the strings. To entice Horace in, Scouse had placed a large piece of cheese right in the middle.

It all sounded great in theory, but the trap was both cumbersome and threatening. It would have to be a very thick mouse to fall for that.

'Oi, Scouse!' I shouted.

There was a pause, then he stuck his head out of the window.

'There are two absolute certainties about your trap. The first is that, if Horace steps into it, you'll catch him. The second is that he won't go within a fucking mile of it.'

By now, several of the fellas were looking out of their windows. They all laughed.

'We'll see, we'll see,' said Scouse. He pulled his head back inside, then carried on prodding at the trap with the broomstick.

Within half an hour, tea had arrived. I ate, then settled down on my bed for the evening with a book. Everyone else on my side of the chokey must have been doing the same, because it was very quiet. Nobody was talking out of their windows.

I felt a distinct sense of anticlimax. No one else had declared an interest in trapping Horace and none of us believed Scouse stood an earthly. It would be funny seeing just how close Horace would go, but it wasn't much to look forward to.

Sometime after about ten o'clock, a couple of fellas started a conversation out of the window. I carried on reading. Suddenly, a shout came. 'Hey, here's Horace!'

There was a scrambling sound as several of us jumped up to stand at our windows. But there was no sign of Horace. Someone started laughing further down the chokey. It was obviously a wind-up.

I was annoyed at being caught out, as well as being disturbed. 'Oi, don't fuck about!' I shouted. 'Otherwise, when Horace does come, someone won't take any notice and might scare him away accidentally.' The logic of this must have sunk in because there were no more false alarms. I certainly didn't fancy jumping up and down all night over wind-ups.

It must have been about midnight when I put my book down and stood up at my window. I stared out into the velvety blackness as the cool night air blew in my face.

Suddenly, I heard the grass rustling at the ends of the path. I saw Horace skip out on to the flags. 'Aussie, here's Horace,' I hissed with an urgency that said this was no false alarm.

I heard Aussie quietly calling to the others and could imagine them all scrambling to stand at their windows.

It was deathly quiet. There was an air of tension, of excitement. We had waited hours for this. No one seriously thought that Horace would fall for Scouse's trap, but it would be funny all the same.

Just as before, Horace skipped, ambled and trotted down the path. Stopping here and there to sniff at the odd scrap, he was totally oblivious to the several pairs of watching eyes.

As he drew nearer to Scouse's trap, I hardly dared draw breath. Standing stiff and motionless, I was terrified in case I knocked something and scared him off. It suddenly occurred to me that there must be seven men standing at their windows, just like me. There wasn't a sound on our side of the chokey.

It wasn't a full moon, but there was light enough for the white plate-cloth trap to stand out in stark relief from its surroundings. The strings lay limply on the flagstones, trailing untidily up the wall and disappearing into Scouse's window

Horace stopped a yard from the trap. He remained motionless for several seconds. That's it, I thought, he doesn't fancy it.

What occurred next happened so fast that it was only by discussing it afterwards that we were able to pick out individual events.

Horace darted forwards into the middle of the trap where the cheese was. Instantly, Scouse yanked upwards on the trailing strings. Horace immediately disappeared from view, enfolded by the rising corners of the trap. As Scouse's arm continued to move upwards, so the whole trap rose off the ground.

It now became apparent to those watching that, from this point onwards, Scouse hadn't thought his plan through. Suddenly, his upwardly travelling arm came into sharp contact with the top edge of the window and stopped abruptly. However, the trap, moving under its own momentum now, carried on rising.

But, with no upward pulling force, it soon became subject to the normal laws of gravity. Reaching the top of its trajectory, which was about level with Scouse's window sill, it stopped.

However, Horace, heavier and more compact than the plate-cloth trap, carried on going. We were astounded to see the fieldmouse suddenly appear again, soaring out of the now motionless trap like some rodent astronaut.

Horace now reached the top of this trajectory, too, a good two feet higher than that of the trap. For a split second, he hung motionless in the air. If Scouse had had the presence of mind, he could have leaned out and caught him in his hand. For Horace, though, the only way was down.

He plummeted earthwards. Landing heavily, his legs splayed outwards as he belly-flopped on to the flags. He immediately leaped to his feet and tried to flee, but he was winded, disorientated and had injured one leg. He ran drunkenly in a tight circle, before straightening out and galloping lopsidedly back up the path.

Suddenly, he swerved to one side as a glass bottle shattered nearby. Someone else had had a plan to catch Horace. Brutal in its simplicity, the planner had intended to take him dead or alive.

Horace careered desperately onwards. He hardly checked his flight as a large black boot on the end of several laces thudded into the path behind him. Another crude but deadly plan. Finally, reaching the end of the path, he plunged headlong into the grass. For a few fleeting seconds, we could hear a considerable rumpus as he trampled all before him. Then there was silence.

The chokey erupted. Men, who had been standing stock still for long minutes silently holding their breath, suddenly reacted quite involuntarily. The sheer ridiculous humour of the spectacle exploded out of eight mouths simultaneously in a co-ordinated shriek of laughter.

The sudden roar of sound detonated into the vacuum of the previous silence. One moment there was the dull hum of absolute stillness; the next, an exploding cacophony of sound.

Once started, it went on and on. Eight men shrieked and roared uncontrollably. I ran around my cell like a man demented, flailing my arms in the air, alternately laughing and gasping for breath.

'Did you see that fucking Horace go!' shouted someone, prompting further spasms of laughter.

Suddenly, we became aware of the night screws running from door to door, looking through spy-holes. They had been sitting quietly in their office, probably nodding off in the still of the early hours. With no warning at all, pandemonium had broken out.

They had experienced many bizarre events over the previous weeks in the chokey, but none so immediately noisy and co-ordinated as this. They must have wondered what we were up to this time.

This added even more humour to the situation. If we had told them the true cause – that the disturbance was the result of us trying to catch a mouse – that would have finally convinced them that we were all quite mad.

As time passed, the volume of laughter died down. But, every so often, someone would break out into another paroxysm and start us off again. I felt exhausted, but also exhilarated. We rarely had cause to laugh so heartily in the chokey.

Now we all talked out of our windows about particular details we had seen, laughing all the while. Fellas from the other side of the chokey began calling across, asking what was going on. There were more gales of laughter as our fellas explained.

I never saw Horace again, but I think I heard him. A couple of nights later, as I was standing at my window, I heard some rustling in the grass near where Horace used to come out on to the path. He didn't appear, but the rustling continued alongside and parallel to the path. Horace was taking the jungle trail. It was much safer.

15 THE BOMB

As Albany and Parkhurst were so close together, whatever happened in one was invariably heard about in the other. The fire at Albany was the talk of Parkhurst long before the 17 Albany cons arrived. One of them, Dessie Walton, was well known to our group. He soon filled us in on the fine details. Dessie mortally hated screws. He also hated nonces, grasses and various other prison minority groups, but his special ire was reserved for the screws. He hated them with a passion that permeated his entire being. It was an obsession with him; he thought about them virtually every waking moment.

A lot of fellas hate in prison – it isn't love that's going to get you through. Many also hated the screws; it was quite normal in the circumstances. But they learned to live with it and didn't allow it to consume them.

Dessie, though, resented their very existence. He took it personally every time they locked him up or otherwise curtailed his freedom. And it wasn't a passive hatred either. Dessie did something about it.

He wasn't a naturally hateful fella; in fact, on the out, he was very happy-go-lucky. Originally from Dublin, he had come to

London in his early teens. Now in his late 20s, you could still hear the Irish in him, but he was as streetwise as any Cockney thief. Tall and rangy, with a shock of jet-black hair, and a handsome rascal's face, with eyes that warned of a quicksilver temper, he could be the life and soul of any pub or party, but he was as irresponsible with himself as he was with others.

No great thinker, he quickly gravitated to the heavy. As soon as he realised that the main requirement for armed robbery was plenty of bottle, he was jumping over bank counters with the best of them. His was a wild firm: they stole fast and lived faster. It was only a matter of time before they were nicked. That it was a ready-eye only added insult to injury. They walked right into a trap and got a good beating as well.

Dessie drew a 15. His free spirit and fiery Irish temper didn't lend themselves to prison. He was only in Wanno a day before he chinned a screw and took a quick trip to the chokey.

He spent a hard four months on E1 before they shipped him to Albany. He arrived full of hatred and found it equally reciprocated by the screws. They were made for each other.

There was always acute tension between the cons and the screws at Albany. It was a constant war of attrition. Many of the cons were rebellious, spirited young fellas doing very big bird; there would be no parole for them. Some of them had been in trouble at other jails before being moved to Albany. The place had acquired the reputation for being the end of the line, a place where troublemakers were sent to be contained.

The regime was very harsh and restrictive for a long-term jail. It was part of the dispersal system, too, which meant that there were many short-termers. The fellas were further aggravated by myriad petty rules and regulations, which were enthusiastically enforced.

Many of the Albany screws were young flash bastards, not long out of training at a local prison. Most of the senior screws were old hands of an older school. They had stewed in their hatred for years and were now thoroughly bitter and twisted. They gave the young screws every encouragement to harass the cons.

It wasn't surprising, given the circumstances and the attitudes on both sides, that it was regularly off. There had been several riots, numerous assaults on screws and regular heavy violence among the cons. Albany was the 'Vietnam' of the prison system.

After one particularly serious disturbance, the Home Office decided that a special long-term wing would be created. Only men doing eight years or over would ·be allowed on it. There would be extra privileges, like there were in other long-term jails, and not so many rules and regulations. The screws hated the idea.

The governor baulked at the thought of having a wing full of what he would describe as his worst troublemakers. There was enough disruption already with them spread out over the five wings. To have 96 hardcases concentrated in the same wing smacked of foolhardiness. The governor amended the plan.

'E' wing was chosen to be the long-term wing. Structurally, it was no different from the other four. It had been built in the 'new style', looking more like campus accommodation than the old galleried Victorian landings.

Each wing had four floors or landings laid out on an X-shaped plan. Three spurs of the X were for cell accommodation, the fourth was a recess with showers, sinks and toilets. A glass-enclosed stairwell ran up the centre of the X, giving access to the other landings.

On the ground floor, a corridor ran out of the back of each wing. Halfway down it was the wing office; further down, the AG had an office. At the end of the corridor lay a one-storey complex of TV and games rooms.

Each wing was identical to the others. With eight cells on each spur, a full wing could hold 96 men. However, the ground floor of 'E' wing had been turned over to other uses: the Welfare had an office in a converted cell; there were several storerooms; a couple of 'hobbies cells'; a screws' tearoom; and another TV room.

'E' wing wasn't unique in this. Some of the others also had

ground-floor cells converted to other uses. What was unique about 'E' wing, though, was the fact that the first landing was reserved exclusively for Rule 43s. Also, as you came up the central stairway from the ones, the door to the twos landing was permanently locked and the glass panels covered with boarding. Although the nonces lived on the same wing, the fellas never so much as saw them. A back stairway led down to their own dining hall and workshop.

This removed another landing from regular accommodation on 'E' wing and made it ideal for the governor's amended plan. Only the top two landings could be occupied. The threes and the fours together could house a total of 48 fellas. This was a much more manageable number, especially when they would be the most troublesome long-termers.

In theory, a long-term wing was a good idea. In practice, it was never allowed to work. Many of the screws disagreed with the extra privileges and relaxed rules. Even though some of them mellowed as they worked regularly in the comparatively relaxed atmosphere of 'E' wing, they were often short-handed and screws from other wings had to be brought in, who found it hard to make an easy transition from one regime to another. Friction was inevitable.

It wasn't only the screws who found the transition difficult. As far as Dessie was concerned, a few extra privileges didn't make the leopard change its spots. When Dessie moved his kit on to 'E' wing, he brought his hatred for the screws with him.

As luck would have it, the move brought him into contact with a kindred soul. Ollie was a short, stocky Scouse, doing an eight for a tie-up. He had had his share of grief at Walton jail, and had arrived at Albany by way of several local nicks. A year in the chokey was enough to confirm in him a mortal hatred of anything in a screw's uniform. It was a marriage made in heaven. Dessie and Ollie soon became close pals. They mixed in with the other fellas well enough, but their mutual obsession served to set them apart from the rest. Many of the fellas took the attitude that, if the screws were leaving you alone, then it was best to leave them alone, too. If Dessie and Ollie believed in the principle of 'live and let live', they certainly didn't think it applied to screws. They began their own personal guerrilla war.

It started low-key enough. Ringing alarm bells was common practice at Albany. There were enough of them all over the place. The screws could never guard them all.

Someone would slip up to an alarm bell when the screws weren't looking, press it, then slip away again. In the control room they could not tell who had pressed it. It just showed up on their board as an alarm, sending every available screw thundering along the corridors towards the source. It wasn't until they got there that they would find it was a false alarm. Albany must have had the fittest heavy mob in the country.

Soon alarm bells were ringing all over 'E' wing. Dozens of hatless and breathless screws were bursting in through every available gate and charging upstairs and along landings. All to false alarms. Dessie and Ollie were long gone.

After a while, they tired of this. It was nothing out of the ordinary to ring an alarm bell. It was always happening. And it was annoying to the fellas to have screws bursting on to the wing all the time. Dessie and Ollie sat down to think of something new.

Dessie noticed that, at certain times, the screws would leave their posts on the landings and in the TV rooms to congregate in the wing office. About eight or nine of them would squeeze into this small office, push the door to and have a cup of tea. The wing could look after itself for a while.

Although everyone was issued with white plastic chamber pots, the majority of fellas favoured a plastic bucket. When it came to having a piss, it didn't make much difference. However, the pots were so small and low that, when it came to having a crap, you had to squat right down. A tall wide bucket was far more comfortable.

Like most of the cons on 'E' wing, Dessie was a clean-living fella. He hated to have to use his bucket, but, if you were locked up and wanted a crap, what could you do? This was something else that made him hate the screws. Every morning, the first thing he would do was empty his bucket down the slops sink and scrub it out.

Now, he got himself a spare bucket. He shit in it, replaced the lid, and left it in the corner of his cell. Over the next couple of days, he shit and pissed in the bucket, then stirred it with a stick. Each time, he would leave it in the corner of his cell.

After ten days, he had a foul-smelling gelatinous goo, the merest whiff of which would cause the strongest stomach to heave. Now he was ready for the next stage.

He took the glass lining out of a Thermos flask and threw the rest away. Using a small jug, he scooped some of the goo out of the bucket and filled the flask lining with it. He bunged the neck with a bit of cloth, then secured it with sellotape. As he wrapped it in an old towel, Dessie smiled in satisfaction at his shit-bomb.

Later that morning, the screws filed down from the landings as usual and went into the office for their communal tea. With Ollie keeping watch in case any screws came in the wing behind them, Dessie crept along the ground-floor corridor towards the office. He paused just before the closed door to pull down an old cut-off jersey sleeve over his face as a mask.

Suddenly, he kicked the door open with a resounding crash. The eight screws seated around the desk first jumped and then cowered, a couple knocking over the cups of tea. Eight pairs of eyes fixed on the masked figure in the doorway.

Before anyone could regain their composure, Dessie hurled the silvered flask up against the ceiling. In the confined space, it detonated like a small bomb. Still reeling from the first shock, the screws threw themselves to the floor as the flask shattered above them. Hundreds of tiny pieces of glass showered down on them, closely followed by a cascade of piss and shit.

Every single one was smothered. It was all over the walls,

cupboards and curtains; hardly a square inch remained untouched. And, before this latest shock could wear off, the smell hit them. A terrible breath-taking, gut-churning stench that had several of them spewing on the floor.

Dessie was long gone. As much as he would have liked to have stood and surveyed his handiwork, he knew he had just seconds to get away. He sprinted along the corridor and up the stairs. He needn't have worried. He was up past the twos before the first screw came out of the office.

It was a significant incident. No one had been seriously hurt, but all eight screws had to go home to shower and change. At first, they considered taking all the flasks away. However, a flask was a valuable possession; a fella could have a hot cup of coffee when he was banged up. In the end, they just settled for leaving the office door open, with one of them sitting in the doorway.

It had been quite a coup. Dessie and Ollie were highly delighted. They talked about it for days and laughed with their pals. But it was a one-off. They wouldn't be able to do it again. They would have to think up something else.

For a couple of weeks, they did nothing. While others were thinking that they had run out of ideas, they liked to think that they were resting on their laurels. To pass the time, they annoyed the nonces.

Although the twos was blocked off, the nonces weren't completely out of reach. Sometimes Dessie and Ollie would go into a cell on the threes, directly above one of them, and stamp up and down for a while, or suddenly drop the locker on the floor. It was hardly exciting stuff, though. They couldn't see the effects of their efforts and, for all they knew, the cell was empty.

The windows of the nonces' cells ran all around the side of the building, just like the other landings. Standing at the window of a cell on the threes, Dessie could look down into the twos cells on the opposite spur. If he could get the angle right, he could throw something at the window. But it was very awkward. You could put your arm out the window, but you couldn't see to aim. Consequently, most shots missed.

Dessie went into the third cell along one of the spurs on the threes. He got Ollie to go around on to the other arm, into the second cell along, directly above the cell of one of the nonces. He lowered a piece of string until Dessie signalled that the end was level with the nonce's window. He marked the length, then pulled it up again. Tying a slipper on the end as a weight, Ollie tossed it across to Dessie, who caught it at the second attempt. He untied the slipper, then retied the string around the neck of a large glass sauce bottle. The sauce had long since been used. He wasn't going to waste good sauce on a nonce. The clear yellowy liquid that filled the bottle would be good enough. It was his week-old piss.

Dessie held the bottle out of the window at arm's length. Ollie pulled the string in until it was just on the mark. Then, with all the panache of a Royal launching a new ship, Dessie slung it down towards the nonce's window.

It arced downwards on the end of the string and struck exactly on the cross bars of the nonce's open window. The bottle shattered with a sharp crack and a shower of glass and piss rained through the window. Satisfied that they had struck another blow against the forces of evil, Dessie and Ollie retired to their cells, content with the evening's work.

Just as in any other military campaign, as one side developed a new weapon, so the other side would move to counter it. Within a few weeks, large wire cages had been fitted over all the nonces' windows. For Dessie and Ollie, it was back to the drawing board.

As in most long-term jails, when the screws sat on the landings, they sat in pairs. There were a couple of chairs and a small table in the corner of each landing, by the central stairwell. Sitting with their backs to the wall, they could scan the recess, watch the stairs and see the entrances to the other three spurs as well. With the level of violence at Albany, this level of surveillance was absolutely necessary.

One day, Dessie noticed that, when a certain pair of screws were on duty on the fours, one of them would sometimes slip downstairs to fetch two cups of tea, leaving the other screw on his own. This one invariably had his nose buried in a magazine, or leaned back against the wall staring blankly into space.

It was about eight in the evening. The day was drawing to an end and it had been a rather uneventful one. Both the screws on the fours fidgeted idly in their chairs, fighting the boredom. In an hour's time, it would be bang-up. Then they could go home.

'I'll get some tea,' said one, standing up. He disappeared down the stairs as the remaining screw settled back against the wall and stared at the ceiling.

Dessie and Ollie crept out of a cell on the fours and tiptoed along the landing. Both had sleeve masks over their faces. Reaching the end of the spur, Dessie peeked around the corner. The screw was sitting back against the wall, barely seven feet away.

With a quick gesture of his hand, Dessie waved Ollie past him. Ollie rounded the corner of the spur at a run, with a large tan-coloured blanket held at arm's length. The screw looked down from the ceiling and everything went dark as Ollie threw the blanket over him.

There were muffled shouts, then sharp cries of pain, as Dessie beat at the struggling form with a wooden table leg. There was only time for a couple of blows; the screws would be coming up from the landing below.

In seconds, it was over. Dessie and Ollie were back up the spur and into a cell. The masks and the table leg went out the window. They sat down at a small table that had two hands of cards dealt on it. Next to the cards were two steaming mugs of coffee. A radio was playing loudly in the corner.

The screws went along the three spurs, looking in all the cells. Everything looked quite normal. All they could do was plan for the future. Never again was a screw to be left on the landing on his own.

Dessie and Ollie were now rapidly running out of options. Not only couldn't they repeat their old tricks, but it was becoming ever harder to come up with something new. Especially something that would surpass their previous efforts. They had their public to think of. Their public – the rest of the cons on 'E' wing – by and large looked on with bemused indifference. Who were they to criticise another con? Especially when the action was aimed at the screws. It didn't affect them and everyone hated the screws anyway. Also, some of Dessie's and Ollie's antics were very funny. Many wondered what they would get up to next. They didn't have long to wait.

Dessie had been toying with an idea for some time. It was a bit extreme, even by his standards, and he hadn't even mentioned it to Ollie. He was sure it could be done though.

There were a couple of IRA fellas on the wing. They kept pretty much to themselves, but got on well enough with the rest of the fellas. The average con didn't approve of their blowing up civilians, but they were staunch enough in the nick, hated the screws and would never grass.

Dessie approached one of the IRA fellas who he knew was a bomber. He asked him about the possibility of making a small bomb out of the materials that were available in the nick. In the workshops there was quite a selection of combustible materials.

The IRA fella told Dessie that he'd have to think about it. Not only would he have to work out the practical details, but also he would have to ask permission from his commanding officer, the most senior IRA man in the jail.

A couple of days passed, then the fella came back to Dessie. He told him it could be done and that he would make it for him. He gave Dessie a list of materials he would need.

It took Dessie about a week to get everything on the list. When he had it all, he handed it over to the IRA fella, who took just two days to make it. He came to Dessie's cell and handed him a small device wrapped in a towel.

There was concern on his face as he handed it over. 'Now, look here, Dessie. I've never made anything like this before. I know it will go, but I don't know how much damage it will do. So don't let it off anywhere near the fellas. I suggest you put it in the big TV room when it's empty.'

This information was music to Dessie's ears. A large smile spread across his face. He rushed along the landing to Ollie's cell to tell him the good news. 'Ollie, me old mate, we're really going to liven those screws up. We've got a bomb to place.'

It was a Saturday morning. There was no work on a Saturday so Dessie and Ollie had all day to place the bomb. Taking the IRA fella's advice, they had decided to place it in the big TV room, even though neither of them expected very much to happen. Just a bang, a flash and a bit of smoke. However, they might as well be on the safe side for their own sakes.

The big TV room was mostly deserted on a Saturday morning. There were only cartoons on and few of the fellas would want to be seen watching them. The TV room was right at the end of the corridor, just past the screws' office. So, if it did get out of hand, it was well away from the fellas up on the landings.

It was mid-morning when Dessie and Ollie strolled nonchalantly along the ones. Dessie had a towel rolled up under his arm, but there was little suspicious in that. He could be going down to the bath-house for a shower or to change his kit.

They passed the wing office and turned into the TV room. It was a big room by prison standards, 40 feet long by 25 feet wide. At the far end was a large TV set up on a shelf and bolted to the wall. Along the length of the room were several rows of plastic-covered armchairs, enough for about 80 men.

The decor was sparse and functional. There were thin faded curtains at the three windows. A low suspended ceiling was covered with smoke-begrimed tiles. There were several tins between the rows of chairs, which served as ashtrays.

While Ollie stayed in the doorway keeping watch, Dessie

hurried to the front of the room. Having pulled a chair under the TV set, he climbed on it and placed the bomb on the shelf behind the TV. He lit the wick fuse with a match and hurried to join Ollie.

Dessie and Ollie walked nonchalantly back along the landing, past the screws' office, up the stairs and into Dessie's cell. They sat down and waited for the fun to start.

Neither of them expected to hear or see the immediate results of their handiwork. They would wait ten minutes, then stroll downstairs again. No doubt there would be screws running about with extinguishers, trying to put the fire out.

Down in the TV room, the fuse burned ever closer to the bomb. Suddenly, there was a thunderous explosion which shook the whole wing. The TV set was blown into a million charred pieces. A massive sheet of flame ran the length of the room, a flash so intense that it instantly incinerated the curtains, the ceiling tiles and every one of the 80 armchairs.

A dense cloud of acrid black smoke poured out of the TV room and funnelled along the corridor. The screws sitting in the office were astounded to see everything outside the door turn black as night. They ran for their lives: out of the office, through the smoke that burned their eyes, and out of the gate, locking it behind them. They stood in the main corridor outside 'E' wing, their eyes running with tears and their faces blackened with smuts of soot. If Dessie and Ollie could have seen them, they would have laughed like drains. However, they had problems of their own.

Like some demonic fog with a life of its own, the smoke poured along the corridor and into every spur on the ones. It shot up the stairwell and on to the threes and the fours. Every spur, every recess and every cell were suddenly filled with a dense acrid smoke. Only the nonces on the twos were spared, because their door to the stairwell was boarded up.

Fellas ran about in a blind panic, coughing and spluttering. What had so unnerved them was that it seemed to have come from nowhere. Only Dessie and Ollie knew what had happened. They had neglected to tell anyone else about the bomb.

A group of about 20 ran down the stairs through the smoke. They knew that the only way out was through the gate on the ground floor. The screws outside heard them coming and unlocked the gate. They led them through the chokey and out into the chokey yard. They left them to sit in the fresh air and clear the smoke from their lungs.

Back up on 'E' wing, a larger group ran up to the fours. There was no way out, though, and the smoke was just as dense. A couple ran into the shower and stood under the water fully clothed, hoping that it would protect them from the smoke. Others stuck their heads out of cell windows, trying to breathe the fresh air while the smoke billowed out all around them. The whole crowd were only minutes from death.

By coincidence, a Works Department screw was repairing a window on the fours. The smoke was no respecter of status, though, and he, too, was trapped. Dropping his tools, he ran down the spur shouting, 'Follow me! Follow me!' He ran on to the adjacent spur that led to the intercommunicating door with 'D' wing. It was electronically locked, of course.

The screw pressed the button on the control box next to the door.

'Yes, who is it?' said a tinny voice from the control room.

'This is Officer Hughes,' said the screw. 'This is an emergency. If you don't open this door immediately, both I and several inmates are dead. The place is filled with smoke.'

There was a slight pause, then the lock clicked on the door. The screw flung it open and ran through into 'D' wing, closely followed by several cons. The air was clean and fresh there. They ran along the spur gulping lungfuls.

A couple returned to the doorway and yelled through the smoke, 'Hey, fellas, along here into "D" wing. The door's open!'

In ones and twos, more fellas came through the smoke into 'D' wing. The main force of the explosion had passed now and the smoke only followed them in wispy patches. Leaving the door wide open, they filed down to the ground floor.

Out in the chokey yard, the fellas had almost recovered. They stood staring up at 'E' wing as the smoke continued to pour out of cell windows, air vents and every crack and crevice in the fabric of the building.

Suddenly, a head was thrust through a window up on the fours. Phil had been asleep in his cell and had just woken up. The smoke filling his cell had panicked him. He had rushed to his door and looked out on to the landing. The smoke had been even denser out there. He had run to his window, stuck his head through the opening and yelled for help at the top of his voice.

A young screw who had been lounging against a wall in the chokey yard, keeping an eye on the 'E'-wing fellas, ran to the middle of the yard. 'Stay right where you are!' he shouted up to the bobbing head. 'Don't move! I'm coming up to get you.'

With that, he ran from the yard into the chokey block. He went back the way the 'E'-wing fellas had come – into the still smoke-filled wing, up the stairs and along to the cell on the fours. He grabbed Phil by the arm and led him to the open door leading on to 'D' wing. When he reappeared in the yard, Phil by his side, the fellas couldn't help but give him a ragged cheer.

By now, all 48 former residents of 'E' wing were sitting in the enclosed yard. Half an hour had passed and the excitement was wearing off. Some of them were becoming restless. They didn't know what had happened, but most of them blamed the screws for it. 'What's fucking going on?' a couple began to shout.

Suddenly, the chief appeared. Motioning for quiet, he addressed them. 'Listen up, men. As you know, there has been a fire. "E" wing is now uninhabitable. Some of you will be going to other wings. Some will be temporarily transferred next door to Parkhurst. The smoke has cleared now. I want each of you to go back on to the wing and collect just those personal belongings that you immediately need. The rest will be packed up for you. Try to be as quick as you can.'

Amidst much muttering and moaning, the fellas filed back on to 'E' wing. As they entered, they suddenly stopped, forming an untidy knot of bodies in the entrance. Amazement registered on every face as they surveyed their former wing. Everything was blackened like the inside of a chimney. Every wall, every floor, every ceiling, every single surface was covered with a thick layer of soot.

Slowly, they moved further into the wing. The entire central stairway was blackened. Every part of the threes and fours was coated. The smoke had got into every cell. All the curtains, bedspreads, books and other personal belongings were thoroughly begrimed. Every budgie lay blackened and dead at the bottom of its cage.

By now, the mood had turned to sullen anger. No one, other than Dessie, Ollie and the IRA fella, knew what had really happened, but a few were beginning to get suspicious. They didn't mind when it was directed at the screws, but this had ruined all their belongings, killed their budgies and nearly killed them into the bargain. It was beyond a joke.

Dessie and Ollie were keeping very quiet. They volunteered no opinions and passed no judgements as they collected their kit together. They were as shocked as anyone. A flash and a puff of smoke was all they had really expected.

As the fellas filed back downstairs again, each with a pile of sooty belongings in his arms, a PO was waiting for them on the ones. In his hand, he held a list of new locations for the men.

Dessie and Ollie joined the queue. When their turn came, they found that Ollie had been allocated to 'B' wing and Dessie to Parkhurst. Whether by accident or design, they could hardly have been sent farther apart.

The two friends walked out of 'E' wing and stopped in the main corridor. They shook hands, their faces screwed up at the parting. 'I'll see you soon, Ollie. Take care of yourself. We had some laughs, didn't we?' said Dessie.

'We certainly did,' replied Ollie, his smutty face cracking into a smile. They turned and walked away from each other, Ollie towards 'B' wing and Dessie towards the chokey and the yard. Suddenly, Dessie stopped and spun around. 'Hey, Ollie!' he shouted. Ollie stopped and turned. 'What the fuck are we going to do for an encore?' They both carried on walking their separate ways, laughing like maniacs.

Thirty-one of the 'E'-wing fellas were relocated on the remaining four wings. The other 17 went over to Parkhurst for a few days. While they were there, a football match was arranged, Albany v. Parkhurst. The remnants of 'E' wing beat Parkhurst's first team.

'E' wing was totally renovated at the cost of several thousand pounds. All the fellas who had lost personal possessions were compensated by the Home Office.

The culprits were never caught.

16 GIVE 'EM A BODY

Robert John Wexler had never read Machiavelli, yet he would have intuitively understood the basic ethos of the creed. Not on any intellectual level, of course – Robert Wexler wasn't in the least cerebral.

However, at a gut level, among his primal urges, it could have made very good sense indeed. Of course, a prince should be feared rather than loved. It had become Robert's main aim in life to be feared by as many people as possible. Because love had never done anything for him, not even to get him noticed, however fleetingly.

His first murder had been largely frustration. And LSD. He could barely remember now the haze that seemed to surround him through that period. He had been just 20 and a Scouse lad in London. If he had thought that the South would be more understanding of his homosexuality than his native North, then he was soon disappointed. London in the mid-Seventies was almost as homophobic as the rest of the country. His kind were still poofs and queers to most people. With that point of view came the scorn and derision. And the emphasis that a queer wasn't a proper man, that he lacked manly qualities.

Robert was already desperately unsure of himself. He realised that his strange looks and tall skinny frame endeared him to few. The secret guilt over his sexuality was the catalyst that triggered the seething rage.

It was ironic that the victim was the one person who had noticed him and shown him some affection. Barry had allowed him to stay at his rundown council flat. They regularly tripped together. They also became lovers. During one trip, Barry had become the personification of the illicit passion that caused Robert so much guilt.

The actual killing had been almost surreal, like some kind of acid flashback. He had observed himself as he plunged the knife again and again into Barry's flesh. The screams seemed so frantic, the blood so vivid.

There had never been any real plan, so Robert hadn't prepared his escape. He was soon caught. The trial at the Old Bailey surprised him in only one respect. He had always known that he viewed the world in a strange way. Surely others didn't feel such pain and despair as a matter of course? But he had never considered himself to be mad. And, as much as he tried to disguise the implications, to be found guilty of manslaughter not murder, because of diminished responsibility, meant that he was officially insane.

The 'hospital order' had sent him to Broadmoor 'without limit of time'. In short, a life sentence in a top-security hospital for the criminally insane. Depressingly, here he found others of his ilk. Men and women obsessed with a particular world vision; one that occupied all their waking moments and stressed them to the point of purgatory.

If Robert had thought that the killing would afford him some new kind of status, would set him over and above the next person, he didn't find it so in Broadmoor. There were hundreds of patients in that hospital who had killed, often more prolifically and in more brutal circumstances than Robert. Whereas before he had been just another faceless misfit in the big city, now he was just another faceless patient in a vast human warehouse.

But Robert had noticed something, had learned something, in the process of the killing. He had long been aware of the dark force that lurked at the fringes of his consciousness, birthed in frustration, nurtured by rage. At times it seemed very similar to rage. It was certainly utterly destructive and almost uncontrollable. He had learned to release it a little at a time. Sometimes its power frightened him. Although it seemed to be of him, he also felt it to be outside him. Part of some greater, infinitely more powerful, force.

But it served its purpose admirably. It drove him and gave him a courage that, although innately self-destructive, enabled him to pursue his vision. That vision wouldn't be realised at Broadmoor though. He had to move on. But how? He was a certified lunatic; it would be many years, if ever, before he could expect to be transferred.

However, he learned from some of the older patients, men who had been there for many years, that you could 'give 'em a body'. It was something halfway between a rumour and an old story, but received wisdom had it that, if you killed someone in Broadmoor and were convicted of murder in an outside court, then you would be sent to do the rest of your sentence in a prison.

It didn't make sense really. For a man, already mad, deliberately to kill another man inside a lunatic asylum must surely be an act of madness. But one old patient told him that it was more an administrative measure than a legal one. The staff at Broadmoor considered that a strict and punitive prison regime would be better able to cope with someone so highly dangerous. It was quite a convenient solution for them.

Robert's first attempt proved an abysmal failure. There were no sharp or heavy weapons at Broadmoor. A victim had to be overpowered and throttled, a difficult task for someone who was hardly a warrior. He thought he had chosen someone weaker than himself. He had gone out of his way to befriend him first, so the attack would be unsuspected. But a strength born of desperation enabled the victim to fight him off.

Robert had spent some time in seclusion. The attack was noted in his hospital record, but he was never charged in an outside court. He resolved to make certain the next time.

However bizarre the personality, it wasn't difficult to find a kindred spirit in Broadmoor. Tom, also in his early 20s and from Liverpool, had killed a drinking partner. The killing was just as senseless and sordid as Robert's. He also shared his drug-raddled physique and nerdy looks.

One way in which Tom did differ, though, was that he had more carefully thought out his personal *Weltanschauung*. Not that it was deeply philosophical. However, it did have a certain order. Tom prayed to the Devil. He had struggled with the black-magic books he had read; he was no scholar. But it struck a chord in him. Not only did it excuse the cruel and selfish things he did, it positively encouraged them.

Robert wasn't at all interested in praying to anyone. He was the deity at the centre of his particular cosmos. However, if black magic was what it took to motivate Tom to join him in the venture, then so be it.

They were generally agreed that they would carry out the killing in the most outrageous and bizarre way possible. They were limited by both the weapons available and a suitable opportunity. They also had to decide on a victim.

Jimmy had already been at Broadmoor for several years. Still in his 20s, he had been sentenced for a string of arson attacks. He was no stranger to mental hospitals, having spent much of his youth in them. But he still had a chirpy good humour, even if he was quite argumentative. He had thought nothing of it when he had argued with a gay friend of Robert's. In the latter's mind, though, it was enough to seal his fate. Tom put it differently: 'The Devil has chosen him,' he avowed.

Finding the opportunity proved more difficult than finding the weapon. Tom had taken his radio to pieces. Part of the frame was a long, flat piece of metal. He spent several nights sharpening it on the stone window-sill. Soon he had a small razor-sharp knife, which he concealed in the radio.

Robert had been secretly watching Jimmy's movements. In truth there was very little to observe. He went to the day room, the ward, the recess, all places that were in clear view of the nurses. Ideally, Robert would have liked some time, undisturbed, with his victim.

Suddenly it dawned on him. Just along one of the corridors, there was a small room that served as a shoe and boot store. Footwear that wasn't worn on the wards was stored here. Actually, it was little more than a deep cupboard, each side lined with footwear stacked on racks. The clue was the racking. Robert reasoned that, if they could get their victim into the storeroom, they could pull the racking out from the wall, so blocking the door. And, by the time the nurses could break their way in, Jimmy would be long since dead.

The plan proved very simple to put into practice. They just waited for Jimmy to collect his shoes to go out on exercise. As he bent over in the store, tying his laces, they burst in.

Robert pulled the racking in front of the door as Tom grappled with Jimmy. Then he joined in. Jimmy was only small and was quickly overpowered. They bound him with pieces of torn sheet. Now they could take their time.

The nurses had run to the store when they heard the struggle. The door wouldn't budge, and the spy-hole had been blocked from the inside. As soon as they determined that it wasn't a nurse being held hostage, some of the urgency went out of the situation. Negotiations began.

To the seasoned negotiator it was already an unusual hostage-taking. They didn't seem to be asking for much. Just to be left alone really, with the threat that they would kill the hostage if the nurses tried to force their way in.

Secure in the store, Robert and Tom began to enjoy themselves. Although tense, both felt exhilarated as they revelled in the power of holding another's life in their hands: They had discussed in detail exactly what they were going to do. And, if they could achieve their plan, they were sure it would gain them the fear and respect they so desired from the criminal fraternity.

Jimmy, helpless and whimpering in fear, was easily intimidated. First they impressed on him that he was going to be tortured and killed. Then they forced grovelling apologies for the slight on Robert's gay friend. As penance, they forced him to perform fellatio on them both. Then they slowly garrotted Jimmy to death.

But they weren't finished yet. They had pondered long and hard on what final unspeakable act they could carry out. One that would grab people's attention and fill them with dread.

'We should eat a piece of his brain,' Tom had suggested.

Now, with Jimmy dead at their feet, he got out his homemade knife.

The subsequent trial at the nearby Crown Court attracted little media attention. The reporters were remarkably restrained. Perhaps it was because the accused were mental patients. You could hardly castigate the insane and moralise to them. To some, the hospital was as much at fault as the culprits: 'It was a scandal that they had allowed such a thing to happen.' But there would be no inquiry. The judge listened to the evidence of the torture and murder, then sentenced them both to life imprisonment.

Robert Wexler was sent to Wakefield Prison. His arrival caused absolutely no stir whatsoever; Wakefield wasn't known locally as the 'House of Horrors' for nothing. There were hundreds of violent and dangerous killers, many of whom had been in the mental hospitals.

As for the enhanced respect and deference he had expected from those professional criminals he so looked up to, the hard men from London and Liverpool still regarded him as a freakish fool. They wouldn't have hesitated to attack him violently had he shown them any lack of respect. And, as he was hardly warrior material, Robert could do little to change the situation.

Robert now realised that he had made a big mistake. It had all been for nothing. His life had changed, but very much for the worse. The harsh and punitive regime at Wakefield didn't compare to the well-resourced, therapeutic regime at Broadmoor. He thought about how he could get back there.

He still had his vision. There was no limit to the number of people he could kill, given a suitably weak victim and the right opportunity. He resolved to kill again. He felt confident, eager even. The rage-like feeling that Tom had called evil was strong in him. It drove him with an almost irresistible force now.

Within a few weeks of arriving at Wakefield, Robert was able to discern who were the most dominant and influential cons. Mostly they were from Liverpool and London. It was the latter who fascinated him though. More sophisticated than their Northern counterparts, they were both professional in their manner and extremely violent, though outwardly quite pleasant at times. How Robert longed to be like them.

But theirs was a closed society. Unless you were from London or known and respected by them, they wouldn't even talk to you. They regarded Robert as just another dangerous nutter, when they regarded him at all. They didn't fear him in the slightest. He was nothing 'one to one', and they moved in tight groups anyway.

Robert focused on one particular group which lived on his own wing. There were four of them: two bank robbers, a gangland killer and, unusually, a Scouse robber. They went everywhere together, as much for personal safety as for the enjoyment of each other's company in a strange jail so far from home.

Robert had managed to get on talking terms with one of the London robbers called Sam, who worked in the iron foundry and got through clean clothes at an alarming rate. Robert worked in the tailor's shop and had altered jeans and shirts for Sam, refusing to charge for the favour. This impressed Sam somewhat, because it was supposedly part of the code that 'your own' never charged each other for a favour. It was also quite convenient.

Robert waited his time. After about a month, during which he had altered several sets of clothes for Sam, he asked to speak to him in private. Sam had always known there was a good chance that Robert would ask a favour in return. But he was sufficiently influential and well off to grant most things. The request, though, surprised him. Robert wanted a knife!

Weapons were often made clandestinely in the foundry where Sam worked. However, it was a very serious matter indeed. Merely to be caught with a weapon could result in solitary confinement, loss of remission and, sometimes, an immediate transfer to a local prison. And, if the weapon were subsequently used in a murder or other serious assault, the maker could be done as an accessory. Consequently, weapons were only made for close friends; always as a matter of duty and rarely charged for.

Robert was way out of line. As Sam gathered himself to volley him, the latter blurted out a reason that gave Sam pause.

'I want to kill a screw with it, Sam. I want to do a screw.'

Everyone hated the screws at Wakefield. It was a brutal, uncaring regime, and the screws enforced the rules enthusiastically. Many were ex-squaddies who had served in Northern Ireland and had become inured to suffering. Needless to say, some hated Republican prisoners. This was only one aspect of their bigotry and prejudice though. They also hated Londoners and blacks with a passion. Some carried a National Front stick-pin concealed behind their lapel, occasionally flashing it at the blacks they harassed.

Sam had a particular reason to hate screws. He had been beaten up by them in a London prison. Not these Wakefield screws admittedly. But, as most screws regarded all cons as being just the same, so were they regarded in return.

A thoughtful gleam appeared in Sam's eye. 'If you say one word of this to anyone, mate, even my pals, me and you'll really fall out,' he said.

'I know better than to say anything,' conceded Robert.

Sam took a couple of weeks to make the knife. Not that the actual job took that long. But, in view of the use to which it would be put, Sam wanted to make sure that no one saw him do it.

Robert was standing in his cell one teatime when Sam hurried in. Quickly, he thrust a rag-wrapped bundle into his hands and hurried out.

That evening, after lock-up, Robert examined it. The greasy rag revealed a long, flat piece of steel with razor-sharp edges that tapered to a point. He bound a strip of cloth around the blunt end to make a handle that was easy to grip. He now had a fearsome weapon. He wasn't satisfied though. Fearing that Sam would never make the knife for him, Robert had bought a piece of hacksaw blade from an acquaintance. Now he used it to cut deep notches into the blade. It would still go in easily enough, but when it was pulled out the jagged edges would catch on flesh and sinew.

Robert hadn't given much thought to which screw he would kill. The prospect was a daunting one. The screws sometimes beat you half to death merely for punching one of them. They made it quite clear that they hardly cared what the cons did to each other, but, if a screw was touched, you were really for it.

Robert had serious second thoughts. His long suit was madness and wickedness, not courage. He came up with a second plan. He would kill as many people as he was able, before the screws could stop him.

He went back to Sam. 'I've decided not to kill a screw,' he told him. 'It'd cause too much trouble. They'd close the nick down and take away all the privileges.' There was a strong element of truth in this, and Sam nodded in agreement. 'I'm gonna kill as many nonces and grasses as I can. So, if you want to give me a couple of names, I'll do them for you.'

Sam was perfectly capable of dealing with his own enemies;

however, he hated nonces and grasses almost as much as he hated the screws. 'Just make sure it is nonces and grasses,' he growled.

It was Friday afternoon in the tailor's shop. Robert sat idle at his sewing machine, having done his quota for the week. Before him, cut paper shapes lay on his work-surface. Carefully he folded them, so intent on the task he didn't see his neighbour looking over. As he finished he sat back. A production line of small paper coffins, each with a cross on the lid, lay in front of him.

Saturday was a day of rest for most cons. They played games, watched TV, cleaned their cells and went on exercise. All the cell doors were unlocked. The cons moved about freely as the screws congregated at the ends of the landings.

Robert was well aware that it was Saturday, but he didn't have recreation on his mind. Tucking the knife carefully inside his jeans, he started out on his mission.

It was just after breakfast, and the wing was quiet. Men still sat in their cells eating their meal. Robert made his way to the landing below and the cell of his mate, Shawn. Well, he wasn't actually a mate, Robert would argue with himself. They were in a tea-boat together. They also occasionally had sex. But he wasn't a friend. Definitely not a friend. Apart from anything else, Shawn was a nonce. In for molesting kids. This hadn't stopped Robert from taking tea and sex with him, but as far as Robert was concerned the category of 'nonce' superseded that of 'friend'.

Shawn was short, fat, fortyish and balding. He hadn't been up long, so he was still sleepy. Even if he had been wide awake, he wouldn't have suspected anything. He certainly regarded Robert as a friend.

As Shawn turned to prepare tea, Robert quickly pulled out the knife and plunged it into his neck. Grabbing the quivering head with one hand, he sawed away with the knife. In seconds it was over. Robert lowered the still gurgling form to the floor. Putting the knife down, he knelt to push the body under the bed. He arranged the counterpane so it hung to the floor.

Robert could relax now. Almost leisurely, he cleaned the gory blade with tissues. Carefully he concealed the knife down the front of his jeans again. He left the cell, banging the door behind him. He went looking for his next victim.

The prison-wise well know the value of a sixth sense, an ability to interpret nuances of meaning, understated tensions and performances slightly out of sync from the norm. It is survival specific for the dangerous long-term jails and mental hospitals. This talent is learned with great difficulty. A failure to do so can cost the unwary their life.

Wakefield was a dangerous jail. Security was designed to prevent escapes rather than stop violence among the cons. There was hardly a day without a serious, violent incident.

Perhaps the mark of the beast was plain on Robert that morning. Maybe the dilation of the eyes, the flare of the nostrils gave it away. For the next two hours Robert patrolled the landings trying to lure victims off to a private place. The inducements were a cup of coffee, a game of cards, the loan of magazines. All offers were politely, nervously rebuffed. Because there was something strange about Robert Wexler this morning. People couldn't put their collective fingers on it, but there was definitely something.

It was nearly noon, and dinnertime was approaching. The wings would be locked up for two hours, but first a count would be made. Shawn wouldn't be visible in his cell. A search would be made and the body found. Investigations would inevitably lead to Robert or, at the very least, he would have to ditch the knife.

But one victim wasn't enough. If he were really to make a name for himself there would have to be more. Frantically, he searched for another victim.

Will had killed his wife, but it was the only criminal act in an otherwise blameless life. Now in his late 40s, he had worked all his life and had two grown-up children. They didn't even write – silent condemnation for killing their mother. They just didn't understand it. He didn't understand it himself. The murder replayed in his mind like a badly remembered dream. Or, rather, nightmare. His life was a waking nightmare now. He was surrounded by all kinds of disturbed and violent people. He had always been a mild man himself.

He knew Robert from the tailor's shop. He was a strange lad in many ways, but their friendship only extended to sharing a tea-boat. He hardly ever saw him on the wing. He was surprised to see him now, standing in the doorway of his cell with magazines in his hand. Robert accepted the invitation to come in, having anticipated it. Will was so polite and easygoing. It was hardly a challenge. But another victim was another victim.

As before, Robert jumped him from behind and sawed through his throat. It might have been Robert's imagination, but from the first thrust it seemed like Will didn't even struggle. Perhaps he had given up on life after he killed his wife.

There was no attempt at concealment now. Dinnertime bang-up was almost upon them, and the bodies would be found. It was time to declare his achievement. He would enjoy the look of surprise on the screws' faces.

PO Wells sat in the wing office on the ones. It had been a busy morning. What with kit change, work parties, exercise and scores of applications, he was ready for the quiet of the dinnertime break. He looked up as Robert Wexler came in. Secretly he cringed. He wondered what madness he would have to deal with now. Wexler was no problem on the wing; in fact, you hardly knew he was there. But he was obviously quite mad. The PO wondered how he had ever got out of Broadmoor.

'What do you want, Wexler?' enquired the PO in a tone that emphasised he had had enough for the morning.

'You're two short up on the landing, boss,' came the mumbled, almost wheedling answer.

The PO looked at Wexler more closely. What was the idiot on about? 'What are you saying?' he demanded.

As he spoke, Wexler removed something from the top of his

jeans and threw it down on the desk in front of him. 'I said you're two short up on the landing, boss.'

The message was clear, but the meaning wasn't. The PO looked down at the desk. His eyes bulged in astonishment and horror. The long dagger glinted cruelly in the bright office light. He could see the pieces of flesh and gore trapped in the grooves.

'Mr Wallace, Mr Wallace,' he cried, jumping to his feet. An intercommunicating door flew open, and his SO ran in. 'Get this man down the block,' he screamed, pointing at Wexler.

Together they walked slowly towards him, ushering him out of the office. 'Come here,' he called at a passing officer. 'Help Mr Wallace escort Wexler to the block immediately.'

The last victim was found first. The PO blanched as the officer announced his discovery. He blanched further when the second body was found. The rest of his day would be spent writing reports and making phone calls.

Sitting in the corner of a cell in the punishment block, Robert hardly felt any different. Admittedly, the zing of adrenalin still coursed his veins, but he knew that was merely transitory. He was just a man sitting alone in a cell. A man who had killed four people now, but in many ways quite an ordinary man nevertheless. Bare walls had no way of showing homage. This time, though, he was sure it would come.

And come it did, but hardly in the way that Robert expected. Over in the hospital they built a special cell, a cell within a cell. There was the outer door, but once inside there was a six-foot space, then bars from floor to ceiling. Behind them was the cell proper. It was like a lion's cage at the zoo, but the lion was to be Robert. He was never to leave it, except to bathe or exercise. On those few occasions when he was unlocked, he would be accompanied by four screws at all times.

The trial was an anticlimax. His guilty plea was a formality. Once again the press was remarkably restrained. The proceedings barely made the national dailies, and the *Yorkshire Post* carried only a small piece. In sentencing him to life, though, the judge stressed the dangerousness of the defendant. And that was it.

Alone in his cage in Wakefield Prison hospital, Robert pondered his fate. He was to be kept in this cell indefinitely. He would never mix with another prisoner. So where was the enhanced status he could now expect from his peers? Where the deference, the respect from other hard and dangerous men? Without an audience, there could hardly be a performance. In the absence of others, there was no such thing as self. He felt his personality begin to crumble. His life was purgatory now.

In lucid moments he mused on the nature of the force that had motivated him, that had driven him. He would call it by the name that Tom had given it now. In his ignorance, his naivety, he had thought he could control the evil. Could mould it to his purpose and achieve his destiny. It had only shown enough of itself to lure him onwards, but its goal was very clear now. Evil was the antithesis of all life. Robert Wexler was a life force. Its intention had been to destroy him all along.

Robert Wexler spent three years in his 'cage', before a television documentary about him forced a change. He was moved to top-security conditions, where he would be kept constantly under close supervision. He remains in prison to this day.

17 THE CENTRE

O f all the prisons in the country, Wandsworth was far and away the most feared and respected among the cons. Other jails might have had their moments – certain incidents or periods when a particularly brutal heavy mob had reigned – but 'Wanno' was in a class of its own.

Home Secretaries might come and go, liberal policies might be enacted, but Wandsworth was immovable and immutable. It was the flagship of the Prison Service. At least in the eyes of the screws if not the Home Office.

Wandsworth was a tight ship. There was no such thing as prisoner power, and as long as most of the screws there drew breath there never would be. It was a hotbed of militants. Their POA was one of the strongest in the country. If there were to be some sort of industrial action, you could safely bet that Wandsworth would be to the forefront.

Wandsworth was a local prison, a remand prison, a top-security prison and an allocation centre all rolled into one. On any given day, you could have as many as 1800 cons banged up. And banged up they would be, for there was little work and less association.

It was often said that you got exactly what you were entitled to at Wandsworth and not a jot more. That was true to a certain extent, but it was the absolute minimum you were entitled to.

The jail served London and the South, but there were cons from all over. Sentences ranged from 18 months right up to natural life. The toughest of the tough regularly walked through its gates. The screws managed to contain them though. Whoever it was, everyone toed the line. This was achieved by a very simple method: brutality. If you got out of your pram at Wandsworth, you could get very severely bashed up.

At the first sign of any trouble the alarm bell would sound. Every available screw would run to its source. This could mean 30 or 40 men, and many of the screws at Wandsworth were big lumps. With no hesitation whatsoever they would steam right in. Never mind who started it, or what the rights and the wrongs of the situation were, they would grab whoever was at the centre of the mêlée and drag them away.

They would be carried bodily across the centre and down on to E1. This was the punishment landing. Here they would be beaten, rammed head first into walls, their clothes torn from their bodies and, finally, thrown naked into a strip cell until the following morning.

On the subsequent Governor's Adjudication, or VC, the screws would all close ranks and lie in unison. To justify the beating, the con would be charged with assaulting a screw. He would inevitably be found guilty and lose six months' remission. You just couldn't win at Wandsworth.

In layout, it was typical of all the old Victorian prisons. Five long galleried wings, 'A' to 'E', radiated off a central hub. There were three separate wings, 'G', 'H' and 'K', but these were used mostly for the nonces.

The centre, the hub where the five wings conjoined was a circular area about 80 feet in diameter. Around the edge was a tiled pathway some 15 feet wide. Right in the middle was a gigantic metal grating, all of 50 feet across.

It was an amazing construction. Made out of cast metal, it comprised several sections. The actual grating was of a strange and intricate pattern. The darkness below was as impenetrable as that of the pit. No one knew what lay beneath.

In itself, in any other halfway sane place, this would just have been an unusual architectural feature. In the hallowed halls of Wandsworth, though, the grating had come to assume an almost mystical significance. Its whole surface had been polished until it shone like burnished silver. Teams of cleaners on their hands and knees buffed away at it all day long.

It shone like some jewel in a dungeon. In the half-light that passed for daytime in Wandsworth, it shimmered in the gloom like a lake of molten metal. To the screws, it was almost hallowed ground. Among the cons, it was known throughout the system as absolutely and totally out of bounds.

Apart from the cleaners, who knelt on cloths, no con's shoe would ever touch it. And, if some new reception happened to blunder on to its outermost edges, every assembled screw would scream at him in unison until he retreated.

Only the screws walked on it. In fact, it was the central point of the jail and the place where the senior screws congregated. You could always find at least one chief, a couple of POs and several SOs standing in a group on the centre.

Often these white shirts would just stand there saying nothing, running their eyes over all who passed. There was something almost reptilian in their total lack of compassion.

The cons had to keep strictly to the pathway when traversing the centre and then only in a clockwise direction. If you wanted to go from 'E' wing to 'D' wing, you couldn't nip across the dozen or so feet between them, the logical route. You would have to make a complete circuit of the centre, past 'A', 'B' and 'C', in a clockwise direction.

And woe betide any con who had his jacket unbuttoned or his shirt hanging out. It wasn't necessarily a nicking. Just a loud and very public bawling out; the humiliation of a grown man in a tone you wouldn't use to talk to a dog. It was far worse than any nicking. And there was always the danger that uncontrollable pride would force you to say something back. Then you would really be in trouble.

Harry was a young fella from Huddersfield. He had come down from the North to try to make it in London. Before long, he had turned to burglary. He wasn't particularly professional at it. When they finally nicked him for one, they charged him with the lot. He was found guilty of about 50. He got five years.

He was like a fish out of water in Wandsworth. There was no prisoner power as such; but he quickly saw that the London robbers were the most influential. On exercise and in the workshops, he heard them talk. He was thoroughly impressed by their attitude and professionalism. He had never met people like them before.

The majority totally ignored him. To them, he was just some thick Northern burglar who didn't have a clue. At the best of times Londoners were very cliquey. Harry didn't fit the mould at all.

In this, he didn't really help himself. There was nothing he could do about his Yorkshire accent, but his general image left everything to be desired. He was dour, unfashionable and scruffy.

Wandsworth was never a fashion parade, but the chaps at least made an effort to look clean and tidy. Through people they knew they would get kit that fitted them. It was possible to have clothes pressed up for wearing on visits. Nothing was more disheartening for a wife or girlfriend than to come on a visit and see their normally immaculate fella done up like a bundle of rags.

Harry was totally oblivious to all this. He didn't get visits, but even if he did style would have been at the bottom of the agenda. None of his clothes fitted. His baggy grey trousers were several sizes too big. He was forever pulling them up from where they had fallen down around his hips. At the bottom they were piled up, concertina fashion, over his shoes.

The shoes themselves were scuffed and dirty. His shirts always had crumpled collars, with several buttons missing. His pride and joy was a large shapeless grey jumper with holes in it. He was never seen without it. There was a rumour that he even slept in it.

His haircut was unfashionably short at the sides and long on the top. Untidy tufts of fairish hair sprouted in various directions. A long ragged quiff hung haphazardly over one ear. The final touch was added by a pair of National Health glasses, through which he peered owlishly.

Whereas bikers and hippies displayed a deliberately dishevelled appearance, Harry was just a mess. A fashion consultant wouldn't have known where to start with him and probably wouldn't have bothered. Small wonder that the majority of the London robbers totally ignored him.

A couple talked to him though. He was immediately impressed that, underneath the hard and violent exterior, they were decent, honourable fellas whom he could trust not to take a liberty. On their part, although they largely treated Harry as a joke, they respected the fact that he was staunch and rebellious. They were reasonably certain that he would never grass and, if ever there were a protest against the screws, then he was sure to be there. Also, with all the slippery bastards about, they liked his simple, ingenuous nature.

Harry quickly came to realise what his strong points were in the eyes of the chaps who spoke to him. He played on them to the full. He set out to wind up the screws on the centre.

Firstly, he greased the long hair on top of his head and combed it straight upwards. In the days of neat, stylish hairstyles he looked like a man who had just had a severe shock. He put on his glasses upside down and set off around the centre.

The four white shirts standing in a bunch didn't take a blind bit of notice of him. They continued talking among themselves, all the time running their eyes over everything. Harry completed the circuit and returned to 'D' wing.

The Londoners who talked to him had been standing there watching. 'I haven't finished yet,' he said as he hurried into his cell.

When he reappeared, his hair and glasses were just the same, but now he had his shoes on back to front, tied on with string. He set out again around the centre.

Once again, the white shirts did nothing. They continued to talk and look around. The discerning, however, noticed the screws' beady eyes focus briefly on Harry as he passed. They had seen a million nutters though. If they pulled every bizarre-looking fella who passed, the place would grind to a halt.

Harry arrived back on 'D' wing again. He was annoyed that he had been ignored, but at the same time he was relieved. He was enjoying himself. The Londoners were standing there laughing, so his reputation as a rebel was increasing. He could imagine them telling their pals.

'I'll show them this time,' he said as he disappeared inside his cell again.

Within seconds he was back. The hair, the glasses and the shoes were still exactly the same, but this time he had a small hearing aid stuck in his left ear. A thin wire ran from it to disappear down the front of his jumper. Turning to the two Londoners, Harry ostentatiously pulled the wire out. It was only six inches long and obviously wasn't connected to anything. He tucked it back into his jumper and set off for the centre again.

This time he walked straight out on to the polished grating, heading across it. The white shirts reacted as if struck by an electric current. As one, the four of them screamed at Harry and waved their arms. A short, stocky SO ran at him, his face contorted in rage. 'Get off the fucking centre,' he screamed.

Harry stopped and looked at him bemusedly. He pointed dumbly at the hearing aid wedged in his left ear. The SO stood and stared, clearly noticing it for the first time. His main weapon had been neutralised. What was the use of shouting at an inmate who couldn't hear you? He could hardly tell him off for walking on the centre either. And from the way this inmate had just pointed at his ear, he was probably dumb as well as deaf. Any communication with him would be difficult in the extreme. It wasn't worth the trouble.

Dismissing him from his mind, the SO waved Harry away, back the way he had come. To make his intention absolutely clear, he put one hand on his arm and gently pushed him in the desired direction.

Harry turned away, back towards 'D' wing. He could feel a smile coming, so he twisted his head away from the SO. As he did so, the end of the wire came clear of the top of his jumper and hung there, swinging freely.

The SO stared at the wire, transfixed. Spinning Harry around, he pulled down the front of his jumper. There was no battery pack or anything; the hearing aid was clearly a dummy.

While all this was going on, dozens of pairs of eyes were on them. The three white shirts, still in a bunch, followed every move. Several screws standing about the centre watched closely. Whenever a screw went to confront a con, anything could come of it. 'Get this man down to E1,' screamed the SO at the top of his voice. Harry stood there paralysed. He was swept up by a tidal wave of blue uniforms that suddenly engulfed him. None of the screws on the centre had missed a trick. They had seen him walk past in disarray. They had just ignored it. Now he had deliberately walked on their centre. If he got away with it, everybody would be doing it. There was a lesson to be taught here. It wasn't a mistake either. Clearly, he was taking the piss.

Harry was carried bodily across the centre by seven screws. With the SO running along behind them, they pushed passing cons out of the way. At a run now, they charged on to 'E' wing. As they headed down the steps to E1, Harry's glasses fell off, followed by one of his shoes.

They rushed him to the end of E1, where the strip cells were. They threw him bodily against a wall. As he landed in a heap on the floor, they kicked at him with their heavy boots and hit him with their sticks.

Dazed and hurt, Harry tried to cover his head with his arms. One particularly stunning blow paralysed him, though, and he felt himself drift away into unconsciousness. The last thing he remembered was the screws tearing at his clothes.

As he lay in a crumpled heap, the screws pulled his clothes off. Those that didn't come easily they ripped to pieces. Then they lifted his naked body by the arms and legs and dumped him in the bare strip cell. They left, slamming the door behind them. It wouldn't be opened until the following morning.

Harry's mind swam back to consciousness. The numbing dizziness was immediately replaced by intense pain. It seemed to be coming from several places at once. He groaned loudly as he rolled over on to his back. Every movement caused his body to scream in protest. Yet, no matter how he lay, the pain raged all over him.

He pulled himself up into a seated position and sat hugging his knees. The memory of recent events flooded back to him, and he felt tears well up in his eyes. It was the effects of the pain, coupled with a degree of self-pity. But he couldn't afford to feel sorry for himself. He still had a night to face, naked in the strip cell.

He crawled over to a board in the corner that passed for a bed. There was a canvas sheet folded on it. Ignoring the stains and the accompanying smells, he pulled it around his shoulders. It wasn't much against the cold of the coming night, but at least it might stop him shivering.

Under the sheet he ran his hands all over his body, examining himself for damage. There were several sore lumps, but nothing seemed to be broken. He hugged his knees tighter, trying to warm himself.

It was no use his ringing the bell. If the screws did answer, it would only be to beat him some more. Staring at the featureless walls surrounding him, he felt the loneliness beginning to close in.

But, at that moment, it was preferable to any company he was likely to get.

In another corner of the cell he saw a lidless piss-pot next to a plastic water jug. Suddenly he realised he was very thirsty. He crawled over to the jug, praying that there would be water in it. It was half-full, but the surface of the water was coated with a dusty film that indicated it had been there for several days. Screwing up his face, Harry took a big gulp. He swallowed it immediately, trying not to register any taste it might have.

He crawled back over to the bedboard; to stand and walk would have been too painful. He lay on his side, covering himself with the sheet. It occurred to him that he was like a wounded animal. This was what the screws had reduced him to.

Strangely, the thought strengthened him. They had degraded him, but in the process they had degraded themselves the more. They were supposed to be the forces of law and order. They liked to look down on the convict lawbreakers, thinking themselves to be morally superior. Yet they regularly committed similar offences. The only difference was that they were never prosecuted for it. For Harry, this only gave justification to his rebelliousness.

Eventually, he must have slept. He woke, cold, stiff and hungry. He lay there for what seemed an hour before the cell door eventually opened. A group of screws stood outside.

'Come on, out you come,' said one.

Harry staggered out, blinking in the brighter light. They shepherded him along the ones and into a normal punishment cell. As the door banged behind him, he saw some clothes piled in the corner.

He dressed and sat in a cardboard chair. Half an hour passed, and the door opened. He was served breakfast, but before the door closed again a screw handed him a small printed form. It was a nicking sheet. As Harry read it, he saw he had been charged with assaulting a screw. No doubt that was to cover the assault on himself.

Another 30 minutes passed before his door swung open again.

It was the doctor, checking that he was fit for adjudication. Harry looked at the drawn face and tightly pursed lips. This doctor was renowned for his lack of compassion. It would be a waste of time complaining to him.

'Are you OK?' asked the doctor in a harsh, nasal voice. There was no enquiry in the tone. No solicitude or any desire to extract information. It was almost as if he were daring Harry to make a complaint.

Harry just grunted his assent. It was no use his saying anything. He wouldn't be believed anyway. Then he would be charged with making a false accusation as well. It was best to say nothing. The doctor turned and left.

Another hour passed. He heard a lot of movement outside on the ones. Sharp, clipped, military-like shouts echoed around the chokey. Suddenly, his door crashed open. A group of six screws stood in the doorway. 'Stand up. Prisoner for adjudication,' one shouted at Harry.

Harry walked to the door. The screws formed up front and back of him. 'Prisoner, march,' yelled the same screw. This show of military precision seemed quite funny to Harry. Very different from the undisciplined beating he had received the night before.

He was marched to stand before a table where a governor was sitting. 'Name and number to the governor,' ordered the screw.

Harry gave his name and number. Hardly looking at him, the governor read out the charge and told him he would be remanded to appear before the Visiting Committee.

'About turn,' demanded the screw.

Almost before he knew it, Harry was back in his cell with the door banged behind him.

The VC was much the same. Two days passed, then he was marched out of his cell again. This time he was taken into a room opposite. It was two cells knocked into one and served as an office. He was marched to stand before a long wooden table.

Two screws stood directly in front of him to prevent him from jumping over the table. As he peered over their shoulders he could see the magistrates seated there.

There was one old boy with a military bearing. He was sitting very erect with a stern expression on his face. The other three were elderly ladies. Their prim faces and neat but unfashionable clothes reflected their thoroughly middle-class backgrounds. The four of them peered over their glasses to look at the dishevelled Harry, as if he were something the cat had just dragged in.

Once again, Harry realised he would be wasting his breath here. 'All I did was walk across their poxy centre, then they beat me up,' he could imagine himself saying. The magistrates would look at Harry, then at the officers, so smart and military-like, standing to attention in their uniforms. His word against that of several screws. It would be no contest.

Suddenly, Harry felt sick of the whole charade. Some justice this. The more he saw of these bastards, the more he felt his rebelliousness to be justified. He just wanted to get it over with and leave the room.

They went through the motions. The charges were read out. The screws gave their evidence. The magistrates peered again at Harry. He was only short and tubby. The officers guarding, towered above him.

'What manner of man could he be that he had attacked six of them?' He read their unspoken question as they stared at him. 'But, then, the place was filled with savages. The officers must have such a difficult job.'

When his turn came, Harry pleaded guilty. He was marched outside while they deliberated. Then he was marched back in again.

In his best military tone the old gent passed sentence. 'Harry S——- you are sentenced to 180 days' loss of remission and 56 days' cellular confinement. Take the prisoner away.'

Sitting in his cell later, Harry mused on his situation: He had been beaten up, lost six months' remission (the equivalent of a nine-month prison sentence) and faced two months' solitary. All for merely walking across the centre. The only consolation was that now he was likely to be shipped out when his punishment finished.

'Just think what I'd have got if I'd done something serious,' he said to himself out loud. Shaking his head he tried to smile. But a smile just wouldn't come.

When his 56 days were over, Harry was transferred to Parkhurst. There he was involved in various protests. He lost more remission and served more solitary. In all his time in prison, though, he had never been violent. Those who knew him well would say that it wasn't in his nature.

It is rumoured that when he was released he went back to Huddersfield. Putting into practice what he had learned from listening to the London robbers, he tried to rob a local betting office with a sawn-off shotgun. An old fella wrestled with him, grabbing the gun. It went off, killing him instantly.

Harry ran out of the shop, with a crowd in hot pursuit. For a while he lost them as he ducked into a church. He reappeared, dressed in the vicar's robes. He was recognised, chased and caught.

At the subsequent trial, he was described by the judge as a cold-blooded killer. He was sentenced to life, with a 30-year minimum recommendation.

Those of us who had known him, and his bumbling, harmless ways, were astounded. We knew plenty who fitted the judge's description; in fact, there were some among us. But not Harry. We mused on a system that could take a petty burglar and change him so much in the space of only four years.

18 THE TREATMENT QUEUE

One classic and enduring image of Parkhurst was the 'treatment queue'. Halfway along the ones on 'A' wing was the treatment room. It was an empty cell lined with shelves and small cupboards. All along these shelves and in the cupboards were various types of medicines. There were glass jars containing liquids of every colour. There were tubs of cream, tubes of ointment and bottles of pills.

Every morning, as soon as 'A' and 'D' wings were unlocked, two hospital screws would appear and unlock the treatment room. They would carry with them a wooden tray with a handle. It contained several bottles of medicines that were too dangerous to leave unattended in the treatment room.

There would always be a couple of fellas waiting outside when the screws arrived. The room had a stable-type door. The screws would push the bottom half-shut behind them, then spend a minute or so arranging the bottles on the shelves. Finally, they would turn to the doorway and place a metal bowl and a stack of plastic medicine tots on the shelf on top of the half-door. This was the signal that they were ready to start serving.

By now quite a queue would have formed, with more joining

every second. Most of them had got straight out of bed. Some would still be in pyjamas, some in trousers and a vest, and a couple in shorts. All were unshaven and thoroughly dishevelled.

Most were on regular medication prescribed by the prison doctor. They would be there every day collecting something. Others would show up when they felt like it and ask for whatever they felt they needed. The screws would hand it out. It was very easy to become a medication junkie at Parkhurst. Almost half the population were on something or other.

As men reached the front of the queue, they would ask for Librium, Valium, Triptycil, Largactyl or some other psychotropic drug. A small medicine tot brimming with coloured liquid would be placed in front of them. They would drink it down and throw the empty tot into the metal bowl. Sometimes, men who had built up a strong resistance to one particular drug had a cocktail of tots lined up in front of them.

The medication seemed to have a similar effect to alcohol in that it shut down whole levels of higher thought. Men walked about zonked out for the rest of the day. Unlike alcohol, though, it didn't have a euphoric effect.

The recurring ritual of the treatment queue was repeated just before dinner and again before tea. There was a final treatment call, mostly for sleeping draughts, at about 8 p.m.

Every single day of the year two hospital screws would be there doling out the drugs. Whatever else might be delayed or cancelled, the men always got their treatment. Some were so dependent that there was a good chance they would run amok if they didn't get it.

Such was the volume of traffic to get treatment that there was a separate treatment room for most parts of the prison; 'B' wing and 'C' wing each had its own treatment room, so did the Security Wing. Outside each, queues would form three times a day. A few would ask for cream for a rash or something for a headache. The vast majority requested one or more of the various psychotropic drugs. They were given whatever it took to get them through another day's bird.

19 WALLY AND THE TURDS

Parkhurst's tin shop was far from being an ideal place to work, but there were worse shops. There were about six of our crowd in there now, all staunch people. We managed to have a laugh, but we also knew what work we had to do. So the screws and civvies left us to get on with it.

Fred soon realised that, of the options available to him, the tin shop would suit him best. We realised this, too, and weren't looking forward to him coming in. We wouldn't have done anything to block his chances; you didn't do things like that. However, it was all academic anyway. As Fred was an 'A' man and a London gangster, one of the AGs attached to the 'labour board' would make the decision.

The labour board duly sat, and we were all relieved to hear that he had been put in the press shop, the one adjoining ours. Whereas the tin shop, which mostly turned out wastepaper bins, was a labour-intensive production line with a tolerable noise level, the press shop was a Dante's *Inferno* of large sophisticated machines designed to bend and tear metal. The noise was horrendous.

I never liked the place, often musing on the thought of lunatics operating dangerous machines. I secretly dreaded the day when there would be some terrible gavolt, and the medics would cart someone away minus an arm or a leg.

We rarely had need to enter the press shop in the course of our work, and as there was none of our crowd in there we didn't go in for social reasons. We were quite pleased that we wouldn't see much of Fred during working hours.

Fred had other ideas though. He was well aware of the distinct lack of warmth towards him from most Londoners, but he was nothing if not thick-skinned. We often joked that you couldn't wound him with an elephant gun.

One of the ways he tried to curry favour with us was to wind up the screws and the civvies. Since we all hated both of these groups, this was a pastime that won him some support. And, to give credit where it was due, he could be very funny at times.

It was very difficult to wind up the screws at Parkhurst for the simple reason that they rarely spoke to us, and we rarely spoke to them. And any screw who stood for being wound up wouldn't have lasted very long.

The civvies, though, were a different matter. In some ways they were in the middle. They had to work alongside us every day and, when necessary, tell us what to do in the most diplomatic way possible. Theirs was an unenviable task.

For the most part they were ordinary working men with a background in engineering. Nothing in their experience could have prepared them for working cheek by jowl with some of the most volatile and dangerous prisoners in the country.

They were given no training in 'control and restraint' techniques, and it was made very clear to them that such things were the sole responsibility of the screws. Consequently, they bent over backwards to avoid antagonising us in any way. All work directions were in the form of requests. All complaints about us were made as sly phone calls, at which stage the screws would appear and take the initiative.

There were only two civvies in our shop, dry, colourless

nonentities whom we treated almost as part of the production process. Relations were always polite and informal, but we never joked with them or otherwise socialised.

In the press shop there were four civvies. They were similarly colourless, but there was one among them, a civvy called Wally Pearson, who fancied himself as something of a mover and a shaker. He prided himself that he could keep the press shop running smoothly. That this was done with a mixture of flattery, slyness and general obsequiousness didn't seem to detract from his good opinion of himself.

Pearson was a tall, portly, middle-aged man with the sharp, pointed features of a wary rodent. His thinning black hair was slicked down tight to his head in a passable imitation of the Joe Loss Thirties' style. This made him seem all the more sleek and rodent-like. All his movements were quick and furtive. He could look you in the eye, but only just.

Not surprisingly he had a reputation for insincerity. He would say one thing to your face, but his real feelings were always delivered by way of behind-your-back phone calls and secret reports. Luckily for our crowd, he rarely came into the tin shop. When he did, he stayed well away from us. This may well have had something to do with the fact that whenever he did appear someone would call out in a loud voice, 'Nitto, chaps! Here's Wally the Rat.'

Pearson must have been warned about Fred. In his own parochial way, he must have been totally in awe of him. The fact was that he now had a notorious and feared gangster in his shop. He immediately resolved to be as obsequious as he could.

Pearson made Fred 'shop cleaner'. Cleaning jobs were quite sought after, as there was little real work involved. Consequently, Fred just wandered around all day and did next to nothing. The ever-present broom was largely a prop to justify his existence.

Pearson also took to calling Fred by his first name. This strategy was absolutely the worst one he could have adopted. Fred always took kindness for weakness. At those times when he wandered into our shop, he would boast about how he had Pearson terrified of him and eating out of his hand. 'You watch me drive him mad,' he promised.

The opening shots in the campaign were comparatively low-key. When Pearson wanted Fred, he would call out a demure 'Fred', delivered *sotto voce*. When Fred wanted Pearson, he would roar out a thoroughly uncouth 'Wally' from any part of the press shop.

Fred then got several other cons to do it. Soon the press shop echoed to shouts of 'Wally' between the crashes and bangs of the machines.

Pearson must have been aware that all the familiarity had got out of hand, but once he had set out on the road to appeasement he probably decided that he would have to put up with the consequences. To take the matter up with a governor now would have got him a rocket for using Christian names in the first place.

The more familiar Pearson got with Fred, the more he bent over backwards to avoid antagonising him in any way. From observing Fred's manner and antics, he was now convinced that he was quite mad as well as dangerous. Pearson would agree with even his most outrageous statements.

Fred took to talking to Pearson about his sister. Now Fred didn't have a sister, but Pearson wasn't to know that. In fact, from the way that Fred went on about her, Pearson was certain that he idolised her. He would listen to Fred emotionally raving about what he would do to anybody who ever insulted or upset his sister in any way. Pearson was no doubt relieved that he would never meet the woman.

One day Fred came into the shop and told Pearson that he had just received a letter from his sister with a photograph enclosed. He asked Pearson if he would like to see it. Realising that he was on very dangerous ground indeed, Pearson said that he would love to. Fred took the envelope out of his back pocket and reverentially removed a small black-and-white photo.

Pearson mentally steeled himself as he was handed the picture. However ugly or unattractive the sister might be, Pearson resolved not to say anything that could be remotely construed as derogatory. As he gazed at the face of a blowsy, middle-aged white woman performing fellatio on a large black penis, Pearson didn't turn a hair. Whatever went through his mind, it didn't show on his face. Pausing as long as he decently could before handing it back, he realised that some remark was required of him. 'She looks like a nice girl, Fred,' he said before discreetly disengaging and hurrying away into his office.

Fred immediately came into the tin shop and told us about it. It really cracked us up. We had been listening to the developing saga and could imagine Pearson squirming while Fred kept a straight face. What really provoked our contempt, though, was Pearson's obsequious remark. We all believed in direct and violent action. Pearson's craven behaviour just highlighted for us the dangers of appeasement.

As part of his general plan to appear a nice fella to the cons who worked in his shop, Pearson brought the *Sun* in each day. He would read it at the ten o'clock break, then allow anyone else to read it as long as it was put back in his jacket pocket at the end of the day. He explained that his wife liked to read it over her supper. This arrangement had been going on for several months before Fred arrived.

One morning, as the fellas arrived for work, it was plain to see that Pearson was distressed. His face was grim, and his normal phoney cheeriness was missing. He hurried about, obviously preoccupied with something, as he started the production process going. As soon as he had done this, he called Fred over. They went into the office together and closed the door.

Pearson had originally decided on a strong line, but in the cold light of day and the presence of Fred his courage deserted him. He settled for sympathy.

'Fred, it was terrible last night,' he whinged. 'I was just getting ready for supper when my wife let out a terrible scream. I ran to the table to find her pointing in horror at the centre pages of the *Sun*. Someone had shit right in the middle and carefully folded it back up again. She was very distressed. Who could have done such a thing?'

Now Fred knew very well who could have done such a thing, for he had done it himself. He had expected this very conversation in fact. For a second he was on the verge of saying, 'Well, you can always expect a lot of shit in the *Sun*,' but thought better of it. A bit of tact was called for.

'Wally,' he said angrily, 'I've got the right fucking hump over this. You're good enough to bring your paper in for us each day, yet some dirty bastard goes and does this. I'm going out into the shop right now and sort it out.'

Fred rushed out into the shop. He hurried behind a large machine and burst out laughing. A crowd of fellas quickly gathered around him. He told them what Pearson had said. They immediately fell about laughing too. He came into our shop and told us, provoking more laughter.

When he returned, Pearson was still sitting in the office with the door shut. The shocked and hurt look remained on his face. Fred hurried in without knocking. 'Wally,' he said, 'I've had a word with the fellas, and they're all agreed that it's a fucking liberty. I can't find out who did it, but it won't happen again.'

That was it. Pearson looked at him as if expecting more, but quickly realised that this was all he was going to get. He seemed somewhat mollified, but all this really meant was that he had swapped his shocked look for a sulky one. For the rest of the day he was unusually distant and withdrawn.

It was late July, and high summer had finally come to the tin shop. We roasted in the unrelenting heat. We opened all the windows and got the screws to open all the doors, leaving just the gates locked. Everywhere was still hot and sweaty though.

In the press shop the temperature was even more oppressive. The machines seemed to blast superheated air into every nook and cranny. Men sat listlessly in any cool corner they could find, but there was no escape from the heat.

Every day, at ten in the morning and three in the afternoon, the shop stopped for tea. A short blast on a siren announced its beginning and end. The cons would huddle in groups over cups of tea or coffee. The civvies retreated into their office to eat the sandwiches and pies their wives had packed for them. They shut the door behind them and forgot about the press shop for the duration of the break.

The four civvies of the press shop shared an office. It was an untidy construction of Perspex and metal panelling. The Perspex didn't have the clarity of glass, and as the civvies moved about inside their images were blurred like an out-of-focus film.

The office was only about 12 foot square, but it was grossly overcrowded with desks, chairs, lockers and cupboards. Catalogues and paperwork were strewn everywhere. Pearson and his men seemed quite at home amidst all the clutter though. They could be seen nibbling at their sandwiches and chatting amiably.

For Fred, however, this was a state of affairs that couldn't be allowed to continue. It was anathema to him that, for a full 20 minutes each morning and afternoon, Pearson could escape from his influence. He resolved to do something about it.

Firstly, he got several clear polythene bags from the store. He took one into the recess with him and shat into it. Then he tightly knotted the bag at the top. He hid it underneath one of the machines. He then got several other cons to do the same. Fred now had a collection of turds, each preserved in its own polythene bag.

Over the next couple of days he would wander into the office with one of the bags hidden in his pocket. He would pick a time when there was only one civvy in there. Waiting until the civvy was busy writing or distracted by a phone call, Fred would suddenly lean over a big filing cabinet and drop the bag down the back. Then he would amble out again.

Soon there were several turds in bags lying behind the big cabinet. There was no chance of their being found, the office was never properly cleaned. Fred knew this better than anyone. He was the cleaner. To move the heavy filing cabinet would be a major operation, and there was no reason to do so anyway.

Fred left the bagged turds lie there for several days. The bags swelled like balloons as the fetid gases expanded in the heat. The knots kept them sealed though.

Fred had taken to walking about the shop carrying a length of stick, with a nail embedded in the end. He told Pearson it was a 'litter stick', for picking up bits of paper without bending down. Pearson didn't care if Fred walked about with a lance, just so long as he left him alone.

Fred ambled into the office one morning, carrying his stick. It was about 20 minutes before tea-break. As the civvy went to answer the phone, Fred quickly leaned behind the cabinet and punctured all the bags with his stick. He ambled out of the office again and went to join a group of fellas huddled behind the machines. They settled down and waited for the fun to start.

The siren sounded and tea-break started. Pearson and the other three civvies went into the office. Despite the heat Pearson still shut the door. It was a symbolic act, distancing himself from the cons and the shop for the duration of the break.

They settled down in their chairs and rummaged through their bags. They took out their sandwiches and pies and put them on the desks as normal. Pretty soon, though, it was obvious that all was far from normal.

First, the youngest civvy, a slight, fair-haired fella in his late 20s, stood up quickly as if coming to a decision and opened all the office windows as far as they would go. He sat back down again and continued eating. But something was still wrong. Then Pearson jumped up and ran to the door. He stood in the doorway, swinging it backwards and forwards like a fan. Leaving it wide open, he went and sat down again.

Suddenly an argument broke out. A couple of the civvies were shouting and waving their arms about. Pearson had gone very red in the face and was shaking his head angrily. Fred was too far away to hear what was being said, but, from the gestures, it looked as if someone had accused Pearson of farting.

Equally suddenly, all four civvies rushed out of the office to stand in a group outside. They continued to argue.

Soon, they became aware that all the cons were looking over at them. Even the screw in the observation box had turned to stare at this unusual sight. Self-consciously, they looked at each other. It was a clear choice between abandoning their tea-break or putting up with the smell. They all filed back in.

In the event it was the shortest tea-break on record. For the 15 minutes that remained they ate in silence, all the while frantically fanning sheaves of paper about in an attempt to dispel the stench.

Fred couldn't get into the tin shop quickly enough to tell us about it. It was the climax of his campaign and a telling victory. We all laughed at the stupidity of the civvies for sitting there in the stink, without realising that something was very wrong. Any con would have recognised the shit smell straight away and suspected a joey.

They were undoubtedly naive, but maybe they weren't suspicious by nature. Perhaps they couldn't conceive that a grown man could do such a thing to them. Whatever the reason, the turds continued to lie behind the cabinet giving off their foul stench.

The civvies avoided going into the office as much as possible now. Phone calls were answered virtually on the run. Break-times were an obvious trial. They took to bringing in air-freshener sprays, but it just made the smell all the more sickly. They rarely took longer than ten minutes for any break now.

Over the weeks, as the turds petrified behind the cabinet, the smell died down. No longer was there the gut-churning stench that would make you want to vomit. There was still a significant smell, but at least it was bearable. Gradually, the civvies extended their breaks until they were taking their full 20 minutes again.

20 THE MACKEREL

Bert Johnson occupied a strange position among Londoners. In general, he was thoroughly disliked and kept on the fringes. On the other hand, though, because of his association with the Twins, an effort was made to keep up appearances. It was nothing to do with the fact that Ron and Reg might get the hump if we turned against him; their contempt for him was well known. It was more to do with maintaining the fiction of a united and interlocking firm of London chaps.

There were two main reasons for Bert's unpopularity. The first centred around his case. Although the Twins themselves were widely feared and respected, as were some of their firm, it was common knowledge that they had several hangers-on with them. The latter weren't feared or respected for themselves. They only got away with what they did because people knew they had the Twins' backing. Bert was one of these.

What really upset people and aroused their contempt, though, was Bert's involvement over Jack 'the Hat' McVitie. Whatever people thought of 'the Hat', and he could be a nasty piece of work when he wanted to, it was known that he and Bert were friends and went about together. That was why the

Twins told Bert and his brother to bring Jack to the party they had arranged.

As game and as crazy as Jack could be, it was highly unlikely that he would have gone alone. He already suspected that Ronnie had the hump with him. Bert asked Jack along, though, well knowing that Jack must be in for a good beating. In the event he was murdered. There was an in joke among the chaps that went: 'If Bert ever invites you to a party, don't go!'

In jail he did little to improve his standing. Most of the chaps were proud men, who tried to conduct themselves with as much honour and dignity as they could. Not Bert though.

He could, however, be very funny at times and regularly took part in various protests. He did his bird easily enough, and you never heard him whining about parole. Nevertheless, he was forever involved in tricky moves and unscrupulous dealings. He just couldn't be trusted.

Among our crowd, he was known as 'the Mackerel', which is an unflattering term for someone who is slippery and underhanded. He wasn't part of our crowd, although he did come into our company quite regularly.

I personally had the hump with him over an incident at the Scrubs. He had been in the chokey with a fella who died under suspicious circumstances. It was alleged that the screws had beaten him up, accidentally killed him and had then tried to cover it up.

There was intense bad feeling about it in the jail. About 300 of us long-termers on 'D' wing had held a sit-down protest. A headline in the local paper read: DID WARDERS MURDER THIS MAN?

At the subsequent inquest, Bert gave evidence that helped the screws out of a tight corner. There was some doubt about the truth of what he said. One particularly radical magazine, *Up Against the Law*, castigated him in no uncertain terms. If he had come back on to 'D' wing, the fellas would have done him. Instead, he had been transferred to Parkhurst.

When I arrived, he had hurried up to assure me that his role at the inquest had been exaggerated. I also found that he had already been accepted by some of the fellas. So, having no hard evidence with me, I decided to let it go for the time being. However, I had arranged for a copy of *Up Against the Law* to be sent to me. When it arrived, I was going to confront him with it in front of the fellas. As things turned out, I never got the chance.

Returning to my cell early one afternoon, I found Stewart and Ralph Baron, a friend and founder member of our firm, waiting for me. I could see that something was up by the serious expression on the face of the usually mischievous Stewart. Ralph, too, seemed on edge.

'Norman,' said Ralph, 'we'd like to ask you something.' He nodded to Stewart, who continued.

'Look, Norm,' he said apprehensively, 'just after dinner I went to slop out. As I came out of the recess, I saw Bert going into my cell. We've been playing a few jokes on each other lately, so I ducked back into the recess to watch what happened. After about 30 seconds, he came out again and hurried away. I was convinced he had set some kind of silly trap for me.

'I hurried back to my cell and crept inside very carefully. There was nothing on top of the door; and I couldn't find anything else that was wrong. So I forgot about it and carried on having a clear-up.

'For some reason, about half an hour later, I decided to check on that two ounces you gave me to look after.' Stewart paused as if he was coming to the bit he found distasteful.

I inwardly cringed, knowing exactly what he was going to say.

'I looked on my bookshelf, behind the books,' he continued, 'and it was gone. It was there before dinner, and no one else had been in. So I don't know what could have happened to it.'

'We know it's a bit strong,' Ralph butted in, 'but you know Bert better than we do. Do you think he could have taken it?'

There was an awkward, embarrassed silence as the three of us stood there looking at each other. This was a very serious matter. Of all the sins that a man can commit in prison, to steal off another con is regarded as the lowest of them all. The presence of nonces and even grasses can sometimes be tolerated, but cell-thieves are usually attacked on sight.

With all the various types of criminal at Parkhurst, nothing ever went missing out of cells. You could, quite literally, leave ounces of snout on your bed with the door wide open, and it would all still be there when you came back hours later.

It was a question of honour. We were all in the same boat. It would be a very weak man who stooped to stealing off other cons just because he was short of a smoke.

Having said that, there was a very severe sanction against cell-thieving at Parkhurst. Rumour had it that a cell-thief had been caught several years previously. The fellas had bashed him, then stuck his hand in the hinged side of a cell door and slammed it. It is said that he lost several fingers.

As much as I would have liked to condemn Bert out of hand, this was something that could utterly destroy his reputation and make him an outcast wherever he went. And there was no conclusive evidence. No one had actually seen him take the snout. Too many people were doing big bird over inconclusive evidence. We often railed against the system because of this. We would be the worst of hypocrites if we judged Bert on similar inconclusive evidence.

'Look, Stewart,' I said, 'firstly, don't worry about the snout. It's only from the book, and we've got about a hundred ounces lying about. Secondly, don't feel embarrassed in any way. It's not your fault. And lastly, yes, I do think he could have taken it, but we've got no real proof.'

I paused to let that sink in. In the back of my mind, I was also thinking that it wouldn't look very good to have one of the London firm exposed as a cell-thief. The various firms of Scouses, Jocks and Paddies would all be laughing at our expense.

I decided to tell Stewart and Ralph about the Scrubs incident. I explained briefly.

'I'm only waiting for a copy of *Up Against the Law*, and then I'm going to confront him with it in front of all the fellas,' I continued. 'I'll do it in the khazi on the compound, then we can all steam into him. That will be the last we'll see of the slag. So, in the meantime, let's keep it to ourselves.'

Stewart and Ralph nodded in agreement.

As an afterthought I added, 'And, for fuck's sake, don't tell Barry about this.' Barry detested Bert. He refused to speak to him and had been looking for an excuse to chin him for ages. On several occasions I had stopped him from doing him.

Stewart and Ralph both seemed satisfied with what had been said. They walked off towards 'A' wing.

At teatime, I wandered across to Dave Bailey's cell, the 'Old Bailey'. Dave, a bank robber and one of the leading lights of our London crowd, was sitting there as usual, with both Ralph and Barry. Barry looked very agitated and red in the face. Ralph looked flushed, and Dave had turned his customary 'whiter shade of pale', as he always did when it was off.

'I've done the slag,' said Barry with absolutely no preliminaries.

Ralph then explained what had happened. He had been telling Dave and Barry about the incident involving Stewart's missing snout. He had just finished when Bert walked in. Barry immediately jumped up and steamed into him. As he punched him into the corner of the cell, Ralph ran over and joined in.

Bert fell to the floor and cowered in the corner. 'What's the matter? What have I done?' he shouted. He started to cry.

Ralph and Barry pulled him to his feet. As Ralph threw him bodily out of the door, Barry kicked him up the arse.

For once, no one was laughing in the aftermath of the violence. It was no laughing matter. We weren't animals who turned on each other for little or no reason. Although, strictly speaking, Bert wasn't one of our crowd, he was on the fringes. He was also a

Londoner. Apart from any other considerations it wouldn't look very good for our solidarity in the eyes of the various other firms.

It could also cause trouble within our group. One of our friends had known Bert since they were kids and quite liked him. Nobody else did, but that didn't mean that they would agree to convict him on wholly circumstantial evidence. There could be a falling out among us, and there were enough potential enemies about without that.

Luckily for all concerned, though, Bert's lowlife nature saved the day. He had gone straight from Dave's cell to the wing office and put himself on Rule 43. Now, whatever the circumstances, he had damned himself. No one of any merit would ever go to the screws and ask for their protection. The mere act of putting himself on 43 had made him a 'wrong 'un'.

We didn't see Bert again. He was down the chokey on the landing with all the nonces and grasses. It was an embarrassing subject for us, so we didn't even talk about it. After a few weeks we heard that he had been shipped out. We were glad to see the back of him.

21 BARON BLUNT

Ralph Baron was the rudest man you would ever meet in your life. It wasn't just that he didn't suffer fools gladly, Ralph didn't suffer fools at all. And, if a fool ever came within insulting distance, he would soon feel the rough edge of Ralph's tongue.

Rudeness was commonplace in prison. Single-handedly, though, Ralph had elevated it into something of an art form. This was why we called him 'Baron Blunt', a play on his surname.

Ralph was just starting a ten. He had been a prolific bank robber, working with some of the best London firms. At 20, he had been the youngest man ever to be sent to Dartmoor. In those days it was seen as the end of the line for hardened, recidivist criminals.

Ralph was shortish, a bit overweight and in his late 20s. His skin was quite swarthy so that he tended to resemble a Cypriot or someone from Mediterranean climes. He also had a riotous mop of bushy black hair. Stewart once called him 'Sooty' as a joke. This was about the only time we ever saw the usually imperturbable Ralph lose his cool. The mischievous Stewart never called him that again.

Ralph was highly intelligent and knew it. At times this made him quite arrogant. However, he was witty, funny and very good company. We all liked him. Ralph was a classic elitist. If you were a London robber with impeccable criminal credentials, then you were OK. If you weren't, then he wouldn't stand you at any price. And he would tell you to your face too. In a criminal subculture that was riddled with hypocrisy, Ralph was like a breath of fresh air. He had his enemies, but these were usually people who had something to hide.

My earliest memory of Ralph was of a day shortly after I had arrived at Parkhurst. I was standing on the ones with Dave, just outside the 'Old Bailey'.

Dave was talking to Kevin, a fella who used to bring him his laundry. Kevin was a big easygoing Londoner, with close-cropped blond hair. He was only 22, yet had a massive body-builder's physique. He was quite slow-witted, bordering on the thick, and was doing a five for a robbery that had been sheer stupidity.

There was no harm in him. He would always do you a good turn rather than a bad one, and there had never been any suggestion that he was a grass. However, he totally lacked any professionalism in the pursuit of crime. Perhaps that was why he looked up to the members of our group with a childlike awe.

Dave was just thanking Kevin for some clean laundry he had delivered, when Ralph swept up. He walked right in among the three of us and took Dave by the arm.

'Dave,' he said, nodding towards Kevin, 'he's a nice fella, but he's a right fucking bore. If you stand for him now, he will be round every five minutes driving you mad. So the best thing is to blank him right from the start.'

With that, he pulled Dave by the arm and led him away. I was left standing there with Kevin, speechless and not a little embarrassed.

This was classic Baron Blunt. I suppose that someone else might have discreetly pulled Dave aside and told him that, if he encouraged Kevin at all, then he could become a pest (as we later found out he could be). Ralph, though, chose to be direct. It was a bit cruel, but this was Parkhurst. The message was that mugs could get you into trouble.

At times, Ralph could be a trifle too direct. He had been looking after two ounces for John and I. Running the book meant that we always had to have 60 or 70 ounces of snout spread about. You were only allowed to hold up to two-and-a-half ounces, so we obviously couldn't keep it all ourselves. Consequently, we spread it around friends and people we knew. Ralph didn't smoke, so he had no snout of his own. He agreed to look after two ounces for us until we needed it.

Ralph occasionally talked to a black fella called Jay. I assumed that Ralph tolerated him for his intellect. He was an educated man, with a courteousness bordering on the unctuous. For that reason I was always uneasy about him. There was nothing I could put my finger on, but, deep down, I didn't trust him.

Jay was doing life with a 15 rec. He wasn't a robber, but black robbers were very rare in those days anyway. It was an unusually heavy sentence for a black man of his intellect. I wondered what his crime could be that it had attracted such a severe sentence.

Ralph lived on 'A' wing, the wing next to ours. As he walked along the threes with the two ounces I had just given him, he passed Jay, who was talking to another black fella called Jackson.

Jackson was one of those fellas who I hadn't really noticed before. He was very tall and thin. He weighed about 12 stone, but spread out over his six-foot-two-inch frame it didn't seem to go very far. He looked all arms and legs. He was a Brummie, doing 15 years for a series of minor armed robberies. In Parkhurst terms, he was a nobody.

I had seen him in the gym a couple of times. In shorts and vest he looked even skinnier. He would punch the bag and clearly didn't have a clue. He held his hands down around his waist and swung wildly. He looked a right wally, but, as they say, punching the bag and fighting are two completely different things.

Ralph passed the pair of them, but only spoke to Jay. He carried on, up to his cell. He had been there about ten minutes when Jay knocked and came in. He told Ralph that, after he had walked past, Jackson had said that he would have to slip in and nick the two ounces.

Perhaps someone less headstrong might have pondered the feasibility of Jackson telling an acquaintance of Ralph's that he was going to rob him. Maybe Ralph should have confronted Jackson and challenged him over it. Unfortunately, though, it was too late for that. The persona of Baron Blunt had sprung into action.

It was early afternoon, and Jackson had just got into bed for a quick nap. Suddenly the door burst open and in ran Ralph. In his hand he had a PP9 battery inside two woollen socks. As Jackson raised his head from the pillow, Ralph struck it a stunning blow. It was quickly followed by several more until Jackson lay unconscious in his bed. Then Ralph ran out again, banging the door shut behind him.

When we came in from work at teatime, the talk was all of Ralph bashing Jackson. If anyone thought that Ralph had gone a bit strong, nothing was said to that effect. We didn't know the full strength of what had gone on. If Ralph were defending the snout we had given him to hold, then he was completely in order. And, whatever the circumstances, our group would stand by him. But Baron Blunt certainly hadn't wasted any time in taking direct action. There was a lot of laughter about the incident.

By the following morning, it was all largely forgotten. Jackson wasn't particularly dangerous, and he had no help worth mentioning. So Ralph wasn't worried by a comeback. That was where the strength of the group was so valuable to us all. Everyone would think long and hard before making a move against any one of us, well knowing that they would have all the rest of the group to contend with as well.

We weren't bullies. We didn't take anything off anyone. We

didn't bother anyone who didn't bother us. But a threat against one was a threat against all.

When we came in from work that dinnertime, you can imagine our surprise to hear that Jackson had bashed Ralph.

We immediately went off to find out how badly he had been hurt. Several of us climbed the stairs of 'A' wing and crowded into his cell.

Ralph was sitting on his bed, more embarrassed than hurt. He had a black eye, which, because of the swarthiness of his skin, didn't look as bad as it might have done. He had also hurt his leg. This didn't explain his bandy-legged gait though. On pressing him further he confessed that Jackson had kicked him in the balls and that they were sore and swollen. The major injury, though, was to his reputation and, by association, to ours too. We asked him what had happened.

Ralph had been walking along one of the landings that morning, when he saw Jackson coming the other way.

As he drew close, Jackson stopped. 'Ralph, why did you do that to me?' he asked animatedly. 'What's it all about?'

'I've got fuck all to say to you,' said Ralph dismissively. 'If you've got anything at all to say about it, we can go into the recess and sort it out.'

The wing was all but deserted. Most of the fellas were out at work. Those who were on the wing were sitting in their cells.

'OK, Ralph,' said Jackson, 'after what you've done to me maybe that's the best thing we can do.'

Jackson walked into the nearest recess, and Ralph followed him. Ralph's brother had a black belt in karate. Ralph had done a bit himself but had only achieved a novice grading. I had seen him in the gym, doing a karate workout on the punchbag. As Jackson shaped up boxing style, Ralph assumed the 'kiba dachi' position, standing square on to Jackson, feet wide apart with his knees bent.

The next thing Ralph remembered was waking up on his bed. Jackson was sitting in a chair beside him.

'What happened?' asked Ralph groggily.

'I knocked you out, man,' said Jackson.

With that, Ralph launched himself off the bed to attack him. He was still weak from being knocked unconscious, though, and his legs crumpled beneath him. Jackson pushed him away and ran out of the cell.

As Ralph finished telling the story, I saw Stewart out of the corner of my eye trying hard not to laugh. To be honest, I felt like laughing myself. I could imagine the situation.

Ralph letting Jackson go into the recess first was mistake number one. The recess was quite dark, with just a tiny window behind Jackson. Ralph had the lights of the wing behind him and would have had trouble seeing the black man in the dark. Jackson would have had no such problem. Ralph was a perfectly lit target.

Ralph's second mistake was to shape up karate style by assuming 'kiba dachi'. If Jackson had realised that it was karate, he clearly wasn't impressed. He promptly kicked Ralph in the balls as hard as he could. The rest was history.

Apart from Ralph's injuries, the immediate problem was that Jackson couldn't be allowed to get away with it. Irrespective of what personal revenge Ralph wanted to take, we wanted our revenge on Jackson for doing one of our group.

It was personal pride, but it was also to do with reputation. There were undoubtedly quite a few who would like to make a move against one or other of our group. But the sanction of an immediate comeback from the rest of us ensured our individual and collective safety. Jackson had to go.

After we were unlocked for association that evening, John, Barry and Stewart came to my cell. Barry was absolutely champing at the bit. He couldn't wait to get at Jackson. We weren't going to wait to see what Ralph was going to do. Anyway, he was still injured. We loaded up with a couple of blades and a short iron bar and set off for 'A' wing.

The major difficulty was that we were going on to another

wing. It wasn't an insurmountable problem, because John lived on 'A' wing and had got across to us. He had walked through the door on the ones when it was opened to allow us through for stage. It was locked again now, though, and wouldn't be opened again until eight o'clock. There was another way, however.

Up on the fives, there was an eight-foot partition, which separated the two wings. We often used to climb over it to go visiting. The screws knew about it, but it wasn't a major security hazard. We were only going from one wing to another.

The four of us climbed the stairs to the fives. Most of our wing screws were down in the office. Those that were on the landings were unsighted for the fives partition.

John and Barry lifted me up, and I poked my head above the partition. I peered into the gloom to see what screws there were about. They were very conscientious on 'A' wing and tended to stand on the bridges. This gave them a commanding view of all the landings.

The bridges were clear, though; I couldn't see any screws at all. As I ran my eyes quickly along the landings, I couldn't see any screws there either. But a movement caught my attention. Then I saw them. There must have been a dozen dark-blue uniforms, standing well back in the shadows of the cell doorways. They were obviously waiting for us.

The screws had heard what had gone on between Jackson and Ralph. They had guessed there would be a comeback from us and knew it would be heavy. Perhaps Jackson had told them himself. He couldn't have been under any illusions about what was bound to happen.

There was nothing we could do for now though. John and Barry lowered me to the landing, and we all returned to my cell. We resolved to get Jackson on the exercise yard the following day.

At exercise time the next day, all four of us were plotted up in the compound, waiting for Jackson to come out. The screws only stayed on the perimeter, so if Jackson came into the crowds of cons milling about in the centre; then one of us could slip up and do him.

The compound quickly filled up. Soon there were over 200 cons running, walking, sitting, standing or playing games. Many of them had heard about the incident with Ralph and guessed there would be a comeback. There were some knowing looks as we loitered about.

Suddenly, Jackson appeared at the compound gate. He came just inside, then stopped. He stood no further than six feet from the bunch of screws by the gate; and that was as far as he was going. Clearly, we had to think up another plan.

The obvious choice was in the cinema. On Saturday night a couple of hundred cons would be crammed into the old chapel up by 'A'-wing stage rooms, to watch the film. Quite a few people had been done once the lights went out. You could crawl along the floor between the rows of chairs, do the business and, by the time the lights went on, be long gone. The cinema at Parkhurst was a very dangerous place.

That Saturday evening, all our crowd went to the cinema. By now it was common knowledge that we were going to do Jackson. Those who hadn't been told that something was up could have guessed from the way that Jackson now went everywhere accompanied by two screws. That, in itself, was something of a face-saver for us.

We got to the cinema early and sat in a row near the back. This gave us a commanding view over the rows of tiered seats.

The place rapidly filled up, and within 15 minutes there were 200 people in their seats. Right at the very end, just as they were about to lock the door, in came Jackson accompanied by two screws. The three of them walked right to the back and sat down underneath the projector, with their backs against the wall. Darkness or no, Jackson was safe for another evening.

By now, we were becoming thoroughly frustrated. It seemed that Jackson was being minded all the time. Short of walking up and doing him in front of the screws, there was nothing that could be done.

We also had the added annoyance of Ralph insisting that it was his row and that he was going to do Jackson himself. We were all for that, but we didn't want to get to a situation where it went on and on until Ralph left it. With us, at least we knew for sure that it would be done eventually.

Finally, we agreed to let Ralph have the first shot. It was no major concession, because no one could get close to Jackson at the moment anyway. However, we knew that the screws wouldn't keep it up indefinitely. They would tell Jackson either to go on Rule 43 or take the consequences.

Now that the ball was firmly in Ralph's court, he came to my cell early one morning and asked what I would use if I were going to do Jackson.

'It depends how much damage I wanted to do,' I said, looking at him closely. Ralph wasn't in my position. He would be going home in a couple of years. He didn't need to miscue and land himself with a life sentence or another lump of bird on top.

I could see from Ralph's manner that he would be satisfied with just knocking Jackson unconscious and putting him in the hospital for a few days. So all that Ralph would need was a cosh of some kind.

It would have to be small and easily concealable so that Ralph could walk about with it on him. But it would also have to be meaty enough to do some damage. Ralph seemed enthusiastic about the cosh.

My first feeling was one of relief that Ralph had decided to dispense with the karate. Our reputation couldn't stand him with another black eye and sore balls again. As it was, the situation was rapidly turning into farce.

I told Ralph that you could make a useful little tool by putting a large stone or chunk of metal inside a couple of socks. It was the same principle as the PP9 cosh he had used, but with a denser payload. Ralph could keep the socks and the object separate until the last moment. The object could be comparatively small, too, provided that it was hard and dense. The centrifugal force of the sock whipping around would give it maximum impact. Ralph liked the idea and asked me to get him a lump of metal from the tin shop.

At break-time that morning, I wandered away from where we usually sat for tea and slipped into the stores. This was where all the various metal-working tools were kept. I couldn't take any of those, though, because they were all on shadow boards. If one went missing, it would leave a very obvious gap.

At the back of the store I found an old tin box full of bolts, screws and washers. Nothing seemed large enough to interest me though. I rummaged through the box and suddenly found a golden-bronze-coloured lump of metal, shaped like an extra-large hen's egg. One end was drawn out, making it look like a large golden teardrop.

At first I dismissed it because it was too small. When I picked it up, though, I couldn't believe how heavy it was. I didn't know from what type of metal it was made, but it was at least twice as heavy as I had expected.

I decided that it would do. I put it in my pocket and walked out into the shop. I went over to a window that had a small hole in its security grille. I dropped it through into some long grass, to be collected later.

That dinnertime, as everyone was returning from work, Barry and I went on to 'A' wing and up to Ralph's cell. He was sitting in a chair, reading.

'I've got it for you, Ralph,' I said. 'Have you got a couple of woolly socks?'

Ralph searched in a box under his bed and pulled out a pair of grey woollen, prison-issue socks. After putting one inside the other, I dropped the golden egg in and handed it to Ralph. He swung it backwards and forwards experimentally. The frown on his face was still registering following his initial surprise at the smallness of the 'egg'.

Suddenly, he swung it viciously against the wall. There was a loud, concussive 'bang', and a deep crack appeared right across the brick. It had, quite literally, cracked in half.

Ralph's frown was instantly replaced by one of consternation. He didn't say as much, but you could tell by his expression that he felt it was too dangerous. He only wanted to hurt Jackson, not kill him. Of course, the trouble was that any blow with the 'egg' was liable to cause serious damage. I had a feeling that Ralph wouldn't use it.

Now the pressure was on Ralph to make his move. He had a bit of breathing space, though, because Jackson was still being minded by the screws.

A week dragged into two. Jackson started to get bolder, wandering further and further from his minders. We had known that they couldn't shadow him indefinitely. Ralph now had his chance. All that remained was for him to take it. But he still hesitated and dithered.

Suddenly, early one morning, Jackson disappeared. He was bound for the Midlands and some accumulated visits. Having had no visits for several months, he was entitled to be transferred to his local prison, where his family could visit him more easily. He wouldn't be back for at least a month.

In some ways, it was a satisfactory conclusion. It was beginning to look like Ralph would never make his move. And, if he did, there was always the danger that he would badly hurt Jackson and get nicked for it. I would have backed Ralph to the hilt, but perhaps he had been a bit premature in doing Jackson merely on Jay's say-so in the first place. I was glad to see Jackson go.

He would be back in a month or so. Then Ralph would have to decide what he was going to do all over again. But a month was a long time in Parkhurst. In between, literally anything could happen.

A few months later, following a sit-down protest on the compound, I and most of our group were shanghaied. Ralph remained though. Jackson duly came back from his visits. Ralph challenged him to another straightener. He lost again.

22 NUT-NUT

Terry Hillman had all the criminal credentials to be one of our crowd; an experienced South London robber, he was doing 15 years for a big payroll robbery. He was staunch enough; there had never been any suggestion that he was a grass. At times he could be a right rebel. He certainly didn't have a good prison record. But a particularly contrary nature set him apart.

He was a burly, powerful fella, balding, with short, curly black hair. He had an aggressive way with him and regularly got into fights. He never went to the gym, so he was out of condition. However, he was a bit of a nutter and would lay into an enemy with whatever came to hand.

One of his problems was that, when in one of his awkward moods, he could fall out with friend and foe alike. Because of his volatile personality, I used to call him 'Nut-Nut'. It was a private joke between us. Terry quite liked the image of being a bit crazy and dangerous.

Of all our crowd, I was the only one who got on with him at all. We had been in a tear-up together at the Scrubs. Having fought side by side, there was a bond of sorts. We weren't close pals, but I was one of his few defenders.

And he needed some defending. At Parkhurst, he had got far too friendly with the screws. He wasn't a groveller or a yes-man by any means. He had a rough, familiar way with everyone and, if any screw had ever got saucy with him, Terry would soon have given him a volley.

He was the number one on the hot-plate. This meant that, among other things, he was in charge of the screws' tearoom. Part of his duties was to brew up for the screws, a job that the vast majority of cons at Parkhurst wouldn't have done. Apart from the fact that the screws were hated and no con would want to make tea for them, it was also seen as quite demeaning to be a screws' tea-boy.

This didn't faze Terry though. In fact, he regularly compounded the felony by making them sandwiches from mealtime leftovers too. He got a few perks in return, but it hardly endeared him to the fellas.

Generally, he wasn't liked. He wasn't publicly insulted, but a lot of people wouldn't speak to him. It didn't worry him, though, because he just surrounded himself with a small group of sycophants. They were mostly weak lowlifes, whom Terry bullied. It was a wonder they stood for it at times. But, like courtiers around a king, without Terry they were nothing.

There were a couple of young screws on the wing, and Terry got on particularly well with them. Under different circumstances, they could have admired his rough rebelliousness. They had both recently left the Army after serving in Northern Ireland. They hated the IRA with a passion.

There were about ten IRA men at Parkhurst, three on our wing. They kept very much to themselves and never gave anyone cause to fall out with them. They were polite and eminently trustworthy. Their crimes apart, they were principled men. I never heard of any of them pulling strokes. In a world where we were surrounded by potential enemies, we had nothing to fear from the IRA.

Some of our crowd didn't like them. Understandably, they strongly disapproved of the IRA's habit of putting bombs in places where civilians could get hurt. Many of the chaps were quite right-wing in their politics. There were more than a few 'Little Englanders'. If a bomb had ever gone off in London injuring large numbers of ordinary people, then our local IRA would definitely have had a severe comeback from the Parkhurst Londoners.

My own personal feeling was that, as they weren't grasses or liberty-takers, they were no threat to me. Parkhurst was full of people who were a very real threat. I would reserve my enmity for them.

There was one particular IRA man who seemed to be the local leader. The one most senior in rank always assumed the role of Commanding Officer.

He was a tall gangling fella, who lived on the landing above mine. He was quiet to the point of being withdrawn, mixing only with the other IRA fellas. If you hadn't known he was IRA, you would never have guessed. Our two ex-army screws hated him. Whether they actually asked Terry to do something about him or whether Terry suggested it himself never came out. What was obvious, though, was that they hatched up a plot between them.

I was lying on my bed one dinnertime, dozing lightly. Everyone was locked up, and most of the screws had gone off for dinner. The wing was very quiet. Over the years, you couldn't help but get into the habit of taking a quick nap over the dinnertime bang-up. There was little else to do, and the large stodgy dinner inevitably had a soporific effect.

From time to time, I could hear laughter from the direction of the screws' tearoom. I guessed that Terry was sitting in there with whichever two screws were on the dinnertime watch. Another habit of his that antagonised many of the fellas.

Almost subconsciously, I was aware of boots going up the metal stairs just outside my door. It wasn't a loud clatter, just the scuffing of leather on steel and the odd squeak of stressed metal. It wasn't unusual. Perhaps someone upstairs had rung his bell and the screws were going up to see what he wanted.

Suddenly, I heard the explosive sound of a cell door opening quickly. Now that was unusual. When the screws were off at mealtimes, prisoners weren't supposed to be unlocked.

It could be a special search or a shanghai, but I hadn't heard any extra screws come on to the wing. Whatever it was, it was something out of the ordinary. Something that couldn't wait until the rest of the screws came back from dinner.

If I had needed any further convincing, the sharp cry of pain confirmed that something was up. I jumped off my bed and ran to press my ear to the door.

The tall IRA man had been dozing on his bed too. Unlike me, he hadn't heard the sound of boots coming up the stairs. Or, if he had, he hadn't paid it any attention. He hadn't heard Terry and the two young screws as they crept along the landing towards his cell either.

The first thing he knew was when the door crashed open, and Terry ran in. He had the sleeve of a jumper pulled down over his face as a mask. As the IRA man rose off his bed, Terry slashed him across the cheek with a Stanley knife. That was the scream that had roused me.

As he threw his arm up to protect his face, Terry hit him across the opposite side of his head with the wooden baton he was holding in his left hand. The IRA man fell to the floor, and Terry continued to beat him.

After pausing just to put in a last couple of kicks, Terry spun round and rushed out of the cell. One of the screws banged the door behind him and slid the bolt home. The whole episode had lasted barely 30 seconds.

For several days, I couldn't find out what had happened. Terry and the two screws obviously weren't talking. If the IRA man went sick with his injuries, no one saw him, and he didn't tell the screws how he had got them. He must have told the rest of the IRA fellas, but they always kept things to themselves.

They never made any sort of comeback. Terry could be very dangerous, and any move against him would have had to be a serious one. Tools would have been used, and it could quite easily have ended up with someone being killed.

Then there was the fact that Terry was a Londoner. The IRA fellas knew that Londoners stuck together at Parkhurst. They weren't to know that very few of the Londoners there liked Terry though.

Finally, Terry obviously had the help of the screws. Looking at it from the IRA's perspective, it wasn't surprising that it was let go.

After about a week, our crowd discovered what had happened. If we had found out immediately, we would have been more incensed. As it was, several other things had occurred in the intervening period. We were still disgusted though. The screws were the enemy. We wouldn't accept help from them under any circumstances. And, as for joining together with them to attack another con, that was completely out of order.

However, the crucial point was that it didn't involve any of our group. We could have picked up the cudgels on the IRA man's behalf on a general point of principle, but similar points of general principle were arising every day. Life in Parkhurst was an ongoing Greek tragedy. We couldn't, and wouldn't, come to the help of everybody.

The important thing was that our firm was strong. Because of that no one gave us a hard time. No one would come at us unless we did something serious to them first. There were far softer targets than us.

The moral was that the IRA man had suffered because he and his crowd were comparatively weak. And, in Parkhurst, weakness was the ultimate sin.

Terry finished his sentence. Over the years his unquiet spirit forever dragged him into violent conflicts in pubs and clubs.

The IRA printed an account of the attack on their member in Parkhurst in their paper An Phoblact. They mentioned Terry by name. It was said that they would take their revenge.

In 2005 he was one of the gang arrested for the attempted robbery at 'The Dome'. Before he could come to trial he died of cancer.

23 MR NICE GUY

If there were one message that was repeatedly driven home at Parkhurst, it was that safety lay with the group. Its corollary was that mixing with mugs inevitably got you into trouble.

Membership of our group did have its risks, but the benefits far outweighed the drawbacks. We were physically safer than most other people in the jail, and that wasn't to be undervalued.

There were no fools in our group. Therefore, we wouldn't be drawn into some major trouble because of sheer stupidity. Admittedly, Barry could be unpredictable, to say the least. But, on balance, his other attributes made him a valued member of the group.

Mick was the oldest of our crowd. At 38 and with an 18-year sentence in front of him, his future looked particularly bleak. He had been a member of the most prolific and successful firm of robbers in the history of London armed crime. The supergrass on the firm had been a childhood friend. This made it especially hard for Mick to accept.

He had an easygoing, likeable personality, but he didn't live nearly tight enough for Parkhurst. He was not only polite and chatty to many of the screws but also on friendly terms with several people outside our group. Quite a few of these were rated as complete mugs by the rest of us. Time and again we would ask Mick why he was mixing with someone or other who had a reputation for being a right berk. Mick would just smile and say that he was only being sociable.

Mick regularly talked to Peter, a young lifer who worked in the tailor's shop with him. Peter was only 22 and thoroughly immature with it. Rumour had it that he was innocent and had taken the rap for someone else. Whatever the circumstances, he hadn't come to terms with his sentence at all and was forever doing stupid things.

He was short, plump and had an innocent-looking baby-face. His fairish hair and blue eyes completed a picture that resembled an overgrown schoolboy.

He didn't win much respect over his friendship with Ron. As the Twins lived in the Security Wing, they rarely came into contact with cons from the main prison. Ron was well known for his homosexuality and, on the occasions when he was escorted through the prison, he would show out to various young fellas. The vast majority didn't welcome the attention. A few of the mugs, though, were pleased to be acknowledged by someone as notorious as he, even if it was only because Ron fancied fucking them.

Peter was one of the latter. A Northerner, he had only read about Ron and Reg in the papers. He was quite flattered that Ron should notice him. He joined the growing band of young fellas who went over to the church each Sunday to pass messages across the pews to Ron.

Peter's closest friend was another lifer called Don. He was in his early 20s and came from the West Country. He was short and squat, with an elaborate, well-greased Elvis hairstyle. The long sideburns and dense designer stubble were an attempt to appear heavy. He worked out on the weights and walked about with an exaggerated body-builder's strut.

This macho image, though, hardly squared with his homosexual activity at the back of the cinema. If anything, it made his posing seem all the more ridiculous. Our crowd had nothing but contempt for him and referred to him as 'Deep Throat'. Barry especially detested him and was forever looking for an excuse to knock him out.

We didn't ever take the piss out of him openly though. He couldn't have a fight, but he could be very dangerous. Only a year earlier, he had got a seven on top of his life sentence for seriously stabbing another con.

Peter and Don had enough neuroses between them to fill a casebook. They could never come to terms with the fact that, in the macho world of Parkhurst, their poofery only brought them contempt. Therefore, they were always doing things to try to prove how tough they were. They were dangerous fools and were to be avoided.

They saw things that our group and others got away with and regularly tried to imitate them. It rarely came off though. If they tried to have a drink of hooch, for example, the 'A'-wing screws would walk right in on them and break it up. Something they would never have tried with our group. This just served to increase their sense of inferiority.

On this particular day, Peter and Don had made some hooch. One young screw, with whom Peter used to joke about, had already told them to get rid of it. Because of the informal nature of his relationship with him, perhaps Peter didn't believe he meant it.

It was mid-evening and time for people to return from the stage rooms and have an hour's association on the wings before banging up. For this period the cells on 'A' wing would be unlocked. Peter and Don had chosen this time to have their drink. With two Thermos flasks full of the hooch they walked along the landing towards Peter's cell.

Two screws were standing on the bridge, near to Peter's cell.

One of them was the young screw. As Peter and Don crossed the bridge, the young screw stepped out in front of them.

At this precise moment the gate at the end of 'A' wing was opened for those returning from the stage rooms. There must have been 50 of us, both 'A' wing and 'D' wing mixed.

The 'A'-wing fellas started to spread out and head up to their landings. The 'D'-wing bunch, with Mick, Barry and I in the lead, headed for the stairs that led down to the ones, on our way through to 'D' wing.

As we approached the top of the stairs, we were on the same level as the bridge that spanned the twos. We could clearly see the two screws standing there, barely 30 feet away, with Peter and Don approaching.

I knew instantly that something was wrong. The signs were almost subliminal, but the two screws seemed to be waiting to pounce, and Peter and Don seemed on edge. A sixth sense picked up on the intangible air of tension.

I was immediately on my guard, but just carried on walking, saying nothing. I wasn't unduly concerned, because Peter and Don weren't friends of our crowd. And, anyway, in a few seconds, we would be down the stairs, passing underneath the bridge as we headed along the ones on our way through to 'D' wing.

Suddenly, Peter turned towards us. As he saw Mick, he called out, 'Mick, have you got a minute?'

Mick smiled his usual 'nice fella' smile and immediately ducked out of the crowd. Straightening his glasses across his nose, he headed along the twos towards the place where the landing met the bridge. Now, I slowed right down. Barry had got it, too, and slowed with me. The crowd of about 20 were forced to shuffle along behind us.

Mick was halfway there when the young screw made a grab for the flask that Peter was carrying. Peter punched him in the face, and they started to struggle. At the same time the second screw pulled out his stick and went to hit Peter with it.

I had no time for either Peter or Don, but now the situation had changed. In Parkhurst, whenever there was a row between a con and a screw, any decent con would take sides against the screw. Even if this meant getting physically involved in a fight. Also, Mick was so close to the action he looked like being involved too.

By now I had reached the top of the stairs. I stopped abruptly and spread my arms wide, grabbing the railing either side. This forced the crowd following me to come to a halt.

'Oi,' I shouted loudly, 'put that fucking stick away.'

The screw stopped in mid-swing. He looked round and saw the crowd of cons standing there. The tight, hostile faces glared at him. The young screw stopped struggling with Peter and stepped back. They both realised that a major incident was only seconds away, an incident in which they could only come off worst.

Taking their chance, Peter and Don brushed past the screws and ran into Peter's cell. There was a banging and scraping as they barricaded the door behind them.

The effect of all this on Mick had been traumatic. One minute he had been bowling along the landing on what he thought was a social call, the next he was in the middle of a punch-up with two screws.

The pleasant smile had disappeared from his face to be replaced by a look of consternation. Fussing nervously with his glasses as he looked over his shoulder, he rapidly backtracked along the landing.

Still looking over his shoulder, he pushed through the crowd. He ducked under my outstretched arms and skipped quickly down the stairs. He hurried along the ones towards the door that led to 'D' wing, continuing to glance up nervously at the twos and the screws standing outside Peter's closed door.

Now that the situation was over, I dropped my arms and descended the stairs at the head of the crowd.

Barry was cursing next to me. 'That fucking Mick, wanting to be Mr Nice Guy all the time. Perhaps now he'll know not to mix with mugs,' he fumed.

Barry was right, of course. Peter had tried to involve Mick, hoping to deter the screws from grabbing the hooch. He had taken advantage of his friendship with him. He would never have tried that with either Barry or me, who didn't so much as speak to him.

We walked through into 'D' wing and entered Mick's cell. He was sitting on his bed, still white around the gills.

'I thought he was going to give me some books,' he said as we came in.

'How many times do you have to be told about having it with mugs?' shouted Barry angrily. The thought of getting involved in a tear-up with the screws on behalf of Peter and Don, both of whom he detested, had really wound him up. For a moment I thought he was going to punch Mick.

If we had thought that Mick had learned his lesson, we were soon disappointed. The following day, he was back to normal. Cheerfully joking with the screws and calling a cheery good morning to all and sundry, he bustled about the landing.

Barry and I watched, but said nothing. Mick had gone down a lot in our estimation. It wasn't so much that he had ignored everything we had said. We just couldn't forget the way he had run off and left us after we had stood by him and his mate Peter. The most basic tenet of our group was loyalty. Where Mick was concerned, though, it was beginning to look like a one-way process. As far as Barry and I were concerned, next time he'd be on his own.

24 THE POOF DOCTOR

By and large, the cons at Parkhurst remained oblivious to any changes of staff. The arrival of a new governor might be remarked on, but such was the barrier between cons and screws that virtually no relationship of any kind grew between them.

The screws actively discouraged any familiarity and kept to themselves. Similarly, most of the cons utterly detested the screws and only spoke to them when they had to. In fact, any con who became too close to the screws would quickly get himself a bad name. Various sanctions would follow, ranging from social ostracism to outright assault.

Exercise time, after the dinnertime bang–up, was the first real chance of the day for the cons to get together. Breakfast was always a hurried affair. The wings were locked off until movement to work, so you couldn't get about the place. On the way to work you would see people from other landings and other wings, but there was little time to talk.

By dinnertime, though, whatever gossip there was had been discussed in the workshops. During exercise, this gossip was passed on, so that by the end of the period you could have a pretty good idea of what had happened in the jail over the past 24 hours.

One exercise time, the talk was all about the new doctor. Although all the rest of Parkhurst's staff were permanent, various local GPs visited to hold morning surgery. You could never be sure which of the four or five it would be, but it didn't really matter anyway, because they would always be guided by the resident medical screws. Each doctor would have his own personal idiosyncrasies, but all would try to ensure continuity and never rock the boat. That was until the new doctor arrived.

Each morning about 20 men would report sick. Mostly it was a waste of time, because they would be fobbed off with pills and medicines. If an operation were needed, then it would be done in Parkhurst hospital. First-class outside surgeons would operate, but it was the level of after-care that worried most cons. It was hard enough dealing with the hospital screws when you were fully fit. So the idea of lying helpless and at their mercy didn't appeal to many people.

The men reporting sick would be let through several gates into a small area adjacent to 'C' wing. Here they would sit on long benches outside the visiting doctor's office. They would go in, one by one, to discuss their problems with him. Also present, would be the hospital PO and another medical screw.

This exercise time, several fellas were going off about the new doctor who had been on that morning. He had cancelled the treatment of men who had been on particular drugs for years. He had also stopped the daily allowance of milk for several people who had managed to wangle a pint of milk a day because of some medical condition.

All this was bad enough in itself, but, to add insult to injury, the new doctor was outrageously gay. Not just effeminate, the fellas emphasised, but absolutely raving. And the mid-Seventies at Parkhurst were hardly liberated times.

By teatime, the jail was in an uproar. All sorts of dangerous lunatics were making dire threats about what would happen if the new doctor stopped their medication. The mere thought of having to go through the day straight made them even more uptight than usual.

The screws, especially the medical screws, were seriously worried. They knew what they could expect when certain cons started to experience withdrawal symptoms that had previously been suppressed by drugs. They also knew that they would be in the frontline when these men joined the treatment queue and demanded their usual medication. Drugging had become official policy at Parkhurst, because it kept people quiet.

The cons in general were very angry. Anything that smacked of a crackdown was like a challenge to them. They were well aware that privileges in prison weren't given gratuitously. They were given to keep people quiet and, as such, had to be fought for. Sometimes they had to be defended. The fact that the clampdown might just be a personal initiative on the part of a new doctor didn't come into it. They didn't draw any distinction between prison doctors and prison management. They were all the same to them.

The following morning, about 90 of us reported sick. They brought us through to the waiting area in batches of 20. It was quite an effective way of registering a protest, because, instead of sick parade being finished in an hour, it would now take all morning. The screws would have lots of extra work to do, which would put them behind in their other duties. And, as an added bonus, we would get a whole morning off work.

I had gone sick out of solidarity with the others. I was rarely ill and had little use for the doctors. However, I also wanted to have a look at the man who had caused all the uproar. The descriptions had sounded so exaggerated that I just had to see for myself.

About half an hour had gone by. There had been a steady flow of men going in and out of the doctor's room. On several occasions there had been muffled screams and shouts. The door would open and the medical screws would gently push the protester out, still shouting abuse at the doctor.

One or two had tried to attack him physically. The screws had got between them and gently edged them out of the room. This was all very unusual, if for no other reason than, in similar circumstances, the heavy mob would have dragged the offender off to the chokey.

At last my turn came. I wasn't on any medication, but I did have some cream for my psoriasis. My excuse would be to ask for more cream. My name was called, and I walked into the room.

The doctor was sitting behind a large desk. Standing either side of him were the two medical screws. They both had grins on their faces, an anatomical feat that I would have previously thought impossible. I was soon to see why.

The doctor was in his late 40s, slim and wearing a suit of pastel beige. It had wide lapels and was entirely too trendy for Parkhurst. He had a long, smooth face and medium-length blond hair that was well slicked down, but curling at each temple.

'Yes, Parker, and what's the matter with you?' he trilled.

Despite what I had already heard, the voice and mannerisms still came as a shock. He spoke in a high falsetto, with accompanying breathlessness. The hand, head and eye movements were all greatly exaggerated.

There were plenty of poofs in Parkhurst, and many of them affected effeminate ways, but none remotely approached the level of high camp of our new doctor. He was a real screaming queen, all high-pitched voice and feminine gestures.

Now, the two medical screws were laughing unrestrainedly. I stood there, thoroughly embarrassed. All thoughts of picking an argument had vanished. I just wanted to get out of the room as quickly as possible.

The doctor couldn't fail to notice the reaction his behaviour was provoking, but he made no acknowledgement of it. He just sat there looking at me, waiting for an answer to his question.

I quickly explained about my psoriasis, secretly praying that he wouldn't ask to see it. I had a patch of the rash on my upper thigh, so it would have meant taking off my trousers. This would have provoked even greater merriment in the two screws. They already seemed to be greatly enjoying themselves.

The doctor listened, then wrote something down in a book in front of him. 'OK,' he said, 'I've renewed the Betnovate cream for another month.'

As he finished, I immediately turned and left the room.

I hadn't had any trouble with him, but there wasn't too much he could do with a request for such a simple treatment. Others, however, continued to be provoked. One got so incensed that he actually dived across the desk and grabbed hold of the doctor's lapels, before being bundled out.

The following day, we heard that the new doctor wouldn't be coming again. It wasn't that his manner had been incompatible with that of a Parkhurst official. There were plenty of others whose manner was hostile, punitive and actively offensive, yet they continued to serve. It was the fact that he had ignored the medical screws' advice and gone against the unofficial policy of prescribing drugs for cons, just to keep them quiet. In his own way the new doctor had been as rebellious against the system as many of us cons.

25 SOMEBODY LOVES A
FAIRY AT 40

Although the new doctor's homosexuality compounded the insult of his attitude in the eyes of many cons, Parkhurst wasn't a hotbed of rampant homophobia. There was a fair degree of live and let live. Hypocrisy apart, the attitude of many of the chaps was that, if the poofs didn't bother them, they wouldn't bother the poofs.

There was always the problem of definition. It was generally agreed that anyone who took it up the bum was obviously a poof. However, quite a few people, at one time or another, in one jail or another, had had their cocks sucked. Did this make them poofs? Most of them certainly didn't think so. Especially as they were either married or strictly heterosexual when outside.

I personally didn't think the issue very important. It was a subject of some embarrassment to me, but, when asked privately, I would offer the opinion that there were many ways to judge a man, and his sexuality wasn't the most important. However, in public, I sometimes echoed the generally homophobic statements of the majority of the chaps.

We were all aware that, as a term of abuse, the word 'poof' didn't have particularly negative or unmanly connotations. There were some poofs at Parkhurst who scored high on all the other manly, non-sexual indicators. Some were very dangerous with a blade. Some could have a right row. Others were very strong on the weights and had good physiques. Many were very staunch and never pulled strokes or grassed. Quite a few were well respected (nobody ever called Ronnie Kray a poof).

Often, when Barry was in a particularly homophobic state of mind, I would take the opportunity to remind him of some of the poofs I had met who were proud, honourable men. One day, just as he was raging about the 'poof doctor', I told him about Micky Blake.

At 42, Micky Blake was getting a bit too old to be a poof. Admittedly, he still had the slender figure of his youth. And his shoulder-length brown hair was still thick and strong, although shot through with grey in places. But his face!

There's an old saying in jail: 'It doesn't show on your shoes.' If it had, then Mick's would have been battered and nearly worn out. As it was, it was his face that had borne the brunt of the stress and strain. What, in his youth, had been a pleasant, almost handsome, if slightly effeminate visage was now deeply lined and worn. Time, that cruellest of satirists, had taken each and every part of the young face that had looked out on the world, and etched age and despair everywhere.

His once smooth forehead was now deeply rutted with lines that made for a perpetual frown. His eyes had sunk deep into a morass of crow's feet until now it seemed as if they peered out from deep pits. The skin was stretched drum-tight, highlighting bony cheeks and jaw, almost as if the skull beneath was trying to force its way through. Its texture was waxy and lifeless; gone was the bloom of youth. Perhaps the saddest feature was his mouth. The loss of all his teeth had caused it to sink inwards, puckering around his lips. He was very conscious of this and would try to shield his mouth with his hands when he spoke. No one, even early-morning visitors to his cell, had ever glimpsed his false teeth.

The once elegant neck was as scraggy as a chicken's, with lined flesh hanging in folds. His Adam's apple, always prominent, protruded almost as starkly as his nose.

It was the face of someone who had been under the most intense pressure. Almost as if the wind had changed, fairytale-like, and a silent scream had been frozen there for ever.

Mick still tried to carry himself like a woman though. He would tilt his head to one side in a coquettish pose. Long, bony fingers would raise a cigarette to his lips in a manner that might have been temptatious a decade earlier. He would swing his hips as he swished on to the exercise yard.

Tragically, it all served to emphasise the cruel caricature of a middle-aged man trying to act like an attractive woman. Whatever had been was gone, and would never be again.

Mick wasn't ideally suited for prison life. No thief or villain, he was basically a straight goer. A disastrous affair with a lover, who had used and abused him, then tossed him aside, had shattered his life. He had killed the fella out of sheer desperation, thinking no further than the act. Not caring what happened next, just so long as the terrible emotional trauma was ended.

The subsequent trial and life sentence had torn the heart out of him. He had plumbed such depths of grief and despair that only his basic life force had kept him going.

In many ways he was already dead. Prison was such a cold, emotionless existence that the pain often seemed to outweigh the pleasure. He had had affairs, but they had all been shallow and unsatisfactory. He had searched for love, his partners for lust.

Now, eight years into his life sentence, the future looked bleak. He still had several years to serve, and then what? The incessant pressure had eaten away at him, eroding the very youth from his body. His sensitive, caring nature was totally at odds with the uncouth, violent people around him. Despite his crime, he wasn't a violent person himself. This put him at all sorts of disadvantages in the prison milieu. He spent whole days looking for just a moment's solace.

Luckily, Long Lartin was a liberal prison. A laidback regime allowed a varied subculture to flourish. There was a widespread gay scene that was more overt than in many jails. Some of the chaps dabbled, some didn't. It was no big deal. No one was ostracised over it. There was all the usual hypocrisy, but nobody was ever bashed just for being a poof.

Having said that, the chaps would never have 'fem' poofs in the company. Those that had their own regular poof would live with them in the domestic situation. But, out on exercise, in the gym, out on the sports field, the chaps would congregate and talk of crime, violence and other macho things. The poofs would congregate on their own. A mirror image of the clubs outside, where the chaps would stand in a crowd at the bar and their women in a group in the corner.

Mick, though, wasn't one of the chaps. He was no thief or villain and had no hard reputation. For him, there was a subculture of poofs who kept to their own company. They weren't dominant or influential in any way. They weren't even a unified group. Regularly, they were harried and harassed by more violent cons.

A group of them generally gathered out on the exercise yard, up against 'E' wing where the path met the main yard. Eight or nine mostly young fellas would stand gossiping and smoking. All were openly gay.

The talk would be of boyfriends and general prison gossip. But mostly it would be of boyfriends. In many ways, Mick was the senior queen. He was certainly the oldest, but he had also served longest in prison.

He was a Londoner and had a reputation for being staunch. There had never been any suggestion that Mick would ever grass anyone. He stood up to the screws too. He had a quick, vicious tongue. Many was the screw who had backed off under a tirade of abuse and innuendo. Mick didn't pull strokes either.

Because of these qualities, most of the London chaps accepted him. There was nothing in it. His sexuality went unmentioned.

Mick wasn't screamingly camp anyway, so there was no embarrassment. There was a degree of mutual respect.

Among the fem poofs, Mick was virtually unique in this. He had no great 'in' with the chaps though. However, as they totally blanked nearly all the other fem poofs, it was significant. It gave him a certain standing.

Unfortunately, it was virtually all he had. Most of the other poofs were quite young. They regularly talked about their various affairs; Mick could only talk. Usually he was on his own. Behind his back, he was regarded as something of a pathetic figure. Recently he had had a fling with Aaron, an uncouth lout of a fella in his late 30s, who was doing life for manslaughter. A country fella through and through, he was no professional criminal. He weighed a strapping 15 stone. With a big bushy beard on an enormous head he could have been a biker. He certainly looked the part and had the attitude. Aaron, better than anyone, realised that the killing had been a pure blunder. The chaps regarded him as a complete berk, although probably a bit of a handful in a punch-up. But he was a big strong fella, possessed of a craziness and a desperation born of his life sentence. If his crime didn't make him the part, then he would act the part to establish his reputation. Aaron was one of the most disruptive prisoners in the jail.

Loud and always arguing with the screws, Aaron was a perpetual bully, who tormented those weaker than himself. He had a habit of playfully punching people, until their arm was bruised and swollen. That it was playfully malicious rather than purely wicked didn't come into it. He made many a young fella's life a misery.

Aaron hadn't been into poofs before he came into prison. His appetites, though, were as uncouth as his manners. In the absence of women, he had to find some way to slake his desires. In his own inimitable way, he took rather than asked.

It wasn't a courtship with Mick. They just happened to be on the same wing, and Aaron pushed himself on to him. At first, it was merely a knockabout friendship. Aaron would walk into his cell and joke and play about.

Perhaps Mick was flattered by the attention. Perhaps the loneliness had grown intolerable. Anyway, Mick encouraged him. Soon he was one of Aaron's possessions.

Once whatever novelty there had been in the relationship had worn off, Aaron treated Mick exactly the same as others in his circle. Because Mick spent more time around him, though, he took the brunt of it. Soon his life was a nightmare. He was constantly at the centre of Aaron's oafish behaviour and brutish desires.

To complain brought playful punches that hurt and bruised. Their sex life was chaotic. Aaron would burst in and take him when he felt like it. Sometimes he would just throw Mick to the floor and fuck him with the cell door wide open. It was hardly a romance. There was no escape for Mick. No one cared enough for him to intercede. To go to the screws would have labelled him a grass. At his wits' end, he demanded a move to another wing. The screws knew what had been going on. Within a day, Mick had moved from 'A' wing to 'E' wing. He would still bump into Aaron about the prison, but they would only meet in passing. He had escaped.

This had all been several weeks earlier. The recent memory was still painful to Mick. For a while, he had been pleased to be on his own. When he stood with the other poofs out on exercise and listened to the trials and tribulations of their lives with their boyfriends, he was glad to be out of it.

The feeling didn't last though. Long hours sitting alone in his cell or in the TV room soon brought back the old familiar emptiness. Loneliness permeated his soul like a bitter winter. It was barely preferable to life with Aaron.

Mick's recent troubles had been no great drama played out on a public stage. The vast majority of cons didn't even know who he was and had remained oblivious to the whole affair. Those who did know had their own lives to lead. If they sympathised, their own situations took all of their energies. They noticed the sad and lonely figure as he went about the jail, but quickly forgot as soon as he passed.

The weather had been brightening up for a while now. Evenings had grown light and the cold bite of winter was gone from the air. Evening association started, and the fellas were allowed out on the sports field for a couple of hours each evening. People who hadn't seen much of each other through the winter months renewed old acquaintances. Impromptu games of five-a-side football proliferated on the Redgra pitch, often with twice that number on each side. Runners strode out around the perimeter of the great field. Men stood in groups talking. Smaller groups walked up and down. People who had been confined to the incestuous, cloying social circle of their own particular wing through the dark months now had the opportunity to make new friendships or extend old ones. In the dead world of Long Lartin, it was a brief period of rebirth.

One evening, Mick was seen talking to a dark-haired young fella close to the Redgra pitch. For those who knew about the recent past and had been used to seeing Mick on his own, it was a significant, if minor, event. When they were seen together the next evening, walking around the field, there were knowing looks and the odd remark. Still, it was no big deal. Neither was a well-known face, with either power of influence. It was hardly the talk of the nick.

As the weeks went by, the pair became inseparable. Whether on the sports field, in the pay queue or in the cinema, there was Mick and the dark-haired young fella. They took to lingering in the corridors together. They could be seen waiting outside each other's wing. People were convinced that Mick had finally found himself a young fella.

In many ways, it was a strange match. Bob P was a Scouse fella in his mid-20s, who lived on the same landing as I did. He was quiet and unassuming. He hung around with a couple of other young fellas and generally kept a low profile. If you noticed him at all, you could be forgiven for wondering what he was in prison for. He didn't seem particularly criminal.

We always spoke in passing, but I was caught up in running a poker table, collecting on our football coupon and generally ducking and diving. Our crowd were all 'A' men and quite notorious. Life was demanding and hectic, as life can only be for someone who aspires to be a face in prison.

It if hadn't been for the fact that Bob was also on the 'A' list, I probably wouldn't have noticed him at all. As it was, I knew he was doing life for killing his girlfriend. In the violent world of Long Lartin, he was very much a lightweight.

Long Lartin was a modern prison involving much state-of-the-art technology. The wings were laid out like campus accommodation, with a central enclosed stairwell running up to the landings.

Each landing was a complete floor, with two corridors of cells either side. Each corridor was quite wide and well lit, although the ceilings were low. At the end was a full-length barred window, through which daylight poured. There were eight cells either side of each corridor.

Bob's was the sixth cell along on the left, two past mine. Consequently, I often bumped into him on the landing or saw him go past as I sat in my cell. Occasionally, he and his mates would have a bet on our football coupon. That was virtually the only real contact I had with him.

As far as I knew, he wasn't into poofs at all. He had never been seen with any of the more infamous ravers, and his name had never been mentioned in any of the regular scandals that blew up.

The first thing I knew of the liaison was when Micky Blake began to appear regularly on our landing. I knew Mick by sight but had rarely had reason to speak to him. I knew, of course, that he was a notorious poof and that he lived on 'E' wing.

It wasn't nosiness. There were good practical reasons for being aware of who came on to your landing. Your cell was a place where you relaxed and your guard could be down. It was an ideal place for an enemy to attack you.

Mick was no threat to anybody though. I noted his constant comings and goings, found out the reason, then thought no more about it. It was none of my business. However, I did wonder what a young fella like Bob was doing with a raddled old queen like Mick. Perhaps he had never recovered from the rejection by his girlfriend.

Now Mick was in his element. His life had a whole new meaning again. He would hurry from his wing or from his workshop to meet Bob. Then they would stroll about, enjoying each other's company.

It had caused quite a stir among the crowd of poofs who regularly met on the exercise yard each day. Mick now had a young well-mannered fella, who hadn't done the rounds among them. He obviously thought quite a lot of Mick and treated him well. Reflecting on some of their own lowlife boyfriends, they wouldn't have minded someone like Bob themselves.

The only negative aspect of the relationship for Mick was that they lived on different wings. For long periods each day, they would be apart, both sitting alone in their respective cells waiting for the wing doors to open so they could be together again. Although to go on another wing wasn't strictly allowed, sometimes Mick would slip upstairs on to Bob's landing. This was when I would see him hurry past my door. It wasn't very satisfactory though. They could only have a few minutes together, and if an unsympathetic screw was on the wing door he wouldn't allow Mick in at all.

Mick decided to try to get a move on to Bob's wing. Other people had changed wings; in fact, he had done it himself only three months earlier. He duly made the application and went before the governor.

The screws knew the real reason behind the move though. They had noticed the comings and goings. They didn't openly encourage such things, but others had got a move for similar reasons. However, Bob was still very young. Perhaps they felt that he should be protected from Mick's corrupting influence. The move was refused.

They still met around the prison. Mick slipped up to Bob's cell on occasions, but the affair now had an air of tragedy about it. Mick complained long and loud to all who would listen about the unfairness of being refused a move. Theirs had become a public and ongoing saga in the life of the institution.

Late one Tuesday afternoon shortly before teatime lock-up, I was sitting in my cell with the door open, eating my meal. Suddenly, there was a shout from the direction of the stairs and the sound of running feet. As I looked up, I saw Mick run past my door. I carried on eating.

Seconds later, there was the tramp of heavy feet as two screws hurried past. I was on my feet instantly. If it was trouble, then it affected me. Friends of mine on the landing could be involved. I came out of my cell and looked along the landing.

The two screws had stopped outside Bob's cell. One of them had his mouth up against the crack of the closed door. 'Don't be silly now,' he shouted. 'Come on out, and you won't be nicked.'

There was no reply. Twice more he shouted out the same command. Still there was no answer. He turned the handle and pushed at the door. It wouldn't budge. He turned to the other screw, and they had a whispered conversation.

Chris, a pal of mine who lived opposite, was already out on the landing. Catching his eyes, I mouthed, 'What's up?'

'Mick's barricaded up with Bob in his cell,' he mouthed back.

The cells were about seven feet long, six inches longer than the length of the bed. If you pulled your bed out across the door and wedged something in the narrow gap, you could effectively barricade your door. All the pushing in the world wouldn't get it open. There was a method. It involved fetching a long, heavy jack and prising the door off. The process would take several minutes and did considerable damage. The door and door lining would be smashed and the opposite wall damaged. Further, it rated as a serious incident and could raise the temperature of the jail. There was always the danger that those inside would fight back. Then rumours of brutality could start, triggering off a major revolt. The screws tried to talk people out first.

It was close to the five o'clock lock-up now though. Neither Bob nor Mick could go anywhere. Perhaps they just wanted to be together for the hour and would come out again when the wing unlocked again at six. The screws left them and walked to the end of the corridor.

I went into my cell and shut my door. Within seconds, I heard the clicks as the computerised locking system locked each door. A screw came along, tried each door handle and looked through the observation flap to check that everyone was inside their cells.

I heard him stop about where Bob's cell was. He rattled the handle then shouted out, 'Are you in there?' There was no reply. I guessed that Bob had covered his observation flap up from the inside.

Six o'clock came, and the sound of clicking ran around the landing again as the doors unlocked automatically. As I came out of my cell, I saw a screw at Bob's door turning the handle. The door wouldn't open, though, so Bob and Mick must still have been barricaded in.

There were knowing looks and some laughter among the rest of the fellas, but it was nothing to do with anyone else. The screw walked away from Bob's door, and everyone else went about their business.

During the evening, I happened to see the chief walk by my door. This was quite unusual as he rarely came up on the landings. As chiefs went, he wasn't a bad fella. He had had all the hard times when he was a young screw down the Moor. Now, in the twilight of his career, he just wanted a quiet life.

Most of the chaps got on with him well enough and called him Percy. He knew where the power lay among the cons and went out of his way to get on with the faces. Sometimes it gave the ordinary screws the hump. Often, he would walk on to a wing and go to the cells of the faces, totally ignoring the screws.

It was good psychology. You always knew that, if you had a problem, rather than having a tear-up, you could go to Percy, and he would work something out. Some screws called it appeasement; Percy called it good management. He certainly averted a lot of trouble at Long Lartin.

At times, he admitted that he quite liked the chaps. He would rather deal with them because at least he knew where he stood. Both shared the outlook of the old school.

I had to smile to myself when I saw him going along to Bob's cell. This wasn't the sort of problem he liked to deal with. No doubt he felt it was all quite embarrassing. You could negotiate with a couple of the chaps who probably wanted some straightforward concession. What did you say to two ravers who just wanted to rump each other?

Nine o'clock came around and evening lock-up. As we returned to our cells, Percy was still at Bob's door. It didn't seem like they were coming out. The electronic locking went on, keeping us behind our doors for the night. There was no sound along the landing outside Bob's door; they were being left together until the morning.

We unlocked for breakfast the following day, and they were still barricaded in. No doubt Bob had stocked up on food and water, but, even so, his two young mates from the cell above had lowered some down.

I secretly wondered what they had done about slopping out. They had no toilet, and it wasn't the done thing at Long Lartin to throw it out of the window. I was sure it must be getting a bit fetid in there. Perhaps true love was sharing the same piss-pot! The work-bell went, and the wing emptied as the fellas went off to the workshops. Chris and I were wing cleaners, so we started on our daily duties. At about ten o'clock, we returned to my cell for our usual cup of coffee.

As we sat there, we saw Percy go by, heading for Bob's cell again. There was a muffled conversation, which gradually grew louder. Then he hurried past again, head down, with an angry look on his face.

He must have spun around, because, suddenly, he was standing in my doorway. 'Look, Norman,' he said, addressing me with no preliminaries, 'I've been as fair as I can with them. I've let them stay in there together all night, even though P—'s an "A" man and should only be locked up on his own. I had to report it to the Home Office. It's rapidly making me a laughing stock. Now, if they're not out by eleven, I've been ordered to jack the door off and drag them out.'

Percy paused, clearly embarrassed by the way he had blurted it all out. Chris and I looked at each other. If either of us had so much as smiled, we would both have burst out laughing. Percy was really in a dilemma. He couldn't leave them indefinitely. Yet, if he jacked the door off, it could lead to an incident that might spark off the jail.

'Can't you talk to them for me, Norman?' he asked. 'Find out what they want. If I can make any reasonable concession, I will.'

He had just tried to put me right in the middle. Reasonable fella or not, there was no way I was going to do a screw's job for him. It could very easily be misconstrued. That was how you could get yourself a bad name.

However, it wasn't unknown for other cons to act as a go-between to resolve a situation to the mutual satisfaction of both sides. There were several factors involved though. I would have to think about it.

'Give me a couple of minutes to think about it, Percy,' I said. 'I'll come down to the office and find you.'

Percy nodded his head and walked off.

As soon as he went, I turned to Chris. 'You know what's going to happen, don't you? At eleven o'clock, the screws will come around and try to lock up all the cleaners. They won't want us about when they jack the door off. We'll have to tell them to fuck off, in solidarity with Bob and Mick. There will be a tear-up, and we'll be dragged away down the block. Then they'll jack the door off, and Bob and Mick will come out like lambs. They certainly won't have a tear-up.'

Chris nodded in agreement. 'Those pair of clowns won't have a fight, that's for sure,' he said. The seriousness of the situation had just dawned on him.

I stood up and walked along to Bob's door. Knocking loudly, I shouted, 'Bob, Mick, this is Norman. Listen, 'cause I want to talk to you.'

There was the sound of movement inside, then whatever was blocking the observation flap was removed. I looked through and instantly regretted it.

There, barely a yard away, was Mick. Twenty-four hours without shaving hadn't improved his looks. He stood in one of his classic poses, cigarette in one hand with the wrist bent, other hand on his hip, with his head tilted to one side. But, horror of horrors, he didn't have his teeth in. The puckered hole where his mouth was looked like someone had just thrown a brick through it.

Bob stood behind and to one side of him. His young face seemed pale and he had an embarrassed, hangdog look about him. He couldn't meet my eyes. I could understand his embarrassment.

Still, that wasn't my concern. People did strange things in prison. We were all under the greatest of pressure. My loyalty wasn't to them as individuals. It was to two fellow cons in trouble.

'Right,' I shouted. 'When they jack the door off at eleven o'clock, are you going to fight them?'

Mick shook his head.

'What about you, Bob?' I queried.

He shook his head too.

'Well, in that case, as you're coming out anyway, you might as well negotiate for some concession now while you're in a position of strength, hadn't you?'

They both nodded in unison.

'But can we trust what they say?' asked Mick worriedly.

'Well, I'm involved now,' I said. 'If Percy goes back on his word, I'll do so much damage that he'll wish he had just jacked the door off in the first place. And he knows I'll do it too. So that's the only guarantee you've got.'

'OK,' said Mick. There was a pause.

'Well, what do you want?' I asked.

He thought for a minute and turned to Bob. Bob hadn't said a word. It was easy to see who made all the decisions. I could safely bet that this hadn't been Bob's idea at all.

Turning back towards me, Mick suddenly came to a decision. 'We know that we'll have to go down the block for a while. We don't mind that so long as they don't shanghai either of us out afterwards,' he said.

'You're sure now?' I queried.

They both nodded their heads.

'Right, I'll go down and tell Percy. You two had better get some things together.'

Chris had been standing close by. He had heard most of what had been said. 'They're coming out,' I told him as I walked past.

I went downstairs to the wing office. The chief was standing inside, talking to several screws. He looked up and saw me. He stepped outside and motioned me into an empty office nearby.

'Well, I've spoken to them, Percy,' I said, 'and they'll come out provided that you guarantee that neither of them will be shanghaied out of the jail.'

'They've got that,' he said immediately. 'You've got my word.'

'The only trouble is,' I continued, 'that I'm involved now. If anything happens, and they are shanghaied, it will make me look very bad. Then I will have to do something personally.'

Percy recognised the implied threat. He knew of the many violent incidents I had been involved in during the recent past. 'Norman,' he said, 'I give you my word.'

'OK, Percy, let them have a few minutes, and they will be down.'

I went back upstairs and along to Bob's door. I knocked and looked through the flap. Mick and Bob both turned to look at me.

'It's me again,' I shouted. 'I've spoken to the chief, and he swears to me that you won't be shanghaied. He's waiting downstairs.' With that, I turned around and went back into my cell.

Chris followed me in. We sat down to finish our coffee, which was now barely warm. About a minute went by and I heard Bob's door open. It closed again; there was the sound of feet shuffling, and Mick and Bob appeared in my doorway. Each held a carrier-bag.

'Thanks for your help,' said Mick sheepishly. Mercifully, he had his teeth in now.

'Yes, thanks,' said Bob from behind him. I waved my hand and nodded my head as if to say, 'OK, don't mention it.' They turned and carried on along the landing.

The following day, I heard that they had been given 14 days in the chokey. It was a bit steep, seven would have done. But I guessed that Percy was getting his revenge.

Over the next fortnight I largely forgot about the incident. I wasn't one to worry about anything, but I was aware that it wouldn't be over for me until they were both back on their respective wings again.

I didn't count the days, but eventually someone told me that they were both up. I hadn't seen them myself yet, but no doubt they were off somewhere together commiserating with each other after the loneliness of solitary. Later I saw Bob up on the landing. Percy had kept his word.

Once again the two lovers were to be seen together all over the jail. Out on the sports field, in the pay queue, at the cinema and on the yard, the two of them, inseparable as always, huddled up together deep in conversation. They had failed in their attempt to be together all the time, but what they had was better than being apart for ever.

26 HITLER'S CHILD

Every working-class area, every generation, throws up a young hardnut, a youth, mature before his time, who is as tough and game as men years his senior. In the early Sixties, Jackie Clark filled this role in London's Notting Hill.

At 19, he was a strapping 13 stone, with a big barrel chest, powerful shoulders and a craggy, dark-shaven jaw. His broken, hook-like nose disbarred him from any claims to handsomeness. With his thick shock of jet-black hair, it even made him look a bit sinister. But he had narrow hips, was very light on his feet, and his jaunty air gave him a devil-may-care attitude.

Jackie could have a right row. He had become the 'daddy' of every borstal he had ever been in, and he had been in most of the tough ones. He had been good at boxing and might have gone far if he'd had the discipline. Even so, with his brawny physique, it gave him a decided edge over most people.

He was a thief and invariably ran with an older crowd than his contemporaries. It didn't really surprise anyone when he finally got four years for a tie-up and went into 'A' wing at the Scrubs. In those days 'A' wing was the boys' wing, where young prisoners under 21, or YPs, were held. All were doing fixed sentences rather than borstal. By YP standards, four was a long sentence. A three was counted as severe and usually came as retribution for several Post Office robberies or scores of serious burglaries.

Jackie arrived just after I did; I was doing six years for shooting my girlfriend. I had originally been charged with capital murder, but the fact that she had a gun too saved me. The manslaughter verdict and heavy sentence made me instantly notorious on 'A' wing. I didn't think that I was particularly tough; there were plenty on 'A' wing who could have done me in a punch-up. But everyone seemed to treat me with a certain deference. I didn't know what they could see that I couldn't, but, as it made life a lot easier for me, I played the role out for what it was worth.

I knew Jackie from outside. I had been in his company a few times, although I usually went about with his younger brother. Also, Jackie had been out with my sister. This didn't make him a member of any particularly exclusive club, though, because many of the local chaps had taken her out. Ann was a stunningly beautiful and intelligent blonde girl of 15. She was sophisticated beyond her years. It didn't last long with Jackie, probably more her fault than his.

This gave me a kind of bond with Jackie. We were both off the same manor, but dozens of others in 'A' wing were from Notting Hill too. The main thing we had in common, though, was that, as our four and six were classed as long-term sentences, we would both be going to Wakefield, the centre for all YPs doing over four years. So we hung around together and got to know each other quite well. By the time we left for Wakefield, we were good pals.

Tony Davey was as different from Jackie as different could be. At six feet three and only 17 years old, his skinny frame made him seem all arms and legs. His greased-back black hair was unfashionably long: His youthful baby-face was spoiled by a longish nose. Despite a certain brashness, he was quite shy. This shyness, as much as his gangling frame, caused him to stoop as he walked.

Tony was very intelligent. He had passed several GCEs at school but seemed to resent these academic laurels as evidence of conformity. For he strongly fancied himself to be a rebel. He was quickly seduced by the simplistic appeal of Fascism and founded the Crawley branch of Union Movement, the organisation behind Sir Oswald Mosley's British Fascist Party. It had small 'bookshops' or offices in a couple of the major cities. It was very much a fringe party, though, a bizarre collection of naive idealists high on faded dreams of empire.

The Crawley branch of Union Movement didn't have much of a grassroots following. In fact, it had six members, all young acquaintances of Tony. He was in charge because he had founded the party. He wasn't a natural leader, though, and his immature silliness soon led to a leadership challenge.

George was a year younger than Tony. He was a small athletic youth with a lively personality. His saucy self-confidence made him the born leader of the group. Before long, there was a palace coup.

It didn't make the local papers, but one day George and the other four told Tony not only that George was now the leader of the Crawley branch of Union Movement but also that Tony was barred from membership. He wasn't summoned before an improvised committee or anything. They just told him to piss off because he wasn't part of their gang any more.

Tony wasn't naturally aggressive, and his lanky build didn't lend itself to feats of physical prowess. However, he was fanatically proud. He had a deeply held code of honour and duty. The pain and embarrassment caused by public rejection, coupled with a sense of perceived inadequacy, combined to give him a murderous resolve. Quite calmly, coldly and logically, he decided to kill George. It wasn't a crime he expected to get away with, so there wasn't a lot of planning to do. There was a process, though, that had a chilling likeness to ritual.

Without telling anyone what he intended to do, Tony made

his preparations. He drew all of his savings out of the Post Office. He spent two weeks drinking every night, lavishing money on a casual girlfriend. Just before all of it was gone, he went into the local sporting-goods shop and bought a hunting knife. It was similar to a Bowie knife and had an eight-inch-long blade.

Tony chose Saturday and Crawley High Street as the time and place of reckoning. There were scores of people about as he walked down the street in the bright sunshine, the big knife tucked in the back of his waistband, hidden by his jumper.

Up ahead he saw George, just as he had known he would. He was being carried along by the inevitability of the situation now. Everything was right. The sunlight bathed him in a golden hue. What finer setting could he have to carry out this honourable act of revenge than right here in his local high street?

A couple of weeks had passed. As far as George was concerned, much of the venom had gone out of the dispute. However, he was disturbed by the sight of a new more confident Tony, carrying himself erect as he bore down on him. He seemed to have the beginnings of a smile curling at the corners of his mouth. It was a knowing smile, born of some secret knowledge. If it had been midnight instead of midday, then George would have been seriously concerned.

The encounter was pleasant enough. From Tony's manner, it seemed like he had forgotten their falling out. His unusually confident mien, though, still made George uneasy. But no sooner had they met than it was over. A couple of sentences were exchanged, and Tony was past him.

George continued on, up the high street. He discounted his fears in such a public place, surrounded by so many people. Directly behind him, though, Tony had spun around and pulled the knife from his waistband. Raising it double-handedly above his head, he plunged the long blade into George's back, the force of the blow causing George to stumble forwards. Tony tore the blade free, plunging George several more times before a final, climatic blow left the knife buried up to the hilt in his spine.

It all happened so quickly. Passers-by stood frozen in shock as the gory tableau played itself out. Leaving George on the pavement in an ever-widening pool of blood, Tony walked casually down the high street, into the police station and gave himself up.

George took a whole day to die, longer than the subsequent trial. That wasn't much of a contest. Tony pleaded 'guilty' and was sentenced to Her Majesty's Pleasure, the juvenile equivalent of 'life'. It wasn't a particularly memorable murder, except for the local inhabitants of Crawley that is. There was one particularly chilling piece of evidence though. It was given by a young policewoman, a strapping country girl. She described how she had stood over George in the local hospital and pulled with all her strength to get the knife out of his back. Tony had meant it all right.

Immediately after the killing Tony had been lodged in the same 'murder charge' ward of Brixton Prison hospital as me. Two things were very plain: The first was that he was quite resigned to being found guilty; the second that he didn't regret killing George one bit.

Tony and I were the only YPs on the ward, the others ranging in age from their early 20s to their late 60s. It was natural enough that we pal up together. It wasn't a close friendship, just two young fellas sharing a common situation.

It soon transpired that I had seen George before. My girlfriend's elder brothers, Phil and Jim, were bodyguards to Sir Oswald Mosley. I occasionally attended meetings with them. One evening, Mosley was speaking at West London's Kensington Town Hall. As the large room filled up Phil and Jim were doing their usual stewards' role, showing some to their seats but others the door through which they had just entered.

The hall was nearly full when two tall young fellas walked in. Both had long black hair, black leather jackets and tight jeans. To

Phil and Jim, long steeped in the thuggish arts but firm believers in proper dress for proper occasions, they looked like two yobbos. Not at all like smart young Fascists; more akin to the anarchist rabble who often tried to disrupt the meetings.

'What do you two girls want?' Phil asked, pleasantly enough, as he stepped in front of them.

'We're from the Crawley branch of Union Movement,' replied Tony, showing the membership card that had come through the post and that he so treasured.

Fellow Fascists were a bit thin on the ground at the best of times. And perhaps they would shape up when they got older. Anyway, they both had valid memberships. Phil showed them to their seats.

I was amazed when this came out in conversation with Tony. Two young fellas from different parts of the country, thrown together by most unusual circumstances. Yet we had met before. Early evidence of the smallness of the criminal world.

I was convicted and left for the Scrubs a couple of weeks before Tony. By the time he arrived, I was firm friends with Jackie. Because of his particularly long sentence, Tony was put in a cell on the ones, close to the screws' office.

If Jackie's sentence, and my own, had attracted interest among the other YPs, then Tony's caused utter dismay. Before he had arrived, mine was the longest on the wing. Now there was a constant coming and going outside Tony's door, as young fellas peered through the spy-hole to have a look at the sort of fella who could murder someone and get HMP.

He was only at the Scrubs a few weeks before they moved him to Wakefield. He didn't do anything very unusual in that time, mostly stayed quietly in his cell. He did indulge in one small act of rebelliousness though.

The screws on 'A' wing were bullies to a man. They took advantage of their relative size and maturity to dominate the YPs.

They were on us every second we were unlocked, and often when we were behind our doors as well. We hated them with a passion. Anything done against them had our heartfelt support.

One of the main ways they would wind us up was over our mail. Strictly speaking, you were only allowed to receive as many letters as you sent out. As we were only issued with two letters a week, there was always an imbalance between incoming and outgoing. For young fellas, many of whom were away from their families for the first time, mail was all important. It reminded them that they weren't forgotten and that someone still cared for them. Equally, many a parent would be thoroughly distraught at the thought of their son being locked up in prison. Their letters desperately sought reassurance that their boy was coping.

This didn't matter a damn to the screws. You would have thought that none of them had ever been a parent themselves. One of the censors was a pure pig. He stuck to the letter of the rule rigidly. He regularly sent back excess mail. In his infinite wisdom, he would also decide whether a relationship was serious and proper. He had stopped several fellas writing to their girlfriends.

He was a morose, bad-tempered Welshman in his early 50s. Balding, with a fat face and even fatter gut, it was hard to imagine anyone caring for him. If he had ever come into prison he would never have received a single letter. Perhaps he realised this and that was what made him so hard where others' mail was concerned. We were convinced that, if he had his way, we would get no mail at all.

Early each morning he could be seen in the censor's office on the ones working through the stack of outgoing mail. He would quickly scan each letter, looking for swearwords or criticism of the prison. Offenders were sent for and their letters handed back with instructions to rewrite. The majority passed his inspection though. These he would moisten with a little rubber roller resting on a damp pad, then he would seal them.

It was a constantly recurring ritual. All outgoing mail had to be in by 8 a.m., before we went to the workshops. The censor always had the mail completed a couple of minutes before work-call. He would finish with an air of finality, putting the roller and pad in his desk drawer.

One morning, Tony came in with his letter seconds before work-call and just after the censor had put away his stuff. Tony apologised for being late and explained that it was an important letter to his mother. With bad grace, the censor snatched it from Tony's hand and started to read it.

Tony left. He paused outside and looked through the crack in the mailbox to see whether the censor was going to put it in the pile of outgoing mail or leave it on the side for tomorrow.

The censor finished reading the letter. He didn't bother to get the roller and pad out of his drawer. He just licked the envelope, sealed it and threw it on the outgoing pile.

A couple of times a week, Tony would deliberately wait until the last minute before hurrying in and handing over his letter. Technically he was still in time, but this didn't stop the censor from giving him a volley. Each time, Tony would go outside and peer through the crack to watch the censor seal his letter. Then he would walk away with a smile on his face.

One morning I saw the smile and asked him what he was so pleased about. He explained how the censor didn't bother to get the little roller out when he brought his letter in late, just licking the envelope to seal it. For the past couple of weeks Tony had been wiping his dick all over the sticky part of the envelope. Then he would rush in at the last moment and hand it to the censor. He would go outside and peer through the crack, just in time to see him lick it. It gave Tony a big thrill to be getting back at him. 'The censor's plating me by proxy,' he would say, laughing.

Jackie and I duly arrived at Wakefield several weeks after Tony. As the only two YPs in an escort of 12, we were processed first and taken over to the wings, carrying our kit with us. 'C' wing was our destination. We were given cells next to each other on the YP landing. There were 50 YPs at Wakefield, and all of them had cells on this landing, which wasn't separated in any way from the rest. Wakefield was the only jail in the country where YPs were allowed to mix freely with adult cons.

After we had put our stuff in our cells, Jackie and I set out to explore our new surroundings. The wing was virtually deserted. We were surprised that the screw who had brought us on to the wing had gone off and left us to our own devices.

We wandered down on to the ones; the threes and fours above us were just bare landings housing rows of cells. Spread along the ones was a snooker table, two table-tennis tables and several dartboards. None was in use. However, we could imagine that this would be the centre of activity come association time.

Along either side of the ones were messes, where the fellas ate their meals. Each mess was two cells knocked into one and contained a few tables and chairs. Four of the messes were reserved for YPs only. We searched out the number of the mess we had been assigned to and went inside. The only difference from the adult messes was that there was a TV in the corner.

Jackie and I came back out on to the ones and just stood, looking around. In truth, we were a bit bewildered. Back at the Scrubs, the screws were on you all the time. Whenever you so much as stuck your head out of your cell, some screw would shout at you. We were surprised at the degree of freedom we seemed to have here. All the time we were half-expecting some screw to appear and start shouting at us, demanding to know what we were doing lounging about.

But no screw appeared. We were allowed to explore at will. There were a few cons about, mostly cleaners. One fella came over to us. He was short, very stocky, with a bushy beard and long hair. Through the hair, we could discern that he was only in his early 20s. The gold ring in his ear was the finishing touch that made him look something like a pirate. Such studied, irreverent disarray certainly impressed me.

Perhaps he was out to impress. It was obvious from our blue jackets that we were YPs. Within seconds of introducing himself, he told us that he was doing double life with a couple of twelves running concurrent. He pointed out others who were also doing long sentences.

I had heard a lot about Wakefield; the cranks and the violence. These fellas who had been singled out to me seemed to be denizens of some strange jungle. I had never met their like before, so I had nothing with which to compare them. They were characters straight out of the Sunday tabloids. It wouldn't be wise to show fear, because someone could take this as an invitation to come on and bully you. However, these were men who had mutilated and butchered like savages, so you couldn't help but fear. I longed for some time to pass so that I would know what was safe and what wasn't in this new and unfamiliar world.

Jackie and I collected our dinners early and went into our allotted mess. We had been there for only a few minutes when we heard the sound of activity out on the wing. The fellas were coming in from work. Suddenly, the door burst open, and two YPs bowled in with dinner trays in their hands. They paused, momentarily surprised by the two newcomers in their mess. Recovering quickly, they slammed their trays down on a nearby table, turned the TV on loud, then sat down to eat.

What immediately struck me was their bounce and arrogance. Back at the Scrubs, their attitude would have brought them instant trouble from the screws. They were positively flash. And so sure of themselves.

I studied them more closely. Both had specially tailored shirts on, with big well-starched collars. They wore tight grey trousers, and their blue jackets were pressed with sharp creases. Most surprising of all, both had long, curly hair with big bushy sideburns. At the Scrubs they would have been prime candidates for the number-one clippers right across the top. They would have emerged from the barbers with a haircut that only began a couple of inches above their ears. I was amazed by the degree of freedom that the YPs seemed to enjoy here.

More YPs came in until there were 12 of us in the same mess. A couple started talking to us, asking where we had come from and telling us about Wakefield. I was still very much on the defensive, but Jackie quickly found his feet. He wasn't intimidated at all. He had nothing to fear from YPs, no matter how long they were doing. He had held his own with grown men.

By his attitude and manner, Jackie began to assert himself. Without saying as much, he let it be known that, if anyone wanted a row, then they could have one. Once again I felt reassured that Jackie was my pal.

Over the next couple of weeks we got to know the other YPs and the place. The regime was very relaxed. We could have all sorts of things that were forbidden at the Scrubs. Although we could mix freely with the adults, by and large the YPs kept to themselves. There was a certain degree of elitism in the fact that we were the 50 longest-serving YPs in the country. That didn't mean that we were the toughest, although many clearly thought they were. Their special status had gone to their heads. The authorities were emphasising that our crimes were too serious for us to mix with others of our age. To the average YP, this was just what he wanted to hear. Consequently, the YPs at Wakefield certainly thought they were something special.

In truth, they weren't. They were in for murder, attempted murder and other seriously violent crimes, but these were largely unlucky one-off affairs. A collection of circumstances and an immature individual carried along on the crest of his passion. A cathartic explosion of violence that was quite out of character. There were scores of young tearaways back at the Scrubs who were tougher and more vicious. Many here were more mental patient than criminal.

Geordie was typical. A baby-faced 16-year-old, all quiffed hairstyle and swagger, he had tried to rob an old man in a Durham park. In the process he had knocked him down, kicked him in the head and killed him. Beneath the bravado, he was still a bewildered and frightened child, trying to cope with Wakefield.

There was one particularly weird fella, whom Jackie and I referred to as 'Burnt-head'. We never knew his name or his offence, but he was the most frightening thing I had ever seen in my life. Other YPs told us that he had thrown a fit a few years before coming into prison and fallen so that his head ended up in an open fire. It had burned off all one side of his face. He was totally bald, and the skin of his head and face was a mass of angry scar tissue. His nose and left ear had melted down to twisted stubs. The corner of his mouth was turned up in a permanent rictus.

That he should have survived to carry with him forever such a nightmare visage was a tragedy in itself. The greater tragedy was the unseen but undoubted scar on his psyche. Yet, whatever crime he had committed, the authorities had seen fit to send him to prison.

There were other sad cases, many more fool than knave. The only distinction the courts had made was to sentence them to very long terms. Looking around me, I began to consider myself both lucky and blessed.

Jackie soon stood out head and shoulders above all the other YPs. He was like a man among boys. He was one of the very few who were married. Without ever throwing a punch, he assumed a leading role. Others deferred to him. His opinion was the one that counted. His was the sun around which the other planets rotated.

Tony had come to see us on the first day. He recognised Jackie from the Scrubs, but only knew him vaguely. Jackie largely ignored Tony, regarding him as something of a fool. Despite Tony's intelligence, he had a talent for appearing gormless. He was certainly immature. His high IQ didn't add any sophistication to his adolescent manner. He didn't command much respect among the other YPs either.

He was friendly with another YP called Mick. Brummie Mick was doing five for Post Office robberies. He was as immature as Tony, but lacked his intelligence. They were well matched. Both liked to play childish tricks and came out with equally childish remarks. Mick had a bit more credibility among the other YPs than Tony did, but only just.

Occasionally, I could have a sensible conversation with Tony. We were both interested in politics and held right-wing views. I soon came to understand his philosophy and his personality. He was a fan of Nietzsche. He believed devoutly in his concepts of *Mensch* and *Übermensch*. He clearly thought himself to be one of the latter. This gave him rights over and above ordinary men.

Honour and pride were paramount in his value system. He wasn't particularly courageous or tough, but it was the fact that he thought himself an honourable man that set him above others.

He saw himself as some undiscovered genius who was yet to find his milieu. The objective observer might find it hard to discern some meaningful criteria to support this. In truth, Tony was a highly intelligent but immature young fella, with a painful inferiority complex. Fascism was just the doctrine to allow him to feel superior.

Tony and Mick would often try to hang around with Jackie and me. Sometimes we would tolerate them, sometimes we wouldn't. Gradually, they drifted out to the fringes of our circle. We spoke to them, but they weren't friends.

There was another Brummie on the YPs called Roy Aston. He was a tall rangy fella, doing eight for attempted murder. He was typically in the Northern yobbo vein, with a greased-up Elvis hairstyle and long sideburns. Skin-tight trousers clung to his long, lanky legs. He was aggressive, arrogant and walked with a swagger that owed more to Hollywood than West Bromwich. Until Jackie arrived, Roy had been the local hardman among the YPs.

One look at Jackie, though, convinced him that he'd come a poor second in any punch-up. From then on, he went out of his way to be friendly. When you got to know him, though, he wasn't such a bad fella. Much of the swagger was a front, and at least he had the backbone to stand up for himself against the screws. He didn't become a bosom pal of either Jackie or me, but he was often in our company and became a friend of sorts.

After a few weeks, I began to feel more at ease at Wakefield, but it was always a bizarre place to me. There were regular violent incidents among the adult cons. I was very aware that I was a youth in the company of grown men – and very dangerous ones at that.

My first fear on arrival, and it was a common one among the YPs, was of the poofs. There were apocryphal tales of YPs who had been lured into adult cons' cells for coffee, biscuits and a chat but had ended up being raped. It had also happened in the showers and recesses.

To most proud young men, still measuring their masculinity against that of others, this would be the ultimate indignity. Something so shameful that, had it happened, it would have to be kept secret. Something so dishonourable that, no matter what the consequences, you would have to kill the perpetrator.

My first act, on my very first night at Wakefield, was to make a blade. We were issued with all-steel, round-ended fish knives as part of our cutlery. I spent several hours filing it on the flagstone cell floor until it had a sharp, tapering point. Any poof who came anywhere near me could have some of that.

As the months passed, I got to quite like Wakefield. The novelty of being treated like an adult by the screws came as a welcome relief after the daily humiliations at the Scrubs. Jackie and I became inseparable. As two young Londoners from the same manor doing time up North, we shared a common background. Neither of us had been that far away from our families before. We were regularly homesick. The cold weather and the Northern accents were a constant reminder that we didn't belong.

We shared our local papers, looking for references to people we knew; just to keep in touch. When we watched *Steptoe* on the TV, the streets of Notting Hill around which it was filmed brought back painful memories. We talked about our families together and read each other's letters. Anything to dispel the sense of isolation that came from being in an alien part of the country.

At about this time, I had a falling out with Tony and Mick. I had had a model plane kit sent in. Now, among the YPs who thought they were trendy, hobbies and model-making were thoroughly naff pastimes. Only boring people with no pals did hobbies. However, as my mother had gone to the trouble of getting it for me, I decided to make it.

I had neither the patience nor the practical skills. The resulting model was an abortion of balsa, paper and glue. Its only use was as a talking-point. Several times, Jackie, Tony, Mick and I stood around it and laughed. It was an inspired foul-up. A craftsman couldn't have made it that way deliberately.

Tony asked me what I was going to do with it. Jokingly, I said I was going to burn it ritually in the recess: a phoenix that would never fly in life and certainly wouldn't rise from the ashes. In the end, I put it on my bookshelf and forgot about it.

Several days later I was coming along the landing towards my cell when I smelled burning. In a world where there was only a limited range of smells, it was instantly noticeable. As I got closer I could see faint wisps of smoke coming from my doorway. I rushed in to find the air thick with smoke. My metal slops bucket was in the middle of the cell and in it the blackened and twisted remains of the plane.

I was instantly very angry. The plane meant nothing to me. I was only going to throw it away anyway, but to burn it in my cell was taking the piss. I immediately guessed who was responsible. It was just the sort of childish prank that Tony would play.

I dumped the bucket in the recess and went looking for him. He must have guessed that I would. I couldn't find him anywhere. By the time a couple of hours had passed and teatime had arrived, I had calmed down a bit. Nevertheless, I caught him outside his mess and gave him a volley. I called him all the childish, silly bastards I could think of and told him he had taken a liberty. 'Just leave me right out in future,' I said. 'Don't even speak to me.'

Later on, Jackie asked me about it. I told him what had happened, but that it was only a trivial matter and not to worry as I had already dealt with it. He didn't fall out with Tony himself, but he was annoyed with him over it.

The next incident came as a complete surprise to everyone. Ignore it as much as we would, we were constantly aware of the interest of various poofs. There were always a couple hanging around the YP landing. Once they realised you weren't interested, though, most of them would leave you alone.

However, it was all thoroughly disconcerting. Here we were, strutting around like young tough guys, yet well aware that there were those who would fuck us like women if they could. Did the fact that I might arouse those kinds of feelings in another man lessen me in some way? Or was it purely a reflection on the other? Most of us resolved this dilemma by arming ourselves with some kind of weapon and staying away from the majority of adult cons.

There was a right raver among the YPs though. Coffee was a mixed-race male prostitute who worked the Bayswater area. She'd been on the game since she was 15 and was mature and sophisticated beyond her tender years. Not satisfied with merely going with her punters, she had set them up to be robbed. Now, at 19, she was doing a four for robbery with violence.

Coffee was very much in demand at Wakefield. Her young mixed-race features hadn't thickened yet and were framed by a bushy, black Afro that predated the style by several years: a sort of Angela Davis with a twelve o'clock shadow.

Coffee made absolutely no bones about her sexuality and swished about in skin-tight grey trousers. She was highly promiscuous. Although she had many lovers among the adult cons, she always went out of her way to try to get hold of other YPs. Youth seemed to hold a powerful fascination for her.

As she came off the same manor as we did, something we shared with no one else at Wakefield, Jackie and I occasionally talked to her. Sometimes we swapped the local papers. We were quite embarrassed, though, by the fact that the only other Notting Hill fella in the jail was a raving poof. We always kept things very formal with Coffee.

The day after I fell out with Tony over my plane, a breath of scandal ran through the YP community. Coffee, usually immaculately turned out, was wandering about with her hair all over the place. From her face and general demeanour, she looked like the cat who had been out on the tiles all night. Never one to keep a secret, she let it be known that she'd had a steamy session with Tony.

People were amazed. It definitely wasn't the done thing. If Tony had had much standing among the YPs, it would have damaged it considerably. As it was, it just confirmed in people's minds that he was a bit of a berk.

A couple of days later, an incident happened between Jackie, on the one hand, and Tony and Mick, on the other. Jackie was sitting in their mess when Mick walked by and accidentally knocked against a table. A cup of water standing near the edge tipped over into Jackie's lap. It was a pure accident, but, in their typically silly manner, Tony and Mick started smirking about it.

Jackie left to change his trousers, annoyed not so much by the soaking as by their laughing about it. When he came back, Tony was lounging in the doorway, but Mick wasn't in the mess. Jackie asked Tony where Mick was. Tony said he didn't know. As Jackie turned away, he saw Mick standing in the doorway of a mess opposite. He was right in Tony's line of sight, and he had obviously known where he was when Jackie had asked.

Angry now, Jackie spun around and punched Tony in the face, sending him flying backwards into the mess. Jackie hurried across the ones and, as Mick backed away, he followed, punching him several times to the head and body. Then he walked away, back up to his cell on the twos.

Neither Tony nor Mick was hurt, but both were severely embarrassed. It meant a considerable loss of face for them in the eyes of the other YPs. They weren't held in much esteem anyway, although they liked to think they were.

The truly amazing thing about the incident was that I didn't get to hear about it. It wasn't surprising that Jackie didn't tell me, because he wouldn't want to get me involved. He was always one to sort out his own trouble without dragging in his mates. And he knew that I already had the hump with Tony. It was common knowledge among many of the other YPs, though, but nobody mentioned it to me. Perhaps they assumed that I already knew.

In retrospect, my ignorance of the incident was a crucial factor in what was subsequently to happen. Knowing Tony like I did, I might have realised how this would have shattered his already fragile ego. I could have guessed how his mind would have seethed in a whirlpool of destructive emotion. The already parlous state of his self-esteem would be further damaged. His self-image as an honourable man could hardly square with being attacked and doing nothing about it. Coming on top of the exposure of his embarrassing liaison with Coffee, no doubt he felt that there was only one thing he could do.

Tony and Mick made an elaborate plan to kill Jackie. They got spare overalls from the clothing store in which to do it. They had a knife and an iron bar made in the foundry. They knew Jackie played football at the weekend. They planned to jump him in his cell after the match.

It was Saturday afternoon, and Jackie was playing for the prison against an outside team. I stood on the sports field watching the match, with two pals of ours from another wing. Benny and Squiz were recently made-up YPs. Now given adult status, they had moved on to 'A' wing. We still managed to see them, though, on the yard and in the workshops.

After the game, the three of us talked to Jackie as he came off. He hurried away to take a shower and I walked to the centre with Benny and Squiz. We stood talking for a while.

Tony and Mick saw Jackie come in. They had been watching out for him from the threes. They saw him collect his clothes and washing gear from his cell, then head downstairs towards the showers.

They slipped down to the twos and went along the landing towards Jackie's cell. They walked as nonchalantly as possible, because directly below on the ones sat dozens of cons watching a communal TV set. Anyone looking up would see them, but they were engrossed in their programme. No one saw them slip into Jackie's cell, pulling the door to behind them.

Jackie took a quick shower. It wasn't long before teatime, and he had things to do. He dried himself, dressed, then headed back upstairs with a towel around his neck. His tired body invigorated by the hot water, he bowled along the landing and strode into his cell.

Mick and Tony were hiding behind the door. As Jackie came in, Mick hit him across the forehead with a massive iron bar. His forward momentum caused him to fall headlong on to the stone-slabbed floor. Tony was on him immediately. In an action replay of Crawley, he repeatedly stabbed him in the back.

Jackie had no chance. There was a shouted cry of pain, then the heavy thud of a body falling to the floor. It alerted some of the TV watchers below. As Tony and Mick slipped out of Jackie's cell, several pairs of eyes watched them go.

They hurried off, each to his own cell. There they changed into clean clothes. Their old ones they dropped into the laundry basket at the end of the landing. Then they went to sit in their mess.

I finished talking to Benny and Squiz on the centre. Calling my goodbyes, I turned on to 'C' wing and headed along the twos towards my cell. I had only gone a few yards when I noticed that Roy's tail, which was at the start of the twos, had its flag sticking out. He had obviously rung his bell to be let out.

It was unusual that he was locked in at all. It was Saturday afternoon, and everyone was allowed to be out on association. Even if he didn't want to come out, he could have sat in his cell with the door pulled to. He didn't have to lock himself in. Sometimes people did bang themselves up, though, usually when they didn't want company. However, Roy was often moody, so it wasn't entirely out of character.

I stopped in his doorway and looked through the spy-hole. Loud rock music was playing inside, and Roy was dancing about and singing. I shouted to him through the spy-hole. He immediately stopped and came over to the door. He shouted for me to get a screw and let him out.

P turned from his door and was surprised to see a screw hurrying towards me from the direction of my cell. Usually you could never find a screw when you wanted one, especially just before tea on a Saturday afternoon.

It was one of our regular landing screws. 'Open Roy's door please, boss,' I said, stepping out in front of him.

What happened next seemed to take place very quickly, almost in a blur. I briefly noticed a shocked, panic-stricken look on the screw's face, as he rushed by.

'I can't,' he said breathlessly. 'Someone's bashed your mate Jackie.' With that, he thrust something into my hands and was past me.

Until then I hadn't even noticed he was carrying anything. I looked down and saw that I was holding a massive iron bar. It was easily as thick as my arm, curled at the end like a shepherd's crook.

I turned to say something, but he was gone, running towards the centre. I felt the cold grip of fear in my stomach. What had happened to Jackie that had frightened him so badly? One instinct compelled me to run the other way; another told me that Jackie was in trouble, and I should go to help him. As I rushed towards his cell, I could hear Roy shouting, 'What's happening,' from behind his door.

At a run now, I reached Jackie's door and plunged inside. What I saw brought me up short. Jackie was lying face up on the floor, in the middle of the cell. A widening pool of blood spread around his head like some fiery halo.

I threw the iron bar into a corner and bent over him. There was a deep dent in his forehead where the knob of the bar had sunk in. This was the source of all the blood I could see. Next to him was a long, bloody skid-mark where his head had first made contact with the stone floor.

He was coughing, trying to get his breath. Gurgled, indistinct words came from his mouth. 'What is it, Jackie? Who did it?' I asked urgently. 'Before the screws come back, who did this to you? We'll do the fuckers.'

'Can't breathe, can't breathe,' was all he could mumble in reply.

I noticed he had his tie on, although it wasn't done up tight. It was the only reason I could see for his breathing difficulties. I loosened it right off and unbuttoned the top buttons of his shirt.

Still he kept mumbling, 'Can't breathe, can't breathe.' If I had known that Tony was involved, I might have guessed at the stab wounds in his back, the ones that were causing his lungs to fill, slowly drowning him in his own blood.

Suddenly, the door burst open. The chief and several screws crowded into the cell, with them the landing screw who had thrust the bar at me.

'Out,' said the chief. 'Get out.'

I tried to protest that Jackie was my pal and that I should stay with him, but I was hustled unceremoniously from the cell.

As I was pushed out, I noticed Roy in the ruck of curious faces outside the door. Some screw had obviously let him out of his cell. He was shouting, 'Who's done my mate Jackie?'

I grabbed his arm. Pulling him along the landing, I whispered, 'Quick, let's try to find out who did it before the screws bang us all up.' Stirrings of revenge were gradually replacing my original feelings of fear and concern.

'I've heard that Scouse fella Purdin saw something,' said Roy excitedly.

'We'll need a tool in case they're still about,' I said. I ducked into my cell to collect my sharpened fish knife, then rushed downstairs towards the YP messes.

Purdin was a YP like us. He shared the same mess as Tony and Mick. As we hurried in, we saw him sitting at a table in the corner. Sitting at another table was Mick. There was no sign of Tony.

Roy and I towered over Purdin threateningly. He was a scrawny-looking fella who was forever moaning about something or other. Now he sat silently, his pasty face white with fear.

'Who did you see come out of Jackie's cell?' I demanded, holding my knife so he could see it.

'I didn't see anything, I swear,' he said, frightened and panicky. Later on I would muse on the irony of one of the attackers sitting across the room from us as we ordered Purdin to tell us who did it.

In the background I could hear the sound of the screws coming round and ordering everyone away to their cells. I put the knife back in my pocket and slipped out of the mess.

There were screws everywhere, shepherding men from the messes and away to their cells. There was a lot of moaning, but the cons knew it had to be something serious. I went up to my cell and banged the door behind me. As I went in, I noticed that Jackie's door was banged up too. They had obviously taken him somewhere.

I sat down and thought about what had just happened. How

had lightning struck so close to home yet again? Once more I was in the middle of a very violent situation. Someone had seriously hurt Jackie. It was a bad injury, but he was a tough fella. I reasoned that, inside a week, he would be back with a bandage around his head. Then the fella who had done it had better watch out. For, if he had needed an iron bar to do Jackie in the first place, he wouldn't stand much chance when Jackie caught him man to man.

I puzzled over who could have done it. The jail was full of dangerous cranks. A few angry words could make a mortal enemy. Perhaps Jackie had said something to someone. Perhaps it was an argument from the football match. There were so many possibilities and no hard evidence. For the time being, all I could do was sit and think about it.

To be banged up so early on a Saturday was unusual. It disrupted my normal routine. I had specific things I did when I was banged up after evening association. I would have to find something to occupy myself with now.

I got my guitar out and started to play. I often played to relieve tension, although I was no great musician. I banged away, more with nervous energy than skill.

In the background I could hear fellas shouting out of their windows to each other, asking what was going on. Occasionally, I stopped to listen. I heard one fella say that the police were going from cell to cell interviewing people.

The thought suddenly struck me that my prints were all over the iron bar in Jackie's cell. I had his blood on me too. I had heard tales about how thick the local Old Bill were. I was already doing a sentence for manslaughter. I pondered the possibility of being fitted up.

But the screw had given me the bar, and he would remember. Benny and Squiz would confirm that I had been with them on the centre. And when Jackie came round he would say that it wasn't me. However, the circumstances were enough to make me view the coming police interview with trepidation.

From time to time, I heard the dull crash of doors opening and closing. Finally, my door opened and in came two local CID. They pushed the door to, sat down and introduced themselves. They seemed friendly enough, but I was very much on my guard. They said that they understood I was Jackie's closest pal and that I had known him outside. I confirmed this, and they nodded in unison, as if satisfied that they were making a concrete start. Then they asked me who could have done it.

Now I was in an awkward position. Even if I had known, I couldn't have told them. I wasn't going to grass anyone, in spite of the fact that they had done my pal. And Jackie would support me in this. He wouldn't want the help of the Old Bill. As soon as he came back, we would sort it out ourselves. However, I didn't want to sound too unco-operative.

I had been sitting on my bed, lounging against the wall. I leaned forward and said earnestly, 'Look, I honestly don't know who did it. It's a complete mystery to me. The first thing I heard about it was when the screw told me.'

They both paused and looked at each other. Nothing was said, but I could read the look: another brick in the wall of silence. As if coming to some unspoken conclusion, they both turned to me, and one said, 'Well, we're not going to mess about with you. You might as well know. Jackie's dead.'

Quite involuntarily, my hands flew up to my face, as a wave of shock and grief gripped me. I couldn't believe it. Jackie, so full of life and spirit. So tough and capable. It seemed inconceivable that he was gone and wouldn't be coming back.

Then other thoughts pushed into my consciousness. What about his wife and young baby? What would my mother think when she heard that Jackie had been murdered in the very next cell to mine? She was already under pressure. This would really worry her. Finally, what about me?

I was in a weird Agatha Christie-type situation now. Someone had murdered my best pal in the cell right next door. I didn't have a clue who had done it.

What would happen if the police didn't get them, and everyone was unlocked again? Would they come after me next, thinking that, as Jackie's pal, I would come after them? It wouldn't be so bad if I knew who they were. At least I could keep an eye on them and be on my guard if they came close. I could strike first if necessary. But it could be anyone.

Every time I went to the toilet, used the shower or went into my cell alone, I would have to be on my guard. I would make my own enquiries. I'd have to. But what a way to have to live. There was nowhere to hide. I was locked in with the killers like a mouse locked up with a cat. I found myself secretly hoping that the police would get them, then felt instantly guilty at the thought.

The two CID were still sitting there looking at me. Only a few seconds had passed. 'Look,' I said in a voice that was more like a croak, 'I really don't know who did it. Jackie never said anything to me about falling out with anyone.'

I told them about speaking to Jackie after the game. I explained that he had gone off for a shower while I stood talking on the centre. I mentioned speaking to Roy, who was banged up. At this point, they stopped me. They seemed very interested at the mention of Roy.

I paused, thinking carefully about what I was saying. I didn't want to drop anyone in it, but surely the fact that Roy was locked in cleared him of suspicion. He was a bit saucy to the screws and had probably told the Old Bill to piss off. Perhaps they just had it in for him. Anyway, he was our pal. It was only right that I should alibi him, especially as it was true.

They asked what he was doing. 'Just dancing about to the music,' I said, and, no, there didn't seem to be anything suspicious in his actions. Clearly, they would have liked more, but there was no more. I moved on to tell of the screw thrusting the bar on me and my running to Jackie's cell and finding him.

Both the CID made notes as I talked. Neither commented on what I had said. Finally, they showed me what they had written and asked me to sign it. I didn't consider that I had said anything of value to them. Further, it should clear Roy of suspicion. I signed.

Their leaving merely emphasised the seriousness of my predicament. I was on my own and would have to deal with the problem on my own. There was always Roy. He had come with me to try and find out who had done Jackie, immediately after I had been thrown out of his cell. Then there were a couple of Londoners among the YPs with whom Jackie and I had been friendly.

Now we were talking about murder though. Perhaps they wouldn't want to know. You soon found out who your real friends were in situations like this. And, irrespective of whatever help I had, as Jackie's pal I would be in the frontline.

I played my guitar again, but now morbid and melancholy. I was too tense to read. Outside you would get drunk, seek the support of your family or console the relatives and share the burden of your grief. Here I could only brood about it in solitude.

Later that evening, the screws brought around cocoa. Nothing was said, so it looked like we would remain banged up for the rest of the day. I didn't mind at all. I wasn't hiding, but at least it would give me more time to figure out what I was going to do. As I wrestled with sleep that night, my mind was full of the images of the day.

The following morning everyone was unlocked for breakfast as usual. I assumed that the police investigation was over. Keeping my sharpened fish knife in my pocket, I slipped out of my cell and headed towards Roy's. Everyone was out on the landings swapping gossip, trying to find out exactly what had happened.

Halfway along the landing, I bumped into Coffee. 'They've got Tony, Mick and Roy down the block for it,' she blurted out, an expression of surprise and shock mingled on her face. She put her hand on my arm in an act of concern, no doubt also showing where her sympathies lay following her recent liaison with Tony.

I carried on to find Hutch, a young London pal of ours. He was leaning on the landing rail just outside his door. We grabbed each other by the shoulders, our faces contorted with emotion. 'The fucking slags,' he said, 'they could only do him on the sly.'

Hutch said that Scouse Purdin had seen Tony and Mick come out of Jackie's cell. He had made a statement. There were other witnesses, too, who had seen other things. But we couldn't figure out where Roy fitted in. He had no obvious grouse against Jackie, unless he had always resented being knocked off the number-one spot by his arrival. He had been friendly right up to the last. If he were involved, then it was the worst kind of treachery imaginable. But I couldn't believe he was. I had seen him banged up. The Old Bill had obviously made a mistake. Perhaps they had segregated him to put pressure on. Maybe they would let him up after a few days.

The fellas in general were angry over what had happened. Jackie was well liked. They admired his spirit. They didn't like the cowardly way it had been done either. If Tony and Mick had come back on the wing, they would have been set about immediately.

I wasn't pleased that they had been grassed, but it certainly resolved a problem for me. If in fact it was them, they would have been looking for an opportunity to do me too. They couldn't afford to take the chance that I would make a comeback. Eventually, I would have heard something. The ensuing tear-up would have been very serious, especially with Tony. Yes, although I wouldn't say as much, I was quite relieved at the outcome.

That afternoon I had a surprise visit. I was taken over to the gate lodge, which was very unusual. As the screw ushered me in, I was surprised to see the governor, and behind him my sister and Teddy, Jackie's eldest brother.

My sister ran forward and threw her arms around me. Tears were running down her face. Teddy appeared at her side. Grabbing me by the arm, he pulled me to one side. His face was tight and white with shock. His eyes had the staring madness of uncontrollable grief and rage.

'Who did it? Who the fuck did it?' he growled, his voice breaking with emotion. He had been very close to Jackie. I explained that I only knew what I had heard. That there were three fellas down the block for it. But that it was all a mystery to me because I wasn't aware that Jackie had fallen out with anybody.

The governor hovered in the background as the three of us huddled together. My sister was clinging to me, crying helplessly. I hadn't been aware that the relationship had meant that much to her. It had been over for some time.

What was already a heavy situation for me was rapidly turning into a tragedy of classic proportions. Once again I mused on the way that bizarre happenings increasingly seemed to be a part of my life. After about an hour, Teddy and my sister left. It was a draining experience for me. They could take their grief outside with them, to dissipate in the distractions of freedom. I would sit and mull over mine like a miser.

Everything that came afterwards was a distinct anticlimax. I missed Jackie's company and the security of his friendship. Then there were the comings and goings of the police. Few of the fellas would tolerate a grass. Jackie was well liked, though, so they didn't feel like having a go at those who had grassed the three down the block. They just ignored them.

Several days later, I was called in for a police interview. I was in a very awkward position now. If I actively sabotaged the prosecution case and Tony and Mick got off, Jackie's family and my sister would never forgive me. However, I wasn't going to do them any damage in court, even if Jackie was my best pal. I would settle things in my own way or not at all.

The police had my statement with them. They read it through to me, including the bit about my finding Roy banged up. It didn't do anyone any harm. I wasn't putting anyone in it. It didn't even mention Tony or Mick. And, as far as Roy was concerned, it placed him well away from the action.

I still couldn't believe he'd had anything to do with it. I'd heard no rumours concerning his involvement. In fact, I was pleased to give that piece of evidence for him. Anyway, it was the truth.

At first I thought I was wanted as a defence witness. That would have been embarrassing for me in the eyes of Jackie's family. It might look like treachery or even that I was involved in some way. The police reassured me that, as mine was all uncontested evidence, in the circumstances I would be listed as part of the prosecution's case. I acquiesced at this not-too-ideal solution. They would only subpoena me anyway, so I had little choice really.

Several months passed, and people largely forgot about the killing. Tony, Mick and Roy had all long since been moved to Leeds. The trial was scheduled for Leeds Assizes.

One morning, about 12 of us were called over to reception. There were five YPs including Purdin. The rest were adult cons. I didn't have a clue who was saying what, but I did know that we were both defence and prosecution witnesses mixed. It had all turned very sour. I didn't feel like talking; I just wanted to get it over with.

A van took us to Leeds Assizes, and we were lodged in cells beneath the courts. I waited for several hours before I was called. I climbed some stairs and, to my surprise, came right up in the back of the dock. Tony, Mick and Roy were sitting with their backs to me, so close that I could have touched them.

I was led over to the witness box. Any court appearance is always an intimidating experience, but the massive chamber of Leeds Assizes was especially so.

As I stood there nervously, I glanced at the dock. Tony was lolling in his chair, sullenly arrogant, with a sour smirk on his face. He had the air of someone who was largely indifferent to the goings-on. However, I could tell that beneath this studied indifference he was enjoying every minute of it.

This was his personal statement. Anyone who messed with him would end up dead. Murder was a statistically unusual act in the early Sixties, yet Tony had done two in less than a year.

Mick was sitting there all pasty faced and afraid. He was only doing a five; a life sentence would be a disaster for him. He definitely wasn't enjoying the proceedings.

Roy was moving restlessly in his chair. It was as if he were having trouble sitting still. He looked outraged, disgusted and frightened all at the same time. Even knowing what I did, it was apparent that he felt he shouldn't be there.

My part was over very quickly. Defence counsel questioned me in detail about my finding Roy locked up. He emphasised the part where I had said that he didn't seem agitated or unusual in any way. Before I knew it, I was back downstairs in the cells again.

Later on, a screw came to my cell. I was surprised when he told me that all three had been found guilty. Tony had stood, still arrogant, as the judge put on the black cap. He had committed two separate murders within the space of a year, which made it a capital offence. He smiled as he was sentenced to death.

Mick stood, cowed and pale, as he was sentenced to life. Roy couldn't contain himself. 'I'm not fucking guilty,' he had shouted as he was also sentenced to life.

Jackie had a big funeral in Notting Hill. There was a long cortege of cars and hundreds of wreaths. A large crowd attended the burial. The manor had turned out in force to send off one of its sons in style. It was extensively reported in the local papers. Yet again I felt a part of local history. To step out of the crowd once was unusual: to make repeated appearances was bizarre.

After a few weeks, Tony's death sentence was commuted to life imprisonment. It would run together with his previous HMP. Several months later the three appeals came up. At the last moment, Tony and Mick abandoned theirs and gave evidence for Roy. By now, another alibi witness had appeared for him. His sentence was quashed. As his other sentence had already finished, he was released.

There was a rumour that, a year or so later, a group of Jackie's friends had slipped up to Birmingham and done Roy. It was said he was seriously stabbed and is now in a wheelchair.

After a few years in Security Wings, Mick spent the rest in normal jails. He was released after about 15 years.

Tony spent many years in Security Wings. He worked out assiduously on the weights and turned his skinny build into a massive physique. He studied on the Open University and got a First Class Honours degree. He was released after 20 years. He was last heard of living in the West Country, sharing a flat with several cats. On a couple of occasions he was invited to lecture on penal matters.

27 THE ALBANY WALL GAME

I had been in the chokey at Albany for over two months. The original 56 days' solitary for my escape attempt (described in Chapter 13) had passed. My situation hadn't changed, though, because, on the day it finished, I was put on Rule 43 for 'subversive activity'.

If I hadn't been used to the perverse workings of the system already, perhaps this would have surprised me. After all, how could I be subversive in solitary confinement? Who could I possibly subvert, other than myself?

In reality, it was just a ploy to keep me in the chokey. The situation up on the wings was still supposed to be volatile. However, the number of incidents had fallen. I suppose the governor wasn't taking any chances though. He wasn't going to allow me back up, or the other 15 or so who were in the chokey with me.

After the madness of the early days of the riot following my escape attempt and subsequent crackdown, life in the chokey had settled down to a steady war of attrition. Things weren't tranquil by any means. We still had regular organised protests, but we no longer stayed up every single night, banging and shouting to keep the screws awake in the nearby quarters.

There were still nights when this did happen. We lit fires and smashed up, when we had anything to burn or break, but protests were organised more around particular objectives.

We weren't going to accept being kept in indefinite solitary under Rule 43. We realised that the worst thing we could do was sit quietly in our cells. That way the governor would be under no pressure to do anything about the situation. We would be left for months and months, possibly years.

Ironically, although Rule 43 wasn't classed as a punishment, it was far worse than being on ordinary chokey. Admittedly, we didn't have to put our bedding out each morning and sit or lie on a hard surface all day. Also, we could have books, newspapers and spend our canteen, if we had any.

But, at least with punishment, you knew how long you had to do. It was always a fixed term of days, and never more than 56, except in exceptional circumstances. With Rule 43, though, it was open-ended. You never knew how long you had to do. We would only be let up when the governor said so and not before. There was no appeal. In the first place they never told you any specific reason why you were on 'subversive'. This made it impossible to formulate any challenge to the decision.

Secondly, the only people you could appeal to were the VC, and mostly they automatically rubberstamped the governor's rulings. So all we could do was perform. We tried to create as much disruption as possible.

There were 20 cells in the chokey. Half a dozen were kept empty for normal punishments, those who would leave the chokey after they had done their time. The rest held us 'so-called' rioters.

Immediately behind the chokey stood 'E' wing. This had been used as a segregation block too. There were still 20 or so fellas held there on Rule 43. When they joined in with us on a protest, it could be both noisy and effective.

Strangely enough, many of the chokey screws had some sympathy with us. The governor had deliberately manned the chokey with older, more decent screws, well knowing that, if he put the heavy mob in, it would be off all the time.

We didn't feel any sympathy for them though. The pressure of trying to survive each day in solitary filled us with a hatred of anything in a uniform. They were grown men. They knew what they were doing. They had seen plenty of men crack up in solitary, kill themselves even. They were as guilty as the rest.

However, there was never any brutality by them. They didn't go out of their way to wind us up. We got what we were entitled to, so we never aimed our protests specifically at them.

Whether this was any consolation was doubtful. They were always the ones subject to the most noise, the immediate effects of disruption and all the ensuing stress. It couldn't have been easy for them, working in the chokey.

Much of their restraint was due to an SO we called Punchy. He was a rugged, stocky fella of about 40 who had once been a boxer. He was tough, fair and could handle himself. There was no brutality while he was on duty.

You could see that he was disturbed by a lot that went on, especially the brutality by the heavy mob up in the wings. Being straightforward himself, he resented the governor's underhanded ways. He wasn't on our side by any means, but if it had been left to him we could have sorted out our grievances without having to perform.

Up on the wings most of the resistance had died down. All the rebels had been removed to the chokey, and the rest had been intimidated by the heavy mob.

There were a group of about a dozen of the latter. All were big fellas, most were ex-services. They went out of their way to provoke people. On a spin, they would rip the cell to pieces leaving possessions all over the floor. They would confiscate things for no reason. Remarks were made about wives and girlfriends.

The regime was very restrictive, with fellas being let out of their cells only for short periods. Any sign of rebellion would be met with instant violence. Several screws would jump on the fella and carry him bodily to the chokey. All the way there, he would be punched, kicked and beaten. Then they would throw him naked into a strip cell, where he would be left for the night.

The following day he would find that he had been charged with assault. On the subsequent VC, he would lose from six months upwards, coupled with 56 days' solitary. It was an effective method of intimidation. Apart from our continued detention on Rule 43, this brutality was the main thing we protested about.

I was in a cell on the outward-facing side of the chokey. There were nine cells on this side, all looking out towards the perimeter fence. The first cell was kept for punishments that came and went. I was in the next cell down.

One morning I heard the first cell door open, then slam. I realised that they had just put someone in there. I went to my window and called out. Within seconds, the fella came to his window and answered.

It was Rob, a Scots fella I knew. He told me he had just got seven days for verballing a screw. Then he told me that Joe Mason, a good friend of mine, had just arrived.

Joe and I were very close pals. We kept in constant contact and knew each other's families on the outside. My pleasure at his being in the same jail was tempered with sadness that he had come to a place that was having so much trouble.

Like me, Joe was doing a life sentence from which he would be lucky ever to get out. He was far more notorious, though, having been involved in riots and escapes in several jails. He was powerfully built, a leader of men, and was held in universal respect by the fellas. Consequently, the authorities feared him.

I couldn't see him lasting long on the wings. Even if he didn't quickly fall out with some of the screws, he would probably come down the chokey in solidarity with me and the rest of the fellas.

By coincidence, I was soon due to go up to the Education

Department for a final tutorial before an important OU exam. The tutor had specifically asked that I should be present. They could hardly bring her down the block to me. They would have to take me up to her class. I just might get the chance to see Joe.

The Education Department lay along one side of a central corridor. On the other side were the entrances to the various wings. The following morning, a screw escorted me from the chokey, past the wings and into the classroom.

Here he left me. I wasn't on my own. There was the tutor in the class and a screw standing out in the corridor. There weren't too many places I could go.

At mid-morning, the class broke off for a tea-break. There was no hot water available in the Education Department, so the fellas went back to their wings. I had anticipated this and had brought a cup with me.

I left the class with all the others. The screw in the corridor didn't notice me, so I walked on to 'C' wing where I knew Joe was. As I stood at the urn filling my cup, I asked a fella to slip upstairs and fetch him.

Suddenly I heard a shout. Joe came hurrying towards me, a broad smile on his face. We hugged each other and quickly exchanged our news. We knew we didn't have long.

He told be how he had just been thrown out of his last jail. I gave him a brief history of the present trouble at Albany. I asked him to stay out of it if he could, but from the way he looked at me I knew that he wouldn't be able to.

By now several minutes had passed. If I didn't return to the class soon the screw would come looking for me. There could be an argument, which might involve Joe. I decided to get back. As I left the wing Joe called after me, 'Take care, Norm. Be seeing you.' It sounded all too prophetic.

The following morning Joe was down the chokey. One of the fellas stopped at my door and told me that he was in the end cell on the inward-facing side of the chokey. He had volleyed a screw.

From the sound of it, he was just looking for an excuse to get down here with us.

Even though Joe was only a short distance away, I was unlikely ever to see him. He would go on exercise with the fellas in the two cells nearest to him. We were only unlocked singly at other times. We would never meet.

Luckily, Punchy was on duty. I knew there was an empty cell next to Joe's. I rang my bell and asked him if I could move. Perhaps because things had been relatively quiet that week, he agreed. He would live to regret it.

Whereas the cell I had just left looked outwards to the fence, my new cell looked inwards on to a small rectangular exercise yard. It was totally enclosed. There were cells running along two adjoining sides. On the other two sides there were blank brick walls about ten feet high.

There wasn't much of a view. In the recent past, though, it had been possible to talk to whoever was on exercise and shout across to the line of cells that ran at right angles to ours.

To the powers that be, though, that must have detracted from the principle of solitary confinement. So they built two breeze-block screening walls, six feet from each line of cells and running parallel to them.

They stood barely seven foot high, topped with a few strands of barbed wire. There was a flimsy, mesh gate at the end of each wall, to prevent fellas from walking behind them and talking to the occupants of the cells. They served no real function, except to block our line of sight. Now our cells looked out on to a blank grey wall.

There were five cells on our side. Joe was in the end cell, adjoining the brick wall. I was now in the next one up. The third was occupied by a young Irish fella. He had only been down the chokey for a few days, and no one knew anything about him. Blackie, in the fourth cell, was a short, dark-haired fella in his late

30s, doing a 14 for numerous armed robberies. He was well known in the system and had been involved in various bits of trouble elsewhere.

Blackie was quite a character, with a lively sense of humour. He sported a big incongruous-looking handlebar moustache. If you hadn't known he was a bank robber, you could have been forgiven for mistaking him for an RAF group captain. He wouldn't have looked out of place in any wartime aircrew.

Next to him was Jeff, a wild young Canadian fella who was game for anything. He was only doing an eight, but his relatively early release date didn't stop him from getting involved in protests. He had short, cropped, blond hair and a fresh, open face. His salient quality was loyalty. He would never leave a mate in the lurch.

The screws' office was next to Jeff's. It stood at the right angle, between the two lines of inward-facing cells. On the other side of it was the gate that led into the yard. Then there was the second line of cells leading down to the recess and strip cells.

The office was as big as two normal cells. It was constantly occupied by the half-dozen screws who usually manned the chokey. Its back wall was Jeff's side wall. He could hear them as they moved about in there.

It hadn't taken me long to move in. My possessions amounted to only a cardboard box containing a bag of sugar, a few books and a wad of letters held together by an elastic band. The cell, of course, was identical to the one I had just left. The only difference was that the bedboard had been torn from the wall, its hinges hanging loose at the back. Some bricks had been removed from around the window reveal, exposing the gap of the cavity wall.

Dropping my box on the bedboard, I went straight to the window and called to Joe. He came to his window. It had been over two years since we had last spoken at any length. I had been out then and used to bring his wife up to visit him. We had a lot to talk about.

Exercise time came around, and fellas were allowed on to the yard three at a time. Over on the outward-facing side I had always been out with Aussie and Gary, the fellas in the adjoining cells. Now I would go out with two new neighbours.

My turn eventually came, and I walked from my cell into the corridor. The screw then unlocked Joe, but that only made two of us. He had gone past the young Paddy. He must have already exercised with two others. I was well pleased. Now the next one out would be Danny. He was in the end cell on the outward-facing side, directly across the corridor from Joe.

This was a double bonus. Not only was Danny one of our own but he was also on the outward-facing side. This meant that, if we wanted to get a message across to the fellas on that side, we could now do so secretly by telling Danny. We could always have shouted across, but then the screws would have heard too.

Danny hurried towards Joe and warmly shook his hand. They had been in some trouble at Hull together, so they already shared a bond. Danny's pale, drawn face lit up in a smile as he walked out on exercise with us.

Danny came from the North of Scotland. He had been an unlikely robber. But his irrepressible spirit and rebellious nature didn't lend itself easily to menial farm work. He had drifted south to Glasgow and got in with some robbers who operated south of the border. His 12 was a long sentence for those times and that part of the country.

In prison his rebelliousness and loyalty to others soon got him into trouble. He was moved to Dartmoor, a hard jail for troublemakers. Here he had several severe beatings and long spells of solitary. His spirit wouldn't let him give in, though, but it seriously affected his health.

Now, four years into his sentence, his tall frame was painfully thin. His natural 14 stone was down to ten. His face was gaunt, with eyes sunk deep into their sockets. It had affected his mental health too. He had a lost, distant look about him. His attention span was short, and he could easily lose track of a conversation. He regularly took large doses of whatever drugs the sick-bay would give him.

His spirit still burned within him, though, but not so brightly. He still had that faithful, dog-like loyalty to others. He wouldn't hesitate to get involved, but now his judgement was suspect. He was easily led. He would loyally follow those who didn't deserve it. His real friends constantly tried to protect him from this. He was regarded with genuine affection by all the chaps.

The three of us walked around the yard in the bright sunlight. Fellas called out to Joe from behind the breezeblock wall. Blackie was an old friend. Stan, Jim and Ernie, also old pals, shouted greetings from the opposite side. Others joined in. If Joe had needed to, it made him feel more at home. It was good for our solidarity too.

Solidarity was very important to us. Few of us knew each other on the outside. All we had in common was our shared situation, our rebelliousness and, generally speaking, a London background.

All of us were spirited and hated the oppression of the screws. The only thing they seemed to understand was that which they ruled by: fear and violence. Well, we were no strangers to violence ourselves. The odds were always heavily in their favour, usually in the order of eight to one. But we had the greater courage, coupled with a self-destructiveness born of the desperation caused by an endless sentence.

An attack on one of us was an attack on all. Although we couldn't join in physically, we would smash on our doors with fists, boots and chairs. If one were punished, others would do the same to be punished likewise. Those on bread and water shared the food of those on normal diets.

We supported each other in every way we could. Joint action was our answer to individual isolation. It was the only way that we had a chance of winning. It was the only action that would force their hand. In the paralysing loneliness of solitary, our loyalty to each other was the only thing that kept us going.

Joe's arrival gave us a much-needed boost. I had already been something of a leader in my own right. To put the two of us together was a definite mistake.

Exercise finished, and we returned to our cells. You could see that Danny was reluctant to go. His loyalty was tinged with sentimentality. He was so pleased to see his old friend Joe, and he resented the return to solitary.

I walked into my cell, banging the door behind me. I slipped off my shoes and padded over to the window in my stockinged feet. The concrete floor was cool after walking in circles around a small yard for half an hour.

I called to Joe, and he came to his window. For a while we talked of Danny. Of how he would always stand by you right to the end. He had already taken so much stick. 'We must try to keep him out of things as much as we can,' said Joe.

This brought us to the inevitable subject. 'What do you fancy doing, Joe?' I asked. 'If we just sit here, Footer will really take his pound of flesh and keep us here indefinitely.'

Joe had already met Footer that morning on adjudication. He was a poor governor by any standards. A short, fat, balding man in his middle 50s, he was hardly an imposing figure in a world where physical prowess was everything.

He had a partially crippled leg and walked with the assistance of a wooden cane. He could often be seen pegging about the jail in a shapeless tweed jacket, constantly mopping his florid face with a large off-white handkerchief.

He wasn't an evil man by any means. He was no sadist and didn't seem to take any pleasure in our suffering. He was just weak. He was caught between the pressure of the POA to cut back on privileges and our demands for better conditions. The POA were always the stronger lobby though. Concessions to us were always made grudgingly, knowing he would have to justify them at the next meeting with the POA. If he had possessed more character and courage, he could have asserted himself.

Consequently, we despised him. When your every waking moment is a nightmare of tension as you grapple with the terminal boredom of unending solitary, it is largely academic whether you are there by the express intention of the governor or merely because he has been forced into it by the POA.

We knew his weakness though. He could be intimidated. This gave us our plan. We would increase the violence of our protests until our pressure exceeded that of the POA. We had nothing to lose. Indefinite solitary would eventually affect our sanity. The strongest mind would crack in the end. So, rather than wait passively, we might as well go down fighting.

Joe took a long time to answer my question. I was beginning to think that he had wandered away from the window and hadn't heard me. 'I don't want to commit myself to anything at the moment,' he said quietly. 'If I say something, I'll have to do it. But I haven't had time to weigh the situation up yet. We'll talk about it tonight.'

That was fair enough. After all, although he had been in the jail a couple of days, he had only been in the chokey a few hours. He would have to consider the various options and the support each was likely to get from the rest of the fellas.

We made desultory conversation for a while. All the time, others were coming out for exercise. Looking along the alleyway between the breeze-block wall and our cells, we could see the gate that led into the yard. As fellas came through we would catch a brief glimpse of them. There were quick waves and short, shouted greetings. It was our only visual contact with the rest of the fellas in the chokey.

Standing at my window, my eye was suddenly caught by something glittering deep in the exposed window reveal. The sun, directly overhead, cast its rays into the darkened gap next to the sill. Right at the bottom, a dull object sparkled at the edges.

I put my arm into the gap. Rough brickwork scratched at my skin. I hesitated slightly at the thought of monstrous spiders lurking in the depths. Gingerly, I reached down with my finger.

I touched something sharp. It moved easily, though, so the object was only small and light. With my arm in the crack, it was impossible to see what I was doing. I gripped something loosely between my thumb and second finger and slowly pulled out my arm.

I was holding the jagged end of a small bottle. The neck was long and smooth. I guessed it must have originally been a tomato-sauce bottle bought from the canteen.

The bottle ended right where the panelled sides would have been. In their place was a ragged fringe of razor-sharp glass. The whole thing was about five inches long. Held by the neck, it would be a wicked tool at close quarters. That it was in the chokey was amazing. No glass of any kind was allowed there, and someone must have smuggled it in among their kit. If it came to a tear-up with the screws now, at least I had a weapon.

I stared deep into the gloom of the cavity to see if there was anything else hidden there. But it was too dark to tell. There was an odd-shaped lump resting on what must have been the bottom. It could have been anything though.

Once again I put my arm deep into the cavity. My fingertips touched against something that moved. I grasped its edge and lifted. As it emerged into the daylight I was surprised to see another broken sauce bottle, identical to the first.

I put them both back where they came from. It was a good hiding place. The screws hadn't found them there. I called Joe to his window. 'Hey, mate, you'll never guess what I've found.' I told him in a whisper about the bottles. 'It gives you something to think about when you come to consider all our options.'

Respecting his wish to discuss it that evening, I went and sat on my bedboard. With my back resting against the wall and my legs crossed, I closed my eyes to think.

Whatever we did, it would have to be extreme: We had been performing for months now, so it would have to be something more than just smashing up or banging all night. We could steam into a couple of the chokey screws, but that wouldn't really solve anything. We would get a VC and some more chokey.

Also it would be embarrassing. Our chokey screws were the older, more decent ones. A couple of them had gone out of their way to make things a bit easier. It would seem ungrateful, even treacherous. Especially as the real villains were the heavy mob up on the wings.

As I ran the various options through my mind, I remembered the two short bars one of the fellas had hidden in his cell. They were a pair of cast-steel hinges, which had fixed a bedboard to the wall. The bedboards were massively heavy, so the hinges had to be meaty too. Each of them was over a foot long and two inches wide. The cast steel was about half an inch thick, so there was some weight to them too.

The side walls of the cells were comparatively thin. You didn't have to be a master bricklayer to work out that they were only half a brick thick. This meant that there was barely four-and-a-half inches of wall between Joe and me.

However, they were built of specially imported bricks, which were unbelievably hard. It was really difficult just to knock in a nail. With ordinary nails, you had no chance – they would bend at the first blow. You needed special 'concrete nails'. And you had to be careful knocking these in. If you didn't hit them dead straight, they would ricochet around the cell like bullets.

So, although the side walls were thin, they weren't weak. We knew that the bricks were of German manufacture: The special razor wire on the security fences was supposed to be made by them too. Trust the Germans to come up with things like these.

We were used to the massively thick walls of the old Victorian jails. The fella next door could scream his head off, and you would never hear a thing. With Albany's walls, though, if you banged on them with your fist they made a hollow, booming sound. You could hear every sound from next door. It made you feel that it wouldn't be too difficult to smash your way through. With a couple of steel bars, there just might be a chance.

Later that evening I stood at my window talking to Joe. We spoke in undertones, twisting our mouths to blur the sound and stop it carrying. We talked in slang and made oblique references to crucial items. It wasn't unknown for the screws to get up on the flat roof of the chokey and lie there listening to our conversations.

By the end of the evening we had three plans, each more extreme than the one before. We labelled them X, Y and Z. Now, once we had explained them secretly to the other fellas, we could refer to them openly just by one of the letters.

Plan X was centred around the two steel bars. Joe agreed that it might be possible to break through the side walls with them. We could wedge our doors to prevent the screws from getting in. This would give us the time we needed.

If everyone on our side agreed, we could smash through into Paddy's, then Blackie's and then Jeff's. By then, there would be five of us. More than would normally get together in the chokey.

Just one wall would stand between us and the screws in the office. By then, though, the heavy mob would be waiting. But they wouldn't have it all their own way this time. They were all right beating people up firm-handed. They'd have the riot sticks, and there would be dozens of them, but there would be five of us armed with steel bars and broken bottles.

We didn't expect to win, but it would be quite a battle. We would get a terrible beating, but we would seriously hurt a few of them too. It would be a major incident and should bring things to a head.

There would probably be a trial in an outside court too. A bit of bird on top didn't mean much when your life or your sanity was at stake. We should be able to bring out about all the beatings the heavy mob had been dishing out too.

It would certainly be a major embarrassment to the Home Office and would get us all moved. We would settle for that. Once we had done our punishment in our new jails, we'd be let up from their chokey. There would be no riot situation to justify keeping us on Rule 43.

Like Plan X, the success of Plan Y depended on a number of people joining in. In fact, the more the merrier. For a hunger strike to succeed, you needed publicity. It was difficult to get the newspapers to publish anything about prisons anyway, what with the D-notice. Individual hunger strikers weren't unusual. But, if eight or ten of us took part, it might attract attention.

Hunger strikes were incredibly hard though. You were in constant pain and ached all over. Weight fell off you, and you got progressively weaker. You would have no strength to fight the screws even if you wanted to. Then there was the danger of doing yourself permanent damage. There was no guarantee that it would work either. Dangerous cons starving themselves didn't excite a great deal of sympathy in most people.

As the hunger strike went on and got progressively harder, there was always the danger that individuals might drop out. And who could blame them? Each man had his limit. It could divide us and harm our unity though. A complete failure could lead to bitterness and the end of the unified resistance.

Plan Z, as befitted its alphabetical position, was the ultimate and most extreme. It was desperation stakes, if all else failed. It was very simple and guaranteed to work. And it involved only Joe and me.

We would come out as if to go on exercise as usual. We would push Andy back in his cell and bang him up. Our chokey screws would back off as soon as they saw the broken bottles we were carrying. We would press the alarm bell and go to wait by the entrance doors. When the bullies of the heavy mob ran in, we would steam into them with the broken bottles.

It was the most desperate of tactics. We should be able to do enough damage to ensure that we were moved out, but we would get the most terrible of beatings. There would probably be charges in an outside court, but it didn't look like Joe and I were ever going to be released anyway.

It was a measure of our desperation that we should even contemplate such a plan. It was a measure of our loyalty and confidence in each other that we should undertake it together. We were men who had nothing. Our futures were bleak and barren, and filled with pain. All we had was our pride, our spirit and our honour. And, as melodramatic as it may sound to free-world people with much to live for, if you had to go down, then you might as well do so fighting the screws with your closest pal beside you.

Over the next couple of days we passed the word around about the three plans. Everyone on our side was in favour of Plan X, which was just as well if we wanted to reach the office. A couple of fellas on the other side said that they were going to try to break through their walls too. Several more said that, at the very least, they would wedge their doors.

Plan Y was even more popular. It was something anyone could take part in, wherever they were located in the chokey and whatever tools they had. It was passively non-violent. And you couldn't be nicked for it either.

Also, it was still one plan away. For the more faint-hearted it was an easy commitment. About a dozen fellas said they would take part. It was good for our unity and morale in that a large proportion of the fellas now felt that they were part of the general protest.

Plan Z met with a stony silence. You couldn't expect men with fixed sentences to get involved in something as extreme as that. Neither Joe nor I would have put anyone in a position by asking them. No one tried to talk us out of it. Everyone knew that it was our decision. After the first mention it was never discussed again. I joked with Joe that they were either impressed by our courage or appalled by our lunacy.

Before we could put Plan X into operation we had to get the

two steel bars. They were in Nuff-Nuff's cell over on Danny's side.

Nuff-Nuff was a strange fella even by Albany's standards. He was as white and as English as any of us, but he had been born in South America. By his own admission, at birth he had been an absolute monster. A cleft palate was the least of his deformities. He had been through over 20 major operations.

The finished product was far from beautiful. He was a big lad with burly shoulders, but his massive head still looked wildly out of proportion. Long, jet-black hair hung down to his shoulders. He had a bad harelip, which pulled his whole jaw out of shape. His speech was equally distorted.

He had a terrible complex about the way he looked. Perhaps to compensate, he always talked very loudly as if to show that he wasn't embarrassed to attract attention to himself. Consequently, his speech came out even more fractured and bizarre. At times it sounded like some large animal snuffling about. Hence the nickname 'Nuff-Nuff', although I always called him John.

When you got to know him, though, he wasn't a bad fella. He was very lonely. He was also extremely demanding of a friendship, but if you were his pal he would do anything for you.

An out-and-out rebel, Nuff-Nuff was always rowing with the screws. This made him popular and respected among the fellas. It brought him more friends and acquaintances than if he had just sat in his cell quietly. Sadly, he was more at home in prison than he ever was outside.

I quite liked him, and we got on well. He wasn't short of bottle, even if he was a bit abrasive at times. Also, he tended to look up to me.

I sent a message over to him through Danny. I knew that he would have liked to use the steel bars himself, but the fellas either side of him didn't want to know. Grudgingly, he agreed that I could have them.

The bars were each wrapped in a cloth and swung from window to window until they reached Danny's cell. He brought them out on exercise, tucked down the front of his strides, hidden by his overcoat. He passed them to me as we came in. I took them into my cell with me.

At nine that evening, the night patrol came on, and the day screws went off. We waited for ten minutes to give them time to get clear of the gate, then we started.

I had made several small wooden wedges. Using the end of the steel bar, I drove them into the gap between my cell door and the metal jamb. I spaced them out, and soon the door was wedged tight. In the background I could hear other fellas doing the same.

If the screws really wanted to get in, they could do so. It would mean fetching big hydraulic jacks and would probably damage the door. But, as it was late at night, with no day staff on, we figured that they would leave us till the morning. After all, we could hardly go anywhere. Or so they would think.

Standing either side of our party wall, Joe and I counted several brick courses up from the floor. Then we counted about a dozen bricks along from one end. Once we were sure that we were starting on the same brick, we began.

With a piece of rag wrapped around one end of the steel hinge, I gripped it in both hands. Standing sideways on, I swung with all my might. The end of the hinge smashed into the face of the brick, sending shock-waves right up my arms.

A dozen blows later, I stopped to survey the damage: The paint had been chipped from the surface and three inches square of bare brick had been revealed. It was going to be a long, hard job.

I could hear the sharp cracks as Joe hit the wall from the other side. From all over the chokey came the sound of various crashes, bangs and muffled thuds. The chaps were hard at work.

All the time fellas were shouting to each other. 'Go on, Ernie, give it some stick.' 'Won't be long now, John, and I'll be through to you.' 'We're coming out, you fucking screws.' Paddy was also shouting encouragement from next door.

Much of it was bravado, designed to keep our spirits up. It was also communication. After all, we were separately locked in our own cells. If the screws came in on someone, he would warn the others.

I started back at the brick. Our plan was to knock one brick out, then it would be easier to loosen the ones around it. But it was so hard. Tiny chips of brick came away. A fine red dust hung in the air. Soon it was in my hair, coating my face and chest and drifting in an ever-increasing circle.

It took all of 20 minutes before I saw daylight through the wall. Another ten saw a half-brick-sized hole gnawed through the brickwork, its deep redness looking like a wound.

Joe and I both paused. It was time to catch our breath and think about the job in hand. No one wanted to be a quitter, but it had taken half an hour to remove half a brick. At this rate it would take a dozen hours to make a sizeable hole.

Already both my hands were red raw. My eyes were streaming, and I was coughing and sneezing from the dust in my nose and mouth. My arms ached and my elbows were exquisitely sore from the constant jarring. Ignore them as I would, the doubts were there.

'Norm, hey, Norm.' I heard Joe's voice coming through the hole. 'Let me shake your hand.' Our hands met in the hole, and we symbolically shook as we laughed at the grandiose gesture.

'Oi, fellas,' I shouted at the top of my voice, 'me and Joe have just shook hands through the wall.' There was some pride there in that we had managed to breach the wall, but it was all very tongue in cheek. It was good for morale, though, and might encourage the others. A ragged cheer went up in the chokey, followed by whistles and shouts.

'Hey, Norm, Norm,' Nuff-Nuff was yelling from the other side.

'What?' I shouted back.

'I've made a little hole, but it's impossible with what I've got.' The booming, distorted voice echoed around the chokey, giving a surreal effect to an already bizarre situation.

'It's the same with me,' bellowed Ernie from across the yard. Other voices joined in to the same effect.

'Don't worry about it, fellas,' I shouted back. 'You've done your best.'

Now it was all down to Joe and me. If it ended right here, the taste of defeat would be bitter. We wouldn't be in the best of spirits to go into a hunger strike. Failure could affect our unity too. As isolated individuals, we would have to sit out our months in solitary.

'Norm, Norm.' It was Joe shouting through the hole again.

'Yeah?' I shouted back.

'Stand back out of the way a minute.'

I stood there puzzled. Stand back out of the way? Why? Surely I couldn't be in any danger? A locked chokey cell had to be one of the safest places on earth. What did Joe have in there, dynamite?

Suddenly, the whole cell shook. There was a deep booming sound that reverberated around the walls. I could feel the concussion through my feet as the floor shook. Then it came again.

This time, half a brick flew out of the wall, narrowly missing me. It shot across the cell and smashed heavily against the opposite wall. Small particles of brick stung my face.

I jumped back into the corner. I was shocked and puzzled. What the fuck was going on?

Bricks flew fast and furiously now. Whole bricks, half-bricks and showers of fragments. Whole sections of the wall fell away. Dust was everywhere. It hung as a red mist in the air. My nose was sore from breathing it.

The booming was deafening. It was like being inside a giant drum. The back wall, against which I was leaning, shook from top to bottom. Then, as suddenly as it started, it stopped.

Voices were calling from everywhere. Ernie, John, Andy, Stan, Aussie were all shouting, wanting to know what was happening. There was concern bordering on panic. No one could conceive of anything that could have that effect in the chokey. A sledgehammer couldn't have made the deep, booming concussion.

As the dust cleared, I peered through the now gaping hole into Joe's cell. He was standing there, begrimed from head to toe. In his arms he had the bedboard, one end resting on the floor. It was incredible. He had been swinging the bedboard against the wall.

Now, a bedboard was a massive construction. There were four planks, each seven foot long by six inches wide, made out of inch-thick pine. An inch gap separated them. Across their back were fixed four, three-by-six-inch bracers. Massive screws held it together.

It must have weighed well over a hundredweight. It was awkward in the extreme, designed so that it couldn't be slung about. Yet Joe had been holding it in his arms and swinging it against the wall.

My own bedboard was lying on the floor, under the mattress and blankets. It was covered with a thick layer of brickdust now. I tipped the mattress and covers on to the floor and dragged the bedboard clear.

I hefted it into my arms, but its weight caused me to overbalance forwards. It was as much as I could do to hold it, let alone swing it.

I lunged towards the wall. There was little momentum, but the sheer weight caused it to smash awkwardly into the brickwork. A few bricks around the edge of the hole, already loosened, fell into Joe's cell.

Four or five times I lunged against the wall. Each time some more bricks came loose, but in nothing like the quantities that Joe had dislodged. I was no physical weakling, but I was no superman either. I stood back to let Joe continue.

Again he swung the bedboard against the wall. The bricks and mortar flew like wild, angry things. The hole yawned in the wall. It was nearly as big as a doorway now. It was large enough to step through.

Joe laid the bedboard on the floor. I climbed over two remaining courses of bricks into his cell. We slapped each other around the shoulders, laughing as tears washed tracks through the dust on our faces.

My cell was devastated. It looked like a demolition site. Brickbats lay everywhere. A thick layer of sandy, red brickdust covered everything. Joe and I were smothered from head to foot.

Joe's cell was a lot cleaner. There was a layer of dust and a few bricks close to the wall, but most of the debris had been knocked into mine. We stood at his window, breathing in lungfuls of clean, fresh air. We snorted as we tried to clear the dust from our nostrils. Our eyes burned from the irritation.

I shouted from the window that we were through the wall. I heard the insistent voice of Paddy coming from two cells along. 'Do mine next. Do mine next, fellas,' the throaty Northern Irish twang rang out.

Paddy was a young fella, who couldn't have been more than 20. He had told us he was doing a five, but he never said what for, and, of course, we never asked.

He had only been in the chokey for about a week. He had been quite restrained, but I felt that this was because he didn't know anyone. Talking to him out the window, I got the impression that he was very scatty and immature. However, he seemed to have plenty of heart.

Whether he realised the seriousness of what he got himself into was a moot point. If he had an obvious fault, it was that he would get involved in anything, no matter how crazy or bizarre. But he was old enough to make his own decisions. And, as his cell stood between us and the office, we welcomed his enthusiasm.

Twenty minutes had passed, and our heads had cleared. Also, the dust had settled in my cell. Joe and I climbed through for the assault on Paddy's wall

I pulled my bedding aside and cleared a space so that Joe had a sound footing. It was difficult enough for him to swing the bedboard without having to balance on bits of brick and other detritus. Joe picked up my bedboard and stepped up to the wall.

'Look out, Paddy, me old son,' he shouted, a smile wrinkling the corners of his mouth. Pivoting backwards and forwards like an

Olympic hammer thrower, he suddenly swung the bedboard against the wall.

Once again, there was a deep booming sound like the ringing of some ancient stone gong. Simultaneously, massive vibrations shook the whole cell. Joe took a couple more swings, then there was a sharp 'crack' as the brickwork ruptured. Bricks started to fall into Paddy's cell as a large hole appeared.

Within ten minutes there was an opening about three foot square. It was big enough for us to climb through. We shouted out to the other fellas that one more wall had fallen. As they cheered we could imagine the effect on the screws.

We guessed that the day staff had been called back on duty. That in itself was a small victory. They wouldn't be pleased to be kept away from their families. It was another blow in our general campaign to remain a problem that wouldn't go away.

We also knew that, with the sort of incident into which this one was developing, the local police would have to be informed. Armed units would surround the jail in case there was an escape attempt. Footer would have a lot of explaining to do in the morning.

Joe and I scrambled through into Paddy's cell and the penultimate wall. Paddy had already cleared a space for Joe to stand in, and his bedboard was propped against the wall that adjoined Blackie's cell. He was highly excited. It looked like he was having more fun than he'd had in a long while.

Once again, I wondered if he really understood what he was getting himself into. Did he realise that what awaited us the other side of the office wall wasn't exactly a welcoming party? The night would end with blood and broken bones, most of them ours.

As we brushed aside Paddy's effusive welcome, we heard someone calling Joe's name. It was coming from outside the window, from the direction of Blackie's cell. Joe walked over to the window. I followed close behind.

It was definitely Blackie's voice, but it was low and indistinct.

Joe could hear it because he was right up against the window, but I could only make out occasional words. I couldn't figure out why Blackie was whispering. Perhaps he had seen something outside his window and was warning us.

Joe turned back from the window, his face grim. He didn't say anything for several seconds. Whatever it was, it had obviously troubled him. I waited with a growing sense of impending disaster.

'Blackie doesn't want to take part,' he announced suddenly.

'What?' I said incredulously.

'Blackie says that he's thought about it, and he'd rather not take part,' Joe repeated matter-of-factly.

'Well, fuck him,' I said angrily, 'he should have thought of that before we started. We need to go through his cell to get to Jeff, and Jeff's all for it. Fuck him. Just smash through his wall, and if he doesn't want to get involved let him make his way down to your cell and sit there until it's all over.'

Joe looked pained. We had expended a lot of time and effort to get to our present point. We were committed now. But Joe was a man of great principle, especially where one of our own was concerned. Blackie had been involved in plenty of things in the past.

'No, Norm,' he said coming to a decision, 'he's entitled to make up his own mind. We'd be out of order to involve him against his will. This is a serious coup. People will get hurt, and there could be further charges. You and I have got nothing to lose. I'm not going to drag someone into something against their will and get them extra bird.'

As angry as I was, I recognised that he had a valid argument. We thought of ourselves as honourable men, especially with regard to each other. It was the screws who were disloyal and unprincipled. If we acted likewise it would undermine our belief in ourselves.

'OK, Joe, I take your point. But all that's really happened is that his arsehole's gone,' I added vindictively.

'Even so, he's entitled to make his choice,' replied Joe patiently.

'Well, what about Jeff? Who's gonna tell him, you or me?'

'Blackie's already told him,' said Joe quietly.

We stood in silence for a minute or so. As the adrenalin rush slowed in our blood so a sense of anticlimax descended upon us. Surprisingly, the normally effervescent Paddy was silent too. As daft as he could be, he realised that he had better keep his peace.

The silence hung in the air like an awkward thing. Joe and I were too close to fall out over something like this. And, anyway, we were still in a serious situation together. Unless we were going to give up and come out peacefully, at some stage the screws would have to steam in. So there could still be a battle.

'What're we going to do then, Joe?' I asked, breaking the silence.

'Let's go back to my cell and talk about it,' he replied. 'And bring your cups.'

He climbed through the hole back into my cell with me close behind. With a puzzled look on his face, Paddy picked up his plastic cup and followed. He must have thought us Englishmen very odd. So violent one minute, yet so calm and civilised the next.

The dust had completely settled in Joe's cell. Paddy and I sat down on some bedding against the unblemished end wall. Joe rummaged inside the cloth in the corner. Turning, he presented Paddy and me with a sandwich each. We had made some earlier, knowing we would need food through the night.

He took our cups and poured orange juice from a plastic bottle. He topped them up from a large white water jug. He stirred each with a spoon, then handed them to us.

This ritual was carried out in complete silence. It was strangely calming, as if it had brought order to the chaos. What could be more civilised than to sit down and eat together, in spite of the bizarre surroundings?

Paddy still hadn't said a word. Once again I couldn't help but think that he felt us English to be very strange. I could imagine him telling his mates back home about it: 'Seriously, boys, I fully expected them to get out some serviettes for us to tuck under our chins!'

For the first time now, I was able to take a good look at Paddy and weigh him up. He was every bit as young as I first thought and typically Irish, with the gaunt face and high cheekbones. His jet-black hair was unfashionably short, his sideboards up around his ears. A thin chest, narrow shoulders and long arms made him seem gangling and awkward. Yet he was only of medium height. His accent was pure 'back of the throat' Northern Irish. His blue eyes sparkled with devilment, and he had a restless energy about him.

I had to give him his due. He was a young fella in a strange country, surrounded by people he didn't know. As an outsider, he must have felt that we owed him no loyalty. Yet he was willing to make a stand with us. I resolved to try to protect him from the worst of what was to come.

Joe sat down with his own sandwich and orange juice. 'Well,' he said, 'we've got a couple of options. We've already done some serious damage. This ranks as a major incident. We could say that we have made our point and come out in the morning.' He paused to chew on a mouthful of sandwich.

'Another option', he continued, 'is that, as we've got this far and are all together, perhaps we should make the most of it. We've got the iron bars. We could tell Footer that we're going to stay in here until he gives us his word that he'll do something about the screws who are giving out the kickings. If he refuses, let them come in, and we'll have a tear-up with 'em.'

Joe carried on eating; he had said his bit.

'Well, I'm in favour of the second one,' I said immediately. 'We've come this far, we might as well finish it. We expected it to end in a tear-up anyway.'

'What about you, Paddy?' asked Joe, looking towards him.

Paddy sat there, mouth full of sandwich, cup halfway to his lips. Clearly, he hadn't expected to be consulted.

But this was a different matter entirely to that of Blackie's involvement. Paddy was in this as much as we were. He would be punished the same as we would, and if it came to a tear-up he would get beaten up too. His opinion now carried equal weight to either of ours.

He might not have been participating in the debate, but he had been following closely. 'Let them fucking come in,' he said without any hesitation.

'Nice one, Paddy,' said Joe smiling. 'We'd better get some sleep and build up our strength. It could be a hard day tomorrow.'

I called out the window, then through the vent in the top of the door, to let the others know what we had decided. A couple said that they would stay wedged up, too, until Footer made a decision to end our confinement under Rule 43. It all added to the pressure on him.

Paddy and I fetched some blankets from our cells and made up a bed each. It would be crowded with the three of us sleeping on the floor, but we had to stay together in case the screws suddenly forced their way in during the night.

My cell was designated the khazi. We put our three piss-pots in there, together with our water jugs and washing bowls. I could hardly complain. Any further mess would be academic.

We said our goodnights and settled down to sleep. We must have been exhausted, both physically and mentally. None of us remembered falling asleep.

I came awake early the following morning, wondering where I was. I woke with a start, the legacy of the fear from the previous night. It hadn't been a relaxed sleep. The shade of Morpheus had provided only a temporary respite. I lay there contemplating the challenges of the coming day.

I was cold and stiff. As I stretched my aching limbs I saw Paddy turn restlessly and come awake too. Perhaps my moving had startled him. All of us were living on the edge. Our nerves were stretched to the limit. Even the tiniest things registered subliminally and rang warning bells.

I got up and stepped into my cell to have a piss. In the cold light of dawn the devastation seemed to stand out more starkly than it had in the half-light of the evening before. If I had needed reminding, it brought back to me the extent of the damage we had done. To my good knowledge no one had ever smashed through the walls in a chokey before. If we surrendered now, it would be many a long day before Footer let me back up on the wings.

I returned to Joe's cell with a pack of sandwiches I had put aside. The outer wrapping of newspaper was thick with dust, but it hadn't found its way inside. Joe was awake now. I gave him and Paddy a sandwich each. We sat there eating, not saying a word.

We could hear the sounds of others waking in the chokey: the splash of water as someone washed in their bowl; a hawking sound as someone else spat out of a window. All the intimate sounds of men going about their ablutions. In prison, you soon learned to live without privacy.

We took it in turns to go next door and wash. We greeted each other cheerily as if to live under such conditions was admirably acceptable. Paddy even whistled and burst into snatches of song. But it was all contrived.

The cold presence of fear lurked in my stomach. Ignore it as I might, it was still there. I would never desert Joe and Paddy, but I dreamed of being a thousand miles away. Everything in my life was pressure and pain now; there wasn't one second's respite. But, although I felt fear, I wasn't afraid of what was to come. I welcomed it as some deadly consummation, but let it just be over.

We heard the screws come on duty for their daytime shift. They immediately checked each cell for the morning count. I heard the screw go to Paddy's cell, then mine, before pausing to stare through the spy-hole at the three of us in Joe's cell.

Twenty minutes later, we heard the breakfast trolley come

around. The smell of the hot food reminded us of our hunger, in spite of the sandwich we had eaten earlier.

The screw knocked on the door and shouted through, asking whether we wanted breakfast, an obvious ploy to get us to open the door. It would take a bit more than a poxy meal to get us to come out. Three voices cried 'Fuck off' in unison.

Later, Punchy came to the door to tell us that Footer would be down to see us very shortly.

'Well, we ain't coming out. So unless he wants to talk through the door he'd better come to the window,' I shouted back. I regretted being so abrupt with him, because he had been a decent fella in the past, and I knew that the present situation bothered him. But the battle lines were clearly drawn now.

'Oi, Norman. What's happening?' Nuff-Nuff's deafening roar made us all jump. Apart from all the other problems, his volume control badly needed adjusting. He was only across the corridor, a couple of cells along.

His shout started others off. I heard Roy, a robber doing 12 years, shouting from the far end, then Ernie and Stan joined in from the other side. Smaller voices could be heard on the periphery. One of our strengths in the chokey was that we communicated well with each other. At the first sign of trouble, we were all up at our windows or doors finding out what was going on.

I shouted across to Nuff-Nuff that Footer was coming down to talk, knowing that my voice would carry to most, who would pass it on to the rest. 'I'll let you know what happens,' I concluded.

Shortly afterwards, I heard the gate into the exercise yard open. It was too early for exercise. I jumped up and looked out the window. Sure enough, Footer and the chief were coming out.

'Hey, Joe, here's Footer,' I called over my shoulder.

'Yeah, well, let's not seem too keen to see him,' he replied.

I stepped back from the window to stand beside him. 'I could always slip up to Paddy's cell and clump him with one of the bars as he comes past,' I said smiling.

'If things don't go right, maybe you can catch him on the way back,' answered Joe.

Suddenly, the short, fat form of Footer filled the window. One hand rested on his walking stick, in the other he held a large white handkerchief with which he mopped his large florid face. He was perspiring heavily. Whether it was the early-morning exertion or the tenseness of the situation, I couldn't tell. And, in truth, I didn't care. He deserved all he got. He knew that his screws were beating people up on the wings. He could stop it if he really wanted to.

'What's this all about?' he asked, looking directly at me.

'Well, guv,' began Joe, but that was as far as he got.

'I'm not speaking to you, I'm speaking to Parker,' Footer interrupted sharply.

I was astounded. I didn't think he had it in him. He knew of Joe's fearsome reputation, yet it had been a deliberate snub. Perhaps the sight of his smashed chokey cells had finally galvanised him. He continued to look at me.

'Well, guv,' I said, deliberately using the same opening words so that he would know that we both spoke with one voice, and it didn't really matter which one of us he spoke to. 'We've made this protest because your screws continue to beat people up up on the wings. It's also about being kept down here on 43.'

He screwed up his face and continued to look at me. Coming to a decision, he said, 'Parker, I won't discuss anything under these circumstances. I want you, or any other representative, to come out and discuss this in a civilised fashion in my office.'

'But what about your screws outside the door?' I countered immediately.

'They won't lay a hand on you, I give you my word.'

'And what about coming back in here afterwards?' I pressed.

'You will be allowed back in,' he assured.

'OK, guv, we'll talk about it and let you know,' I said, trying not to sound too dismissive. It must already have been quite humiliating for him to have to come to us. Governor's call-ups usually worked the other way around. And it was all happening in front of the chief and the assembled screws. Although we were in the driving seat now, it wouldn't always be so. I didn't want to antagonise him so much that his desire for revenge outweighed his better judgement.

Footer and the chief walked back up the alley bounded by the breeze-block wall. I turned to Joe and Paddy. 'Well, what do you think?' I asked.

'Once you're outside that door there's no guarantee that he'll keep his word,' said Joe gravely.

'I know that, Joe, but if they do jump on me they'll know that the rest of you won't come out without a fight,' I reasoned.

Joe didn't look convinced. His experience was that logic and rationality rarely found a place in official thinking. Paddy didn't look convinced either; Irish or not, he knew he was safe in here. Outside the door there were dozens of screws with big black boots, who would love to jump all over his head. His look said that only a daft Englishman could even be thinking about it.

'I'll ask the others,' I said.

I pulled a chair up close to the door and stood on it so that my mouth was level with the ventilation holes. 'Fellas,' I shouted, 'Footer wants someone to come out and talk to him about it in his office.' There was a deathly silence.

'And who's going to do that?' asked a voice that sounded like Roy's from down the landing. It was an obvious question.

'I'll go out. But, listen, fellas. If they take any fucking liberties with me, don't come out. Make them break their way in and smash the fuckers with everything you can lay your hands on,' I shouted back defiantly. I knew the screws were outside in the corridor and could hear every word.

There was no argument or alternative suggestions. 'OK, you screws, move away from the door, and I'll come out,' I shouted again. 'Danny, let me know if they're clear.' I put my eye to the vent holes and could see that there were none opposite. Danny would do the same.

'You're OK, Norm,' came Danny's shout.

I jumped down from the chair and turned to Joe. 'Take care, mate,' I said as we shook hands.

'You take care,' he replied passionately, as he grasped my hand in both of his.

'Take care, Paddy,' I said as I turned to shake hands with him too.

He shook my hand vigorously but said nothing. I could see dampness in the corner of his eyes and emotion working his face. We had known each other only a short while, but there was a strong bond. We would sacrifice ourselves for each other, and there was something noble in that. I knew that, if asked, both he and Joe would willingly walk in my place.

I didn't have a lot of time to think about it, but I mused that ordinary men in the free world would rarely experience comradeship such as this. Their lives were filled with all the mundane treacheries that working men lapse into just to get by. Conformity could become, by insidious degrees, dishonourable. I would embrace my rebelliousness even if I got my head kicked in during the process.

We levered the wedges from the door jamb with the handles of our plastic knives. 'OK,' I shouted through the crack, 'someone unlock the door.'

I heard the sound of footsteps, then a key turned in the lock. The footsteps receded. With Joe and Paddy standing guard with a steel bar each, I pulled the door slightly open and peered through the crack. I could see Danny's door and the blank wall at the end of the corridor. There were no screws.

I pulled the door wider and quickly stepped outside. I heard it shut behind me and the wedges being hammered in again. I turned to look up the corridor. It was black with screws. From two doors up, screws lined either side right the way up to the office.

In the open area before the office, there were dozens more. Each stood stiffly to attention, eyes staring fixedly to the front.

Light glistened from shiny black peaks. Serried lines of shiny black toecaps winked from the floor. Grim, pasty white faces stared starkly from a background that was unrelievedly black.

Suddenly I felt exhilarated. The fear was driven from me in a rush of adrenalin. The sheer overkill of the intimidation had the opposite effect. There would be no shame in being overwhelmed by this multitude. If all this was for my benefit, it was quite a tribute.

I walked between the sombre honour guard, an arrogant, confident mouse overshadowed by the lines of threatening cats. The whole chokey had gone deathly silent. I could imagine all the fellas listening apprehensively at their doors.

Not one screw said a word. No one made the slightest hostile gesture. Yet as I passed I felt their hatred as a physical thing. They would have loved to leap on me and batter me senseless. But they were under orders.

Coolly, calmly, looking straight ahead, I walked towards the open office door. There was no swagger. I wasn't going to take advantage of the situation. I didn't only represent myself; the fate of others depended on the outcome.

Inside the office, Footer sat behind the desk, the chief at his shoulder. I walked to stand on the plastic mat just before them. I heard someone close the door behind me.

'Well, what's the matter, Parker?' Footer asked, without any preliminaries.

'You know what's the matter, guvnor,' I replied. 'Your screws up on the wings keep beating people up. Then they charge them with assault to cover themselves.'

'Which ones?' Footer asked.

I reeled off the names of the six worst culprits. 'It will only stop when you move them out. And that's what me and the fellas want,' I said.

'Give me a couple of days to look into it, but in the meantime you'll have to stop this protest.'

That was as much as I was going to get from him. 'OK, guvnor, I'll go back and tell the fellas.' I turned and headed for the door.

There were two screws standing just inside. One opened it, and I walked out. All the other screws were standing just as I had left them.

I walked back down the landing. As I neared Joe's cell, a single screw stepped over and put his key in the lock.

'It's OK, Joe, open the door,' I shouted out.

There was the sound of wedges being removed again; the screw turned the key and walked away. The door opened, and I stepped inside.

I didn't exactly say, 'Thank fuck for that,' but I certainly felt that way. However, it was all pressure. The situation we were still in had yet to be resolved.

Joe and Paddy welcomed me back. I told them what Footer had said. He hadn't rejected our demands out of hand. He had asked for names and time to consider the situation, so it was an inquiry of sorts. And what else was there to do? Our plan to smash through the walls until we got into the office couldn't proceed now. We had no food and dire conditions. A hunger strike would be hard enough without being wedged up three-handed in a wrecked cell.

And, if the screws left it for a few days then forced their way in, we'd probably be too weak to do much about it. The logical course of action was to come out and await the outcome of Footer's investigations. We could always go on to Plan Y if he reneged.

But it wasn't always down to logic. Pride and, above all, morale were important too. Every day of resistance was a personal sacrifice. It was easier to cower in your cell and retreat, but that way lay the death of the spirit. And spirit was everything.

It would have to be talked over anyway. We weren't the only ones wedged up. It would be a group decision. Perfect democracy, even though some would be swayed by others.

I pulled a chair close to the door again. I climbed up and put my mouth to the ventholes. 'Fellas,' I bellowed, 'this is what Footer said. He asked me for names. I told him the six worst, and I said they had to be moved. He said he would look into it. In the meantime, he wants us to come out. What do you think?'

'What do you think?' shouted Roy. 'You're the ones in the worst trouble. They'll come in on you first.'

I turned to Joe and Paddy. 'I'll carry on, if anyone wants to carry on,' said Joe peremptorily. 'But it wasn't much use you putting yourself on offer if we aren't going to give him a chance to do something. If he fucks us about, we can still go on and do the hunger strike.'

That was exactly my sentiments. I looked at Paddy, and he nodded in agreement. In some ways the abrupt halt at Blackie's wall had left a sour taste. We had psyched ourselves up for a big showdown. Anything else would be an anticlimax. We wouldn't be sorry to be out of this situation.

Anyway, it was hardly defeat. We had smashed through two of their special German brick walls, a victory not short on symbolism. We had kept the screws out of their beds all night. Old Bill surrounding the nick had turned it into a major incident. And Footer's small and overstressed heart had had another couple of worry lines added to it. Any honourable settlement deserved consideration.

'Us three think we've made our point for now,' I shouted to Roy. 'And if Footer double-crosses us we'll go right ahead with Plan Y.' I thought that just about summed it up.

'That's all right by me,' shouted Roy immediately.

'And me,' grunted Nuff-Nuff. Other voices joined in in agreement.

'I'll ask Ernie, Stan and the others on the other side,' I shouted as I stepped down.

The other side agreed. Most of them had heard me anyway. I climbed back on the chair. 'Looks like we're coming out,' I yelled.

There was the sound of banging as fellas knocked their wedges out. Then it was just a matter of sitting there until the screws got around to unlocking you. I guessed they'd do us first. They would want to get the worst of the situation over with.

Sure enough, Joe's door opened, and there was Punchy. 'I hope we're going back in these cells after they've been repaired,' I said before he could start.

Punchy looked anguished. He had come this far peacefully. I suppose he figured that once the bedboards were screwed to the wall again, and we'd lost our steel bars, there would be no danger of it happening again. It wasn't much to concede. He agreed.

Our protest must have unnerved Footer, because none of us was nicked for damaging the walls. The reasoning must have been that, if we performed like this in the relatively better conditions of Rule 43, what would we do on punishment? It was an admission of weakness and the first sign of concessions.

Unfortunately, it was also the last. The fat weakling had known all about the gang of screw bullies. They represented extreme opinion among the screws, but to discipline them would bring a screws' revolt. We were the weaker party, or so he thought. He did nothing.

A couple of days went by. We had never known the Works Department to move so fast. Usually, they were a byword for ineptitude and delay. On the third day, Joe, Paddy and I were shown back into our original cells.

We might have known that the Works hadn't performed any architectural feats. We expected bare, new brickwork and wet cement. What we didn't expect was a massive rusty steel plate bolted either side of each hole.

It was straight out of *The Works Book of Bodges*. It was both ugly and impractical. The latter because we could now hear every sound in the next cell. Paddy, Joe and I would be having some rather public bowel movements from now on.

It was also dangerous. The one massive bolt stuck three

inches clear of the plate. All the better to brain yourself if you stood up quickly.

We didn't intend to stay though. Three days had passed now, and there had been no changes. Word from up the wings was that the screw bullies were still about. Footer had double-crossed us.

That evening, as we shouted across to each other, it was agreed that we should move on to the next stage. Plan Y was imminent. It wasn't an easy commitment for anyone. Hunger strikes were exquisitely painful. They were a severe risk to your health. How far would each man go?

Once you started, you were committed. To stop would be to admit failure. Different people had different strengths. If fellas dropped out one by one, it could damage morale. And we had already failed with Plan X.

For Joe and me, it was especially significant. On the other side of Plan Y, the spectre of Plan Z loomed. We had already committed ourselves. We had meant it when we said it, knowing and accepting the implications. The chaps were nothing if not men of their word. We would have to follow through.

But we had a couple of days' grace yet. It was no use our going on a hunger strike unless it got some publicity. And the Home Office would play it down for all they were worth. They would give out a totally spurious reason for our protest and underestimate the numbers involved by a fifth.

Stan was expecting a visit in three days' time. I was going to write a letter to a newspaper, setting out our grievances and the names of the people involved in the hunger strike. Stan would smuggle it on to the visit and slip it to his visitor. The visitor would hand it in to the London offices of a national newspaper. Then the Home Office would be under pressure from within and without.

In the meantime, we had three days to play with. We weren't exactly in a festive mood, but perhaps the thought of the pain and discomfort that was to come made us thankful for this brief period of respite.

That night all of us whose cells faced on to the yard were at our windows. It was warmish, with hardly a breath of air. In the velvety black sky above, myriad stars twinkled in perfect focus. The bright moonlight lit the yard with an unearthly glow. It was an idyllic, almost enchanted setting. As a Hollywood film set it would have smacked of cliché.

We played Twenty Questions and other guessing games, shouting backwards and forwards across the yard. Paddy joined in enthusiastically. He had fully found his feet now. His recent involvement in the 'wall' protest had increased his standing among the fellas. As far as anyone was concerned, he was one of us now.

In some ways this was a double-edged weapon. Paddy was a natural extrovert. He was a talented singer, mimic and teller of jokes. His effervescent personality coupled with his boundless enthusiasm rapidly turned the proceedings into 'Paddy's Chokey Show'.

He was funny, though, and diverted our attention from darker thoughts. If he was a bit over the top, then we could tolerate that. Different people handled chokey in different ways. The important thing was that, should there be any trouble, Paddy had already proved he would stand with us. Virtually everything else was insignificant.

A couple of hours passed. Interest in the guessing games waned. There were extended lulls in the conversation. Sometimes we would go for ten minutes, just standing there in the silence, soaking up tranquillity.

Suddenly, Paddy started to sing. His high, sweet voice arose out of nowhere. It carried clearly right across the yard. He was singing 'Kevin Barry', that Republican anthem so rich in pathos. It was early days for the IRA in England; they were still a comparatively minor irritant. All politics apart, we were enchanted by the beauty of the performance.

I had the strange feeling that I was sharing a memorable experience. Among all the pain of solitary confinement, in a bleak and unhappy place such as the chokey, it was a magic moment. It struck a chord in me that would resonate down the years. An exquisitely beautiful experience made all the more so by the squalor of the surroundings. The only tragedy was that it would soon pass, leaving no trace for posterity.

Paddy finished the song. No one spoke. It seemed a sacrilege to break the silence, as if it would somehow break the spell. Taking his cue, Paddy launched into another one. This time it was a rousing rebel song.

It was great entertainment. Paddy was as good as any professional I'd ever heard. With no amplification or musical backing, he held us spellbound. When he was done, we all said our goodnights quietly and went to bed. It was a fitting end to an evening. Anything else would have been a gross anticlimax.

Over the next couple of days, I was exposed to Paddy's complete repertoire. On Blackie's side there was a brick wall: between Paddy and me a pair of massive metal plates, which acted like sounding-boards. I was the more accessible audience.

No TV watcher myself, I was soon familiar with all the jingles. According to the others, Paddy's mimicry was masterful. He had them spot on. I couldn't have told the difference.

There was one particular jingle that soon burned in my brain like a raw nerve. It was a biscuit advert that, on TV, must have been preceded by drums and the deep, deep voice of a Red Indian.

I would be lying on my bed, dozing lightly, a common enough state in the chokey. My face barely inches from the metal plate. Suddenly there would be a deep roll of Indian war-drums as Paddy beat on the plate with his knuckles.

In the background could be heard the chant of the Braves, 'Umba, daba, umba daba, umba daba, umba daba.' Finally, Sitting Bull himself would cut in. In a deeply resonant and sepulchral tone he would intone, 'Who put the figs in the Fig Rolls?'

Now it was all very funny stuff – the first time. It was brilliant mimicry, but it frightened me. (When your nerves were stretched as tight as mine, you didn't need to be awakened by the disembodied voice of Sitting Bull.) After about a dozen times, though, it began to pall on me. Soon, I could cheerfully have strangled him.

On another occasion, I was sitting reading when a very cultured, upper-class English voice rang out next door. It was answered by the typically sing-song voice of the Indian subcontinent. The throaty tones of a Northern Irish voice joined in, closely followed by the higher-pitched Dublin accent.

Suddenly, the broken diction of pure Cockney cut across the babble: 'Cor, fuck me. All these poxy foreigners in 'ere. All we need now is a fuckin'Yank.' Immediately, the deep, rolling tones of the Marlboro advert answered, 'Say, did somebody call my name?'

It was hilarious. It actually sounded like there were several different nationalities in the cell next door. I had a professional entertainer for a neighbour.

Unfortunately, I wasn't always in the mood. Often, he would bring me back from some deep reverie where I was lost to the world. Once again, the harsh realities of the chokey would flood in. My only consolation was that the pain and discomfort of the impending hunger strike would slow him down a bit. Even Paddy would find it difficult to sing and joke when he was starving to death.

Stan duly had his visit, and the letter was smuggled out. The following morning, ten of us refused breakfast. The screw looked at me quizzically when I told him I was on hunger strike. 'I've still got to put your meal in,' he said. I knew that was part of the rules. I stepped back, and he put the metal tray on the floor. Plan Y was under way.

Even though it was the first meal I would miss, I realised I would soon feel the effects. I was so used to being fed at specific times, day in, day out, that if a meal were to be delayed by only half an hour my stomach would quickly feel hunger pains.

I started as I intended to carry on. I picked up the tray and pissed on the porridge and bread and jam. However long the tray stood in the corner now, I wouldn't be tempted to eat from it.

By mid-morning, the hunger was a gnawing pain in my stomach. I went on exercise with Joe and Danny as usual but felt cold. Without food for fuel, the body couldn't keep warm. We walked and talked of anything except food and the nascent hunger pains. I was pleased to come in, but even back in the cell I couldn't get warm.

Dinnertime arrived, but instead of being a welcome break in the monotony it was a time of trial. Never had the bland prison food looked so appetising. The screw took the piss-soaked breakfast tray out, wrinkling his nose as he did so. The pungent urine smell wafted across to me. I could do without living with that in my nostrils all the time. I resolved not to foul the meals again. Will power would have to be enough.

Received wisdom had it that if you drank plenty of water it allayed the worst of the hunger pangs. I drank it by the pint, but in my chilled condition all it served to do was to make me piss constantly.

Teatime came and went. The meal sat in the corner to tempt me through the night. As I lay on my bed trying to read, the insidious food smells titillated my nostrils. I told myself that, if I had just the tiniest taste, that brief satisfaction would be enough. But I knew that it would only make it worse.

That evening we talked out of our windows as usual, but our hearts weren't in it. It was cold standing there in the night air and the hunger pangs were so fierce that I felt sick.

To add to my discomfort, a mild headache started. It registered almost subliminally, only occasionally forcing its way into consciousness. But I was aware that it was there.

Hunger kept me from sleep. I couldn't keep my mind from the

pangs. My body seemed to ache in several different places simultaneously. Only by screwing myself tightly into a foetal position beneath the covers could I temporarily escape it. Eventually, in the early hours of the morning, sleep born of exhaustion overtook me.

I woke the following day and was immediately aware of the low-level ache that suffused my whole being. If I had thought that the pangs would be restricted to my stomach then I was sorely mistaken. There was an aching, yawning chasm in my gut; but that vied for attention along with my headache and a bone-deep chill.

I felt listless as I walked on exercise. I realised that, within days, strenuous physical activity would be out. It wouldn't be too long before even walking was beyond me.

Contact between us had dropped to a minimum now. No one seemed to have the enthusiasm to start a conversation. Thankfully, Sammy Davis Jnr next door was also suffering. There were no songs, no impersonations and no Red Indians selling Fig Rolls.

As the third day dawned on our misery, I found that the hunger pains had abated somewhat. Someone had once told me that the first three days were the worst, after that the pangs died away. Well, they certainly hadn't died away yet, but they had become more of a dull ache throughout my body.

As time passed, Punchy had been looking increasingly strained. His face was white and drawn as he supervised the delivery of the meals. He had been on duty every day since the latest trouble began. Perhaps he was refusing leave until the problem was resolved.

Late on the afternoon of the third day, my door opened suddenly, and Punchy hurried in. 'Look, Parker,' he said, 'I've seen the governor and told him that, if he doesn't do something shortly, I and my staff will refuse to man the block. I told him that, so far, your protests have been passive and not aimed at us. But that soon you would have no alternative but to turn on us. He has told me that if you stop your hunger strike you will all be moved. Either you or Joe will go tomorrow; the other one two days later and the rest of you after a week. Just as soon as arrangements can be made. He's given me his word on this, and I give you my word on it too.'

From the look on his face, you would have thought that it was Punchy who was under all the pressure. But he was a caring man and couldn't conceal a grudging respect for us. Also, he wasn't a bad judge of men. He knew that we were determined not to give in. He realised that we were running out of options. Our protests were becoming increasingly desperate.

It sounded like an attractive solution and about the best we were going to get. Especially for Joe and me. But we were in this with the rest. Joe and I might be moved, then no one else. They would think that they had got rid of the ringleaders and that the protests would end. The rest might be left there for months. 'I'll have to talk to the others, guv,' I said. 'We've discussed everything else between us.'

'That's OK,' said Punchy. 'I'm going around to everyone personally so you all know exactly what's happening.'

He went out. Seconds later I heard him open Joe's door. I waited for him to finish and come out again. I called Joe to his window. 'Well, what do you think?' I asked.

'If they keep their word it's a victory of sorts,' Joe replied.

I called through the doorvents to Roy, Nuff-Nuff, Danny and the others opposite. They were all of the same opinion as Joe.

'I ain't worried about changing the jail,' I shouted. 'I'm not fighting for all those fuckers up on the wings who haven't got the arsehole to stand up for themselves. I'm only concerned about us. We're the ones in the chokey.'

The fellas shouted their agreement and said that they were willing to take the chance that they would be moved.

Joe and I then called over to Ernie, Stan and Jim and the rest on the other side of the yard. They were unanimously for the plan. I rang my bell, and Punchy came and opened my door.

'So, we've all agreed to stop the hunger strike. But, if Footer double-crosses us again and goes back on his word, then the fellas that remain here won't stop tearing up,' I finished defiantly. I regretted it as I said it. The threat brought an almost imperceptible hurt look to Punchy's face. He was a proud man who had gone out of his way to behave decently. 'By the way, guv, the fellas appreciate what you've done for us,' I added quickly.

Punchy acknowledged the concession and implied apology. 'OK, Parker,' he said, 'I wish it hadn't come to all this.' He turned and left.

That night we were all up at our windows. There was almost a holiday mood, brought on by thoughts of our imminent departures. On my part the euphoria was genuine, because, as one of the first two to go, I was confident that I would get out. Apart from Joe, the others must have had their doubts. But they were putting on a brave face about it.

Paddy was in fine form. He sang all his most rousing rebel songs, told dozens of jokes and did impersonation after impersonation. My spirits rose even further at the thought that, very shortly, I would never have to listen to the Fig Roll Indian again. It was all forgiven now though.

Joe and I talked late into the night. In one way it was a sad time for us, because it was a parting of close friends. For years we had kept in touch through messages carried by mutual friends. And, finally, when we had got together in the same jail, it had to be Albany in the middle of a riot.

Joe and I inhabited a strange world. We were men who carried all our emotional baggage with us. The outside world was a far and distant place. Seeing our families once a month for a two-hour visit only served to increase our sense of isolation and loneliness. Our souls were sustained by just a few strong bonds of friendship.

But we were warriors in a harsh gladiatorial school. The most crucial requirement was strength, in all its forms. Strength to survive the physical rigours of solitary confinement, beatings and bread and water. Strength to survive the emotional vacuum in which we existed. We were spiritual sailors, for ever condemned to sail the seas with no port to call home. In the final analysis we were lonely, lonely men. For Joe and I, there would be sadness in our parting.

I woke early and lay there in the darkness. Instead of the usual pain and despair, there was hope in my heart. I savoured the thought that even if I didn't go today then Joe would. But I had a strange feeling that it would be me.

I heard the screws come on duty. I felt my heart quicken. The breakfast trolley came around. Just before my door closed Punchy told me that I would be moving right after breakfast.

Suddenly my problems were over. Wherever I was going, I wouldn't be on subversive 43. I was embarking on a whole new adventure. The only news that could have cheered me more was that I was to be released.

I went to my window and called for Joe. I told him I was going, and he was genuinely pleased for me. 'Take care, Norm. I don't think I'll be far behind you,' he said. 'I'll drop you a card when I get settled.' It was an emotional moment. There was nothing else to say.

My door opened, and there stood two screws I hadn't seen at Albany before, I guessed they were part of the escort from another jail. I picked up my few belongings and walked out after them.

I went to Joe's door. I banged twice with my fist. 'I'm off, Joe,' I shouted. I turned away quickly as he called his muffled reply. 'Danny, John, Roy, Jeff,' I shouted as I passed along the corridor. 'You all take care. And, don't forget, NO FUCKING SURRENDER.'

Several voices called out in reply.

As I reached the gate leading to the yard, I called to Ernie, Stan and Jim down the other corridor. With their farewells ringing in my ears, I walked out into the yard, the two screws beside me.

The open sky and fresh air were invigorating. I breathed deeply, and my heart filled with hope for the future. I walked away from a part of my life that I would never see again. By comparison, the future looked rosy.

Two days later, as promised, Joe was moved to Wandsworth. A week later, Roy followed him. Over the next month several others went too. However, that was the lot. Footer double-crossed us in the end. The half-dozen that remained were kept in the chokey for over a year before they were moved. One of them, Jim, was to be shot dead by armed police several years later, rather than come back to prison.

28 OF ESCAPES, PRINCIPLES AND PRISON POLITICS

Of all the Albany rioters, I had come out of the situation the best. Whereas others had gone to tightly run local prisons or long-term jails that were experiencing their own problems, I went to the Scrubs.

In many ways Wormwood Scrubs was a strange jail. Firstly, it served a multitude of penological uses. 'A' wing alone housed three distinct categories of prisoner. There were those who had come from all over the country to await operations in the prison hospital. Then there were those awaiting allocation to other prisons. Finally, in an area partitioned off from the rest of the wing, there was the Segregation Unit. This contained men doing punishment for infractions of prison rules.

'B' wing was the boys' wing. Here, prisoners under 21 awaited transfer to various Young Offender institutions. The wing was notoriously volatile. Apart from all the mischief that 300 teenage boys could cause during the day when they were unlocked, the nights were literally bedlam. Many stood at their windows until daybreak, singing, calling out messages and shouting abuse at each other.

'C' wing, also notoriously volatile, housed both remands and those awaiting allocation. With men kept three to a cell, there could often be upwards of 500 prisoners on the wing. The remands would be ferried backwards and forwards to court on a daily basis. Those awaiting allocation ranged from men doing nine months to those doing life. The short-termers would go to jails all over the country; the lucky among the long-termers would get a place in 'D' wing, after spending several months on a waiting list.

'D' wing was the long-term wing. It housed over 300 men doing from five years to life. The prisoners were, in the main, carefully screened and selected. Many were 'stars', who had never been in prison before. The rest were mostly well-behaved, model prisoners. There was rarely any trouble. Apart from the fact that the cons were carefully selected, there were many benefits from being on 'D' wing.

Firstly, the wing was very relaxed and easygoing. You were unlocked from 7.30 a.m. until 9.00 p.m. and enjoyed a range of facilities and privileges that were the envy of many long-term jails. Perhaps the greatest benefit, though, was that the Scrubs was in the heart of London. This meant that Londoners could get their visits easily and generally keep in touch. Lastly, the parole rate was quite good on 'D' wing.

I had noticed on my travels through the system that the authorities allowed these pockets of relatively civilised conditions to exist. It wasn't done for humanitarian reasons, but rather to encourage and control. At the first sign of trouble on 'D' wing, the perpetrator would be immediately shanghaied. He might spend a short time in the Segregation Unit beforehand, but, ultimately, he would be transferred to another, much worse, jail.

In the light of all this, it might seem strange that the authorities had seen fit to send me to the Scrubs from the riot-torn Albany. Perhaps they didn't intend for me to go to 'D' wing. Most likely, the right hand didn't know what the left one was doing, as usual. However, there was an unofficial policy whereby a particularly troublesome prisoner was put in among a well-behaved prisoner population. The logic was threefold. The troublemaker would discover it difficult to find other like-minded cons; he just might learn to enjoy the good facilities and fear to lose them; and, lastly, some of the good behaviour of the vast majority might just rub off on him. Ergo, my transfer.

I duly arrived in Scrubs reception, still on the 'A' list; in patches from my Albany escape attempt; half-starved from the hunger strike and with a disciplinary record that could hardly have been worse.

There was an immediate problem. 'C' wing's governor refused to have me on his already volatile wing. This left only two options: the Seg or 'D' wing. Now, comparatively speaking, the Scrubs' Segregation Unit was a decidedly lightweight operation. It served a convict population that was relatively well behaved, with particularly troublesome prisoners being transferred out. The chokey screws didn't have to regularly restrain and control men over periods of time. There was little brutality.

It didn't make much sense to put me in there. If I had proved too much for Albany's extremely robust chokey, I wouldn't last five minutes in Scrubs Seg. So it was to be 'D' wing.

There was another immediate problem. Although 'D' wing housed men on the 'A' list, it didn't accept those in patches. So, in the continuing spirit of conciliation and accommodation, I was taken out of patches and moved over to 'D' wing.

Now, even on the well-behaved 'D' wing, there was a small group who were to be considered the chaps, by others, as well as by themselves.

As in every other jail, membership of this elite club was largely self-proposed. Fellas nominated themselves by their deeds or their attitude. Acceptance was solely determined by whether or not the rest of the chaps acknowledged you. Objective criteria were arcane and obscure, but, generally speaking, if most chaps in good standing considered you to be a tosser or a slag, it was either social ostracism or the river. There were, however, occasional, isolated wannabe chaps who belonged to an exclusive club of one.

This all gave rise to an extremely high level of gossip, intrigue and general backbiting. Any macho, sexist notions I ever had that gossiping and backbiting were purely the preserve of women were soon dispelled after a few years in prison. Of all the mental pressures, 'prison politics' rates among the highest.

Luckily for me, though, being accepted was one problem I definitely didn't have. I was doing life for my second 'gangland' killing; I had been in riots, escapes and hunger strikes; I was partially deranged because of a depressive mental illness, and I was violent on a regular basis to anyone at all who upset me. I wasn't the ultimate chap but, if there had ever been elections to a national committee, I could probably have got myself nominated.

I didn't get a standing ovation or a ticker-tape parade along the ones, but small groups of London chaps wandered over to welcome me. Some I knew personally, others were friends of friends.

I soon learned that one of the most valued privileges at the Scrubs was to 'dine out', if you wanted to. This meant that you could eat your meals at communal tables placed crosswise along the length of the ones. About three-quarters of 'D'-wing cons took advantage of this privilege. There were about 20 tables. I soon found out that the elite among the Scrubs chaps dined out on tables 4 and 13.

To the uninitiated, it might have seemed that table 4 seated the cream of the cream. Freddie, of the Kray gang, was capable, influential and well respected. Three of the Great Train Robbers, Gordon, Jim and Buster, were there largely by virtue of the respect their crime had attracted. Frank and George were two experienced North London bank robbers. Then there were a couple of young wannabe chaps, who basked in the reflected glory.

As the leading lights of table 4 were mostly middle-aged and well behaved, they were looked on by everyone as a calming influence. This could hardly be said of table 13, where the other concentration of the chaps dined out.

Billy G had recently arrived from a dirty protest at Parkhurst. A strong, honourable and determined man, the authorities feared him the most.

Alan had been in the Parkhurst riot and had been severely beaten by the screws. Now that an action for damages was pending, he had been transferred to the Scrubs to keep him quiet.

Jim and Pat were both prolific armed robbers whose cases had attracted widespread publicity. Tommy, also an armed robber, was one of seven brothers in a large North London crime family. Martin, barely 21, had been a family friend of Ron and Reg and a junior member of 'the Firm'.

Apart from Billy G, all of table 13 were quite young. Together with Billy G, they shared his volatility and hatred of the screws. They obviously thought me to be a kindred spirit. I was invited to join them on table 13.

For myself, I was quite relieved to be in a cushy jail for a change. The protests, solitary confinement and hunger strikes at Albany had taken it out of me. I felt I could do with a period of relative peace to regroup and gather my strength. My first priority was still to escape, but it didn't have to be right away. In the meantime, I could re-establish contact with my family and friends through visits.

One of the positive aspects of being moved from jail to jail was that it gave you a comprehensive frame of reference, allowing you to compare levels of security. Escape from the purpose-built long-term jails was very difficult because you were confronted by every security measure possible. However, in the older prisons many of the security measures had been grafted on, so there were occasional gaps or shortcomings.

I quite enjoyed weighing up a new jail. Glaring weaknesses were very few and far between, one had to look deeper. With a combination of De Bono's 'lateral thinking' and my own homespun philosophy, I usually managed to find some chink in the armour though.

In security terms, the Scrubs was trying hard to come to terms with the new breed of resourceful and desperate criminal. These were prisoners who had both a very long sentence, one from which they might never get out, and a large accumulation of wealth. For them, escape was virtually the only option. Or so you would think. In reality it was amazing how few actually gave serious consideration to it.

For many, the trauma of the trial and the subsequent long sentence had knocked the fight out of them. For others, once they had settled into a relatively cushy prison regime, they switched off. They weren't living, by any stretch of the imagination, just existing at a very basic level. And once they had got into this rut, it was very difficult to get out of it. Apart from anything else, they just couldn't bring themselves to face the rigours of solitary confinement, bread-and-water diets and the other sanctions that went with a failed escape. Further, it takes a bit of bottle to try to escape, and they just didn't have it any more.

For myself, I had several advantages. I had grown up in and around West London, so I knew the area around the Scrubs very well. I actually went to school only a hundred yards away. I knew the layout of the inside of the prison well, because I had served an earlier sentence there, in 'A', 'C' and 'D' wings. I could call on help from many of the chaps in 'D' wing. I could also call on help from friends outside in the form of having a getaway car left outside on the day of the escape. With these advantages in mind, I felt quite confident.

The major obstacle to escape from the Scrubs, and most other security jails for that matter, was a 20-foot-high wire fence that ran all around the perimeter. It stood about 16 feet inside the outer perimeter wall and was festooned with rolls of razor-sharp barbed wire. Trembler-bells were fixed to the wire fence panels at regular intervals, so that any movement would set off an alarm.

The whole of the outer perimeter was scanned by closed-circuit TV cameras. At night, powerful lights on high poles provided an illumination that was brighter than daylight.

At strategic points around the jail were positioned observation posts, which were constantly manned. Screws with dogs criss-crossed on permanent patrol. Thus far, the Scrubs was as secure as any jail I had seen.

However, there were a couple of weaknesses, one of which immediately excited me. The outer perimeter wall was a massive stone construction. To its top had been fixed a large plastic canopy, like an inverted gutter. This was to prevent a rope and hook finding purchase. But the wall wasn't very high, only about 16 feet. In the corner, where two walls met by 'D' wing, it stood only 14-foot high. Further, a camera had been fixed on top of the wall, its thick, black, plastic cable hanging down inside. This meant that anyone who could get beyond the wire fence would only have to raise themselves about 12 feet off the ground to be able to grab the plastic cable. This was a major flaw in the outside perimeter.

The other, more general weakness was that major repair work was always going on, as the Scrubs was such an old jail. This meant that there was a vast stock of tools, ladders, building materials and so on. None of this was left lying about, by any means. However, it did raise possibilities.

I was put to work in the laundry, part of an old ramshackle, brick-built complex that stood in the yard between 'C' and 'D' wings. Most of the complement of tables 4 and 13 worked in there too, so I realised that it must be a comparatively good number.

Next door to the laundry was a paint shop. It was shared by cons on a painting and decorating course and the Works Painters Department. There were several ladders in there. By day they were supervised by four Works screws. By night they were chained and padlocked to a wall inside the barred and gated shop.

On close inspection of the inside of the laundry, I could see that the paint shop and the laundry had originally been one building. A partition wall had been built to separate them. The partition was plasterboard fixed to wooden framing. However, I suspected that there might be some hidden steel reinforcing. I would never be able to tell until I smashed through the plasterboard though. So I would need a pair of bolt-croppers, just in case.

Suddenly, I had the basic kernel of my plan. If I could get into the laundry outside working hours, I could then break my way into the paint shop and get at the ladders. A hammer was all I would need to knock the padlocks from the securing chains. Then I could drag the ladders through into the laundry and on to the fence. But how was I to get into the laundry?

My cell overlooked one side of the laundry and, specifically, the gate through which we would enter. Long hours of observation confirmed that the gate was never locked on the double. It was single locked, of course, and a padlock was fastened through a hasp. However, the security PO on his rounds never locked the gate with his doubles key.

I always took particular interest in the movements of the security PO in whichever jail I was in. Most strategic gates were doubled, but they always had to leave a few that were in constant use. From my seat at table 13, I noticed that they didn't double the gate at the far end of 'D' wing until quite late in the evening. Works screws with small parties of cons would often leave by this gate. An added bonus was that this gate wasn't under direct supervision all the time. It was partly obscured by a large TV set on a stand. Admittedly, there were often upwards of a hundred cons watching the TV but they were so intent on what was on the screen that they hardly looked at movements through the gate.

My plan was beginning to fall into shape. Possession of a single key would allow me to slip out the end gate of 'D' wing. The outside end of the wing wasn't covered by the cameras, nor was the small yard between 'D' wing and the laundry gate through which I intended to enter. I could knock the padlock off, unlock the gate, break through the partition, drag two ladders – one large, one small – through into the laundry, exit through the gate I had entered and take a run at the fence. Provided I didn't run smack bang into a dog patrol, I could be up and over the inside fence before the screws could get to me.

One thing was immediately apparent. Apart from a gate key and several other necessary items, I would need at least one fellow escapee. He would carry the second ladder.

This proved to be a major problem. I needed someone who was brave, sensible and physically fit. Brave, to face the prospect of clambering over high barbed-wire-strewn fences and walls; of being savaged by guard dogs, shot at by armed-police-response units outside and beaten up by screws if we failed. Sensible, in that they wouldn't let anyone know by words or deed what we intended to do. Physically fit, to do all the carrying and climbing.

These stringent criteria narrowed it right down. There were very few who fitted the bill. And those who did fit didn't want to go, either because they had settled into their sentence or had done long enough to get to a lower-security establishment, where escape would be much easier.

Fortunately, a partner wasn't that immediate a problem. I had many other things to do that would take weeks if not months. I would just carry on and hope that I would either find the right person or they would arrive from another jail.

I set about trying to get a singles gate key. Every screw had one, as did Works screws, probation staff, chaplains, nurses and teachers. All had to move freely around the prison to go about their daily tasks. I wouldn't try to steal an actual key. They all had to be checked and handed in at night, and a missing key would spark off a full alert. They would change every lock in the jail that the key fitted, so it would be of no use to me anyway.

But if I could get an impression of a key, then smuggle it out, have a key made and smuggle it back again, that key would get me through any undoubled gate in the jail.

In the sex-starved world of prisons, romance is always in the air. Mostly it is imagined. Attractive and not so attractive female nurses, teachers and probation staff fuel the fantasies of many a frustrated con. Occasionally, the attraction is mutual.

It just so happened that one of the young wannabe chaps on the fringes of our table-13 group was having an affair with a teacher. She was a young blonde girl, who most of us had never seen because she didn't leave the education block. The relationship had progressed through secret glances, whispers and clandestine touching, to full-blown sex in a book cupboard. Needless to say, Jimmy, our young Lothario, saw fit to share every intimate detail with his circle of friends.

I wasn't particularly interested. My old-fashioned values caused me to baulk at the idea of Jimmy betraying a trust so flagrantly. If I had harboured any further doubts that he was exploiting the woman, these disappeared when it came out that he was getting her to fetch things in. First, it was just tobacco, then it progressed to bottles of drink. Experience told me that it wasn't going to last very long.

I would never have asked her myself, but the prospect of spending the rest of my life in prison concentrated my mind wonderfully. Through an intermediary, I asked Jimmy to get an impression of a key from her. Ever keen to ingratiate himself with the chaps, Jimmy obliged. She brought in a small piece of cuttlefish, pressed several indents of her gate key into it and handed it to Jimmy.

Now I had my impression, all that remained was to get it out. I bought a large soft-toy teddy bear from one of 'D' wing's hobbies enthusiasts and hid the cuttlefish inside. The toy was handed out on a visit and passed to an expert key-maker friend of mine.

While I awaited the return of the finished key, I set about finding the rest of the things I would need. At least one of us would have to look like a screw as we walked out of the gate at the end of 'D' wing. Luckily, this was only a minor problem. We washed all the Works screws' overalls in the laundry. There were dozens of sets of the brownish boiler suits, and there was little check kept on them. It would be easy to put a set in my personal laundry and carry it over to the wing when required.

The cap would be slightly more difficult. If a screw's cap went missing, there would be a full-scale search of the whole jail. For someone to keep it could only mean that they wanted to impersonate a screw.

Caps did go missing on a regular basis, however. Often, when the screws ran to answer an alarm bell, their hats would fall off. Mischievous cons sometimes took them and ripped them to pieces. The remains could be found in the recess or strewn about the yard. Occasionally, the cap badge would be kept as a souvenir and hidden.

Not much went on in the jail that our group didn't get to hear about. It just so happened that a friend of ours on 'C' wing had ripped a cap apart a few days previously and hidden the badge. He sent it over to us, and I hid it in the laundry. Just to be on the safe side, I asked him to get another one. Within a week he had obliged.

Now I had the badges, the actual caps would be no problem. We had access to cardboard, black material and plastic, so one of the hobbies enthusiasts could soon make a couple up for us.

As for the rest of the uniform, we could get screws' shirts from the laundry and the black boots we wore differed little from theirs. I was confident I could now deck at least two of us out as passable imitations of Works screws.

Going through my plan step by step, the next requirement was a hammer to knock the padlock from the laundry gate. There was a small toolkit kept in the wing office for minor emergency repairs. If some con wanted to knock in a nail, or hang a poster in his cell, he could always borrow the hammer. It had to be returned by nine o'clock bang-up, but by then it would all be over for my escape anyway.

The bolt-croppers for any hidden reinforcing in the laundry

partition were a big problem. They were so obviously a major escape aid that they were carefully supervised. However, we did have several pals on the Works. One of them was actually based in the laundry. There was a small storeroom he and his Works screw used as an office and tearoom. In the corner was a cabinet containing tools. Not a pair of bolt-croppers, unfortunately, but our pal said that he used them regularly and could leave a pair in the cabinet overnight. It would bring him some heat after the escape, but they had been left there before.

There was no doubt that my faith in human nature had been damaged by the selfishness and cruelty I had witnessed in jail. In extreme circumstances, the ruling creed was often 'Every man for himself'. However, there was always a small group of men who were loyal and honourable; who would sacrifice themselves for others with little thought for their own welfare. In helping me with my escape, men who hardly knew me put themselves at considerable risk, and for no reward other than my heartfelt thanks. One could only feel humble at such times.

From a material, logistical point of view, I was now ready to make my escape. The key was finished outside and could be brought in at a few days' notice. Everything else was in position. But I still didn't have a partner. No one had arrived, and, search as I might, I couldn't find anyone suitable and willing on 'D' wing. Suddenly, though, it all became academic.

One morning, as we crossed the yard for work in the laundry, I noticed a large lorry filled with scaffolding parked next to the wing. Several civilian contractors stood about under the watchful eye of a screw. As we returned from work at dinnertime, partially erected scaffolding skirted the base of 'D' wing. From friends on the Works I found out that the roof and the whole of the outside of the wing were to be renovated. The work would take several months.

At first I thought this might be a boon. The scaffolding, boards and ladders were all ideally suited for an escape. I just might find an opportunity. The reality, though, was that the scaffolding brought new and vastly increased security around 'D' wing. Special observation boxes were set up, more lights erected and patrols increased. Any hope of escape was gone until the work was over.

Several months passed, long frustrating months. There was always the possibility that some trouble would arise in which I might get involved. I had been shanghaied before. It could easily happen again. Time really was of the essence.

On the positive side, though, I had now found a partner. In fact, I had found three. Ian Down was a young North London robber, doing 25 years for a string of bank robberies in Scotland. He was part Scots himself and filled with the Celtic warrior spirit. Just a few years into his sentence, he had already been involved in several tear-ups and escape attempts. We were made for each other.

Ian was instantly enthusiastic about the escape. He came to work in the laundry, so he could clearly see the full extent of the plan. Then he settled down with me to await the removal of the scaffolding.

With two of us involved, there were now two opinions. Ian pointed out that, provided we could find suitable people, four would be an ideal number for the escape. A Works party comprising a screw and three cons would be quite normal, leaving the wing after tea. Even if it were seen crossing the yard and entering the laundry, it would excite no interest. More importantly, though, when we ran at the fence, Ian and I could carry the ladders while the other two could mind us off against any screws we might bump into.

Admittedly, those carrying the ladders would be first up the fence and have the best chance of getting away. However, it was quite a touch to be put into someone else's escape. And if we didn't bump into a patrol right away, there was a good chance we would all get out.

Although we had many things in common, Ian and I had quite different personalities. I burned with far more bitterness and anger than him. I was hostile and stand-offish; he was outgoing and friendly. There was no problem. Ian's way worked for him; my way worked for me. We were both surviving, when others all around us were going under.

Malcolm was one of Ian's circle of friends. His youth, clean-cut looks, good manners and intelligence made him seem out of place in prison.

However, the placid exterior belied a fiery nature. He was courageous, brave and extremely determined. He was also a libertarian.

I thought I was well informed about all the various political creeds, but this was a new one on me. It turned out that Malcolm was somewhere to the left of the revolutionary Marxists. This hardly sat well with my own right-wing views, but, as Ian pointed out, we were only going to escape together, not run for office.

Apparently, Malcolm had firebombed his local Tory-run town hall; this kind of direct action was virtually unknown in the early Seventies. Political terrorism was still largely in its infancy. He had carried on his protests in prison and had spent months in solitary. He had lost most of the remission on his ten-year sentence. His aggression, though, was directed only at authority. I found him to be extremely pleasant and friendly. We got on immediately.

In many ways, Gerry Kelley was quite similar to Malcolm. Tall and slim, with long black curly hair that framed a pasty baby-face, he looked more like a college student than the leader of the IRA team, who had bombed the Old Bailey a couple of years earlier.

Terrorism didn't sit easily with the chaps. Many were working-class 'Little Englanders' and quite conservative in their outlook. So, while nonces, grasses and slags were clearly beyond the pale, terrorists occupied a grey area. However, there was no violent antipathy towards them. They were either acknowledged or ignored.

One saving grace for Gerry, as far as the chaps were concerned, was that he had bombed the Old Bailey. That symbolic strike at what was, for us, a hated symbol of oppression endeared him to quite a few. The further knowledge that he had come within a whisker of blowing up New Scotland Yard, too, added to his popularity. Quite a few of us had contemplated doing just that at one time or another.

On a personal level, I found him to be pleasant, intelligent, shy and extremely naive about crime. Before the actual bombing, he had never committed a criminal act in his life, not even a minor one. Ironically, he was strongly against conventional criminal activity *per se*.

This latter fact was only revealed to me during one of our infrequent 'escape committee' meetings. We had been discussing what we were going to do after the escape. The IRA was relatively unorganised in England at this time. Ian and I were to provide the getaway vehicle and the safe house. Gerry had promised us help to get away overseas.

This meant that we would spend several days in the safe house before leaving. As neither Ian nor I had any money, we had been discussing a bit of work he had been looking at before his arrest. It was a large general Post Office in North London. A determined team could take upwards of a hundred grand. This would come in very handy for our future lives on the run.

I asked Gerry and Malcolm if they would like to join us in the venture. There was a stony, embarrassed silence. It transpired that neither had stolen anything in their whole lives before; both were ideologically opposed to stealing and, lastly, in Gerry's case, the IRA wouldn't approve.

I was astounded. Here were two men who would think nothing of blowing up public buildings, yet they baulked at armed robbery.

'Malcolm, think of it as redistributing wealth in an oppressive capitalist society,' I said with just a trace of irony.

Embarrassed, he shook his head and refused to be moved.

'Gerry, you can give your share to the IRA.'

Equally embarrassed, he mumbled, 'I'm a bomber, Norman, not a robber. There's others do the robbing.'

The logic of this Republican division of labour largely escaped me. I was on the verge of asking if there was anything in their respective party manifestos that prohibited escaping and possibly bashing a screw on the way out, but I refrained. Ian had reassured me that both were keen to take part.

Now there were four of us awaiting the removal of the scaffolding. At long last, the renovation finished and the contractors started to dismantle it. However, we suddenly had another problem. Three Libyan terrorists had been arrested, and they were lodged in 'A'-wing Seg. As a direct result, security at the jail was increased. Unmarked cars full of armed police encircled the jail day and night. We wouldn't be able to make a move until the Libyans were transferred.

More months passed and the Libyans were finally deported. The jail was returned to normal. We readied ourselves to make our move.

At first it was just a wild rumour. Soon the whole nick was buzzing with the story. A young fella had been killed in the Seg.

I found it hard to believe at first. 'A'-wing Seg was quite civilised as punishment blocks go. There were no systematic, regular beatings. However, Steven Smith had definitely died in a punishment cell in the Seg.

The trouble had started on 'C' wing. Steven, barely in his 20s, was doing four years. He was backward rather than mentally retarded. With his nerdy looks and National Health glasses, he was more inadequate than criminal. He was awkward and argumentative and regularly fell foul of the screws.

He had been taken to the Seg after his umpteenth argument with a screw. The official version was that he had died sometime during the night. They said he had been found hanging from his window bars. There were several discrepancies though. Further rumours were coming from the Seg that he had been beaten up.

Whatever the real facts, the authorities didn't help themselves with their subsequent secretive behaviour. With feelings running high, they didn't want to carry the body out through 'A' wing, past cells full of prisoners. So they put Steven in a sack and carried him down the narrow, circular staircase at the rear of the Seg. Once in the yard, they put the sack in the back of an unmarked van and drove out of the prison.

The whole episode lacked a certain dignity. It smacked of a cover-up. Several lifers remarked that it was similar to details in their own cases. A further surprise came when it was revealed that the body was quickly cremated and, it was rumoured, without the permission of the family.

The jail was now in complete uproar. Men who had been quietly doing their time were vociferous in their protests. There was a move for something to be done. A sit-down protest was mooted.

The inquest was quickly convened. When the story was reported in the press the headline in the local paper read, DID WARDERS MURDER THIS MAN? Conflicting evidence was presented. One prisoner from the Seg said that he had heard a scuffle, then silence. Another said that Steven had asked him for a cigarette during the night, yet his family and friends swore he had never smoked in his life.

A rope was presented, made from torn pieces of canvas sheet. When asked to tear a strip off the same sheet, the 19-stone exhibits officer was not able to do so. Yet Steven was frail and had a partially crippled hand. There was more in a similar vein, all quite suspicious.

However, the Prison Service closed ranks as usual. In the final analysis it came down to the word of a prisoner against that of a prison officer: The jury returned an 'open' verdict. It wasn't what the authorities wanted, but it was all they were going to get. As far as they were concerned, the matter was closed.

Back in 'D' wing it was far from closed. We hadn't expected

anything from the inquest. It was all part and parcel of the system. And the system always worked to protect itself. The only justice we would get was that which we made ourselves. We decided on a sit-down.

Within the circle of our 'escape committee' we were astounded at how accelerating events had overtaken us. We were intent on escaping; that would be our personal statement against the system. Suddenly, though, there was a major matter of principle at stake. We had to take part. Enthusiastically, we joined in organising the protest.

The following day over 300 men sat down in 'D' wing. There were scattered protests on other wings. The prison ground to a halt, and several wing governors came to negotiate. It was a significant incident.

As much as I felt my violent nature to be indefensible, at heart I considered myself to be a reasonable, even honourable man. Surely, even the Home Office could see the rightness of a protest about a murder, albeit one committed by screws. I didn't expect a commendation for my part in the protest, but I didn't expect outright condemnation either.

Two days later, early on a Saturday morning, I was shanghaied. Ten screws came to my cell; I was taken to reception, loaded into a van and sent on my way to Parkhurst. The following day Malcolm was shanghaied to Gartree. In disposing of two of the ringleaders of the sit-down, they had unwittingly disposed of two would-be escapers.

There were still two left, though, and Ian and Gerry were determined to carry on. Ian knew the whole plan and where the various materials were to be obtained. The escape was scheduled for the following Saturday.

During the week, Ian put aside two sets of screws' overalls and two shirts. He had checked them for size, and they were a good fit. He retrieved the two badges. Back in his cell he set about making the two caps to go with them. As he left the laundry late on Friday afternoon, he carried the overalls and shirts with him.

Saturday dawned, with Ian and Gerry readying themselves for a visit. Later, as Gerry sat with his wife, Ian discussed last-minute details with a cousin. He told him where the car was to be left and at what time. As he got up from the visit, he took the key from his cousin and hid it in his mouth. The rub-down search proved to be no problem.

The afternoon seemed to drag on interminably. Both stayed out of the way in Ian's cell lest some fluke attract attention to them. When tea was finally served, neither could face it.

With tea over, the wing settled down to an evening's association. Some went to their cells and banged up; others sat playing cards and talking; the remainder played games or watched TV. At the far end of 'D' wing, beyond table 13, a hundred men sat impassively in front of the big TV set.

Inside Ian's cell on the ones, he and Gerry put on their disguise. They paused momentarily as a friend stopped by to give them the hammer he had borrowed from the wing office. Then, with a few quick adjustments to the hats, they were ready. Ostensibly, the fellas on table 13 were sitting quietly, playing cards. In reality, they were scanning the wing, watching the movements of the screws. Suddenly, the nearest screw was down by the centre and out of clear view of the end gate. The signal was given.

As nonchalantly as they could manage, Ian and Gerry strolled from the cell. They passed table 13, circled the body of men watching TV and approached the gate. Without looking back, Ian opened the gate with the key, walked through with Gerry, then locked it again.

Their passing hadn't gone unnoticed though. A couple of the TV watchers had stood up and were sheepishly making their way back towards the main body of the wing. All of the complement of table 13 now stood up and glared at them. 'Sit down,' they mouthed. The offenders returned to their seats.

After the warmth of the wing, the cold evening air felt stimulating. Staying close to the end of the building, Ian and Gerry headed into the enfolding darkness, across the small yard to the laundry gate.

With one quick movement Ian knocked the padlock from its hasp. He had acquired the knack robbing wagons as a child in the goods yard near his North London home. Using the key again, he let them both into the laundry, before locking the gate behind them. He rested the broken padlock back in its hasp. It would pass a cursory inspection.

Together they broke into the Works store, forced the tools cabinet open and got their first surprise. There were no bolt-croppers. Ian quickly ran to the partition. The plasterboard disintegrated with his frantic attack, revealing the second surprise. A reinforcement of thick steel mesh stood between them and the paint shop. With only the tools they had, they wouldn't be able to get the ladders.

Gerry looked deflated.

'Think, think,' cried Ian, screwing up his face and clenching both fists. He glanced around the shop.

There, against a wall, stood a pair of steps. They were only eight foot high though. Ian cut the retaining ropes and laid them flat on the floor. Now they were 16-foot long, but one of the eight-foot sections comprised just two lengths of wood.

Next, Ian turned to one of the massive tables that were used for folding sheets on. The strutting underneath was criss-crossed with wooden slats. He broke several of these free, then, with Gerry holding the whole construction steady, he nailed them across the steps as rungs. Finally, he fixed a length along each side of the steps to keep them open and rigid. Now he had a slightly rickety 16-foot ladder.

That should take care of the first fence. But he needed something for the wall. He scoured the shop again.

He tipped another of the massive tables on to its side, revealing long pieces of thick strutting. Having cut two eight-foot lengths free, he laid them side by side on the floor. Once again, he nailed wooden slats across them. He now had another makeshift ladder. They were ready for the move to the fence.

This next part would be largely a hit-and-miss affair. They didn't have a vantage-point from which to observe the comings and goings of the screws. They would just have to wait until a patrol went past, leave it a couple of minutes, then go and trust to luck. They watched as the screw with the large black German shepherd passed the end of 'C' wing.

Silently, they followed their passage across 'C'-wing yard. They disappeared out of sight behind the blank end wall of the laundry, only to appear again crossing 'D'-wing yard. Finally, they went behind the end of 'D' wing and out of sight.

Ian counted up to 100, then opened the gate. Each carrying a ladder, they ran side by side to the nearest part of the fence. In the deathly quiet Ian threw the longest ladder up against the fence. In his mind, he could imagine the turmoil that was soon to come: the lights, the sirens, the panic in the control room. He started up the ladder.

The plan had been for him to go up first; the flimsy ladder wouldn't hold two. However, in the heat of the moment, Gerry climbed beside him. There was a grating sound as the foot of the ladder sunk into the gravel, then a sharp snap. Part of one leg had broken off, and the ladder slipped sideways.

With a strength born of desperation, Gerry threw the ladder he was carrying clear over the fence. Reaching upwards, he grasped the top of a panel and heaved himself up. He wobbled precariously on the top, swung over, then dropped to the ground.

For Ian, though, it was all over. Gerry stood a good five inches taller than him. When the ladder broke and slipped sideways it sounded Ian's death knell. Stretch as he might, he just couldn't reach the top of the fence now.

'Go on, go on,' he cried at Gerry, pausing on the other side of the fence. Immediately galvanised, Gerry grabbed the short ladder and made for the corner where the walls met.

Sirens were blaring now; there was the sound of running feet; cons were shouting encouragement from the wing. Gerry was oblivious to it all. Carefully, he placed the ladder against the wall. Gingerly, he climbed upwards. Relief flooded through him as his fingers clasped the thick black camera cable. It was all behind him now as he hoisted himself up to sit astride the wall.

'Stay right where you fucking are.' The voice seemed to come out of nowhere.

Startled, he gazed around, blinking in the harsh glare of the outside floodlights.

'Sit still.' The voice came again.

There, below him on the road that ran alongside the prison stood a man wearing a dark suit. Next to him stood another, similarly attired. Both were facing him, legs apart, arms outstretched towards him. As Gerry focused more clearly, he saw the guns they were holding in their hands.

He looked back inside the jail in time to see several screws surround Ian. He watched as they led him away. He turned again, as he heard a noise outside, further up the road. A van with a flashing blue light sped towards the two men on the ground. With a deep sigh, Gerry threw back his head and stared at the heavens. So much space, so much distance. He mused that this was probably as close as he would get to freedom for a very long time. With a shrug of resignation, he hoped it would be enough to sustain him through the long months of solitary that were to come.

Ever the warrior, Ian continued to rebel throughout his sentence. Tear-up followed tear-up, escape attempt followed escape attempt; he was moved from jail to jail. Finally, the flesh failed the spirit. In his 16th year Ian suffered a severe mental breakdown. For a long while, his sanity hung in the balance. It was four more years before he was finally released, damaged in mind and body.

He lived in much reduced circumstances for several years, the poverty and the drugs exacerbating his already parlous mental state. Often roaming the streets in this deranged state, he had a heart attack and died in 2003.

Not long after the Scrubs escape, Gerry Kelley was transferred to Northern Ireland. He escaped from the Maze in a mass break-out. He was recaptured in Holland, only to be freed again. He is now a member of Sinn Fein's executive committee. He was elected as an MP and is often seen at the side of Gerry Adams at public engagements.

29 THE FOOD PROTEST

From a con's perspective, if there was one thing that was good and positive about Parkhurst, it was the degree of solidarity among the cons in the face of a threat from the screws.

There was always a high level of violence between the cons – in fact, the place absolutely bristled with hostility. But some action by the screws that threatened the average con's lifestyle could unify individuals and factions who might normally detest each other.

In many ways, Parkhurst was a concentration of rebels drawn from all over the country. Heavy violence was the common thread that ran through most of the population, rather than a shared professionalism in the pursuit of crime. If Grimsby or Ramsgate or Truro ever threw up a hardnut, a dangerous wild man who was a legend in his locality, you could safely bet that he would eventually find his way to Parkhurst. And these men would be strong, silent types, rather than swaggering braggarts. So you never knew who you were dealing with. That was why it didn't pay to throw your weight about. You could come very severely unstuck.

One topic that could regularly unite all the diverse elements was the food. Generally, it was no better and no worse than many other jails, but this was no recommendation at all. It was uniformly dull, and it was clear that the cooks had no interest in turning out good food. They were just going through the motions from day to day.

The potatoes were often badly cleaned, insufficiently cooked and, when mashed, full of lumps. The greens were regularly stringy and overcooked. The meat dish could be full of fat and gristle, the gravy lumpy and greasy. The duff was often stodgy and not cooked through. At least once a week there would be no sugar in the custard and it would be thin and runny, with a consistency more like soup.

Every day, at least one part of the meal was thoroughly unpalatable. There would be moans, curses and the occasional governor's application in the morning. But, when there was a conjunction of all the above-mentioned culinary mishaps, there could be trouble.

On this particular day, the cook had surpassed himself. It was as if the legacy of his general indifference had finally culminated in this most abysmal of meals. Every component part was ruined in one way or another. And what was so surprising to the hardened con wasn't so much that the cook had managed to fuck everything up, but that he still saw fit to send the meal on to the wings. Clearly, he was taking the piss.

It was us serving orderlies who noticed at first. As we took the lids off the trays and canisters, the experienced eye couldn't miss the drastic drop in quality from previous meals.

Since we would be in the frontline when it was served up, we wanted to distance ourselves from responsibility for it as much as possible. We would also have to eat it ourselves, so our complaints were heartfelt.

'Look at this lot of shit. I'm not serving that up,' said one.

'Where's the PO? He should see this garbage,' said another.

The SO had been hovering in the doorway to his office, as he usually did when meals were served. He never served the food himself – that was done by the other screws and several inmate orderlies – but he was always on hand because mealtimes could be a flashpoint for trouble.

Scores of people would be milling about in a confined space. Fellas who didn't particularly like each other could find themselves together in the meal queue. There were dozens of ways that trouble could start.

The SO came up to the hot-plate and looked into the food containers. By now, the fellas in the queue had crowded around, 40 or 50 people all shouting and cursing. It was a situation that could easily turn nasty.

The SO was the same one who had been on the night Barry Hurley – 'Top-cat' – hit the screw with the table. His thin pale face looked tight and drawn. His narrow shoulders and slight frame seemed to shrink as the baying mob closed in. He hadn't caused this problem, yet he was the one who would have to try to sort it out.

He waved his arms in the air to quieten people down. Then, raising his voice to be heard above the din, he shouted, 'I'm going to phone the kitchen!' With that, he spun round and hurried into his office.

The crowd still continued to shout and curse. The orderlies and the screws who were to have served the meal stepped back from the hot-plate and leaned against the wall – a physical act to distance themselves from responsibility for the food.

A couple of minutes passed and the SO came out of his office again. Raising his arms once more, he shouted, 'Lads, I've phoned the kitchen and tried to get the meal replaced, but the cook has refused. I'm sorry. I tried to do something about it, but it's out of my hands.'

As he finished, a cacophony of screams and curses rang out. A few of the real nutters were shouting about smashing up the wing. A sea of angry, distorted faces mouthed insults that were lost in the general din.

'Let's just bin it,' shouted someone above all the rest. 'Let's all tip our meals in the bin.'

This was a traditional form of protest over bad food. Provided everybody did it, it could be a significant action. One that would make the governor sit up and take notice.

A metal dustbin was pulled out from the recess and set in the middle of the landing, just past the end of the hot-plate. The fella who had made the suggestion picked up a tray and stepped forward to be served. We servers stepped away from the wall, up to the hot-plate. As the fella walked past, we put a portion of each part of the meal on his tray. When he had collected it all, he walked over to the dustbin and tipped the lot in. Leaving his tray on a nearby table, he headed for his cell.

Now other fellas collected their meals and tipped them into the bin. Some remained standing about the landing afterwards. There was a degree of euphoria, because something was being done about an injustice. On so many other occasions, we had had to suffer it.

More men came in from work. They saw the crowd gathered around the hot-plate area and the dustbin set in the middle of the landing. They couldn't miss the electric atmosphere.

'What's going on? What's happening?' men would ask.

'We're all binning the meal 'cause it's crap,' would come the reply.

The fella would collect his meal, then tip it into the bin. A few threw their trays in as well.

One of the last to come in was Big Mick. Mick loved his food. He would eat in as many food-boats as he could, but then he was a big fella. He had often said that the one form of protest he couldn't get involved in was a hunger strike, arguing that you were only weakening yourself when you should stay strong to resist the screws.

As Mick collected his meal, he watched the fellas in front of him throw theirs into the bin. He walked to the bin and tipped his in likewise. Then he turned towards the crowd of fellas standing around.

'This is a lot of bollocks,' he said angrily. 'You all make one over a bit of poxy grub, when you should be doing something about parole. Nobody's getting it here. If you really want to protest about something worthwhile, protest about the parole system.' With that, he threw his empty tray against the nearest wall and stormed off to his cell.

Later, in the 'Old Bailey', we talked about the food protest. Insofar as everyone had refused their meal, it had been a significant success. Also, we had been told that the cook was putting on a special meal of eggs, chips and mixed grill for tea. So we had made our point.

Big Mick wasn't impressed, though. 'Give it a week,' he said, 'and it will be back to normal again. What gives me the hump is that everyone sits about doing nothing about their parole knock-backs.'

Mick had a point, of course. But it was no good just one jail making a protest; it would have to be co-ordinated. The question was: How could you get all the various rebellious individuals in other jails to take part on the same day?

'Doesn't Geoff go on home leave next week?' I asked suddenly.

'I think so,' said Ray, 'but what's that got to do with it?'

'Well, Geoff's one of those anarchist types and he's associated with that prisoners' rights magazine *PROP*. We could get him to put a bit in *PROP* calling for a national day of action over the parole system,' I suggested.

There was a few seconds' silence. Clearly, the rest of the fellas weren't too impressed with the idea.

John spoke first. 'And do you think that the fellas in other jails are all going to have a protest just because *PROP* tells them to?' he asked with heavy sarcasm.

'No, I don't,' I replied, 'but it's worth a try. Once one jail starts, others might join in. I'll ask Geoff anyway.'

Later that day, I spoke to Geoff Coggan about the idea. In his late 40s, he came from a totally different background to the rest of us. A distinguished-looking gentleman of about 50, his flowing grey locks made him look more like a senior civil servant than a prisoner. He was articulate, learned, very well spoken and passionately into radical left-wing politics. He was doing a five for fraud, but always insisted that he had been fitted up for political reasons. He wasn't violent at all. However, we respected the way he stood up for what he believed in. In his own way, he was an out-and-out rebel who fought the system every inch of the way.

I told him what I had in mind. I said that, even if he couldn't get it into *PROP*, perhaps his friends could pass the idea around by word of mouth.

It wasn't that the left-wing crowd had much credibility with the average prisoner, because they hadn't. They were viewed as thinkers rather than doers. But they had the organisation to get the message around.

Geoff was very enthusiastic. It was just the sort of thing that he loved to get involved in. He was quite flattered that I had come to a comparative lightweight like him for assistance. He promised to do all he could to help.

Within a few days, we had forgotten all about it. Other events had occurred that occupied our attention. Geoff duly went on home leave. When he returned, he came up to me and said that he had set things in motion.

I told our crowd about it, but it was all too abstract for them to get excited about. Soon, the demands of everyday survival in Parkhurst took all our energies and we largely forgot about it.

30 THE SIT-DOWN

About two months after the food protest, we came in from work one dinnertime and all the talk was of the rooftop protest next door at Albany. It had said on the radio that 20 to 30 men were on the roof, protesting about the parole system.

If you listened carefully out of a cell window, you could hear their faint shouts, carried on the wind. This gave us a sense of immediacy and an added sense of involvement. Very soon, all of Parkhurst was enthused with the spirit of revolt.

Our crowd immediately congregated in the 'Old Bailey'. Everyone was there, and all those on the fringes of our group dropped in, too. The big question was: What should we do?

Some were all for staging our own protest at once. Others argued that it would be best to put the word around so that the action got maximum support.

Personally, I couldn't make up my mind what was best. If we did something straight away, we could capitalise on the excitement generated by the publicity over Albany's protest. However, there would be people here at Parkhurst who wouldn't know what was going to happen and might miss out.

If we waited, everybody would know about it. Tomorrow was

pay-day, so everyone would be well stocked up with food and tobacco. On the debit side, though, the longer we waited, the more the enthusiasm might wane. Albany's protest might suddenly come to an end. And, last but not least, the screws might take some pre-emptive countermeasure, like keeping us locked up for a few days.

Further group discussion was cut short by the need to collect our dinners and bang up. We agreed to continue when we were unlocked again.

Over the bang-up, everyone was tuned in to any news broadcast they could find. The Albany sit-down was mentioned several times. When we were unlocked for exercise, the fellas were even more fired with enthusiasm.

The overwhelming consensus was that we should do something in solidarity with the Albany fellas and not leave them to stand on their own. The wider the protest, the less likely it would be that the riot squads would be sent in to cosh everyone up.

While we were waiting for the screws to let us out of the wing, John called me aside from the main group. 'What are we going to do about the book?' he said quietly.

John and I ran the only book in the jail. Not only would our regular punters expect a bet, but if we didn't show, even for one day, then someone else might come forward and start their own book.

'We'll carry on as normal,' I replied. 'There's no guarantee that there will be a sit-down this afternoon anyway. If the majority are against it, it will be put off until tomorrow. It's only a matter of me taking out my paper and the snout bag, and I've got them with me anyway.'

The wing gates were opened and we all filed out. The crowds made their way down the hill and into the compound.

John and I took up our normal position on the edge of the football pitch, next to the khazi. We were immediately surrounded by several of our regulars. Sit-down or no sit-down, the committed punter wasn't going to miss a bet.

I collected the betting slips and the snout and put them in the green cotton bag. I marked the amount and the punter's initials in my paper, alongside the horse backed.

It was all done quite openly. The screws were aware that John and I ran a book. As long as there was no trouble, they let us carry on. They knew that, in any long-term jail, there had to be a book to keep all the gamblers quiet.

Now that we had taken some bets, I personally didn't want the sit-down to begin that afternoon. If there was a sit-down, it was likely that John and I would be shanghaied or put in the chokey for a couple of weeks. Then the winning punters wouldn't get paid. I didn't want it to seem that we had taken their bets under false pretences.

After about half an hour, Dave Bailey and Big Mick walked up. 'The majority of people want the sit-down right now,' said Dave. 'They're not worried about being prepared. They'd rather do something while the feeling is strong.'

'That's OK by me,' I said, and John nodded in agreement. We had always said that we'd go with the majority and, in my heart of hearts, I felt it was the right decision.

As exercise came to an end and the screws unlocked the gates to the shops, we both moved backwards on to the grass of the football pitch. We lay down in the strong, hot sunshine. As I looked around, I could see about 50 fellas doing likewise.

I could see scores more filing into the shops. Nothing was said to them. There was no abuse. It was their decision. However, it was in times like these that you found out who would stick by you and who wouldn't. Most of those filing into the shops were deliberately staring at the ground so that no one could catch their eye.

Suddenly, the paths were deserted. Everyone who was going had entered the shops. The screws were still standing around the walls and fences bounding the compound, puzzled that the 50 men on the grass hadn't moved. Usually they would be moving across the compound, shepherding the remaining stragglers into the shops.

I sat up and looked at the group on the grass more closely. Our crowd was well represented, but Barry was off on a visit and Ray just hadn't showed. The Paddies and the Jocks were well represented, too. Strong, hard men who didn't say very much but just acted. They were very staunch.

All the nutters who you would have expected to be there were there, sitting quietly on the grass. If there was going to be a row, we were in very good company.

At some unseen signal, the screws suddenly moved away from the perimeter and closed in on the football pitch. They stopped at the edge.

A portly PO and the chief stepped on to the grass and walked between the groups of men. They made their way to where our group were sitting.

'What's happening then, boys?' asked the chief, an old hand who had been in the service for years.

Some of our group looked at me. I had a reputation for being good with words. They wanted the reason for our protest to be put across properly.

'Well, guv,' I began, taking their cue, 'we're sitting down in protest at the way the parole system is run and also in solidarity with the fellas on the roof at Albany.'

The chief's face was a picture. He had seen protests over food, brutality and living conditions. All immediate, personal things that could be negotiated, one way or another. But this was a political protest in the sense that it challenged a national decision-making process, one which, incidentally, he wasn't part of. He wouldn't be able to concede anything on this. He just stood there and said nothing.

In the period before the '69 riot, there would have been little hesitation. Massive reinforcements would have been brought in from other jails. Then they would have steamed into us.

But, post-'69, they didn't want any full-scale battles. Especially at Parkhurst, the cradle of the riot. So, for a while, we could expect to negotiate. But a point would come when their patience would run out. Then they would come in and get us.

We weren't looking for a full-scale tear-up with the screws. Neither side would win any medals. We just wanted to register a strong enough protest and show some solidarity with Albany.

The chief shrugged, then, together with the PO, walked back to the line of screws. He set them to stand at various points on the perimeter. Then he left the compound, probably to confer with the governor.

We continued to lie on the grass. It was a beautiful summer's day and we were out to make the most of it. It looked like the screws were going to leave us alone for a while, so we might as well relax while we could.

Looking around the pitch, I could see all the others stretched out, too. Everything seemed so peaceful, so normal that it hardly felt like a confrontation.

You could imagine people hearing on the radio that 50 dangerous prisoners were carrying out a sit-down protest at Parkhurst. They would expect a group of tight-faced cons, confronting lines of equally tight-faced screws in riot gear. It could well come to that eventually, but, for now, we were content to rest and gather our strength for what was to come.

I had taken almost 30 ounces in bets before exercise had finished. The snout was in the green cotton bag, which I had under my head as a cushion. Suddenly, the thought struck me that many of the fellas would be without a smoke. Tomorrow was canteen day, so most of the smokers would be down to a few dog-ends by now. Yet I, who didn't smoke at all, had 30 ounces of tobacco as a pillow

I rolled over and spoke to John. 'Look, mate, we've got all this snout wrapped around us, which we'll lose anyway if we're moved. So how about we give the fellas a smoke? We can't just sit here with this lot while they haven't got a dog-end.'

John immediately agreed. I stood up with the bag and walked to the nearest group. I asked each fella if he smoked. To those who said, 'Yes', I gave half an ounce.

I moved from group to group, doling out the snout. When most of it was gone, I came back and handed the rest to John. He would share it with our crowd.

As I sat down again, I couldn't help reflecting that the screws would now think that our group had paid the rest to take part. They had a talent for misconstruing quite innocent behaviour.

The afternoon wore on. Soon it was 4.30 and time for the shops to turn out. Radios crackled and screws who had been standing against walls and fences stood erect, feet apart. The gates leading out of the compound were opened.

Ideally, the screws would have liked to keep us isolated. They didn't want us to talk any more cons into joining us, but there was no way to get those working in the shops back to their wings without their walking past us.

Our group made themselves busy. We spoke to the rest and asked them to try to get as many as possible to join us. So, if they knew any of the fellas coming out of the shops, they should try to encourage them to take part.

The first of the returning workers emerged from the shops. They came almost reluctantly, mostly staring at the ground. Each of them knew that this was a protest that every con had an interest in. But, just as in so many walks of life, they had neither the courage nor the determination to take part.

There were no jeers from us. The last thing we wanted was an obvious division among the cons. The ones who wouldn't take part would have to live with it. The next time they moaned about something, someone would remind them that they would have to put up with it because they certainly didn't have the bottle to do anything about it. The next time they swaggered and gave it the rebel bit, someone would remind them of the occasion when they had swallowed it and left their mates to do the fighting for them.

The fellas sitting on the grass began calling to men leaving the shops. 'Hey, Tim, how about it then?' and 'Jimmy, are you with us?' Occasionally, a man would step off the path and hurry to join us on the grass. A ragged cheer would break out and a smattering of applause. Then they were all gone.

About 20 had joined us, pushing our numbers up to 70. There were about 350 cons in Parkhurst, but, bearing in mind that this had been a spur-of-the-moment protest and many men couldn't get in the compound because they were in a different part of the prison, 70 was not too bad. It was a large enough number to ensure that, if the screws did try to use force, there would be a full-scale battle. The screws would win, of course, but they could well do without all the ensuing publicity.

The new fellas mingled in with us. Many of them hadn't realised that a sit-down was taking place. Others had thought that it would be so badly supported that it would be a non-event.

As the euphoria brought by our increased numbers wore off, we suddenly realised that we were hungry. We didn't need the sight of fellas leaving work for tea to remind us that it was time to eat. Having been fed at certain set times, year in, year out, the body had become programmed to expect food at these times. A mere half an hour beyond a mealtime brought sharp hunger pains and an empty feeling.

But there would be no food for us. The screws were hardly likely to fetch our tea out to us. They obviously didn't expect the protest to go on for very long, but, if it did, one of their main strategies would be to starve us out.

No one complained about being hungry. If a few missed meals were the worst that we would suffer over the protest, we would be well pleased. If anything, it heightened our sense of martyrdom.

As the evening approached and shadows began to lengthen, all the screws withdrew from the compound, although a sizeable posse clustered outside the main gate leading to the wings. Clearly, they did not want to be at close quarters with us in the dark. The police had the whole jail surrounded now anyway, so there was no need for them to be inside the compound with us. We weren't going anywhere.

Now that we had the compound to ourselves, we ventured off the pitch to explore the extent of our territory. Although we were all committed to stand and fight together, there was little camaraderie yet. Mutual suspicion and hostility were too deeply ingrained for them to break down completely over the space of a few hours.

Our group wandered about together, as did groups of Jocks, Paddies and Scouses. We greeted each other and shared jokes when we met, but I got the impression that, if it was off, each group would try to outfight the others as a matter of honour. And that was no bad thing.

As darkness fell, it grew cold. Many of us had come out in T-shirts and thin jackets. We would have to find a way to keep warm. The obvious solution was to get inside one of the shops. But they were all locked and the windows barred.

I walked over to the tin shop with Big Mick, Dave and Jeff. We peered through the grimy windows at the familiar interior. As we stood outside in the evening chill, it looked very inviting.

On my own, I wandered around the outside of the shop, looking for a weak point. In the gathering gloom, I saw a couple of fellas standing at a side window. They had raised the sliding sash, but this had done them no good at all. A massive set of bars covered the whole window

As I drew closer, I saw that they were two IRA men I knew. As we greeted each other, I looked closely at the bars. At first sight, they seemed impossibly secure. There were about ten of them in a grille, all an inch in diameter. The whole lot must have weighed a couple of hundredweight. However, it was the grille's very weight and rigidity that was its weakness, for the whole thing was set in a wooden surround. Over the years, the wood had rotted and the weight of the grille had pulled it out a fraction from the surround. You could get some movement by pushing it back in tight.

I pushed the bottom corner in and, placing both feet against the wall, suddenly yanked the grille outwards with all my strength. In truth, I was sure that nothing would happen. To my surprise, it immediately came a full inch away from the surround.

Another determined yank pulled it three inches clear. A final pull had the whole grille hanging lopsidedly in the shattered frame.

The Irishmen were looking at me in amazement. They hadn't noticed the rotten surround. Recovering quickly, first one, then the other pulled himself over the sill and dropped out of sight inside. I followed close behind.

Strangely, it seemed lighter inside the shop than out. A bright moon cast an eerie glow over deserted workbenches and machines. I felt the illicit thrill of being somewhere I wasn't supposed to be. Normally, each time you entered the tin shop, your every move would be closely watched.

I made my way towards the civvies' offices. Mostly, I had food on my mind. Perhaps I might find some packets of biscuits in the desk drawers. Then there was warmth. Perhaps there would be an old mac or overcoat hanging behind a door.

There was nothing. Nothing that could be of any use to us. Even the stone, metal and concrete of the building generated no warmth to make sleeping inside more attractive.

Suddenly there was someone in the offices with me. Tina, a raver off 'B' wing, had climbed into the shop after us and was ransacking drawers and cupboards.

Whereas I had searched carefully, Tina was tipping over filing cabinets and emptying out drawers on to the floor. The noise in the empty shop was awesome. Tina was taking this opportunity to damage a small part of the system she hated so much.

I wandered out, back into the main body of the shop. I was just in time to see the two IRA fellas lever the wooden door off the stores. It fell with a resounding crash, revealing a darkened interior lined with racks and racks of tools.

They rushed in and grabbed armfuls of hammers, chisels and files. Carrying them to the open window, they shouted out into the darkness. Shadowy figures appeared and the Irishmen passed the tools out to them. Soon, nearly everyone was armed with something or other. Now, if the screws attacked with riot sticks, we could meet them on something like equal terms.

Next, the two IRA men started to remove the lock from the storeroom door. I couldn't see the logic in this. It would cause so much trouble once the screws discovered it was missing. They would have to change every lock in the jail. Then, any measurements the IRA fellas had taken would be useless. And any homemade keys would no longer work. However, it wasn't for me to tell them not to do it. I climbed back out the window, into the night.

For a while, I joined Big Mick and Dave, just walking up and down the compound in the moonlight. After so many years of only being out in daylight, it was quite a novelty to be enfolded by the darkness. We had experienced so many bad things in broad daylight that the dark held no fears for us. If nothing else, it was a place to hide. Albeit temporarily.

About 20 fellas had climbed on to the roof of the tin shop. There was always the possibility that the screws would come in under cover of the darkness, so this was an easy position to defend. Not much could be seen through the velvet blackness, but it would be the same for both sides. All we on the ground could see on top of the tin shop were bulky shapes, silhouetted against the night sky.

Somebody suggested that we build a fire. It seemed the obvious thing to do to keep warm. There was an abundant supply of wood around the buildings. Nothing substantial or more than a couple of feet long, but the general detritus of petty repair jobs.

Several of us set about gathering armfuls and stacking the wood in an ever-growing pile. One old boy seemed particularly taken with the idea. He scurried about enthusiastically, chuckling all the while.

Dick was in his 60s, but was still strongly built, with a massive bony jaw and totally bald head. He was simple, cheerful and mostly harmless. However, he had an uncontrollable passion for setting things on fire. A country man, he had worked his way up through sheds and small barns, graduating to cottages and, finally, houses. For these last conflagrations, they had given him life. If the governor could have seen Dick rushing about in the darkness in pursuit of arson, the odds against him ever being released would have lengthened considerably.

The fellas up on the roof had mostly settled down for the night, huddling in nooks and gulleys. Suddenly, there was a burst of dazzling brightness as the summer-dried wood of the bonfire roared into flame.

A cheer went up all around the fire. Fellas started shouting across from the roof. Some scrambled down to get to the warmth. Eventually, we all slept fitfully. We had to get as much rest as we could. Tomorrow – or was it today now? (None of us had a watch.) – could be a hard day.

The last thing many of us remembered was Dick's shadowy figure rushing back and forth to the fire, ever replenishing the pile of wood stacked by its side.

The brilliant brightness of the morning couldn't mask the early chill. We woke up stiff, cold and hungry, but most of all hungry. Some fellas were already up and moving. Going to the khazi in the tin shop, drinking from the water tap outside or just walking about, flapping their arms to keep warm.

Fellas called out to each other. The discomfort of sleeping rough was quickly replaced by the exhilaration of still being free. Not free of the prison admittedly, but free of the narrow confines of a cell.

'Well, are we ready for them today?' called one of the Jocks rousingly.

'Let them fucking come,' growled one of the Scouses in reply.

It might be early, but there was nothing the matter with our spirit.

I stood up and stretched my legs, looking around the compound as I did. It had been untidy before. Now, with bits of wood broken off buildings and branches snapped off bushes, it was devastated. The compound always looked like a building site, but now it was starting to resemble a demolition site.

Among all this disorder, there was one well-tended area that stood out. Over to the side, between two small concrete paint stores, lay a group of four garden plots.

Any two cons could apply for a garden plot, and they would be given one of these to look after. It wasn't much of a coup. The soil was dry and barren. Long, taffy grass grew everywhere. Three of the four plots lay untended and overgrown.

The fourth, though, was a well-ordered undertaking with neat lines of shoots thrusting through well-watered soil. There were short stakes with twine strung between them and the earth had been tilled into long, straight rows. It was an oasis of fecundity in a sea of sterility.

'Whose fucking garden is that?' I shouted out.

Fellas looked over to where I was pointing.

'It's Nijam and his boyfriend's,' someone replied.

I knew Nijam Hussain. I had been on remand at the same time as he and his brother Arthur. They had kidnapped and murdered a newspaper executive's wife. It was said that they had fed her body to the pigs.

Arthur was the devious, driven one. Nijam had been only 19 and easily led. He had had a hard time in jail, where he came across as juvenile and weak. He and his mate were always reluctant to get involved in any sort of rebelliousness against the screws. Sure enough, they were nowhere to be seen on our sit-down.

'Well, if they ain't out here, then they're no fucking good.' I said. 'So I don't feel bad about robbing their garden. Anyone know what the different things are?'

I walked towards the plot. A couple of the Paddies walked with me. 'Here's potatoes and carrots. There's peas and onions there. Over here there's lettuces and some small marrows,' said one.

'OK, so let's pull them all up,' I continued. 'We'll wash them under the tap and peel them. If someone can find a large container, we'll boil them up and make vegetable broth.'

We set about harvesting the vegetables. We trampled through the twine and canes, tearing anything green from the soil. A couple of others joined in and soon we had a sizeable pile of mixed veg.

One of the Jocks had climbed into the tin shop and found a massive metal cooking pot with a broken handle. It was quickly washed, filled with water and set on the embers of the fire. Also from the shop came a score or so of old cups that belonged to the various tea-boats. They, too, were washed and set by the fire.

The vegetables were peeled and thrown in the pot. A long metal ladle appeared from somewhere and was used to stir the ingredients vigorously. Soon the pot was bubbling away merrily. Sharp appetites were set on edge by the aroma. Cold hands longed to clutch a hot cup of broth. Cold and empty bellies yearned for a warm meal.

After what seemed like an age, the pot was lifted from the fire. The steaming contents were ladled into the long line of waiting cups. Since there were nowhere near enough of these to go round, we ate in shifts, the first shift burning their lips so as to finish quickly and not prolong their comrades' wait.

By 8.00, the sun was up and blazing. It was going to be a long, scorchingly hot day. Men were already wrapping bits of wet cloth around their heads and faces to protect skin that was unused to so much sun and fresh air.

By 9.00, we were besieged by flies and every other insect that could crawl, hop or fly. We regularly doused our heads under the tap now, but it was a very sticky, uncomfortable morning.

One of the fellas had brought his radio out with him, so we were able to hear a mention of our sit-down on the local radio. It might not have been apparent from where we were standing, but the eyes of the county, if not the country, were upon us.

The compound was overlooked by a hill which carried a public road. We could see the tops of cars going past, about 500 yards away. Suddenly, a coach pulled up close to a hedge and a couple of dozen holiday-makers got out. They immediately started to wave to us. Heartened by this spontaneous show of public support, we waved back.

We were all well aware of the thoroughly devious nature of the prison authorities. They weren't averse to blatantly lying when it suited their purpose. To discredit us, they were quite capable of announcing that our protest was over something quite different and unreasonable. I decided to state our grievance clearly and unambiguously.

Malcolm Simpson was a young fella who, although serving his first sentence, had been sent to Parkhurst for his rebelliousness. He was well mannered, highly intelligent and ferociously committed. He hated the system and all it stood for. A political activist before it became fashionable, he described himself as a libertarian. He would never have dreamed of committing such a capitalist crime as robbery, and his gentle, easygoing nature prevented him from committing unprovoked acts of violence. However, this hadn't prevented him from bombing his local town hall.

In the England of the early Seventies, Malcolm was way before his time. At only 19, he had been sentenced to ten years. He was now well on his way to losing all his remission through fighting the screws and taking part in various protests.

His finest quality was his loyalty. If Malcolm said he was with you, then he would remain right to the last. Most of the London crowd thought him a bit naive when dealing with the realities of getting by in a working-class milieu. We had a simpler solution than revolution: we stole to beat the system.

For what I had in mind, Malcolm was ideal.

I climbed into the paint shop and went into the rifled store. There were pots of paint and several brushes on a shelf. I took a large pot of black paint and a wide brush.

I went into the recess and took the roller-towel from its rack. I climbed back outside with the lot and handed the roller-towel to Malcolm. Together, we climbed to the top of the tin-shop roof.

The side of the roof facing the road was a full 100 feet long by 25 high. The pitch was less than gentle, but not precipitous. Its colouring was a convenient shade of off-white, ensuring that the black paint would stand out in stark relief.

In my right hand, I had the open tin with the brush inside. Around the left, I wound the end of the roller-towel. Malcolm was holding the other end. He sat across the ridge, with his feet braced against the roof. He leaned backwards as he lowered me down. I knew that he would let himself fall before he would let me go.

The fall wouldn't have killed me. But the 25-foot roll down the roof, followed by the 12-foot drop to the ground would have done me no good at all. It wasn't merely the prospect of rolling on the ground covered with black paint that bothered me. Should I break something, which was quite likely, I would have to leave the protest and trust myself to the tender mercies of the waiting screws. Clearly, I couldn't afford to fall.

I knelt against the sloping roof. Precariously balancing the paint pot between my knee and the slope, I painted a big black 'P'. Malcolm swung me across for the next letter. Twenty minutes later, the legend 'PAROLE IS A FARCE' screamed out at passers-by. We climbed down to join the others.

By now, a lot of fellas felt that we had made our point. We had publicised our protest and shown solidarity with Albany. We couldn't hold out indefinitely. For a start, we had no food and, if we did force the screws to come in and get us, many of us would be badly beaten, with criminal charges to follow.

We decided to call a meeting. With all 70 of us sitting in a large sprawling circle, men voiced their opinions.

There were quite a few fellas who had only a couple of years to do. Mick said that it would be a liberty to drag them into a riot unnecessarily. The screws would make sure that they would be the ones to get more bird on top. Extra bird was insignificant to men who weren't getting out for a very long time.

Mick thought we had made our point. So did I, for that matter. We had kept the screws out of their beds all night, had an interesting time and could feel rightly proud that we had made a stand.

The vast majority of opinion was with Mick. There was one lone nutter, though, a man more fool than rogue. Mossy was only doing a five. To his credit, he had had a row with the screws at Wandsworth and got a terrible beating for his trouble, so he wasn't a complete poser. 'I think we should stay out indefinitely,' he said.

Perhaps he meant it. Maybe he had a death wish. But his opinion had to be considered.

I had been sitting quietly, listening to the arguments. 'Listen, Mossy,' I interjected, 'what you want to remember is that there are men here who won't be able to walk in and leave you on your own. They'll stay out here and get their heads kicked in, not because they believe in your cause, but because they won't leave you to fight the screws alone. So try to be a bit fucking responsible, eh?'

That seemed to shut Mossy up and we got down to discussing what we would demand in return for coming in peacefully. We wouldn't be able to demand too much, but a bath, some clean kit and a hot meal shouldn't strain their generosity too much.

We shouted across to the gate for them to send someone over to talk. Within five minutes, the gate opened and the deputy governor, the chief and the security PO walked towards us.

The fellas had asked Mick and myself to negotiate for them. It was a scene straight out of *High Noon* as we advanced across the pitch for a rendezvous in the centre circle.

Just as I was beginning to feel slightly silly, there was the sound of running feet behind us. The 'Manchester Yank' appeared alongside, panting heavily. No one had asked him to come along. He was widely regarded as a complete berk.

A tallish, rangy fella in his late 20s, his unfashionably shaven head gave him a menacing look. Unfortunately for him, all he had was the look.

He said he was a Yank from the Bronx. He certainly talked in what even we could tell was an exaggerated American accent. Every now and again, though, the flat sounds of Manchester would come through. When he had finally confessed that he had been born in Manchester, that settled it as far as we were concerned. We were all convinced that he had only been to the Bronx on holiday. Consequently, we always called him the 'Manchester Yank'.

A couple of months previously, he'd had a row with a fella while playing football. As he had run off at the mouth, the fella had butted his front teeth in. Afterwards, he strode about all menace and macho, but with a gaping hole where five front teeth had been. Any credibility he'd ever had had vanished with his teeth.

The six of us met within the centre circle, as symbolically neutral territory as we were likely to find.

'When are you coming in?' asked the Dep with absolutely no preliminaries.

'That depends on you,' said Mick, just as quickly.

'What do you want?'

'A bath, a change of kit, a hot meal and a guarantee that there will be no stick after we come in,' I broke in.

'You can have all that. I give you my word,' the Dep said immediately.

'It's ten o'clock now. We'll come in at noon,' said Mick.

It was all over. Both sides were relieved that there had been no sticking points. We nodded briefly and turned to leave.

'And no fucking funny business or your screws will get hurt,' shouted the Manchester Yank aggressively.

This was completely out of place. It could easily have provoked the sort of response that could have escalated into a tear-up.

'Shut up,' said Mick with genuine anger. He didn't suffer fools at all, especially in dangerous situations such as this.

The Manchester Yank instantly got the message and fell silent. He walked back with us, eyes downcast, a crestfallen look on his face. We returned to the circle of fellas and told them what the Dep had said. There was general agreement that we had got as much as we could expect.

As noon approached, we saw the gate at the far end of the compound open and about 20 screws step just inside. They split into two ranks to form a gauntlet. In the gateway stood two more screws, blocking the exit. Behind them, we could see even more screws.

The first con walked towards the gate. He entered the gauntlet, but had to stop when he reached the two screws standing in the gateway. One of them rubbed him down thoroughly to make sure he didn't have anything hidden on him. They were well aware that we had broken into the shop store and had armed ourselves with the tools. Soon, more cons were funnelling down the gauntlet to be rubbed down, two at a time. Once through the gate, each man was led away by two screws towards the bath-house.

This was an old one-storey building about 70 yards from the compound gate. It had rows of baths and showers either side of a central gangway. As each man went in, a screw handed him a towel, soap and whatever clean kit he wanted.

The capacity of the bath-house being only about 40, it was soon full. Back at the compound, the screws stopped letting men through, leaving them to mill around inside for half an hour until the bath-house cleared. Then the second and final batch was allowed through.

Any reservations we had about coming in were quickly dispelled. The screws weren't going out of their way to be pleasant, but there was no abuse or provocation either. Neither side wanted it to end in a tear-up now.

The hot, soapy water quickly relaxed our aching bodies. It soothed skin burned by overexposure to too much sun and wind. It eased limbs stiff from a night sleeping rough.

We slipped into clean, fresh clothes, discarding the sweaty, begrimed ones we had been wearing. It was a cleaner, more relaxed body of men that emerged from the bath-house.

Each of the three wings had set up their hot-plates to receive their men. There were trays of steaming food, with lines of screws waiting silently to serve it. Apart from them, the wings were deserted. All those who hadn't been out on the protest had already been fed and locked away.

The meal was above average in quality and the portions were generous. After collecting his meal, each man was led away to his own cell and banged up.

After the euphoria of being free for a day, returning to our cells was a distinct anticlimax. As each of us sat eating alone, we realised that we had plenty more of this to come. We had had our fun; now the piper would have to be paid.

The hot bath and large meal had an instant soporific effect on me. I undressed, climbed into bed and instantly fell asleep.

I was wakened by the sound of tea being served. I could hear the clatter of men going up and down the steel staircase and the hubbub of their voices.

Suddenly, my spy-hole cover swung open, then darkened as a face pressed against it.

'Are you OK, Norm?' asked a voice I immediately recognised as Barry's.

'Yeah, I'm fine,' I replied, hurrying to my door.

'I can't stay long,' he continued. 'There are dozens of screws all over the place. I'm going now I've got your address. I'll be in touch if you're moved. Take care, Norm.' With that, he was gone, leaving the spy-hole cover swinging.

As the sound of doors banging and feet hurrying about the landings died away, my door was opened.

'Slop out and collect your tea,' said the screw standing there.

I went straight to the hot-plate to get my meal. There were dozens of screws standing all around the ones. I saw Jeff and a couple of others getting water from the recess. It seemed that the screws were letting us out only four at a time.

The hot-plate screws put the food on my tray as I passed. Not a word was spoken. I filled my mug with tea from a nearby urn and went back to my cell, slamming the door behind me. Clearly, us protesters weren't going to be allowed much freedom.

I settled down for a long boring evening. I took some of my Open University books out and started to study. What a life-saver my degree course was. Soon I was lost in the world of 16th-century Florence.

Dimly, in the background, I could hear the sound of radios. The thick Parkhurst walls muffled all but the loudest of noises. The wing was unusually quiet. There would be no association for anyone this evening, the innocent being punished with the guilty.

Just after 8.00, my door opened. There stood Nut-Nut, with a couple of screws hovering in the background. He had a trolley with a tea urn and a tray of buns on it.

'Do you want some tea and a supper bun, Norm?' asked Nut-Nut, smiling broadly.

I wasn't in a smiling mood, but I held out my cup to be filled from the urn. Then he handed me a bun that would have been a roll other than for a few currants embedded in its surface. I shut my door on the last human contact I would have that night.

31 THE CHOKEY

The following morning, the same performance was repeated for breakfast. The rest of the wing were slopped out and fed first, then we were led out four at a time.

There was still no hostility from the screws. Our protest was over. It had ended peacefully, so no violence was expected now. I slopped out, collected my breakfast and banged my door behind me.

When the screws returned from breakfast, they unlocked the rest of the wing. Once again, landings rang to the thunder of working boots and the shouts of men as they called to each other across the wing.

I heard a gate slam back against a wall and a booming shout of 'Down for labour!' They were letting the rest of the fellas go to work. They were trying to get the jail back to normal as soon as possible.

The wing grew quiet again as the last of the fellas left. Then there was the sound of more doors being unlocked. My door swung open.

'Slop out,' said the screw, 'then make your way to "B" wing

for adjudication.' With that, he walked off to open the next cell.

I had already tidied my cell and packed most of my kit into the large boxes I kept under my bed. There was a good chance that I would be transferred now. They usually got rid of the supposed ringleaders.

I emptied my pot in the recess, put my breakfast tray out and picked up a thick book that I had always meant to read when I had the time. I'd have plenty of time to read it in the chokey.

There were about two dozen other fellas slopping out. All of them had been involved in the sit-down. We gathered on the ones, laughing and joking. Much of the high spirits was contrived, though. After the heady excitement of being free on the compound, there was an underlying sense of defeat: the screws were in complete control again.

Big Mick came strolling along, smiling broadly. It was a brittle humour shielding his barely concealed anger. But he wasn't going to let the screws see him looking miserable. We greeted each other, then walked out the gate together and along the corridor to 'B' wing.

Soon, the two dozen from our wing were standing on the ones of 'B' wing. There were no other cons about. Those who weren't out at work had been locked away. But there must have been 40 screws, all standing quietly against the walls.

There was a wait of about ten minutes, then a name was called. Tom, a pal of ours, walked towards the open gate that led into the chokey. As he disappeared from view, we could all imagine his feelings. The claustrophobia as the gloom of the dungeon-like landing enfolded him. The low ceiling, the dim lighting shielded by metal grilles and the parallel lines of cells with their vaulted arches above. He would pass the office on the left, opposite the recess. The door would be open at the far end of the landing, but the gate locked. Daylight would stream in, but reach only a short way until it was smothered by the gloom, making the chokey seem all the more subterranean. And his heart would sink a bit more.

Apart from being physically foreboding, Parkhurst chokey had a formidable reputation. This was where the heavy mob of screw bullies had regularly beaten up men before the riot. There was no organised brutality now but, if you played up, you could expect a kicking and a night in the strip cells. And, if you continued to be violent, there was always F2 landing in the hospital. There you could be beaten, drugged and left for days in a strait-jacket, with the ever-present threat of certification and a move to Rampton or Broadmoor hanging over you.

If only a fraction of the stories that were told about those two places were true, there really was hell on earth.

A couple more fellas went through the doorway. Then my name was called and I walked forward.

Just inside, two big screws were waiting. They formed up on either side of me and escorted me along the landing.

About three-quarters of the way down, a door was open. We paused outside while one of the screws rubbed me down thoroughly. He flicked through the pages of my book to see that nothing was hidden there. His main concern was for some kind of weapon. It wasn't unknown for someone to try to attack the governor on an adjudication.

I was ushered through the open door to be met by two more screws, even bigger than the first two. 'Prisoner, stand on the mat, face the governor and give your name and number,' said one.

They kept in front of me as I entered the cell. The adjudication room was just two cells knocked into one, but there was a unique feature: all along where the communal wall had once been was a row of thick steel bars stretching from floor to ceiling. It was like the frontage to some lion's cage. And there, on the other side, sat the lion.

The sedentary crouching didn't disguise his air of menace. The Dep was well known for his lack of feeling. He was no mere administrative wimp, either. A burly ex-rugby player of about 35, he had also trained in karate.

He wasn't particularly brave, but in a one-to-one encounter he could be quite a handful. He also had some style. He would stroll about all over the jail accompanied by the chief, looking for all the world like Edward G Robinson playing the part of a prison governor.

I stopped on the mat and faced him. '083395 Parker, guvnor,' I said, speaking over the shoulders of the two screws who stood between me and the bars. They were playing it a bit strong. What did they think, that I could prise the bars apart and get through? More likely it was to prevent my jumping forward and spitting at the Dep.

He read out the charges quickly, then nodded to the chief who was standing on his left.

'How do you plead?' asked the chief, stepping forward.

My guilty plea came as no surprise to anyone. I could hardly deny being on the sit-down. As for anything else, they would find me guilty anyway, whatever my evidence. And I was damned if I was going to beg for mercy. Cruel, cowardly bastards, I despised rather than hated them. They wouldn't get any weakness out of me.

'Fourteen days' cellular confinement and 14 days' loss of pay,' said the Dep without further ado.

'Prisoner, about turn!' shouted the chief.

I turned and the two screws marched me out of the adjudication room.

We went a short distance along the landing to a cell. They ushered me in, then banged the door shut behind me.

I stood and surveyed what was to be my home for at least the next two weeks. The cell was about eight feet wide by ten feet long. Three of the four walls were painted brick, dull beige in colour, aged and peeling in places. The outside wall had been rendered and strengthened, and was all of three feet thick. It had been sprayed with a smooth grey fleck.

A small window was set in a sloping reveal, high up the wall.

The steel framework held a dozen small panes of thick glass, begrimed and spotted with paint. Two of them could be slid sideways, revealing two openings through which fresh air could enter. Beyond the steel-framed windows, three thick steel bars ran horizontally across, their ends embedded deep in the brickwork. In consequence, it was a window in name only. Light and air seemed to struggle to penetrate its massive defences.

The two side walls were bare and totally featureless. The inner wall had a heavy steel-clad door and frame set into it. Towards the top of the door was a glass spy-hole, shielded on the outside by a metal cover that could be swung aside to allow the screw to look in. For surreptitious observation, there was a small hole drilled in the middle of the cover.

To the right of the door, at head height, a bell-push was set in the wall. This was to be rung only in emergencies. Yet the screws invariably took so long to answer that any true emergency was liable to prove fatal. Above the bell was a hot-air vent.

The ceiling was arched and slightly vaulted, the bare brick painted a dull white. In the middle was a light, its metal housing and grilled glass allowing only a modicum of brightness to suffuse the cell. At night, you had to strain to read by it. It could be turned on and off only from the outside.

The floor was black-painted concrete. Its cold, unyielding surface gleamed dully in the half-light, perfect counterpoint to the dull whiteness of the ceiling. Between the heaven and hell of these two morbid architectural extremes lay only featureless walls.

If the cell's decoration was minimal, the furnishings were decidedly sparse. A heavy metal bed lay tilted against the wall. There were no springs, just crossed slats of black-painted metal. It would be far more comfortable to lie on the floor than on the bare slats.

The bed stood hardly a foot high, so that, when you lay on it, it felt as if you were sleeping on the floor. But this bed wouldn't be used for sleeping for a while yet. There were no sheets, blankets, pillowcase or pillow. For a man on punishment, these were removed at breakfast-time and weren't returned until after tea. The authorities weren't going to allow me the luxury of lying in bed all day.

Against another wall stood a small wooden table with flimsy legs. Next to it was a wooden chair of similarly fragile construction. In one corner of the cell lay a large plastic washing bowl. Inside was a small square of silvered metal which passed for a shaving mirror. Clustered around it was a partly used bar of White Windsor soap, a shaving brush, a stub of shaving soap and a toothbrush.

Next to the bowl stood a gallon water jug made out of white plastic, scratched and grimy. Beside it was a blue plastic mug, containing a plastic knife, fork and spoon. A plastic chamber pot squatted a few feet away. It was dust-covered, with ominous yellow discoloration showing through the semi-opaque, off-white material. I walked over to it and gingerly lifted the lid. Thankfully, it was empty, but its sides were encrusted with a yellow scale. I resolved to scald it out with hot water as soon as I could get to the recess.

Replacing the lid, I surveyed my domain. It didn't amount to a lot. There was little comfort and negligible stimulation. I was going to be very bored. I was immediately grateful for the thick book I was still carrying.

I was aware of a sinking sensation in my stomach as my mind came to grips with the prospect of 14 days in solitary. I was already bored. There would be nothing to do in here, nothing to make sense of my day. No company, no one to put on any kind of front for. This would be a dangerous deprivation, for in the absence of others there is no such thing as self. Loneliness would erode the personality as surely as water eroded stone. I felt a rising tide of panic. It was a familiar feeling in the first few minutes of solitary. What if I couldn't handle it? What if it cracked me up? Others had taken a way out through madness or suicide.

A hot surge of anger put paid to these negative feelings. I would survive this. It was only 14 days. I had done far longer in solitary before. The time would pass. It was just a question of settling in and working out some sort of daily routine for myself, however minimal.

Suddenly I heard the muffled voice of Big Mick calling my name. He was somewhere just outside my door.

'Over here, Mick,' I shouted through the crack between door and jamb.

The booming voice sounded close now. 'I'm on my way, Norm. They're slinging me out and fucking good job, too. I don't know where I'm going, but I'll be in touch. Take care of yourself.'

I shouted back a quick 'Good luck, Mick,' and then he was gone. I immediately felt the loss. Mick was a tower of strength, a rallying point. He was a strong ally in any jail.

I sat down in the chair, my book in front of me on the table. I tried to lose myself in reading, but, within ten minutes, the unyielding hardness of the chair became a persistent distraction. In the background, I could hear the slamming of the occasional door as others began their chokey. It wasn't much of a consolation, but at least I wasn't completely alone.

Just before noon, I was unlocked for dinner, its arrival heralded by the familiar sounds of a dinner trolley being unloaded. The crashes and bangs of metal containers being slung on to the hot-plate were like gunshots.

I collected a plastic plate, bowl and some cutlery from a pile on a nearby table, got my meal and returned to my cell.

There were several screws standing about, but nothing was said to me and there was no overt hostility. I didn't stare, just ran my eyes over them quickly, familiarising myself with their faces for future reference. These were the enemy's frontline troops, at the cutting edge between con and institution.

I couldn't help noticing one particularly big screw. He stood all of six foot five and weighed in at about 16 stone. Unlike most screws, he was both muscular and athletic. He was in his late 20s, but had a much more youthful face. From the white shirt he was wearing, I could tell he was an SO. He seemed young for such a rank, especially in the chokey at Parkhurst which was no easy sinecure. This strapping giant looked like he could handle himself, though. And, from the confident, almost arrogant way he carried himself, you could see that he wasn't intimidated at all.

Suddenly, his name came to me: Allsop. He had a reputation for giving out a bit of stick whenever it was off. He was a cruel man, but he also had courage, the quality that made the fellas hate him all the more. The vast majority of screws were easily cowed in a one-to-one situation, so they were despised rather than feared. In many ways, Allsop was like one of us – and therein lay the threat.

The other screws were typical of their kind. Whether late 20s or early 40s, a flabby chest rested on a fat gut, which counterbalanced an enormously fat arse. For them, happiness was pear-shaped.

Lazy men, their sedentary lifestyle and relatively high standard of living quickly translated into a major weight problem. They were reminiscent of prize porkers fattened up for a county show. Small wonder that so many of them had heart attacks when running to alarm bells.

As far as human contact was concerned, I was better off in solitary. There would be no word of comfort from them, and none wanted for that matter. I banged my door behind me and sat down to eat my dinner.

As I ate, I could hear the muffled sounds of more doors opening and closing as others collected their dinners. Then there was the sound of several pairs of boots marching down the chokey; a babble of voices; the clang of the gate as it was shut behind them; then silence. The screws had gone for their dinner, leaving just one in the office. There would be no doors unlocked now, for any reason, until they came back.

Sitting there eating, I could hear voices outside my window. Two fellas were shouting to each other. Generally, sensible cons didn't converse out of windows. There was only a limited amount you could say without giving away some information to whoever else might be listening. And, if it wasn't something important, it could wait until another time. On normal location, where you were out for most of the day, only a very weak person would need someone to talk to over bang-up.

But, in the chokey, it was different. You were locked up on your own all the time. You didn't get the opportunity to talk to anyone. So, when it was quiet, fellas could have a sensible conversation out the window and pass an hour or two.

As I listened more carefully, I could distinguish the voice of old Dick, he of the inflammatory bent. It sounded as if he was directly above me. Then I heard the voice of the Manchester Yank coming from right next door to me.

'Oh, bollocks,' I said loudly and quite involuntarily. It was just my luck to have the Yank next door. You could bet your life that he'd make a mug out of himself. He'd either get a dig off the screws for being mouthy, then fold right up, or he would start whingeing. However long it took, I was sure that solitary would get to him. I would end up doing his chokey as well as my own.

I put my chair by the window, then stood on it. With my head level with the window, I could hear both of them quite clearly. As far as old Dick was concerned, a sensible conversation was out of the question. The Yank wasn't much better and he was brash and noisy to boot. Neither qualified as company. If I did ever hit a particularly low point and needed someone to talk to, neither of them would be much help.

Sure enough, the Yank was whingeing already. 'How the fuck can they justify 14 days down here, when I didn't do any more than all those doing 14 days in their own cells?' he whined with his Manchester-Bronx twang.

I realised that there must have been far too many punishments for them all to be lodged in the chokey. The majority of fellas had been lucky enough to serve it out in their own cells.

It was also unlikely that the chokey was full with protesters. They wouldn't want to concentrate too many of us in the same place. Although their strategy would be to split us up as much as possible, this did not include the ringleaders and those they thought were the hardcore. They would be isolated in the chokey to avoid any further trouble.

Suddenly, a voice cut into the conversation. It was Tom. A London robber in his early 20s, he was doing a 12 for a bank. He wasn't the most active or successful bank robber you would ever meet, but he was game and genuine, if a bit naive.

He was above me, to my left, probably next door to old Dick. I would be able to talk to Tom easily enough *and* have a sensible conversation.

'Hey, Tom,' I shouted. 'It's Norman.'

'Where are you, Norm?' he shouted back.

'Underneath old Dick,' I replied. 'What did you get?'

'Fourteen days down here,' said Tom. 'Alec's next door and John's downstairs but over on the other side.'

That was a piece of information I was interested to hear. Initially, I was pleased that I would have John's company, however fleeting, because we were close pals, but, when I thought about it, I was sad that he was down the chokey at all.

He was a strong man in many ways, very brave and staunch. He was also very highly strung. He had regular panic attacks and had to resort to the Valium. He needed the weekend hooch parties just to let go and relax. To stay sane, he had to be active and doing something. I knew that the long hours just lying on his own would soon get to him. I could read and work out. John would read fitfully and then ask for his medication, which he could have virtually on demand.

'How long did you get, Norm?' Tom's voice stirred me from my thoughts.

'Same as you, 14 days,' I replied.

'Hi, Norm,' shouted the Yank enthusiastically from next door, as if I'd accidentally forgotten to acknowledge him when I had spoken to Tom. 'Those mother-fuckers have got me down here for 14 days too,' he added as much in exasperation as in anger.

I inwardly winced as he butted into our conversation. I knew that I wouldn't be able to ignore him for two whole weeks, and I suppose I was trying to delay it for as long as possible. The last thing I wanted to do was to encourage him.

Before I could reply, the Yank shouted, 'Hey, why do you think they've got us down here, when all the others are up in their cells?'

'Because they haven't got the room down here for everyone and they think we're the ringleaders,' I shouted back, drawn against my will into conversation with him.

The Yank had already secretly suspected this. He just wanted his own worst fears confirmed.

'But what have I done that's different?' he called plaintively.

'Well, it couldn't have helped your walking to the middle of the football pitch with me and Mick and then giving the Dep a volley, could it?' My sarcasm had a touch of venom.

The Yank was beginning to realise that being a spokesman and leader wasn't all glory. 'What about old Dick then?' he shouted, as if pleading a case.

I wanted to tell him that I really didn't give a monkey's about why he thought he was down here, or the injustice of it. The plain fact was that he was down here and he had better come to terms with it as quickly as possible. But all I said was: 'They obviously saw old Dick enjoying himself with the fire. He burned everything he could get his hands on.'

'Well, I'm not standing for it,' shouted the Yank forcefully, the old bravado back in the act. 'I'll see the governor. I'll get in touch with the embassy,' he cried defiantly.

I nearly said that I didn't know that Manchester had an embassy, but thought better of it. Instead, I said, 'The governor won't do you any good. It was his man who put you down here in the first place. And, as for the embassy, you'll find they don't carry much weight here.'

He wasn't to be denied, though, and kept ranting on about what he was and wasn't going to do. If nothing else, it effectively ruined any further conversation between Tom and me.

'I'll speak to you later, Tom,' I shouted, and stepped down from the window.

I put the chair back by the table and sat down to read. The book was *The Occult* by Colin Wilson, a massive paperback. It was a fascinating, scholarly work, something that needed solid bouts of reading. It was just the sort of book for the chokey, provided that you had the intelligence to understand it. You could spend a couple of hours reading a chapter, then spend another couple wrestling with its philosophical implications.

Suddenly, there was the clash of keys and the sound of the chokey gate slamming back against the wall. Then there was the thunderous roar of several pairs of metal-tipped boots on the landing as the screws returned from dinner.

Along the landing, a cell was unlocked. After a pause, there was a sudden splash as someone emptied his pot into the slops sink, followed by the sound of running water. He was washing his pot out, filling his water jug, cleaning his plate and bowl. It was amazing how quickly you learned to distinguish each sound of life in the chokey. There was a short delay, then more splashing of water. The second trip was probably to empty a washing bowl or dustpan. The fella was lucky. In chokeys like the one at Wandsworth, you only got one trip to the recess. Washing bowl, jug, plate, pot and anything else had to be precariously balanced for the single journey.

More doors opened and closed. Then it was my turn.

'Slop out,' said the screw as he opened my door. It was purely ritual; I didn't have to be told.

I emptied my pot, filled my water jug and washed my plate and cutlery under the hot tap in the recess. Two trips were all I needed. I didn't rush, but I didn't deliberately dawdle either. There were other fellas waiting.

I went back and banged my door. The boredom had been broken by slopping out, but it was hardly an event. Now it was back to more of the same: reading, day-dreaming and dozing.

Twenty minutes passed and the chokey went quiet again. I could hear a couple of fellas talking out of their windows. I was wondering if we were going to get exercise on this first day, when my door was suddenly unlocked.

'Come to the office and check your kit,' said the screw.

The fact that they had removed all my kit from my cell on the wing indicated that I wasn't staying at Parkhurst. I was well pleased. I had detested the place from the start. However, there was no guarantee that I would be moved quickly, and sometimes, if you were due a lengthy stay in the chokey, they would bring all your kit down anyway. I followed the screw to the office. There on the table was a large grey, metal-framed cardboard box and a bundle of bedding. The screw took the lid off the box and we went through the contents. There were packets and jars containing tea, coffee, milk, sugar, jam and various other canteen stuff. There were toiletries, a couple of pairs of prison shorts, some socks and a pair of trainers. I was relieved to see my big black Hacker radio in one corner.

We opened the bundle of bedding together and inside was all my OU stuff, some other books, underpants, papers and pens. I was pleased to see the OU things. Not only would they provide me with something to do to pass the time, I had an exam due in a couple of months' time.

'You can have your soap, toothpaste and course books,' said the screw, 'but you can't have the rest while you're on punishment.'

I picked up everything I was allowed and returned to my cell. For a while, I had something interesting to do. I stacked the course books on the floor, against the wall. I flicked through some old assignments in a folder. I counted the sheets of clean foolscap in another folder. I tried out several pens. I had everything I needed to continue with the course.

Suddenly, there was a gruff, barking shout of 'Norman!' from outside my window I immediately recognised John's voice. I carried my chair to the window and stood on it.

As I peered through the small opening, I could see John's face looking up at me. He was in the first exercise yard, the one closest to the building. His face broke into a smile as he saw me.

'Hello, Norm. This is a lot of bollocks, ain't it?' he said, finishing with his usual hacking laugh. He was pleased to see me. It gave him a lift. Good friends were so important in situations like these. We provided moral support for each other.

'Are you OK, John?' I asked, reassured by the old familiar laugh.

'Not really. I can't find anything to do. I just keep pacing up and down.'

'Find yourself some books. They've got a library down here,' I advised.

'I tried that for a couple of hours, but, if I read for too long, it gives me a headache.'

We chatted about what news we had. Of our crowd, Big Mick had been shipped out, Tom and Alec were down the chokey with us and the rest were doing their punishment up on the wing.

Suddenly, a voice cut into our conversation. The Yank must have been dozing and had woken to hear John's voice outside. 'Hi, John,' he said, his exaggerated accent distorting John's name almost out of recognition.

His familiar tone surprised me. He certainly wasn't a pal of John's; in fact, he hardly knew him. He knew he was a face, though.

Like most of our crowd, John didn't suffer fools gladly, if at all. He didn't have to live next door to the Yank for the next two weeks either. His short, chilly reply – 'All right, mate' – was sufficient to inhibit even the Yank's ebullient personality. He didn't interrupt again.

When Tom called down to John seconds later, it was a different matter entirely. Tom was one of us and John liked him. Soon they were laughing and joking together.

Then Alec called out from further over to the left. Between them, he and Tom had plenty of news, having been talking out the window to the fellas above them. These were 'B'-wing cons who hadn't been involved in the trouble, and they gave us a direct line of communication into the main prison population. We now had a way of getting messages back and forth to our pals on 'D' wing.

John's exercise period was soon over. The half-hour had flown by. As he was leaving to go in, he stopped and said, 'What happens after the 14 days are up, Norm?'

'I was hoping you wouldn't ask that,' I replied. 'Things should have quietened down a bit by then. They won't want their block filled up with us indefinitely. But if there's still any tension, they'll keep some of us down here on 43.'

'Bollocks to that,' said John as the screw called him in.

The Yank was up at his window immediately. 'Hey, Norm,' he shouted urgently, 'what was that about Rule 43?'

I hadn't been thinking about the Yank next door. If anything was sure to galvanise him, it was the possibility of having to do more time in the chokey.

'It's only a possibility,' I replied. 'If they think there could be further trouble, they'll keep the ringleaders down here on Rule 43.'

'But I'm not a sex case and I haven't asked for protection, so how can they do that?' There was desperation in the Yank's voice now.

'I'm talking about "Good Order and Discipline" – you know, subversive 43,' I explained.

'And how long can they keep you down here on that?'

I let the Yank's question hang in the air. I wasn't trying to wind him up. I could handle the chokey, just about, but the Yank, he would struggle and I'd take no pleasure in watching him crack up.

He was a right berk, but at least he had made one with the rest of us. He would be another casualty of the system and the screws would be secretly pleased. The process of his cracking up would unnerve the rest of us, too. It was amazing how personal suffering made you empathise more keenly with another's. It wasn't impossible that it could be me that would crack up someday. By God's grace, I was strong at the moment. There was a steely bitterness born of hatred. There was a self-belief born of arrogance. But it might not always be so.

'They can keep you down here as long as they like,' I answered quickly.

There was a short pause, as if the awful truth was taking time to sink in.

'But that's ludicrous!' the Yank wailed.

Ludicrous, eh? Well, that was a word I hadn't expected him to use. 'Ludicrous it might be,' I said, 'but they can do it.'

There was a long silence. It was just the opportunity I needed. 'Speak to you later,' I shouted and climbed down from the window Hardly had I sat down at my table than the door opened.

'Exercise,' said the screw

I got up and walked unhurriedly to the door. I was longing to be free of the claustrophobic confines of my cell, but I didn't want to give the screw the satisfaction of seeing my eagerness.

I went along the landing towards the gate, then turned left along a narrow passage. Suddenly, I was through a door and out into the fresh air.

Immediately to my left was a wire gate, which led into what looked like a walled cage. This must have been the yard John had been in. In there now was a fella I didn't recognise, walking up and down. I was shown into an adjoining yard. As I walked in, the wire gate clanged shut behind me.

The exercise yard I was in was little more than a large cage, about 24 feet long by 12 wide. Its four walls were constructed of breeze-block, about eight feet high. Stretched across the top was a wire mesh. It would have been perfect for a chimpanzee. For a human, though, it was too small: 24 paces completed an entire circuit.

But the fresh air was sweet in my nostrils and the sky was bright and boundless through the mesh. Although my body was imprisoned, my spirit soared and expanded. It strengthened me and recharged my spiritual batteries. It was far, far better than being locked in my cell.

As quickly as John's exercise period had seemed to pass, mine seemed to go even faster. I had no watch, so I couldn't be sure, but it certainly didn't seem like half an hour.

All too soon I was back in my cell with the door banged shut behind me. The old familiar panic seized me involuntarily. The body knew it was unnatural to be confined like this. But there was no alternative for me. However much I disliked it, however much I couldn't handle it, I would stay locked up.

I quickly threw off my depression. The fresh air had cleared my head. It had also given me an appetite, and I was looking forward to tea.

I read for a while. I could hear the fellas talking outside the window, but I didn't get up and join in. Standing at the window, talking, could provide a welcome break, but after too many hours, the novelty wore off. I would save it for the long evenings when I would be locked in, uninterrupted, until the following morning.

The familiar crashes and bangs of metal containers being offloaded from the meal trolley disturbed my reading. Even the thick walls and metal doors couldn't do more than muffle the sharp sounds that reverberated around the chokey. In another setting, they might have been accompanied by the appetising smells of hot food. Here, though, the food was plain and overcooked, and whatever aroma there might have been had long since dissipated.

The sound of doors opening and closing could be heard again until, at last, mine opened. I went to the hot-plate and collected my tea, the last meal of the day.

Strangely, the trips outside my cell now became almost counterproductive. Instead of revelling in the stimulation of temporary freedom, my mind focused on the sharp feeling of loss when, once again, my door banged shut behind me. The exercise period had, in retrospect, been especially traumatic. The fresh air and open space had seemed only to emphasise the claustrophobic confinement of my cell. I didn't even contemplate refusing exercise, however. Despite the mental pain, the exhilaration of half an hour's comparative freedom had lifted my spirits.

The screws went off for their tea and the chokey fell silent again. I slowly ate my meal within my own private universe, thinking of the long evening to come.

I finished eating and returned to my studying. It was hard to concentrate though. The peace and solitude were there all right, but so was the underlying tension. As surely as water eroded the hardest stone, solitary living eroded the personality and the self-control that went with it. It hadn't reached the stage yet where I was consciously, physically fighting to control a rising sense of panic, but I was aware that it was there.

It inexorably gnawed at me and kept me as taut as a bow. Sharp sounds made me jump. Tension in my neck and shoulders translated into a low-level muzzy headache. Studying under these circumstances was like trying to read with a radio on full blast.

The screws returned from their tea and it was time to slop out again. Once more I went out, emptied whatever needed emptying and filled my water jug.

'Collect your bedding,' said a screw who was standing nearby. He pointed to a cell across the landing. I pushed the door open and walked in. Leaning against one wall were perhaps a dozen mattresses. Bereft of their usual white cotton covers, they were really no more than large rectangular pieces of foam. Against another wall was shelving holding pillows, pillowcases, sheets, towels, blankets and bedspreads.

'Take one mattress, one pillow, one pillowcase, two towels, two sheets, three blankets and one bedspread,' said the screw from behind me.

It took two journeys to get it all across the landing and into my cell. I slung the mattress on to the iron bedstead and stacked the rest on top.

'In the morning, after you slop out, put the mattress back where it came from and stack your pile of bedding somewhere on the shelves. Remember where you put them, then you'll get the same bedding back that night,' advised the screw.

I resolved to remember well. I could handle most deprivations, but I was scrupulous about personal hygiene. I didn't much fancy sleeping on someone else's dirty sheets.

As the door closed behind me, I knew that that was the last time I would leave my cell until the following morning. Yet it was only 6.00.

Outside the window, I could hear Tom calling to Alec. I climbed on to my chair and joined in the conversation. Talking bolstered our spirits. However, we realised it was all too little. As soon as we stepped down from our windows, the loneliness would be on us again, an insidious coldness that chilled the human spirit. Away from the warmth of human contact, one could only dwell on the unnatural state of loneliness. The voices of others seemed to sound further and further away as one retreated unwillingly into the ice palace of total isolation. And, of course, in the act of withdrawing, one advanced ever onwards towards that ultimate state of loneliness: complete madness.

Yes, the spirit could die, there was no doubt about that. And, afterwards, the soul would die, too. The will to live would slowly, inexorably wither away until the pain of living far outweighed the pleasure. Then death would become a welcome and merciful release. Almost an adventure, a last and final odyssey.

Although I was nowhere near that low state yet, I could comprehend it. Luckily, I was strong. A fierce arrogance fired my spirit, causing me to be contemptuous and dismissive of weakness in others. Those others would break long before I would. Yet that gave me no cause for comfort, because their breaking would diminish me also. All of us in the chokey were entwined in a complex web of support that was completely involuntary. Just souls in torment, giving each other sustenance as and when we could.

As we talked, suddenly a new voice joined in. The flat Northern tones of Leeds came from the cell to the left of me.

"Ello, lads, it's Harry. Any news of Geoff?'

Harry was a very strange lad. A short, stocky fella in his mid-20s, he was doing a five for a string of burglaries. He was totally lacking in charisma and most of the London crowd thought him a bit of a wally.

In this respect, he didn't help himself. Whereas many of the fellas had at least a pair of tailored jeans, a smart jumper or a decent pair of trainers, Harry was always scruffy from head to toe. It wasn't from neglect. Rather, he just didn't acknowledge the importance of style. He wore a baggy pair of bib-and-brace overalls spotted with paint, topped by an equally baggy and shapeless grey jumper. At its neck could be seen the crumpled collar of a prison shirt. A battered and scuffed pair of prison shoes encased his feet. His haircut was the sort you would get on reception to one of the big local nicks if you weren't careful. Unfashionably short at the back, it gave way to long, fairish strands that constantly fell across his eyes. A round-framed pair of National Health glasses completed the naff look.

Yet underneath this unimposing exterior was a lively mind, a strong sense of decency and a steely determination. You might not want Harry at your party, but, if there was going to be any trouble, he would be excellent company.

Not that he was violent, but, if he believed in the rightness of your cause, he would stand with you. And, if he stood, he wouldn't back down. Never mind the household names; the success or failure of every prison protest depended to a great degree on the Harrys of this world.

'Hello, Harry,' I said. 'How are you?'

'A bit hungry,' he replied. 'I'm on hunger strike.'

'What's that for?'

'Well, I got 14 days like the rest of you, but I thought I might as well put a bit of pressure on them as well.'

He said this with no sense of drama, but as if what he was undertaking was something quite trivial and commonplace. The difference between him and the Manchester Yank was immeasurable. If Harry said he was going through with it, you could be sure he would.

'I'll give them a couple of days, then I'll refuse water as well. That'll worry them,' he added.

No doubt it would, I thought. Whereas you could last for weeks on a hunger strike, to go without water would bring a crisis within 48 hours. What was particularly dangerous about this strategy, though, was that, since the screws were so uncaring, they could well let it go too far before they did anything.

Some con dying because of deliberate self-neglect wouldn't bother them. The publicity and all the forms to fill in would be a terrible hassle, though. This was the only reason they would be liable to act.

Before I could reply to Harry, he said that Geoff had told him he was going on hunger strike, too.

Geoff – who we had got to circulate the idea of a national day of protest against the parole system – was also a bit of an eccentric, definitely not in the chaps mould. Doing five years for frauds he always swore he was innocent of, he revelled in any chance to challenge the authorities. He was completely non-violent, but possessed a store of inner strength not readily visible to the casual observer.

Although I admired Harry and Geoff's courage and determination, a hunger strike wasn't for me. I had already tried that route a couple of years earlier at Albany. It wasn't the discomfort that deterred me. I just tended towards a more active, violent approach. It got results more quickly. Also, Harry and Geoff were doing comparatively short sentences. They could afford to take a few chances with their health. Very soon they would be out, eating decent food and free from the heavy prison pressure.

I had to keep my strength up. The chokey and the screws would weaken me enough without my deliberately adding to the burden. I still had a long way to go, at least another ten years. This was just one minor battle in what would be a very long and arduous campaign. If I took to starving myself on anything like a regular basis, my health would deteriorate very quickly.

However, with both Harry and Geoff on hunger strike, our collective bargaining position was strengthened considerably. The last thing we wanted was for the situation to go off the boil. If any degree of normality returned, we could well be in for a long spell in the chokey.

Alec and Tom would keep us informed of what was happening up on the wings, from their contact with the 'B'-wing fellas above them. And, from what they were saying, nothing was going on. The other punishments were locked in their cells, but all the rest of the cons who hadn't taken part were wandering about as normal. If they hadn't joined us in the first place, we could hardly expect them to take the initiative now.

The one heartening piece of news was that someone had heard on the radio that there had been questions about our sit-down in the House, and it was said that the Home Secretary was going to make a statement. Albany and several other jails were still on the roof. So, although we felt isolated in the chokey, we knew we weren't entirely forgotten.

From conversation out the window, it transpired that no one had seen Geoff go on exercise that afternoon. Both Tom and Alec had a clear view of the cages, so he could hardly have slipped by unnoticed. Harry hadn't been allowed to go on exercise because he was on hunger strike. From that, we knew for certain that Geoff must be on hunger strike, too.

I must have stood for a couple of hours, talking out the window and listening. The conversation was often banal. You could hardly have an intimate chat when you were shouting out a window. And, with the Manchester Yank constantly butting in, it was often difficult to have a conversation at all.

The Yank was suffering already. He hadn't been half a day in the chokey yet and he was whining about how bored he was. He said that he didn't think he could handle 14 days of this.

With mine being the closest cell, he would constantly ask my advice and, quite gratuitously, tell me all his troubles. Many a time I nearly gave him a volley. He would be out in a few years, while I had over a decade to do, and here was he, whining to me!

However, I knew he was struggling, and it wouldn't take too much out of me to give him a lift now and again. There was, after all, always the chance that he would top himself. He wouldn't be the first suicide in Parkhurst chokey. If that happened, it would be a heavy blow to the morale of us all, reawakening, as it would, those unanswered questions about our own mental states. Questions we constantly put to the back of our minds. So I would suffer the Yank, as much as I could.

Outside on the landing, I heard a door slam and the familiar squeal of the meal trolley. At this time of night, it could only be the supper bun and a cup of tea. It seemed as if we had been up at our windows for several hours, yet the tea trolley told us it was only 8.00.

Doors opened and closed, the sound of the tea trolley getting closer. My door opened and there was the chokey orderly. He was just another con, but you had to be careful of cons who worked in the chokey. The screws always chose those they trusted, which meant that we couldn't. Quite often it was one of the protection 43s who lived upstairs.

The orderly was an obsequious-looking individual, plump, in his late 20s, with constantly moving eyes. The screws could certainly pick them. He looked just the sort of fella you could never trust. He rang all my subliminal alarm bells.

'Tea, mate?' he asked, smiling at me weakly.

I walked to the door holding out my pint plastic mug. He filled it from a large silver urn set atop the trolley.

'Supper bun?' he asked, pointing to a tray of brownish lumps next to the urn.

I put my hand out and he gave me one.

'Goodnight,' he said, as the screw closed the door and slid the bolt home.

I hadn't acknowledged him except for a succession of grunts. I despised the bastard. He was one of the enemy and, given the least excuse, I'd chin him. But I wouldn't go out of my way to do it. There were too many sly ways he could get back at me. Fouling my food before I received it was one. It would be best to just remain anonymous as far as he was concerned.

The tea was awful, unsweetened and weak, and the brownish lump which was the supper bun really didn't bear closer inspection. I was hungry, though, so I ate and drank the lot. It would fill a hole for the night and allay the hunger pains that were already gnawing at me. There were 14 hours between tea and breakfast. As I finished, I couldn't help thinking that it would have been a feast for Harry and Geoff, who hadn't eaten all day.

I made up my bed, taking my time. I carefully folded sheets and blankets to produce the most comfortable lie in the circumstances. My bones were aching from being pressed up against the hard wood of the chair all day. There hadn't been too much pleasure during this particular day, so to undress, slip between clean sheets and lie comfortable and pain free was something to look forward to.

I called my goodnight out the window to the fellas still talking, and got into bed. As I stretched out, I luxuriated in a brief moment of comfort. Moments such as these were all the pleasure I could look forward to.

It was still only just after 8.00. The light wouldn't be turned off for over two hours yet. If I tried to sleep, it would disturb me and, if I did sleep, I would probably wake in the early hours of the morning and lie there in the dark, wide awake.

I picked up a course book and, once again, I was among the Borgias and Machiavelli. They would all have had trouble surviving in Parkhurst. However, after my experiences, I would have sailed through the treacherous times of 16th-century Italy.

I read for a long time. The chokey had grown very quiet. The fellas had stopped talking out their windows, and I could hear the measured tread of the night patrol as he went from cell to cell. A couple of paces, the sharp rattle of the lock and bolt being checked, the grating sound of the spy-hole cover swinging backwards and forwards, the click of the light switch, then more paces. It had its own rhythm. If you were lying in your cell awake, you could measure the approach of the bringer of darkness.

I welcomed his arrival. I became enfolded in the gloom, which blacked out the details of the hated cell that had tortured me all day. It heralded the coming of unconsciousness and escape from all the cares of the waking mind. Sleep was a merciful, if temporary, release. I dozed off.

I seemed to have been asleep for only a short while when the light suddenly came on. It was amazing how you never anticipated the arrival of the bringer of light. He was never welcome in the chokey. Apart from eyes squinting in the sudden glare, there was the immediate realisation that another day of pain was just beginning.

It was an effort to get out of bed and start my ablutions, but my rage and arrogance served me well as I swung into the routine. At least, while you were doing something, you didn't have to endure the tedium of boredom.

After about 20 minutes, the screws came on. There was much banging of gates, jangling of keys, stamping of feet and whistling. It was almost like some military drill. In fact, many of the screws had been in the forces, and they liked to start the day with a bit of order and discipline.

Two screws came round to do the count. The bolt was drawn back with a bang. Numbers were shouted the length of the chokey. It went quiet while the SO phoned the numbers through and waited for the reply. Then the phone rang and the screws unlocked the first man for slopping out.

The second day passed identically to the first, except that there wasn't the excitement of the mass adjudication. The morning seemed to drag on interminably.

About an hour after breakfast, I did my workout. I had a cast-iron rule for survival. Wherever I was, whatever the occasion, I did my workout at 9.00 every Monday, Wednesday and Friday morning. It was the absolute core of my physical and mental discipline.

I did half an hour of running on the spot, then strict sit-ups and leg-raises in non-stop frantic rotation. It left me drenched with sweat and totally exhausted, but it fired up my spirit, strengthened my will and readied me for another day in prison.

I could hear the Manchester Yank knocking on the wall, but I ignored him. Once started, I wouldn't stop for anything. Part of the discipline was not accepting any excuse for a rest.

I finished and, kneeling astride my washing bowl, washed my body down with astringently cold water. The Yank chose this moment to knock again. I continued to ignore him.

When I had dressed, I got up at my window and yelled out, 'What?'

I could hear the Yank scrambling to get on his chair. 'What were you doing, Norm?' The nasal drawl had changed into an almost perpetual whine, now tinged with concern. I couldn't believe this fella. He would have been able to hear the gentle thumps and grunts as I went through my workout. He hadn't heard my door open, and there had been no screams or angry shouts, as there would have been if the heavy mob had steamed in. What did he think I was doing? Fighting silently with some ghostly visitor?

'Working out,' I said with what I thought was commendable patience.

'That's a good idea,' he responded enthusiastically. 'I'm going to do that myself.'

'Good,' I encouraged, 'it will take out some of the tension, give you an appetite for the food and help you get a good night's sleep.'

The Yank didn't ask me for details of my workout, despite the fact that he knew I had been into fitness for years. His old know-it-all persona had temporarily asserted itself again.

I had seen him in the gym. He walked without posing, with his muscles tensed, but he really didn't have a clue. I anticipated that any workout he designed would be very unbalanced and of little use.

For about ten minutes, there was a succession of bangs and crashes from next door. The air was rent with loud grunts of exertion and the explosive expelling of breath. The Yank was putting on quite a performance. If he was going to work out, he might as well let everybody know about it.

I didn't mind the disturbance at all. If nothing else, it kept him busy and away from me. He would sleep well tonight and, who knows, he might keep it up. Then he would be stronger in spirit and less in need of my psychiatric ministrations.

The noise stopped and there was silence for about ten minutes.

'Norm.' It was the Yank again.

'Yes,' came a sibilant hiss from me.

'I still feel very tense,' whined the Yank.

I considered several caustic replies before rejecting them. 'Well, read, write something, close your eyes and try to relax,' I cajoled. 'We're all bored and tense. It's just a question of handling it.' With that, I got down again.

Later in the morning, I heard John calling me from outside the window. He was in the first exercise yard again. I climbed on my chair. 'Norm,' he whispered, drawing as close as he could. 'We can't stand for this. I've had a word with some of the fellas and we're going to steam into the screws.'

Now this was a very desperate plan indeed. As we were only let out one at a time, it would mean each man steaming into the screws on his own. There were always six or seven screws on duty and they were all big lumps. You might get a few good digs in but, in the end, you would get a good kicking, a VC and more chokey.

It would be a very game thing to do. Not many men would have the nerve. I thought that I could strap up to do it if pushed, but I certainly didn't fancy it. And, as for finding several more to do likewise, I wouldn't count on it.

'Who have you got?' I asked.

'There's Tommy, Alec, old Dick, the Yank, Geoff, the chokey orderly and me,' whispered John.

I conceded that Tom and Alec were game enough to try, but the rest definitely weren't up to it. And, as for the orderly, I couldn't believe that John had even asked him. For a start, he was a protection 43. I couldn't see him making tea for the screws one minute, then attacking them the next. I guessed that John must be feeling pretty desperate. He had a lot of trouble with his nerves. Valium was his preferred medication. He was a long-standing member of the treatment queue. I had feared that his highly strung nature would bring him under pressure sooner or later. In many ways, he was a wild, brave, strong man, but he couldn't handle the pressure of solitary.

I felt deeply for him. He had become a good and loyal pal. But I couldn't do his chokey for him. His being on the other side of the block to me meant that I couldn't even shout to him occasionally to cheer him up.

'Why don't you have a word with Dr Cooper?' I suggested. 'He has called you up regularly, so, strictly speaking, you're his patient. Try to get a move into "C" wing for a while.'

'I ain't going in with those fucking nutters,' retorted John immediately.

'Well, the tear-up isn't on, John,' I said. 'Only a couple of those you mentioned will make one.'

'What are you going to do?' he asked me.

'Look, there's nothing we can do together, except a hunger strike and I'm not doing that. I think they are going to 43 me at the end of the 14 days. If so, there's something I'm thinking of doing, which I can only do on my own. I'm not going to commit myself right now, because then I'll have to do it regardless.'

I paused to let that sink in. There was a moment's silence, then John launched into a tirade. He was going to write to his MP, his brief, his family doctor and anyone else he could think of. By the time his exercise had finished, this was the course he was decided on.

My own plan was far more simple and direct. I knew from past experience that the Dep had to make his rounds each morning. At some stage, he would reach the chokey. Each door would be opened and the Dep would say 'Good morning' and ask each man if he was OK. It wasn't done out of concern; it was just a part of his daily duties. It was while on his rounds that the Dep was most vulnerable. He only had the chief with him, a big slow-moving man. The Dep also always came up close to whoever he was speaking to.

I resolved to return the Dep's 'Good morning' each day and be generally pleasant. I would lull him into a false sense of security. Then, if I was put on Rule 43, I'd put my plan into action.

As he came around one morning, I would say, 'Excuse me, guvnor, can I have a word with you?', smiling disarmingly as I stepped forward. Then, as he turned to face me, I would punch him in the face as hard as I could. If I could get in a few more digs, I would. I wasn't particularly out to hurt him, but it had to be a significant assault that would bring disciplinary charges.

I'd probably get roughed up a bit, but, strangely enough, in that respect I was probably safer attacking a governor than a screw. I would certainly be slung in a strip cell for a couple of days. On the subsequent VC, I would be sentenced to more solitary, but the important thing and the whole object of the exercise was that I was certain to be transferred to another jail.

There was an unwritten rule that anyone who assaulted a governor had to be moved out. It was probably something to do with the fact that the Home Office didn't want to be seen to leave the offender at the mercy of his victim. Anyway, it was a hard-and-fast rule and one sure way of getting a transfer.

Later that morning, I heard the Dep coming round. There was the sound of doors opening, the chief's shout of 'Stand up for the governor!', a muttered greeting and the crash of the door slamming shut again.

The sounds grew closer. I was standing just inside my door. I wanted them to get used to my being up close to them. The door flew open. The chief shouted his order even though I was already standing, and the Dep stepped into the doorway.

'Morning, Parker. Everything OK?' he asked, standing square on to me, not the slightest bit intimidated. You had to hand it to him. He might stroll about like Edward G Robinson, but he had nerve.

Up close, he was a short, stocky, bullish man. His former rugby-playing activities, coupled with his karate training, would make him quite a handful in a punch-up.

There was an apocryphal tale of a well-known face who had run out of a chokey cell at Hull and punched the Dep flush on the chin. He had shaken his head and immediately punched him back, knocking him headlong back into his cell. He hadn't even nicked the fella for it. I didn't want that to happen to me. To be mugged off like that could ruin your reputation and make you a laughing stock. And, if the Dep didn't nick you and you weren't moved, you, like the fella at Hull, would have to stay and face it.

I resolved to hit the Dep flush on the side of the jaw with my best right hook. The secret would be to catch him unawares. I was sure that, so long as he didn't see it coming, I could deck him.

I began to practise the punch, standing with my legs apart and my hands raised as if in conversation. Then, quickly switching my weight from one foot to another and pivoting at the hip, I would whip my fist over in the tight arc of a right hook.

I repeated it over and over again, talking all the while. 'Now look here, guvnor.' *Crash.* 'Excuse me, guvnor.' *Bang.* Soon it all came together in one easy motion. All I had to do now was get it right on the day.

We went through the same old routine of exercise periods, talking out the window and slopping out. Whatever novelty value there had been on the first day had now long since gone. Everything was total boredom. The Yank was almost climbing the walls. All bluff and bravado had disappeared. Twenty times a day I reassured him that time would pass, that it would soon be over and he would be back on the wing.

It was all to no avail. He now spent most of his time up at the window, whining to whoever would listen. That morning, my ear pressed up against the crack in my door, I had listened as the Dep came to the Yank's cell on his morning rounds. His pleading and whingeing were pitiful. My pride would never have allowed me to do that, but the Yank was weak.

I didn't want to aggravate matters by having a go at him over it. To some extent, I was now living out the Yank's drama with him. He really did sound like he might kill himself. As the fella nearest and the only one to whom he could turn, I could hardly let him go ahead without, at least, trying to do something.

In the afternoon, they came and took Harry away. I heard his door open, some muffled conversation, then he was gone. We all assumed that they had taken him over to the hospital because of his hunger strike. It was for the best, really. If he was taken bad, he had more chance over there than here in the chokey.

On the third day, an event took place that reminded me that, although isolated in my concrete cocoon, I wasn't safe from harm. The outside world that I was increasingly rejecting could still intrude – and violently.

It was mid-evening and I had been standing on my chair talking out the window. Tom had been gently ribbing old Dick about the bonfire. Dick was chuckling excitedly as he relived moments that had been passionately exciting for him. Soon, he was shouting half-remembered details out the window, between roars of laughter. If anyone had ever suspected him of being halfway sane, his virtuoso performance as he rose through the octaves on his way to total loss of control would have convinced them otherwise.

I was standing there, laughing to myself, wearing only my underpants. Suddenly, the door burst open. I jumped down from the chair and turned around. Allsop was standing just inside the doorway with two other screws right behind him.

'Stop shouting out your window!' said Allsop aggressively. From a world of almost complete solitude, I was now in the middle of a very nasty situation. This was our first test of wills. Allsop knew all about me, knew of my reputation as one of the ringleaders. The outcome of this confrontation would determine whether I would be left alone for the duration of my stay. If I completely backed down, I could expect him to give me a hard time. Whenever I left my cell, he would be at me, chivvying me along and trying to humiliate me.

Yet it was a formidable challenge. Allsop himself was a giant. The two screws with him were squat, powerful men in their early 40s. Their coarse, corpulent faces had all the compassion you would expect of crocodiles. They were fully clothed and wearing steel-toed boots. I was virtually naked.

I walked halfway across the cell towards them, then stopped. Psychology was all-important here. If I had backed up against the wall, my fear could well have encouraged them to come forward. As it was, they weren't intimidated at all. The odds were too strongly in their favour for that. But my walking towards them had made them uneasy and not so totally in control of the situation.

'I know someone was shouting, guvnor, but it wasn't me,' I said, looking directly at Allsop.

He glared back. He wasn't willing to admit that he had made a mistake and he couldn't be sure that I wasn't lying. He couldn't just leave it like that, though. It would look like he was retreating.

'Well, if it is you, you'll spend the rest of the night in the strip cell,' he threatened.

I stood there, looking at him but saying nothing. I hadn't said anything to challenge him, so he could withdraw having made his point. There would be no loss of face for him. I had been threatened by him and seethed inwardly. But, standing there in my underpants, there wasn't too much I could do. I had stood my ground, though, and he hadn't humiliated me. I would have to settle for that.

Allsop and the two screws backed out, eyes fixed on me. The door slammed with a resounding crash. My heart was beating noticeably. It was a defeat of sorts but, in the circumstances, not much of one.

On the fourth morning, we had some good news. Tom shouted down that some of the 'B'-wing fellas above him had heard the Home Secretary on the radio saying that there was to be a review of the way parole operated. In future, it would be granted more widely.

We all shouted and cheered. We had actually achieved something. Our sacrifice wasn't in vain. We, and all the other protesters in the other jails, had changed the parole system. Enthused as we were, though, it still didn't alter our present situation. We knew there would be no amnesty for the protesters, irrespective of the rightness of their cause.

Day now followed day, in endless repetition. By the end of the week, it was difficult to pick out previous, individual days. They all seemed to run together in an uninterrupted succession of routine trivia.

I was aware that a strange shift had occurred in my mental outlook. Whereas, before, I had felt that I was a part of the world, increasingly I felt that the world was external to me. My cell was so totally and utterly familiar that it was almost as if it was an extension of myself. I could lie on my bed and allow my consciousness to expand to fill every cubic inch of space. This was my own personal universe and I felt as if I was plugged into the very fabric of its boundaries.

I grew to hate interruptions by the screws. Whenever they opened my door, the hatred would well up inside me. They were intruders into my private world and I was relieved when they went away again.

My hatred was also directed against the world in general, that world that had left me on my own to deal with the rigours of solitary. A basic self-preservation had taken over. By continuing to deny that I needed such things as comfort, company, stimulation, I had almost reached the state where I actually believed it. It was all a defensive mechanism to relieve the pain.

I wondered what lasting damage all this would do. To stand aloof from the world, cut off from all caring relationships, would create a cold, uncaring man. I pondered the irony of one prison psychiatrist labelling me a psychopath. Because, if a psychopath is someone who is unable to form meaningful relationships with others, then solitary confinement is just the process to develop psychopathy.

If, by this point, I was beginning to hurt, then the Yank had become like a whipped and broken cur. His personal struggle with loneliness was now a public event. He broadcast it out of his window like some melodramatic and repetitive TV soap. I cringed each time I heard it. There was pathos there, but each of us was wrestling with our own dire problems.

John was getting very strung out, too. His exercise sessions were intense and painful. He had written letters to literally dozens of people, but his situation hadn't changed one bit.

The thing that really bothered each and every one of us was the implied threat of Rule 43 after we had finished our 14 days. Seven days in the chokey can be a much-needed rest. I knew of lots of fellas who, when the pressure got too much, would deliberately get put in the chokey for a week.

Fourteen days' chokey was no great problem either. The second week would drag a bit and you would be glad when it was over, but it wouldn't kill you. With Rule 43, though, you had no target to aim for. You couldn't simply hold on for a specific length of time, because you didn't know how long you had to do. It could be a month, two months, six months, two years. Slowly, very slowly, the second week passed. The Yank didn't know whether to be elated that the 14 days were coming to an end or distraught at the thought that he might be 43'd.

Daily, in excruciating detail, he and I went through exactly what he had said to the Dep on the fateful day of the sit-down. The more he analysed it, the more sanitised it became. He was strongly of the opinion that to continue to isolate him as one of the ringleaders would be an outrageous liberty. I forbore to point out to him that the authorities took liberties all the time. But the Yank must have realised this anyway, hence his growing apprehension.

As much as I might have wished otherwise, I was aware that, with Big Mick gone, I would be thought of as the main ringleader. If anyone was going to be 43'd, it would be me.

Each day the Dep continued to come around. The number-one governor was a weaselly-looking individual. One half-decent shot would put him on the floor. Unfortunately, though, it was the Dep who invariably did the morning rounds. I continued to practise my conversation punch: 'Er, excuse me, guvnor.' *Crash.*

If anything, the Dep had taken to lingering that second or so longer at my door, probably to delay as long as possible his daily encounter with the Yank. There was no holding back for the latter now. His whingeing and pleading were quite unrestrained. There was a good chance that they would let him up to the wings just to get rid of him.

On the evening before the end of our 14 days, we were all up at our windows until quite late. The Yank actually sounded almost cheerful. It wasn't that he had been told anything – they never told you you were on 43 until the moment your punishment ended. It was more a case that he couldn't accept the awful prospect of limitless months of more solitary, so he dismissed it as a possibility.

I hoped for his sake that he was right. I was almost sure that I wouldn't be so lucky.

We eventually shouted out goodnights and climbed down from our windows. As I lay in bed, I thought how nice it would be to know that this was the last night I would spend in this cell. Back on the wing, I would still be in a cell, but there would be all the stimulation of the events that passed for social life in Parkhurst. I longed for all the work involved in running the book. I smiled to myself at the thought of the reunion in the 'Old Bailey', as all the fellas swapped their news. My body yearned for a good weights workout in the gym. There was bound to be some hooch down, so we would have a party at the weekend. Small stuff really, but infinitely more stimulating than lonely weeks in solitary.

The following morning, I woke with a sense of foreboding.

I slopped out and was fed in the same way as previous mornings. I had to put my bedding in the store, which could have been taken as a good sign. You were allowed your bedding all the time on 43 because, officially, it wasn't punishment. So it didn't make much sense to put it away at 9.00, if I was going to get it back later in the morning. However, logic had no place in Parkhurst. More likely, the governor hadn't told the screws what he intended yet.

Soon, there was the sound of the Dep coming on his rounds. I could imagine each of the fellas standing as I was, tensely awaiting his arrival. Just a few words from him could make so much difference. The Yank must have been pacing his floor like a maniac.

My door swung open and in walked the Dep. I was standing just inside and he came right up to me. You had to give it to him, he didn't hide behind the screws. And, if I had my way, this would be his downfall.

It wasn't grudging admiration that was running through my mind, though. Mentally, I dropped my right knee, rotated my hip and smashed my fist into the side of his face. My heart raced with nervous anticipation. I prayed I would get it right. A tap was no good at all; he wouldn't even nick me for that. I'd spend a couple of days in the strip cell, then there would be endless months of 43. I focused as hard as I could. With luck, I would break his jaw

'Morning, Parker,' the Dep said energetically.

'Morning, guv,' I replied, trying to appear relaxed but feeling as tight as a coiled spring.

'I've got good news and bad news,' he continued.

Thankfully, he didn't ask me what I wanted to hear first. I was only paying a fraction of my attention to what he was saying anyway. All systems were running the attack programme. The moment he said the fateful words, I would strike.

'The bad news is that I can't let you back up on the wing. The situation is still too volatile,' he said.

I teetered on the edge of chinning him, but a tiny voice advised that I might as well hear the good news first.

'Before your friend Joe left the Security Wing here,' he went on, 'he asked me to do him a favour. Now I've always respected Joe. We go back a long way together. So I said that I would. He asked me to help you out if I could.'

I couldn't believe this incredible crap I was hearing. The Dep in avuncular mode was something I just wasn't prepared for. Although I didn't believe a word, it was sufficiently bizarre to grab my attention.

'You're going to have to stay down here a little while longer,' he continued, 'but I promise you that, in 14 days' time, you will be moved to another jail.'

By now, a sardonic smile had curled the corners of my mouth as utter disbelief showed in my face. Surely he didn't expect me to go for this? It was all just a ploy to keep me quiet for another two weeks, then he would delay and play for more time.

'I give you my word,' said the Dep reassuringly, as he saw the look on my face. 'Anyway, you're down as the one who took the lock from the tin shop, so we want you out of the jail.'

It was this last sentence that finally convinced me that he was telling the truth. The IRA fellas had taken the lock, but I had been in the shop at the time. It was amazing some of the things I got blamed for. It was as if no one else had a mind of their own. I was well pleased, though. I didn't mind this being on my record as long as it got me out of the jail.

'OK, guv,' I said. 'Two weeks it is then.'

He turned on his heel and left, banging the door behind him. Mixed emotions raced through my mind. On the one hand, I felt that I had swallowed my pride by not chinning him; on the other, I felt that I had done the sensible thing because I was going to be moved anyway. If he kept his word, that is. However, even if he didn't, I could still chin him in two weeks' time.

I stood there deep in thought, not moving. Suddenly, I heard my name being called.

'Hey, Norm! Norm, ya there?'

Slowly, I climbed on my chair. My mind was still in a turmoil. I didn't need any of the Yank's problems.

As soon as he heard my voice, he launched into an account of his conversation with the Dep. His unrestrained joy all but drowned the old arrogance, but not quite. 'And I said, "Now look here, Dep,"' prattled the Yank, before going on to deliver his final ultimatum.

The outcome was that the Yank was to be allowed back up the wing. I knew the conversation hadn't gone anything like the way the Yank was telling it. If I hadn't been mulling over my own conversation with the Dep, I would have listened at my door again. I didn't doubt that the Yank had been on his knees.

I was happy for him, though. He certainly couldn't have gone on much longer. At a more selfish level, I was thankful he was going. He had nearly driven me crazy.

Almost as an afterthought, the Yank asked what had happened to me.

'I'm on subversive 43,' I said matter-of-factly.

There was a prolonged silence. Perhaps the Yank had fainted at the thought of what he had so nearly missed, but then I would have heard the crash as he fell off the chair.

It was a very sombre Yank who spoke next. 'Gee, Norm, I'm so sorry. I promise I'll send you lots of books and magazines down,' he said with genuine concern.

'Hey, Norman.' Tom's voice sounded from above. 'Me and Alec have been 43'd too. Old Dick is going up, though.'

I felt sorry for Tom and Alec, but at least I'd have some company.

'Norm.' Tom's voice came again. 'The orderly just told me that John has been 43'd, but Tina is going up.'

Tina? I hadn't even known that Tina was down here with us. No one had seen her. She must have been upstairs, but over on the other side. She hadn't taken one single exercise period. She was one crazy, stubborn fella.

I was particularly sorry to hear about John. All the time he was down here, I would be worried about him as well as me. There was always the chance that he would crack up and steam into the screws. Then I would have to make one, too.

I would be going anyway now, so I was content to keep my head down for a couple of weeks. I wasn't looking forward to John's next exercise period. He would be straight over to my window.

Shortly after the Dep finished his rounds, I heard them open the Yank's door. He must have been all packed and ready, because he came out immediately.

'Boy, am I glad to be getting out of here,' I heard him say right outside my door. Then he was gone.

About ten minutes later, my door was opened.

'Collect your bedding, Parker, you're not on punishment any more,' said the screw.

You could have fooled me, I thought as I crossed to the bedding store. I could have my bedding, my radio and a few other luxuries, but I would still be locked up in solitary 23 hours a day.

After I collected my bedding, the screw called me to the office. My box of property was on the desk again. I was given my radio and the various canteen goods I'd had in my cell on the wing.

The radio would be a great boon, especially in the long evenings. I would tire of constant music quite quickly, but a play on Radio Four would take me out of Parkhurst for a few hours. The bag of sugar would make all the difference to the tea and porridge and the jars of jam would turn the bland slices of bread and marge into a treat. It was amazing how comparatively minor creature comforts could assume such importance in the chokey. There was so little to look forward to that you anticipated every pleasurable experience, no matter how small.

I went out for exercise, depressed that the two-week cycle I had just finished was beginning all over again. The only positive aspect was that I would be going in two weeks' time – if they kept their word. Once again, exercise was over all too quickly. No sooner had I got back to my cell than John was at my window. As expected, he was really uptight. John realised better than anyone that he couldn't handle solitary indefinitely. A month's solitary would be like a lifetime to him.

I had done six months at Brixton and three-and-a-half months at Albany, so I knew just how much it took out of you. By the end of both periods, I was a long way out. I felt that they had changed me irrevocably, more so than any physical abuse ever could. That would have been active and of relatively short duration. Solitary was passive and agonisingly long. It taught you the true meaning of loneliness, an exquisite torture that attacked the mind rather than the body.

The longest fined punishment you could get was 180 days'

solitary, though, in certain riot situations, a couple of these could be run together. With subversive 43, however, there were instances where men had spent two to three years in solitary.

Once again, I advised John to use his relationship with Dr Cooper to get out of the chokey. The doctor was a very powerful man in Parkhurst and could do virtually what he liked. He had even bailed Ron and Reg out of trouble several times.

This time there was no argument from John. He knew that this was the only way. It was no shame having a psychiatric problem in Parkhurst; all the best people had them.

The second fortnight dragged by even slower than the first. I still talked to Tom and Alec out the window, but it was difficult to find things to talk about now. Also, it was cold standing at the window in the night air, and it made your legs tired. More and more, I listened to the radio and read.

Strangely enough, I actually missed the Manchester Yank. A pain he might have been, but at least he was a distraction. We had heard from our crowd that, for the first couple of days, he had strutted about the wing as if he had organised the whole protest single-handedly. However, perhaps because a screw had warned him that he could be sent back down the chokey, he suddenly went very quiet.

We also heard that, on the day they let the Yank, old Dick and Tina up, Harry and Geoff were allowed out of the hospital. So everyone was back on the wing except for John, Alec, Tom and me. I had never seen myself as a martyr, but this was the role I was increasingly being cast in.

Towards the end of the third week, Dr Cooper got John transferred to the hospital, but into a ward instead of into 'C' wing. This was a much better deal as it was more likely to be temporary. Residents of 'C' wing tended to be long-stay.

Now, days passed at an agonisingly slow pace. The daily round of workouts, meals, slopping out and exercise was repeated *ad nauseam*. I had gathered all my strength behind a final push to complete the month. I refused to consider the prospect of treachery and further months of solitary.

The last Sunday was the longest day of my life. When I awoke on Monday, I was only one day away from the deadline. As the Dep passed on his rounds, I got the usual 'Good morning' and a cryptic 'I haven't forgotten.'

The trouble was that that wasn't specific enough for me. What hadn't he forgotten? That I was going to be moved at some stage or that I was going to be moved tomorrow? To me, there was a world of difference between the two.

Later that evening, my door opened and there was Allsop. For the first time, he didn't seem aggressive or threatening.

'Parker,' he said, handing me my box of property, 'here's all the stuff you couldn't have down here. You're going to Long Lartin in the morning, so you might as well pack everything tonight to save time.'

With that, he turned and was gone. It was a decent gesture. He had confirmed that I would be going in the morning. In bed that night, I was filled with elation. The torment was nearly over.

I woke early and lay in the darkness, impatient for the day to begin. I could feel the excitement in me as I anticipated the events to come. My release from solitary, a trip through the countryside, my arrival at a new jail and the meeting with friends old and new. To someone who had spent the past month entombed in a ten-by-eight-foot cell, that was a great adventure indeed.

As soon as my light came on, I was up. I washed, stacked my bedding and tidied my cell. I was ready to go before breakfast was even served.

I shaved, ate every scrap of porridge and forced down four slices of bread and jam. I didn't want to travel on an empty stomach. I heard the screws go off for their breakfast and sat down to wait, impatient for their return.

It was a long hour, but finally I heard the stamping of their boots. I looked around the cell to see if there was anything I had forgotten. I had already said goodbye to Tom and Alec the night before, immediately after Allsop had told me I was going in the morning. There was nothing else to do.

I ran my eyes over the walls of the cell for one last time. I took in all the minute details that I had become so familiar with. They would be etched in my memory for a long time.

Suddenly, my door opened and it was time. Quickly, I slopped out, stowed my bedding in the store and put my plate and bowl by the hot-plate. I picked up my box of belongings and walked towards the open gate of the chokey.

A green Transit van with darkened windows was backed up to the gate, its rear doors open. Several screws stood in front of them. My box was searched, I was rubbed down, then I was handcuffed to a screw. The security PO checked the cuffs, then I got into the van. I noticed that my other boxes of property from reception were already stacked inside.

We taxied through the grounds and into the gate lodge. I didn't recognise any of my escorts. They seemed quite relaxed, without any obvious hostility. I guessed they were from Long Lartin.

As we drove out the gate, I felt the shade of Parkhurst slip from my shoulders. It was a part of my life that was now dead for ever. I actually felt some optimism as I looked forward to what was to come.

GLOSSARY

AG, Assistant Governor.
'A' list, the highest security category.
Albany, top-security jail on the Isle of Wight.
association, recreation period when prisoners are allowed to mix.
bang-up, lock-up.
bird, prison sentence, time.
bit of work, a criminal venture, i.e. a robbery.
blade, homemade knife.
blagger, armed robber.
blank (to get a), to be snubbed, or to be refused something.
block, punishment block (*see also* chokey).
book, horse-racing book.
bridge, in a prison, a short landing running across the wing, joining the two long landings on either side.
brief, solicitor.
Broadmoor, top-security hospital for the criminally insane, in Berkshire.
centre (the), the 'hub' where the wings of a Victorian jail meet.
chaps, an almost mythical grouping of criminals whose ethos

includes: professionalism in the pursuit of crime; loyalty to others of their kind; hatred of and non-co-operation with authority; and courage. Many aspire to membership, few qualify.

chief, chief officer; the most senior uniformed officer in the jail.

chokey, punishment block (*see also* block).

civvy, civilian instructor.

'E' man, someone on the 'escape list', placed there for having escaped, attempting to escape or being suspected of planning to escape.

face, notorious or influential criminal with some standing within the criminal fraternity – i.e. 'to be a face'.

firm-handed, to be in a group or crowd.

food-boat, arrangement where several prisoners chip in to cover the expense of a shared meal.

fours and fives, in a prison, the fourth and fifth landings.

Gartree, top-security, category-A prison near Market Harborough.

gavolt, rumpus.

GBH, grievous bodily harm.

on the out, outside prison.

glassed, to be hit with a glass (usually in the face).

go into one (to), to throw a violent tantrum.

Good Order and Discipline, *see* Rule 43.

grass, to inform, an informer.

heavy (the), armed robbery.

heavy mob (the), the riot squad.

hooch, homebrewed booze.

hot-plate, industrial oven used to keep food hot.

hump (the), mood of aggressive depression.

Jack the Hat, Jack McVitie, murdered by Ron and Reg Kray.

joey, small parcel, usually of contraband.

khazi, toilet.

long-firm, a type of fraud.

Long Lartin, top-security jail in the Midlands.